Historical Society of Watertown

Watertown Records

Historical Society of Watertown

Watertown Records

ISBN/EAN: 9783337143725

Printed in Europe, USA, Canada, Australia, Japan

Cover: Foto ©ninafisch / pixelio.de

More available books at **www.hansebooks.com**

WATERTOWN RECORDS

COMPRISING

East Congregational and Precinct Affairs

1697 to 1737

ALSO

RECORD BOOK OF THE PASTORS

1686 to 1819

PREPARED FOR PUBLICATION

BY THE

HISTORICAL SOCIETY

BOSTON
DAVID CLAPP & SON, PRINTERS
291 Congress Street
1906

PREFACE.

This, the fourth published volume of Watertown Records, comprises the only two volumes specially devoted to ecclesiastical affairs now extant. The records of congregational and precinct affairs are in the one book, entered the one at the beginning, the other at the end of the book which has been reversed. The pastors' records are those of a book kept by the Rev. John Bailey, Henry Gibbs, Seth Storer, Daniel Adams, Richard R. Elliot and Convers Francis. The many pages of the record devoted by Pastor Bailey to his pious meditations, ejaculations and hints upon Bible texts, the Committee has not deemed to be of sufficient present interest to be now reproduced. Of the many pages occupied with his remarks made at Communion services, only a few selected portions are given, to indicate their general character. As he intended them to serve only as private memoranda, he wrote them in a much abbreviated form, using the common abbreviation of "y" in place of "th" with most all words beginning with those two letters, using the Greek "X" *i.e.* "Ch" for Christ, "I. X." for Jesus Christ, and "H. G." for Holy Ghost, and others then readily understood by him at least.

         BENNETT F. DAVENPORT,
         CHARLES F. FITZ,
           Committee of Publication.

[WATERTOWN RECORDS.

East Precinct Congregational Affairs.]*

[2] At a great and Gen[ll] Court, or afsembly for his majesties Province of Mafsachufets-Bay in New-England, began & heild at Boston upon Wednesday the 29th of May 1700—and Continued by feverall Prorogations untill Wednesday the 12th of February following, for accomodateing and Ifsuing the difterrences relating to the fupport of the miniftrey in the middle and easterly parts of Watertown, Refolved and Ordered that there be a fubfscription throwout the whole town of Watertown, The farmers excepted, In order to the fupport of the miniftre in the old and new meeting-houfe, that there Perfons & Eftates who fubfcrib for fupport of the miniftrey at the Old meeting-houfe be liable to be afseffed thereto and no where elfe, and that there Perfons and eftates who fubfcribe for fupport of the miniftre to the middle-meeting-houfe be liable to be afsefsed thereto and no where elfe, that fuch who refufe to fubfcribe to the miniftre at either meeting-houfe shall be liable to pay to the miniftrey of the meeting-houfe ftanding within the bounds of the military Precinct where thay dwell, that each fociety be Impowred to Choofe a certaine number of men to afsefs them, and thofe to be upon oath that the feverall fubfcribers shall enter their names at or before the twentieth of may next before Sam[ll] Hayman and Tho: Brown Esq[rs] two of his majesties Juftices within the County. S[d] Justice Hayman to appoint the time and Place in fd: town to take the fubfcribtion of such the Inhabitants as shall be prevented of subfcribing at the time, or times fo to be appointed as afores[d] by reafon of their being then ought of town, or detained by ficknefs, shall have liberty to subfcribe before the town Clarke at any time before the twentieth Day of August next coming, that this order Continue in force untill the end of feven years next, or untill the Inhabitance of both faid parts of the town shall mutually agree to fupport the miniftre in any other manner, and that all actions suets & controverfies Relating to the meeting-houfes, or miniftre in the faid town of Watertown Doo ceafe untill the accomplifhment of fuch fubfcribtions confented to.

   Isaac Addington Secretary.   William Stoughton.

* See vote of Oct. 20, 1701, on p. [11] concerning keeping records.—Eds.

[3]

Decemb^r 9th 1685. At a Gen^{ll} town meeting. Voted that Endeavours should be ufed to hier an houfe for the minister, Voted, That the selectmen with Corp^{ll} Bond f^r shall be a comitte to fearch ought a Place that may be hired for the minister and make return to the town.

A true copie taken ought of Watertown third Booke of Records.
 p^r Munings Sawin town clerk of Watertown.

Feb^r 12th: 1685. The town being called together by order of the comitte aboves^d The town did then Declare by a vote, That, if a number of Perfons would build a convenient houfe to entertaine the minister in neer to this meetinghoufe, that then the town will pay them that build it Rent for the s^d houfe, untill the town doe agree and have actually Removed this meetinghoufe, or built another in the Room of this more convenient for the Inhabitants fomewhere else where the town shall agree upon.

A true copie taken of Watertown third Booke of Records. [p. 28.]
 p^r Munings Sawin town Clerk for Watertown.

Alfo it was agreed by a vote of the town that that Peace of town land lying between Old Goodman Sawin's land upon the east, and the Path leading from Pastor Sherman's houfe to the burying Place on the west, and between the two highways north and south shall be to fet the afores^d houfe upon, the builders allowing the town refonable sattisfaction for it out of the Rent of the houfe, the f^d land being about five acres more or lefs.

A true copie taken of Watertown third Booke of Records. [p. 28.]
 p^r Munings Sawin Clerk for Watertown.

Paid by	lb	s	d		lb	s	d
Mr William Bond Esqr	13	09	01	Stephen Coolidg	03	12	00
John Bond	04	09	00	William Shattuck	04	03	09
John Morfe	03	01	00	Joseph Hastings	01	06	06
John Woodward	03	03	00	John Traine fen^r	02	12	06
Jonathan Brown	07	08	00	John Perry	01	09	06
John Sawin				Tho Traine	01	19	00
William Goddard fen^r	04	04	00	Serg^t Jno Coolidg	08	07	03
Gregory Cooke	04	18	03	Wido Mary Smith	02	10	00
Nathan Fiske fen^r	03	15	00	Jno Knop fen^r	05	19	00
Samuell Eddy f^n	03	18	06	Micael Barstow	03	05	06
Capt Jno Sherman	00	13	00	Widow Eliz: Faning	02	14	00
Corn^t Jno Hammont	11	10	06	Capt Nat^ll Barsham	05	07	07
John Kimbol	02	01	04	Deacon Wm Bond	03	18	00
Nethaniel Bright	03	14	05	Nethaniell Coolidg	05	19	03
Marten Townend	02	19	00	En^{en} Sam^{ll} Thatcher	05	04	05
John Chenry	03	02	02	Caleb Grant	01	17	06
Elliz Barron	02	16	00	Jofeph Grant	02	06	00
Mr Jno Bisco	05	01	09	Christopher Grant	01	16	00
Tho: Bisco	02	11	00	Mr Ric Norcrofs	06	09	11

Deacon Jnº Bright	-	-	06	16	11	Deacon Jnº Stone	- 04 12 10
Joseph Mason	-	-	03	12	03	John Straton senr	- 06 13 11
David Church	-	-	02	13	06	Nicolas Wyeth	- 01 06 11
Corpll Roger Wellington		04	04	00		Simon Stone sen	- 06 09 01
Samuell Livermore	-	-	06	06	04		
Jonathan Coolidg	-	-	02	16	00		

[4]

At a Genll town meeting by adjornment the 14th of October, 1690: The town by there vote did manifest their earnest defire that Mr. Henry Gibbs might be treated witn in order to his being a conftant help to the town, not only for the Prefent, but for the futer alfo, so that thay might not be deftitute of the word nor Ordinances of Christ if god shall pleas to Continue him amongst us.

Voted by the town that the Deacons together with Capt Sherman & Leut. Bond shall treat wth mr Henry Gibbs, and to Returne his anfwer at the Genll town meeting next enfuing.

A true copie taken out of Watertown third booke of Records. [p. 42]

pr me Munings Sawin Town Clark for Watertown.

At a Genll town meeting Novembr the 3d 1690: At this meeting Capt Sherman & Leiut Bond together with the Deacons being sent to treat with Mr Henry Gibbs about his being a help to the town in the worke of the miniftrey and his anfwer is as followeth to wit. that he locketh upon it as a call from god, that hath Inclined the town to be fo unanimus in their calling of him, and therefore is willing to attend the fd. worke as god shall enable him, The town also accepts his anfwer herein, and did by a vote of the town declare that this Day his time began as unto his fallerry, as is above written.

A true copie taken of watertown third booke of Records.

pr Munings Sawin Town Clerk for Watertown.

At a Genll town meeting by adjornment the 16th of Novembr 1691. Voted at this meeting that the town doe renew their call unto the Reverend Mr Gibbs That he would Continuue to carry on the worke of the miniftrey amongft us, according unto there former Call, as appeares upon Record. The town by their vote, choofe Mr William Bond, Capt Warren, Simon Stone, for to treat with the Revd Mr Henry Gibbs to come amongft us to carry on the miniftrey.

A true Copie taken out of Watertown third booke of Records. [p. 45.]

pr Munings Sawin town Clarke for Watertown.

Perſuant to a vote of the town Paſsed at A Gen[ll] town meeting the 4th of February 1695/6 legally warned, wherein wee the ſubſcribers wer deſired to provide a miniſter to Preah the word of God in the new-meeting-houſe, and treat M[r] Henry Gibbs in the firſt place for his acceptance, wee have accordingly treated the Rev[nd] M[r] Henry Gibbs once and againe, and he hath Refuſed to preach with us as o[r] miniſter, or ſo much as one day as other miniſters did afterwards. Dan[ll] Warren, ſen[r] Caleb, Church, and Phillip Shattucke.

     A true Copie taken of Watertown third book of Records for Watertown [p. 111.]
      p[r] Munings Sawin town Clerk for Watertown.

Voted at a Gen[ll] town meeting the 20th ot Decemb[r], 1695, legally warned, it was voted by the town that wee doe Renew our Call to the Rev[d] M[r] Henry Gibbs. In order to his being fixed amongſt us, in the worke and office of the miniſtrey for the town, to officiate in the new-meeting-house, according to the advice and determination of the hon[d] Committee, bareing date May 18th 1693.

     A true Copie taken of Watertown third Book of Records. [p. 107.]
      p[r] Munings Sawin town Clerk for Watertown.

[5]
In anſwer to the Propoſals made in thoſe votes Preſented to me by Cap[t] Warren, Isaac Mixer j[r] and Benjamin Gearfield one the 23[d] December 1695.

Being ſenſible that there is great diſsatisfaction in the town with Refferrence to the meeting wherein thoſe votes wer paſsed, I feare it might prove uncomfortable ſhould I accept my Compliance therewith and accordingly I am adviſed to decline the matter, till ſuch time as caer be taken to remove the ſd diſsattisfaction, not doubting, but that this being effected which I earnestly pray that god would in his own time grant it would much conduce to the mutuall comforte and advantage. Watertown february the 4th 1695/6. By Henry Gibbs.

     A true Copie taken of Watertown third booke of Record. [p. 108.]
      p[r] Munings Sawin town Clerk for Watertown.

[6, 7 & 8] Blank.
[9]

Jan[r] 8th: 1696/7 The Brethren and Inhabitants of the east end of Watertown, being aſsembled did by Vote make Choice of Simon Stone to keep a Record of all votes that paſsed that Day, and ſo from time to time of what might be voted in after meetings by the above s[d] Company.

Item. Voted at the same meeting that thay would still continue to maintaine the Revd Mr Henry Gibbs, as thay did for the last year, Provided he will continue with them in the worke of the Ministrey in order unto a settlement with them in the office of a Pastor (as soon as God in his Providence Shall make way for the same) in the old Meeting-house.

Item: It was Voted in order to the promoteing of a settlement, that some Persons be Chosen & Impowred to act for the s^d Society in moveing to the Neighbour Churches for advice & assistance, and any sower of those Prsons to call a meeting when they shall se occation, the Prsons so chosen were, Capt Nathaniel Barsham, Lieu^t John Hammonde, Mr Richd Norcrofs, Dr Palsgr. Wellington, Joseph Sherman, Nat^{ll} Bright, and Simon Stone.

Octob^r 1697 At a meeting of the subscribers to the maintenance of Mr Henry Gibbs, Joseph Sherman, Nat^{ll} Bright, and Serg^t Thatcher wer Chosen to be assessors for Mr Gibb's salary, and also Robert Goddard was Chosen Commission^r to take their Invoice.

Item. It was voted at the s^d Meeting that every Poll should be Rated at 12^{lb}. Cattle according to the Countrey Invoice. Plowing land and Mowing land at ten shillings p^r acre, Housing ye highest not exceeding sower pounds, the lowest not less than ten shillings.

Item. It was voted that 12^{lb} be allowed for wood for Mr Gibbs, and that such as brought in wood should be allowed for walnut eight shillings, and for oak seven shillings p^r Cord.

Item. It was voted at s^d Meeting that every one bring in his money by Contribution Paper^d, and that all lose money should be Reconed for the use of the society when thay shall call for it.

Octo^r ye 5th 1698. At a meeting of the Inhabitants of the Easterly part of Watertown vizt Those who subscribed to the maintenance of the Ministrey there.

Simon Stone was Chosen moderato^r for s^d Meeting.

Item. A sallary of sixty five pounds besides houseing & fireing was Granted to Mr Gibbs according to agreem^t for the Ensuing year.

Item. Mr Nathaniel Bright, Serg^t Thatcher, and Corp^{ll} Sherman wer Chosen assessors, also Robert Goddard was Chosen to take their Invoice.

Item. It was voted that the 65^{lb} aboves^d should be paid by Contribution and that every on should put in their money paper^d, and that what money came in Loose or unpaper^d Should be to the use of the Society.

Item. Capt Barsham & Serg^t Bond wer Chosen Collecto^{rs}.

Item. It was voted at s^d Meeting that 12^{lb} Should be added to the 65^{lb} aboves^d to Provide Mr Gibb's with wood and to be put in the rate therewithall.

Item. That the aboves^d summs should be proportioned according to the Rules observed the last year.

Item. It was voted at the aboves^d meeting that one sixt part of s^d sums be p^d by ye middle of next November.

Feb: 4: 1700/1 Item: Then paid in to M{r} Henry Gibbs in full of what was granted to him for the carriing on the work of the miniſtrey for the year begining October the fift 1698, being ſixty five pound with houſing & firewood according as is above granted.

Novemb{r} the 7{th} 1698. At a meeting of the Subſcribers aboveſ{d}, Voted that Joſeph Grant should mend the glaſs, and Joſeph Child the Caſements of the meeting houſe, and bring in their accounts at the next meeting and that the Society would ſe them paid for the ſame.

Item: At the ſ{d} meeting there was granted to Serg{t} Chadwick for looking after the Meeting-houſe for the year past and enſuing three pounds.

Novemb{r} y{e} 16{th} 1698 At a Meeting of the Inhabitants of the east end of Watertown.

Voted, First that we will elect appoint and authorize, ſome P{r}ſons from among o{r}ſelves to transact ſuch matters as relate to our further ſettlem{t} w{th} respect to maintaining of the publick worship at the old meetinghouse which Persons shall have power either to Petition on our behalfe, when & to whome they shall ſe needfull, or to anſwer in o{r} name to any ſuch Petitions, or complaints which may be offered & exhibited to our diſadvantage.

Item: We Elect, appoint & authorize for y{e} ends aboveſ{d} Cap{t} Barsham, Corp{ll} Sherman, W{m} Shattuck, D{r} Wellington, Lieu{t} Bond and Nathan{ll} Bright.

[10]

Octob{r} y{e} 4{th} 1699 At a meeting of the Inhabitants of the east end of Watertown to agree upon the way of gathering M{r} Gibb's maintenance there being granted to him as his ſallary & for wood 77{lb} There was then Choſen Simon Stone Moderato{r}. Choſen to take an Invoice Nathan Fiske, Choſen aſseſsors. Nathan Fiske, Serg{t} Beeres and Sarg{t} Thatcher, choſen Collectors Deacon Barsham and Deacon Bond.

Item. Voted that the meeting be adjourned untill monday the 23{d} Instant that care may be taken for the Pastors wood, and to agree how to raiſe the ſ{d} Rate, and take account of the Collecto{rs} of the money p{d} into the Pastor the year Past.

Novemb{r} y{e} 27{th} 99 At a meeting of the Inhabitants of the east Congregation in Watertown for the raiſing of the miniſters Sallary It was voted that every head should pay ſix ſhillings.

Item: That the rate should be raiſed as to Chattles & lands as it was the two former years.

April 19{th} 1700 Then p{d} to the Revd. M{r} Henry Gibbs: for his carriing on of the work of y{e} miniſtrey as it was granted October the 4{th} 1699 the ſum of ſixty five pounds, with ſufficient fire wood which was in full according as it was granted.

Octob^r 2^d 1700   At a meeting of the Inhabitants of the east-end of Watertown to agree upon the way of gathering Mr Gibb's maintenance, Chosen moderato^r Simon Stone.

It^m: Voted that we do grant to the ministers maintenance this year enfueing the fum of 77^{lb} a fixt part being for wood at the fame price as formerly.

It^m: That each head shall pay fix fhillings and all other rateabl estate according to the contrey Invoice.

Chosen to take the Invoice Serg^t Coolidg.

Chofen afefsors, Serg^t Beeres, Enf^n Thatcher & Corp^ll Fiske. Chosen Collecto^{rs} Deacon Barsham & Deacon Bond.

Novemb^r ye 27th 1700   At a meeting of the Inhabitants of the east-end Precinct by adjournment.

Voted that we will meet at the houfe of Serg^t Ric: Collidg on the 18th day of Decemb^r next enfuing for to have an account of the arrears of the minifters rate of the two last years, and to fe what the Company will doe concerning the defpofing of the lofe money, and alfo to Chofe a Clerke.

Decemb^r 18th 1700   At a meeting by adjournment Enf^n Sam^{ll} Thatcher was Chofen clerke, and the meeting adjourn^d untill Jan: 14th 1700/1.

Jan: 14th 1700/1   By adjorn^t At a meeting of the Inhabitants at the east end of Watertown, It was voted by s^d Society at the aboves^d meeting that the loofe money according to ou^r former votes to be difpofed of by the Cociety and now in the hands of the Collecto^{rs} be given to Mr Gibbs—except fo much of it as to Clear the Rates of thofe removed, which cannot be obtained, but are certainly lost and the rates of thofe who appear to be certainly unable to pay the same.

Also Doct^r Palsgrave Wellington, Lt Jonas Bond and Corp^ll Nathan Fiske were Chofen & appointed to Joyn wth the Collectors to effect the difpofial of s^d moneys according to the above written vote, and for further bifinefs which may accur it was voted that the meeting be adjorn^d to be heild at at the houfe of Mr Nathaniel Bright on the fecond Monday in Feb^r 1700/1 at five of the Clock afternoon, and Capt Nathan^{ll} Barsham was Moderat^{or} of the aboves^d meeting.

Feb^r 10th 1700/1   Nathan^{ll} Bright was Chofen Moder^{tr} and the meeting adjorned untill Feb^r the 17th next at fix of the Clock afternoon at the houfe of Capt Barsham, to finish the aboves^d worke.

Perfuant to the aboves^d vote Jan^r 14th 1700/1 Doct^r Palsgrave Wellington Lt Jonas Bond and Corp^{ll} Nathan Fiske wer Chofen & appointed to Joyne wth the Collecto^{rs} to examin and effect the defpofall of the loofe money—there returne is as follows.

An account of the defpofall of the money gathered for the maintenance of the ministre of the east end of s^d town, both that which was loofe, and that which was papered, and that which was given in by rate, and that which was given in otherwife.

[11]

Feb^r ye 10th 1698/9   Then paid by the aboves^d Collecto^{rs}, and comitte by order of s^d company out of the loofe money to Mr Henry Gibbs for the making up his fallary for the year past, two pounds thirteen shillings and fix pence, and of the rate money fixty two pounds fix shillings and fix pence, which maketh fixty five pounds, which is in full fattisfaction and wood to content for faid year, and there yet remaines ungathered for the ufe of s^d companey, in arreres of s^d year fix pounds, ten shillings and three pence.

For the rate made in the year 1698–9 for the maintenance of the miniftry in the east end of Watertown, was made 77^{lb} 14^s-08^d and ought of the fame rate was paid 60^{lb} 5^s 2^d and ought of the loofe money 04^{lb}-14^s-10^d which maketh fixty five pounds in money and wood to full content, and there yet remaines in arrears ungathered for the ufe of said Companey, nine pounds thirteeen shillings & fower pence.

It^m voted   In exfplaination of the vote made Octob^r the 2^d 1700 that the rate to be made shall be raifed as followeth, that Poles shall be rated at fix shillings P^r head, horfes at three pounds P^r head, oxen at three pounds P^r head, cowes at two pounds P^r head, swine and sheep at fower pounds P^r fcore. Improved land at ten shillings P^r acre and west land at five shillings P^r acre, and houfing at fower pounds the highest, and the lowest not under ten shillings, and the rate to be made for mending the meetinghoufe glafs, and the paying the fexton's fallary to be made by the afsefsors Chosen for the Prefent year.

Itm   Voted, that when and fo often as there shall be occation for the Inhabitants of the east end Precinct of Watertown to be called together, it shall be in the power of Mr Simon Stone, and Capt Nat^{ll} Barsham to call them together.

Feb. 17th 1706-7   Paid to the Reverend Mr: Henry Gibbs in part of what was granted to him for carrying on the work of the miniftrey as it was granted Octob^r the 2^d 1700. the fum of sixty pounds, fixteen shillings and eight pence.

Octob^r ye 1st 1701   At a meeting of the Inhabitants of the easterly Precinct of Watertown, being orderly to grant a fallary for the upholding of the miniftre in s^d P^{r}ecinct, and for the Chofiing of afsefsors, Collecto^{rs} and other officers. Mr Simon Stone was Chofen Moderat^r to cary on the worke of s^d meeting.

It^m Voted that each head shall pay fix fhillings.

It^m: Voted, that we do grant for the minifters maintenance for the year enfuing the fum of 77^{lb} a fixt part being for wood.

It^m.   Voted, that the remainder that the heads do not amount to fhall be raifed by the fame rules the province tax is.

It^m: Chofen for afsefsors Nathan Fiske, Lt Jonas Bond, and Sam^{ll} Livermore.

Voted, That Capt Nat^{ll} Barsham & Deacon Wm Bond be colectors for the minifters rate.

It^m : Munings Sawin Chofen Clerk for s^d fociety, John Chadwick fn^r Chofen to looke after the meeting-houfe, and to be allowed for it one pound and ten fhillings.

Voted that all thofe that will cary in wood to Mr. Gibb's doe it by the first wednesday in Novemb^r and if that do not fufficiently bring in a fupply, then the Deacons to take money out of the Salary granted and buy wood for his fefonable fupply, unlefs Mr Gibbs will fupply himfelfe, and take the money as it comes in.

Octob^r ye 20th 1701   Voted, that Capt Barsham carry the afsefsors before lawfull authority, to be fworn to the faithfull difcharge of their offices.

It^m : Voted, that the s^d Rate be p^d in as formerly, by a Conftant Contribution on every Sabbath day (only all p^rfons to come down to the table, to the box) and all money to be paper'd.

It^m : Voted, that Munings Sawin lay ought three shillings of the s^d focietie's money to purchafe a booke to keep the s^d Societies Records, and to tranfcrib there former Records into s^d Booke.

It^m : Voted, that the s^d fociety take caer and order all there youth, that at the publique worship of God on the Sabbath Days, thay fit in the feats appointed for that end, so that they may be under the infpection of the tything-men.

It^m. Voted, that this meeting be adjorned to the first monday of Decemb^r next at fower of the clock in the afternoon, to be at the houfe of Mr Nath^ll Bright, In order to heer the accompt of the Minifters Rate.

Decemb^r ye 1st 1701. At a meeting at the houfe of Mr Nathl Bright, the account of what was unpaid in the ministers rate in s^d Precinct and there remained unpd. 13^lb.

Alfo the rate made for the year enfuing was then brought and Read to the cociety, which amounted to the fum of feventy five pounds, and five shillings, and it was comitted into the hands of the Collecto^rs to gather, vizt Deacon Nat^ll Barshan & Deacon Wm Bond, according to the vote at the meeting octob^r the 1st 1701.

Feb. 17th 1706/7   Then Paid to the Revd Mr Henry Gibbs for his carying on of the worke of the miniftrey amongst us in the year. octob^r the first 1701, as it was granted, paid in part of the fume of fifty nine pounds two shillings and three pence, and in fier wood according as it was granted.

[12]

Octob^r ye 7th 1702 At a meeting of ye east-end society for the granting of the ministers sallery. Voted that we will give to the ministers maintenance 77^lb a fixt part for to provide wood.

It^m Voted, that the Rate to be raifed for s^d money shall be according to the rules the P^rvince tax was ordered to be made by (excepting heads;) which are to be fet at fix fhillings P^r head.

Lieu^t Jonas Bond, Sam^ll Livermore, and Mr Nat^ll Bright wer Chofen afsefsors to make s^d rate.

Deacon Nat^ll Barsham & Deacon Wm Bond wer Chofen afsefsors to gather s^d Rate, and pay it in to the minister of s^d Society.

Munings Sawin Chofen Cler.

Serg^t Jno Chadwick Chofen to locke after the meeting-houfe, and the s^d fociety to allow him for his fervice one pound and ten shillings.

It^m: Voted, that the youth which attend ye Publick worship of God on the Sabbath days ftill continue to fitt in the places appointed for that end.

It^m; Voted that there shall be a rate forthwith made of fower pounds, three pound whereof to pay ferg^t Chadwick for locking after the meeting-houfe for the year paft, and the year enfuing, and twenty fhillings for the mending the meetinghoufe glafs this P^{r}sant year.

It^m. Voted, that the s^d afsefsors make s^d rate, and comitt it to Dan^{ll} Benjamen, who is chofen to gather it and pay it in for ye ufes afores^d.

It^m. Voted, that Serg^t Jno Chadwick and Dan^{ll} Benjamen take caer and get the meeting houfe glafs mended and to be p^d ought of the rate made for mending the glafs, voted, that ye s^d rate be p^d according to the way stated the last year.

It^m Voted, that one fixt part of the rate granted for the miniftrey be p^d in at or before the first monday of Decemb^r next for to provide wood.

Alfo at s^d meeting Jofiah Goddard gave an account of A rate comitted to him to collect in the year 1700 as follows

        Paid to Jofeph grant   01^{lb}–07^s–09^d }
        Paid to John Chadwick 02 –16 –11 }

Jan: ye 5th 1702/3. At a meeting of the east end fociety, at the houfe of Mr Nat^{ll} Bright.

Voted, that the Collectors should fpake with Tho: Rider, and fe whether he will pay the whole part of the rate due to Mr Gibbs from Watertown old Grift miln for the year begun the 6th of octob^r 1701. that then the s^d fociety will baer him hearmlefs for paying to any others for s^d milnfe for ye aboves^d.

It^m: Voted, that the rate to be made for Mr Gibbs for this p^{r}sant year, be made according to the act for makeing the Province tax this Prefant year.

It^m. Voted at s^d meeting that Mr Simon Stone & Capt Nat^{ll} Barsham, do on the next lectu^r day Post up on the old meeting-houfe door, that the Inhabitants of the easterly society of Watertown do give a meeting at said meeting houfe on the 15th day of this Instant January, at one of the Clocke in the afternoon, to take caer to repaire s^d meeting houfe, and to Chofe a comitte to fe the worke done.

Jan: ye 15th 1702/3 At a meeting of ye east end cociety at the old meeting-houfe in Watertown. Voted that Mr Simon Stone should be modera^{tr} for s^d Meeting.

It^m. Voted, that we will grant a rate, a quarter part of the fum of feventy feven pounds, towards the repairing the old meeting-houfe in s^d town, and that there be forthwith a rate made, at or before the 25th of march next enfuing by the P^{r}sant afsefsors.

It^m: Voted, at s^d Meeting that Capt Nat^{ll} Barsham Doct:

Paslgrave Wellington. Serg^t Ric: Coollidge are chofen a comitte to fe that the s^d worke be fefonably and well don.

It^m, Serg^t Jabez Beeres was chofen Collector to demand and gather in the s^d rate and pay it in to the aboves^d comitte by the 25th of march afores^d for the end aboves^d and no other.

It^m: Voted, at s^d meeting that all the loofe money that is given in on the sabbath days Contrebutions for the maintenance of the miniftrey shall be given to Mr Gibbs over and above his fallary.

Feb^r 17th 1706/7 Paid to the Reveren^d Mr Henry Gibbs by the Collectors, in part of what was granted to him on october the feventh 1702. for the Carying on of ye worke of the miniftrey amongst us, the fum of fifty pounds fourteen shillings and fix pence, and in wood according as it was granted.

[13]

October 6th 1703. At a Gen^{ll} meeting of the Inhabitants of the east end of Watertown, Mr Simon Stone was Chofen Moderato^r.

Item. Voted that we will give to the Ministers maintenance 77^{lb} in money, a fixt part whereof to be to provide wood, at feven shillings Pr Cord.

Item. Voted, that the rate to be raifed for f^d money shall be made according to the rules this P^{r}sant province is made by.

Item. Voted, and Choofen for afsefsors to make f^d Rate Sam^{ll} Livermore, Obadiah Coollidg and Nathan Fiske.

Item. Chofen for Collectors to gather & pay in f^d Rate to the miniftrey of s^d end Capt Nat^{ll} Barshan & Deacon William Bond.

Item. Munings Sawin Choofen Clerke, and Thomas Coollidg Choofen to looke after the meeting-houfe, and sweep it for the year enfuing, and to be allowed one pound & ten shillings for his fervice.

Item. Voted, that the contribution be ftill. continued on the Sabbath days, and all the money to be papered, or written upon.

Item. Voted, that this meeting be adjorned to the first Wednefday in November next, to one of the clocke in the afternoon of s^d day at the old meeting-houfe, to confider of sum way to get in the arrers that are yet unpaid to the miniftrey belonging to ye east end of s^d town.

Novemb^r ye 3^d 1703. At the aboves^d meeting by adjornment, In order to take caer about geting ye aboves^d arreres for s^d ministrey maintenance, it was adjorned to the second wednesday of s^d Novemb^r to one aclocke of the s^d day at the old meeting-houfe, Capt Barsham to give notice of it the next Sabbath Day after exercize.

Novemb^r 10th 1703. At the s^d Meeting by adjournment, Capt Net^{ll} Barsham was Choofen moderato^r for faid meeting.

Iteim. Munings Sawin was Choofen to take caer that the afsefsors Choofen to make the ministers rate for this prefent year, be fworn as the law directs.

Item Voted, that the collectors draw ought a list of ye names of all fuch perfons as have not p^d and made up their acc^{ts} for there proportion of y{e} ministers Rate made for the year 1702. in order to comit it to the Conſtable to gather.

Item. The abovefˡᵈ meeting is adjorned to the houſe of Corpˡˡ Natˡˡ Brights to be on the firſt monday of Decembʳ next, to five aclocke in the afternoon, to confider further about yᵉ arrears of the miniſters rate.

Decembʳ the 6ᵗʰ 1703. At a meeting at the houfe of Corpⁿ Natˡˡ Brights by adjornment Corpˡˡ Bright was Choofen Moderatoʳ.

Fcb: 17ᵗʰ 1706/7. Paid to the Reverᵈ Mʳ Henry Gibbs by the Collectors, and Conſtable Samuell Jeniſon, In part of what was granted for the carying on of the worke of the miniſtrey amongſt us, in october the fixt, one thouſand ſeven hundred and three, the ſum of fifty ſeven pounds twelve ſhillings and nine pence, and in firewood in full as it was granted.

[14]

Augᵗ 30ᵗʰ 1704. At a meeting of the Inhabitants of the easterly part of Watertown In order to take caer that the miniſters ſallary be pᵈ in according to the grant.

Item. Voted, at ſᵈ meeting, that the rate granted for the miniſters maintenance for this preſant year 1704, in the east end, have forwith a warrant affixed to it, by the preſant aſseſsors that made ſᵈ Rate, and that the ſᵈ rate with the warrant to it, be forthwith commited to the conſtable in ſᵈ east end, to gather in what of ſᵈ Rate is unpaid, to the Reverᵈ Mʳ Henry Gibbs, by the firſt wednesday of octobʳ next hence enfuing the date hereof.

October yᵉ 4ᵗʰ 1704. At a meeting of the east end Inhabitants of Watertown In order to rais a maintenance for yᵉ miniſtry in sᵈ east end. Mʳ Simon Stone was Choofen moderatoʳ for ſᵈ meeting.

Item. Voted at sᵈ meeting, that we will give to the maintenance of the miniſtrey in ſᵈ end for the year enfuing 77ˡᵇ in money, a fixt part whereof to be for to provide wood, at 7ˢ Pʳ cord.

Item. Voted that the rate to be raiſed for ſᵈ money ſhall be made according to the rules that this pʳsant Province tax is made by.

Item: Voted, and Chofen for afseſsors to make ſᵈ Rate Samˡˡ Livermore, Nathan Fiske and Munings Sawin.

Item. Voted, and Chooſen for Collectors to gather in ſᵈ Rate, and pay in the fame to the miniſter of sᵈ east end Capᵗ Natˡˡ Barsham and Deacon William Bond.

Item Voted, that the aſseſsors ſhall affix a warrant to ſᵈ Rates and comit it to the Conſtable to gather and pay to the minister of sᵈ end, that is to faie what is unpaid by the firſt wednesday, of october next enſuing the date hereof, the collectors to give the account of what is unpᵈ to the Conſtable.

Item: Voted and Chooſen for clerke Munings Sawin, Thomas Coollidg Chooſen to to locke after the meeting houſe and ſweep it, and to be allowed for his ſervice one pound ten Shillings.

Item: Voted, that the Contributions be continued upon the Sabbath days and all money contributed to be papered, or written upon.

Item: Voted, at s{d} meeting that the Clerke doe enter into the booke purchafed by fd east end of Watertown, all fuch votes & agreements as have pafsed in f{d} cociety Refering to the fupport of the miniftre in f{d} east end of Watertown.

Feb{r} 17{th} 1706/7 Paid to the Rever{d} M{r} Henry Gibbs by the Collectors, and Conftable John Chadwick, in pat of what was granted for the fupport of the miniftrey amongst us: Octob{r} the fourth one thoufand feven hundred and fower, the full & Juſt fum of fifty feven pounds three shillings and two pence, and firewood in full according as it was granted.

[15]

March 26{th} 1705. At a meeting of the east end fociety in Watertown. Voted that for the further promoteing & carying on the worke of Repaireing the old-meeting-houfe, in f{d} cocietie, we do defire the Collector forthwith to goe to thofe perfons that have not p{d} equall proportion with their Neighbours, and alfo carry with him a fubfcription that fo all may pay there equall proportion, or otherwife fubfcribe and pay as thay thinke meet.

July 23{d} 1705. At a meeting of the east end Inhabitants of Watertown, and s{d} meeting was adjorn{d} to the first wednesday of october next

October y{e} 3{d} 1705. At a meeting of the Inhabitants of the easterly end Inhabitants of Watertown orderly warned & met.

M{r} Simon Stone was chofen Moderato{r} for s{d} Meeting.

Voted, at said meeting, that we will give to the maintenance of the miniftrey in s{d} east end societie for the year enfuing 77{lb} in money, one fixt part whereof to provide wood at feven shillings p{r} cord.

Voted, that the aboves{d} rate shall be made according to the rules Prescribed in the law for the making the last Province tax. Choofen for afsefsors at s{d} meeting Samuell Livermore, Nathan Fiske and Munings Sawin.

Voted, that s{d} afsefsors shall perfix a warrant to s{d} Rate and comit it to the constable to gather and pay the aboves{d} fum to the ministrey of s{d} east end cociety by the first wednefday of September next.

Voted, that the Contrebution be ftill continued on the Sabbath day and Deacon Net{ll} Barshan and Deacon William Bond to receive s{d} contrebution: and pay it in to the Minister of s{d} cociety, and all s{d} money to be Papered or written upon.

It{m} Munings Sawin was chofen clerk at s{l} meeting.

Thomas Coolidg choofen fexton to locke after the meeting houfe & to Ring the bell for the year enfuing, and s{d} cocietie doe allow him for his s{d} fervice two pounds.

Voted at s{d} meeting, that the Gen{ll} meeting for the granting the minifters sallery shall be as formerly on the first wednesday of october annually for s{d} cociety, and that the clerke of s{d} cociety post up the warning on the meeting houfe Door on the sabbath day before s{d} meeting, and all fuch officers as may be thought necefsary for the ends afores^d of makeing gathering & Recieving s^d Rates according to our ufuall custom.

Voted, at s^d meeting that the aboves^d afsefsors shall make the rate for the sextons sallery this year, and alfo we do defire the abovs^d Deacons to gather s^d rate, and allfo the remainder of what is due of the last years rate to the sexfton, and pay it in to him.

Jun: 17th 1706 At a meeting of the Inhabitants of the easterly cociety in Watertown orderly warned and meet in order to take caer to gather in the arrears of the ministers rates and fuch other concerns as may be thought needfull.

It was voted at s^d meeting, that the constables vizt Samuell Jenifon and John Chadwick Senr forthwith gather in the arrears of the ministers rates comited to them to gather, and pay in the fame forthwith according to the warrants.

Voted at s^d Meeting, that we doe defire appoint and Impower Deacon Nathaniell Barsham and Deacon William Bond & Enfign Samuell Thatcher to gather in what of the arrears of the ministers rates, which are ungathered, before the rates wer comitted to the constables to gather.

Voted, at s^d meeting that Deacon Net^{ll} Barsham Deacon Wm: Bond and Mr Nat^{ll} Bright be a comitte to enter into said cocieties booke of Records what thay may think nedfull, by the clerk of s^d cociety.

[16]

Octob^r 2^d 1706 At a meeting of the east end Cocietie or Congregation in Watertown Orderly warned and mete.

Jonas Bond Esqr was Chofen Moderato^r.

Voted at faid meeting that we doe grant a rate of ninety Seven pounds in money for the minifters maintenance, in f^d focietie, for the year enfuing, twelve pounds of f^d fum: to provide wood for f^d Ministrey, at feven shillings Pr Corde, twenty pounds of s^d fum which is more that our ufuall rate is in Confideration of o^r Pastures prefent Circumftances by sicknes & weeknes.

Voted at s^d meeting that ye f^d Rate be made according to the Rules in ye law for the makeing the last Province tax, with a warrant affixed to it to be comitted to the Conftable in ye east end.

Voted at s^d meeting and Chofen for afsefsors to make s^d Rate, Sam^{ll} Livermore, Nathan Fiske and Munings Sawin.

Voted at f^d meeting that the Contrebution be ftill Continued as ufually it hath been in f^d cociety on the Sabbath days.

Voted at f^d meeting & Chofen for Clerke for f^d society Munings Sawin. Chofen for sexton Tho: Coollidg, and to allow f^d sexton for his sallery for one yere next enfuing two pounds money, and f^d afsefsors to make a Rate and affix a warrant to it, to be gathered by the Conftable in f^d Cocietie.

Voted at f^d meeting That ther fhall be a Contrabution four times this year, that is to saie every qurter of a year on the Sabbath day, the Decons to give notice of it the Sabbath before.

Said meeting is adjorned unto the first monday in December next to one of the Clooke in the afternoon of s^d day.

At a meeting of the east end Cocietie or Congregation the 2ᵈ day of December 1706

Capᵗ Barsham was Chofen Moderatoʳ.

Voted At sᵈ meeting, That we doe nominate, appoint & impower Jonas Bond Esqʳ and Samuell Jenifon to anfwer to what may be objected by any of said Societie neglecting to pay their ministers Rates in fᵈ cocietie.

Voted At fᵈ meeting and Chofsen as an adition to the first three afsefsors to make fᵈ Rate, John Coollidg and Samuell Jenifon.

Voted and Chofen at fᵈ meeting to treate wᵗʰ the Reveᵈ oʳ Pastoʳ Mʳ Gibbs, In order to gaine help to Carry on the worke of the miniftrey amongst us for the pʳsent, Mʳ Simon Stone, Deacon Barsham & Decon Bond.

December 16ᵗʰ 1706 the above granted rate of 97ᵗʰ was made & comited to Constable John Straton Juʳ to Collect & gather in, Pʳ Samˡˡ Livermore, Nathan Fisk & Munings Sawin afsefsors.

Octo: 1: 1707 At a meeting of the east end Societie or Congregation in Watertowne, Orderly warned & met,

Capᵗ Jonas Bond Esqʳ was Chofen Moderatoʳ for fᵈ meeting.

Voted at sᵈ meeting that we do grant a Rate of 77ˡʰ in money for the maintenance of the miniftrey in fᵈ Congregation for the year enfuing, twelve pounds of sᵈ Rate for to provide wood for the minifter of sᵈ cocietie.

Voted That sᵈ Rate be made according to the rules in the law for the makeing the last Province tax, this Prefent year.

Voted And chofen afsefsors to make fᵈ Rate, Lieuᵗ Samˡˡ Thatcher, Mʳ Palsgrave Wellington and Samuell Jenifon.

Voted and Choofen Sexton for the year enfuing, Thomas Coollidg, and to be pᵈ by two Contrebutions on the Sabbath Days, The Deacons to give notice of it the Sabbath beforehand.

Voted And Choofen for clerke for fᵈ Societie for the year enfuing, Munings Sawin.

Voted That the Contribution be still Continued on the sabbath days as formerly.

Voted That the Deacons, or one of them give notice to fᵈ congregation the Sabbath before each quarter of sᵈ year is ought That so Persons may make up by Contrabution each quarter Part of sᵈ Rate, the next Sabbath following.

[17]

Novembʳ 12 1707. At a meeting of the Inhabitants of the easterly Congregation in Watertown, orderly warned and meet.

Voted That we do defire, nominate, appoint and Impower, thefe severall Genᵗ to be a Comitte to Confider & advife what steps may be thought most Proper to be taken for our futer, honorable and Comfortable settlement in fᵗ Congregation, by Prefering a Petition to the honᵈ Genˡˡ Court now fiting in Boston, vizᵗ Capᵗ Jonas Bond Esqʳ Leinᵗ Jnᵒ Hammond, Mʳ Palsgrave Wellington, Mʳ Netˡˡ Bright and Capᵗ Netˡˡ Barsham, are Chofen for the ends abovefᵈ.

Jan: 7th 1707/8 At a meeting of the Inhabitants belonging to the easterly Congregation in Watertowne orderly warned and meet together.

Cap‘ Jonas Bond Esq‘ was Choofen Moderato‘

1 voted. By said Inhabitants that thay will Choofe a Comitte to take an account of the Deacons of what is behind of the minifters rate in arrears, in thofe years before f⁴ rates wer Commited into the hands of the Constables, and to make there Report of what thay find to f⁴ Precinct at there next meeting.

2 voted. That Samuell Livermore, Richard Coollidg and Nathan Fiske be a comitte for the ends abovef⁴.

3 voted. That f⁴ Meeting be adjourned unto wednesday the 14th of January Currant at one of the Clocke in the afternoon.

What is above written are the severall votes Pafsed at f⁴ meeting. Attest Jonas Bond Moderato‘ of f⁴ meeting.

At a meeting of the east end Cocietie in Watertowne legally warned the 7th of January 1707/8

Voted. That M‘ Bright be choofen Moderato‘.

Voted That thay would choofe a committe to audate accounts between thofe that are charged to be behind in the ministers rates. And the Deacons from the year 1697 until 1702/3.

Voted That Cap‘ Jonas Bond, Sam¹¹ Livermore, Richard Coollidg, Nathan Fiske, Doct‘ Wellington be Choofen for the ends afores⁴ and to take account of the Deacons of strangers money.

Voted That the meeting be adjorned untill the 11th of February 1707/8.

[18]

At a meeting of the easterly Cocietie or Congregation in Watertown Feb‘ 11th 1707/8 M‘ Net¹¹ Bright was Choofen Moderato‘.

The Comitte appointed to audate accounts with the Deacons Refering to the loofe money, and we received an account of, 19ᵗʰ–10ˢ–10ᵈ, which money was delivered to ou‘ Reverend Pastu‘ M‘ Henry Gibbs.

S⁴ meeting is adjurned unto the 18th day of this Instant Feb‘ at one of the Clocke in the afternoon.

At a meeting of the east end Cocietie or Congregation in Watertowne Feb‘ 18: 1707/8.

Voted That the Committe Chosen Jan: 7ʰ 1707/8 to take an account of the Deacons of what is behind of the ministers Rates in arrears, in the year befores⁴ Rats wer Comitted into the hands of the Constables. Doe forthwith Indeavoure to get in the remainder of the same, and alfo to Recon with any fuch as are behind in f⁴ Rates, and alfo doe allow f⁴ Comitte to abate fuch part of s⁴ arrears as thay shall b sattifffyed ought to be abated, (That is to say if the same be don within three months next hence enfuing the date hereof), and if any of them that are faid to be behindhand in f⁴ Rates & arrears will give their oaths before a lawfull authority that thay have already pᵈ a part of the whole, then the same shall be allowed pᵈ.

At a meeting of the easterly Cocietie or Congregation in Watertown the 7th of June 1708

Capt Jonas Bond Esqr was Chosen Moderatr for sd: meeting.

1. Voted That the last Rate made for the Support of the ministrey in sd: Cocietie be forthwith Commited to Constable Nathan Fiske to gather, and he to Issue & make up his accounts of the whole of said Rate at or on the first wednesday of october next.

2. Voted and ordered that the sd: Constable give an account of what part of sd Rate is not exspended in Carrying on ye worke of the ministrey in sd cocietie to the Reverend Pastur Mr Henry Gibbs, by the abovesd first wednesday in octobr

3. Voted and Choofen to be added to the Comitte for warning of meetings in sd Cocietie Deacon William Bond and Samuel Eddy sr and what sd Comitte shall agree upon & send to the Clarke of said Cocietie in writing shall be accounted sufficient warrant for sd Clerk to post up in writing.

4. Voted That we do Desire Deacon Natll Barsham, Deacon Wm Bond, Mr Natll Bright & Saml Eddy sr to procure som Person or Persons for the carrying on of the worke of the ministrey in sd Cociety for ye next & last quarter of the present year, upon as resonable terms as may be.

[19]

5. Voted At the sd meeting, that som further steps may be taken for the more honorable & comfortable support of the Minittrey in sd Cocietie or Congregation.

6. Voted That for that end we do Desire the former Gentn Imployed as a committe for sd worke to take and use such methods for the ends abovesd as thay may thinke most proper. Vizt Capt Jonas Bond, Lieut Jno Hammond, Mr Palsgrave Wellington, Mr Natll Bright & Deacon Netll Barsham.

Octobr 6 1708 At a meeting of the easterly Cocietie, or Congregation in Watertown Orderly warned & meet.

Mr Netll Bright was Chosen Moderator for sd Meeting.

Voted 1 That we do grant a Rate of 77lb in money for the maintenance of the ministrey in sd Societie.

Voted 2 That sd Rate be made according to the ruls for making the Province tax this year.

Voted 3 And chosen for assessors to make sd Rate Lieut Saml Thatcher, Saml Jenison & Josiah Goddard.

Voted 4 And Chosen Clerk for sd Cocietie for the year ensuing Munings Sawin.

Voted 5 And Chosen for sexton to Ring the bell & sweep & locke after the meeting-house, Tho: Collidg, and to be pd by a Contribution at twice in the year.

Voted 6 That the Contrebution be still Continued on the Sabbath days.

Voted 7 That we do desire the Comitte Chosen Jan: 7th 1707/8 to take an account of what money is quite lost, with the names & sums of each Person, and bring in ye account to the next meeting.

Voted 8 That we do defire Serg^t Jno Chadwick & Dan^ll Benjamen to take caer that the glafs in the meeting-houfe be mended, and bring in their account to the next meeting.

Voted 9 That the f^d meeting is adjorned to the first wednesday in Decemb^r next, at one of the Clock at this meeting-houfe.

[20]

Decemb^r 1st 1708 o At a meeting of f^d Cocietie by Adjornment.

1 Voted at f^d meeting that we do add to ye rate granted October the fixt, 1708, eight pounds in licke money, being to make up what money is quiet lost, from the year, 1703, to the year 1708.

Voted 2 Voted that there be a contrebution to gather money on the Sabbath day for the payment of the mending of the meeting-houfe glafs, (and if any over plus be) to be left in ye Deacons hands for the ufe of f^d Cocietie, the Committe to give notice for f^d Contrebution the Sabbath before.

Voted 3 That we do defire Capt Jonas Bond Esqr Deacon Net^ll Barsham, Deac: W^m: Bond, Mr Net^ll Bright, Munings Sawin, and Serg^t Jno Chadwick, To give o^r Reverend Pasto^r Mr Henry Gibbs thanks for his gift to f^d Cocietie.

Voted 4 That Mr Gibb's gift to ye f^d Cocietie be entered in ou^r Booke of Record for f^d P^rcinct.

To Jonas Bond esq^r Mr Palsgrave Wellington, Mr Sam^ll Livermore, Mr Richard Cooledg, Mr Nathan Fiske, The Comittee appointed by the Easterly Precinct of Watertown, to take acc^tt of the arrearages Due to the miniftry of f^d P^rcinct.

Gentlemen, Pleafe to inform the Inhabitants of your Precinct, That I freely Remit twenty Pounds of the Arearages due to me, for Preaching unto them: vizt eighteen pounds twelve fhillings and five pence, of what was due before octob^r 8: 1703. and one pound seven shillings and seven pence, of the Rate Comitted to Constable Jno Straton, which offer of mine, if accepted by the P^rcinct let it be entered in the book of Records belonging to the same.   yours to serve,

Watertown Nov: 30: 1708.   HENRY GIBBS.

[21]

Octob^r 5: 1709 At a meeting of the Easterly cocietie or Congregation in Watertown Orderly warned & meet:

Voted 1 That we do grant a rate of 77^lb in money for the maintenance of the Miniftrey in f^d congregation, twelve pounds of said fum to be for to provid wood for the miniftrey, at feven shillings Pr Cord.

Voted 2 That f^d Rate is to be made according to the Rules for making the Province tax this Prefent year, and that the afseffors affix a lawfull warrant to f^d rate and Deliver it to the Constable in f^d cocietie sesonably.

Voted 3 and Chofen for afsefsors to Make f^d rate, Corp^ll Sam^ll Jenifon, Cler: Jofiah Goddard & Henry Spring.

Voted 4 And Chosen for Clerk for s{d} cocietie or Congregation Munings Sawin.

Voted 5 And Chosen for sexton to Ring the bell and sweep and lock after the meeting-house Tho: Coolidg, and to be p{d} by two Contrebutions within the year.

Voted 7 That a contrebution be still continued on the Sabbath Days for the ministre of s{d} Congregation.

Voted 8 That we do appoint Deacon Nethaniel Barsham, Deacon W{m}: Bond and Sam{ll} Eddy s{r} to be a Committe to warn meetings for s{d} cocietie or Congregation when & so often as there be occasion.

9 Voted That we do adjorne the aboves{d} meeting to the first monday of Decemb{r} next at ten of the Clock in the forenoon, To take caer for the paying for mending the old meeting-houfe glafs, and fuch other Concerns as s{d} meeting shall se occation for.

At a meeting of the Easterly Precinct by adjornment the 5{th} of Decemb{r} 1709.

Voted That we will have a Contribution upon the 3{d} Sabbath day of this Instant December in order to gather money to pay for the mending the meeting-houfe glafs, and for the mending the Bel wheel, and som other arreers due to the sexton.

Voted That s{d} meeting be adjorned to the third moirday of this Instant month, to take account of what money is gathered, and to pay it to the Creditors, And to se if the Cocietie will Confider of som method for placing of the meeting-houfe.

At a meeting of said societie by adjornment the 19{th} of Decemb{r} 1709.

	£	s	d
The Deacons gave account of the Contrebution money	01	14	07
P{d} To Ephraim Cutter Ju{r}	00	08	00
to Joseph Coollidg	00	06	00
to Sert{s} Jn{o} Chadwick:	00	01	00
to Daniel Benjamen	00	01	00
to Joseph Grant	00	18	07

Voted That we do defire the severall Gent{n} viz{t} Nethaniel Coollidg s{r} Samuel Eddy sen{r} Nethaniel Bright s{r} Sam{ll} Thatcher s{r} Joseph Sherman and William Chattuck s{r} to sit at the table.

Voted That we do defire Cap{t} Bond and the Deacons to give the aboves{d} Gent{n} notice of the aboves{d} vote.

The aboves{d} meeting is Defolved by Cap{t} Bond Moderat{r}.

December{r} 20{th} 1709

Then Receivd of Munings Sawin in y{e} east-ends behalfe for the mending the meeting houfe glafs, the fum of eighteen shillings and seven pence I said Received P{r} me

his
JOSEPH X GRANT.
mark

[22]

Octob{r} 4{th} 1710. At a meeting of the Easterly Societie of Congregation in Watertown Orderly warned and met, Cap{t} Jonas Bond esq{r} was Chofen Moderat{r}.

Voted 1 That we do grant a rate of seventy seven Pounds for the support of the ministrey in said Congregation for this Present year; Twelve pounds of s^d seventy seven pounds to be for a supply for wood for the ministrey at seven shillings P^r cord, Provided it be brought in by the last day of March next, And such as do not bring wood by the last day of March as afores^d that their part of ye rate shall be paid in money, or otherwise to the ministers acceptance.

Voted 2 That the rate be made according to the Rules for making the Province tax for this P^{r}sent year, And that they do affix a warrant to s^d rate according to law, And to deliver said rate to the Collector sesonably.

Voted 3 And Chosen for afsessors to make s^d Rate as aboves^d Sam^{ll} Jenison, Josiah Goddard and Henry Spring f^r.

Voted 4 And Chosen Clerk for said Cocietie, Munings Sawin.

Voted 5 And Chosen for sexton Tho: Coolidg, to take caer of ye meeting-house, and to be p^d for his service by two Contrebutions as formerly.

Voted 6 That the Contrebution be still Continued on the Sabbath days.

Voted 7 And Chosen for a Committe Deacon Net^{ll} Barsham, Deacon Wm Bond and Samuel Eddy f^r To warn s^d Cocietie together when & so often as their may be occation.

Voted 8 And Chosen for Collector for to gather in s^d rate Jonathan Stone.

Voted 9 And Chosen for receiver of the aboves^d rate, Mr Net^{ll} Bright, to receive in and pay out said Rate for the ends and use for which it was granted, Rendering an account of the same to s^d Cosietie. And also said Mr Bright is Chosen to call the late Constables to an account belonging to s^d Cocietie That have had the ministers Rates Comited to them to gather. That have not issued and made up their accounts according to their warrant And to pay in the same to the Reverend Mr Henry Gibbs.

Aprill 3^d 1711. The aboves^d Rate was made and Comitted to Mr Jonth Stone Collecto^r to gather and pay in to Mr Neth^{ll} Bright Receiver amounting to the sum of 77^{lb}–12^s–09^d.

       Pr Henry Spring
       Josiah Goddard &
       Sam^{ll} Jenison assessors.

[23]

October 3^d 1711. At a meeting of the easterly Cocietie or Congregation in Watertown orderly warned and meet.

Voted 1 That we do grant A rate of 80^{lb} for the support of the ministrey in s^d Cocietie or Congregat^n for the year ensuing, Twelve pounds whereof is to provide wood for the ministrey at eight shillings P^r cord.

Vot 2 That the s^d rate be made according to the Rules Prescribed for making the last Province tax, and that ther be a warrant affixed to s^d rate according to law, and to deliver said Rate to the Collector sesonably.

Vot. 3 And Chofen for afsefsors to make f⁴ Rate, John Coollidg, Josiah Goddard and Nathan Fiske.

Vot: 4 That we Choofe Deacon Neth̅ Barsham, Deacon Willm Bond & Samll Eddy fr a Committe, for f⁴ Cocietie for the year enfuing.

Vot: 5 That we do Choofe Jonathon Stone Collector to gather & pay in s⁴ Rate to the Treafurer or Receiver.

Vot: 6 for Treafurer or Receiver of f⁴ Rate, Mr Nethll Bright, who is to receive in and pay out f⁴ rate for the ends for which it was granted, and to render an account to the f⁴ cocietie fefonably.

Vot: 7 That we do Choofe Munings Sawin Clerk for f⁴ cocietie for the year enfuing.

Vot: 8 That we do Choofe Tho: Coollidg sexton, and to be p⁴ by two free Contrebutions as formerly.

Vot: 9 Voted that the Collectors Shall annually make up their accounts with the Prsent Treafurer or Receiver, or his or their fuccefsor in f⁴ office of their severall rates.

Vot: 10 that the Contribution be ftill continued on the Sabbath day as formerly.

Votd 11 That we do defire Mr Netll Bright & Munings Sawin to take caer to find out how much the feverall Rates did amount too that have been made of late years for the fupport of the miniftrey in f⁴ Cocietie or Congregation, and when f⁴ rates wer made, and by whome, and when comited to the feverall Conftables, In order to the more effectuall & spedy gathering the arrears of said rates.

Voted 12 That the meeting be adjorned to the first monday of November next at on of ye Clock in ye afternoon. In order to Confider of fom way to mend the Meeting-houfe glafs, and to know the cocieties mind (whether they will add anything towards his late loffes by fier) in the Prsent Rate, or whether they will give him a free contribution once or moer in ye year.

Novembr 5 1711. At a meeting by adjormt

Voted 1 That we will have a free Contrebution fower times in this Prsent year Infuing, for the Revered Pastor Mr Henry Gibbs, for the repairing of his buildings, and fuch other ufes as he shall fe caufe.

Vot: 2 that we will add twenty shillings to the abovesd rate last granted for the miniftrey to mend the meeting-houfe glafs.

Jun: 13th 1711/12 At a meeting of the easterly Cocietie or Congregation in Watertown Orderly warned and meet, for to defpofe of a certaine Contrebution in the hands of the Deacons.

Voted That we do freely give the f⁴ Contrebution to our Reverend Pastor Mr Henry Gibbs.

[24]

Mar: 17 1711/12 At a meeting of the Inhabitants of the Easterly Congregation in Watertown orderly warnd and meet.

Voted 1 That the money that was over and above the Purchafe of the Pastur land Purchafed of Mrs. Judith Allen (being five pounds & five shillings) we defire Mr Nethaniel Bright one of the Committe, to keep it while fuch time as the fubfcribers fe caufe to call for it, if their should be a prospect to purchafe more land or lands.

Voted 2 That the Deed of the lands Purchafed for the ufe of the miniftrey in f^d congregat^n be lodged with their book of Records.

Voted. 3. In anfwer to the subfcription fent from feverall of the Inhabitants of the middle Part of Watertown, and left with the Rever^d Mr Henry Gibbs, Bering date Feb^r 1711/12 And fome Propofals made to them againe, which wer Read and voted at this said meeting.

Voted, 4 That we do defire Maj^r Jonas Bond to communicate the same.

Voted, 5 That all the Rates belonging to the estate of Benj^a Wellington Dece^d, which wer due to the miniftrey in ye aboves^d Congregation (in the hands of any Constables untill this Prefent year be all Crost and difcharged.

[25]

May, 26th 1712. At a meeting of the Inhabitants of the Congregation at the east-end of Watertown, orderly warned and meet together.

1. Voted. That we will Choofe a Committe to Represent us at the Great & Gen^ll Court, Upon the second Wednesday of their next feffions, which will be ye 4th of June next, Being the day appointed for the hearing of the Petition of Sundrey of the Inhabitants belonging to the easterly Military & Companey of said town, Baring Date March, 17th 1711/12 And make fuch defence against said Petition as they shall think most Proper. And alfo to Addrefs his Excellency and ye Great and Gen^ll Court, for a Better & Lasting Settlement of the Congregation in the east end of s^d Watertown.

2. Voted And Chofen for the ends afores^d to Be a Commite to Reprefent o^rfelves in the f^d Court, Maj^r Jonas Bond esq^r Mr Joseph Sherman, Mr William Shattuck f^r, Mr Nethanial Bright, Mr Palsgrave Wellington, Mr Sam^ll Livermore, Mr Nathan Fiske, Capt Nethaniel Barsham & Mr Richard Coolidg.

[26] Blank.

[27]

Watertown, May: 29. 1711.

We the fubfcribers, Inhabitants in s^d town, being very senfible of the great want there is of better accommodations to the Miniftrey in the East-End of s^d town; as to Pasture land & meadow: And being alfo very free & willing to contribute for the Purchafing of Lands; either Pasture, meadow, or both, for the accomodating of the Revd Mr Gibbs, who is our prefent Minifter, & of fuch as shall succead him, in the work of the Miniftrey in s^d Congregation: And there being now A Prospect off Purchafing some Lands, for the ends afores^d we do freely & voluntarily subfcribe, engage & promife to pay the feveral fumms affixed to our names into the hands off Deacon William Bond, Mr William Shattock fr and Mr Netll Bright A Comitte to be by them laid out for the ends aforesd of which fumms we do engage to pay the one halfe within a week, and the other halfe within fix months after the date hereof, giving to sd Persons full power as a committee to act & transact in that matter, and to Receive a Deed or Deeds, in our names, of Lands purchafed with ye money, hereunto subfcribed, and said lands to be & remaine, for the ufe of the miniftrey of said Congregation.

	£	s	d		£	s	d
Mr Henry Gibbs	02	00	00	Jonas Bond esqr	02	00	00
Richard Coollidg	01	00	00	Netll Barsham	02	00	00
John Bifco	01	00	00	Samuel Thatcher	01	10	00
John Chenery	00	12	00	Netll Bright	02	00	00
Oliver Wellington	00	15	00	Samll Eddy fr	00	12	00
Samuel Holden	00	10	00	William Shattuck	01	00	00
Isaac Holden	00	10	00	William Bond	01	10	00
William Shattuck Jr	00	10	00	Munings Sawin	00	15	00
Joseph Holden	00	10		Nathan Fiske	01	10	00
Joseph Coollidg	00	10	00	Jonathan Stone	01	10	00
John Abbut	01	00	00	Josiah Goddard	00	15	00
David Stone	00	10	00	Daniel Benjamen	01	00	00
Robert Goddard	00	15	00	George Lawrance	00	10	00
Thomas Bond	00	10	00	Josiah Perry	00	10	00
Samuel Hastings	00	10	00	Ebenezer Stone	00	06	00
John Straton Jur	01	00	00	Benjamin Eddy	00	12	00
Samuel Straton	01	00	00	Joseph Sherman	00	05	00
Mrs Elizebeth Bond	00	05	00	Henry Mils	00	15	00
Samuel Livermore	01	15	00	Palsgraue Wellington	02	00	00
Danll Smith	01	00	00	Henry Spring	01	00	00
Danll Livermore	01	00	00	Samuel Jenifon	01	10	00
Timothy Barron	00	10	00				
Thomas Learnard	00	10	00				

[28] Blank.

[29]

October, 1. 1712. At a meeting of the Easterly Congregation or Precinct in Watertown Orderly warned and affembled, Mr Natll: Bright was Chofen Moderator.

Voted. 1 that we do grant a Rate for the fupport of the Miniftrey in fd Congregation of 82lb. fourteen pounds of said rate to be for to provide wood for the minifter at nine shillings Pr Cord. Provided the Genll Court do not other wife order the Raising of sd Rate.

Voted. 2 For affefsors to make fd Rate, Nathan Fiske, Jno: Coollidg, and Daniel Livermore.

Voted. 3 And Chofen for a Comitte for fd Precinct Deacon Natll Barsham, Deacon William Bond and Mr Natll Bright.

Voted. 4 & Chosen for Receiver or Treasurer Mr Nat^{ll} Bright.
5 Munings Sawin Chosen Clerk for 1^d Precinct.
6 Chosen for sexton Tho : Coollidge & to be p^d for his worke by two Contrebutions as formerly.

The aboves^d meeting is adjorned to the third Monday of November next, to Consider of what may then further to be acted. 1^d meeting to begine at two of the Clock of s^d Day.

October 5. 1712. Rec^d of the Collect^{rs} of the Rates for the Ministrey at the east end of Watertown and of other Persons, in full of all Dues to the Ministry from Oct, 6. 1711, to the sixt of Octr one thousand seven hundred & Twelve.

Rec^d ₩^{r} me
Henry Gibbs.

Novb^r 17th 1712 At a meeting of the Easterly Congregation or P^{r}cinct in Watertown by adjornm^t : Voted at s^d meeting that we do desire our former Comitte Chosen to Represent us in the affaire at the last Gen^{ll} Court, to lay the Result of s^d Court, before the Committe Chosen by the westerly or middle congregation in sd Watertown as soone as may be, and to desire sd committe to give us an answer of what they Intend to do in said affaire. The aboves^d Gen^{ll} Courts act was Read at the aboves^d meeting, and was voted to know ye minds of s^d easterly Congregation, who did Declare our willing submission to and compliance with s^d courts 1^d order. Baring Date the 4th of Novemb^r 1712.

Feb^r 2^d 1712/13 Watertown,

At a meeting of the Easterly P^{r}cinct in Watertown orderly warned & meet.

Voted   That we do Choose, appoint & Impower These severall Gen^{tn} following vizt Maj^r Jonas Bond, Capt Net^{ll} Barsham, Nethaniel Bright, William Shattuck s^r Doctor Palsgraue Wellington, Richard Coolidge, Nathan Fiske and Sam^{ll} Livermore To be a committe to Represent This Precinct at the meeting warned by order of the select men of this town on the fourth of this Instant : to hear the advice of the Gen^{ll} Court relating to the support of the ministrey & to take effectuall care y^t ye publick worship of God be honourably maintained amongst us. And at s^d meeting to declare our willing submission to & compliance with the late order of the Gen^{ll} Court bering date Novb^r 4th 1712. Relating to the support of the ministrey in the two precincts of ye town according to what was formerly voted by us, and entered in our Booke of Records. And also at s^d meeting to enter a Protest in our names (if need be) against any vote or Proposals that may ther be made, or offered to supersed, Infring, Invalidate or annull the s^d order of the hon^d Court, or to Retard the effectuall execution of it. And further to declare in ye name of the Precinct that we Judge it an affront to the hon^d Court, and Injurious to the peace of the town to clogg ye execution of s^d Order, or to pretend & endeavour by a Maj^r vote of the Enhabitants of the town to oblige or ensnare us, or any others of the town, who are desirus to submit to s^d order, unto anything of a differrent Import. And furthermore we desire our Committee abovesd to Insist upon it that the assessors of the town be forthwith set on worke to assess the sum mentioned in first order of Court for ye ends and in yr manner therein Specified. And to deliver a copie of this our vote to the moderator that may be assigned for said meeting.

[30]

Voted. That the Treasurer use the utmost of his endeavour to get in what of Arrears yet Remaine in the Constables hands by the 20th day of this Instant february, and to make report of his doings therein at our next meeting.

Voted. That we desire Majr Jonas Bond, And Mr Netll Bright, or any others that are willing to meet with Stephen Cook this day to agree wth said Cook, Reffering to sd Cooks Rates as they shall se meet.

[31]

March: 17th 1712/13 At a meeting of the Inhabitants of the Easterly Precinct or Congregation in Watertown Orderly warned & meet.

Voted 1 That we do choose Samuel Livermore to be an assessor in the stead of Daniel Livermore to make the Ministers Rate for the prsent year for sd Precinct, granted on the first of october, 1712.

Voted 2 That we will have a free contribution, on the first Sabbath day of may next ensuing, for to pay the arrears due to Mr Gibbs, which arrears are sumthing doubtfull to be gotten.

Voted 3 That we will Choose a comitte to Represent us at the next sitting of the Genll Court, in Order for any matters in Refferrence to the late order & advice of the Genll Court bearing Date Novembr 4th 1712.

Voted 4 That we do desire our former Comitte, Chosen the 26 of May, 1712, vizt Majr Jonas Bond, Mr. Joseph Sherman, Palsgraue Wellington, Netll Bright, Capt Barsham, Wm Shattuck, sr Samll Livermore, Nathan Fisk & Ric. Coollidg. they or the Major Part of them, to Represent us in what may be to be further acted in Refferrence to the aforesd order & advice.

Voted 5 That we are free and willing to pay our part of the Quarter of a year Sallorry. . . . . . Due to our Reverend Pastr Mr Henry Gibbs for preaching to ye whole town a quarter of a year, according to the towns votes, which Quarter began the 6th of November, 1695.

Octobr 7 1713. At a meeting of the Easterly Precinct or Congregation in Watertown Orderly warned & met the 7th of October, 1713. Majr Jonas Bond Chosen moderatr.

1 Voted that we will Choose A committe to Reprsent our selves, and to apply themselves to the select men of said Town, or else where as shall be thought needfull, To see that the Act of the honorable Genll Court, and the vote of the Town in June last past be put into effectuall execution for the Support of the Ministry in Watertown.

2 Voted that we defire the comitte Choofen the 26th of may, 1712 for the ends aboves'd viz't Maj'r Jonas Bond, M'r Joseph Sherman, M'r Palsgrave Wellington, M'r Nat'll Bright, Cap't Nat'll Barsham M'r Will'm Shattuck, M'r Sam'll Livermore Nathan Fiske & Ric: Coollidg

3 Voted & chofen for a Comitte Cap't Nat'll Barsham Deacon W'm Bond & M'r Nat'll Bright.

4 M'r Nat'll Bright Chofen Receiver for y'e Minifters Rate.

5 Munings Sawin Chofen Clerk for said Precinct.

6 Tho: Coollidg Chofen fexton, and to be p'd by two Contributions as formerly.

7 Voted that we will have a contrebution on the first Sabbath day of every month for the year enfuing, and what is gathered shall be set off in their Ministers Rate.

8 Voted that y'e third Wednesday of this Instant october be appointed for fuch as are willing to cart wood for the ministrey of said P'r'cinct.

9 Voted that this meeting be adjorn'd to the second Wednesday of November next, and to begine at one oclock in the afternoon.

Watertown Oct'r 6, 1713, all Dues for the Miniftrey at the East End of f'd Town paid for the year Past.   HENRY GIBBS.

Watertown Novemb'r 5'th 1713 Rec'd of the feverall collectors of the Rates for the Miniftrey att the East-End of s'd Town, and of P'rticular Persons included in s'd Rates, the full of all dues To the Miniftrey of the East Congregation, From the time of their being seperated from the other part of s'd Town, unto the fixt of Oct'r one thoufand seven hundred & eleven.

           Rec'd I say in full

                    P'r me

                       HENRY GIBBS

[32]

11: Nov'ber 1713. At a meeting of the Inhabitants of Easterly Precinct or Congregation in Watertown the 11'th of November, 1713. By adjornment.

1 Voted, that the Treafurer or Receiver for the Ministers Rate of s'd Precinct do forthwith take effectual caer and Quicken up the Constables & Collectors forth with to finish & make up their accounts with the said Treafurer.

Decemb'r 14'th 1713. At a meeting of the Easterly Precinct or Congregation in Watertown Orderly warned & meet the fourteenth Day of December, 1713.

1 Voted that we do grant a Rate of fourteen pounds for the Rever'd M'r Henry Gibbs for his fallery for preaching to y'e s'd Congregation for two months: viz't from the 7'th of October last past untill the fourth of December currant. And alfo we do grant fourteen shillings more to be added to the fourteen pounds for to make up fum lofe in y'e Rate last Committed to Jon'th Stone, to gather for the said Congregation.

2 Voted, That we do Choofe Nathan Fiske, John Coollidg

and Samuel Livermore aſſeſsors o make the ſaid Rate and Deliver it with a warrant affixed to it, unto the Collector.

3 Voted and Chooſen for Collector to gather ſ{d} Rate Robert Goddard.

At a meeting of the Inhabitants of the Easterly Congregation in Watertown Orderly warned & met the 6. of october 1714. Maj{r} Jonas Bond was Choſen Moderator for s{d} meeting. Choſen for the comitte for the year enſuing Cap{t} Nat{ll} Barsham, Deacon William Bond & M{r} Nat{ll} Bright. Choſen for Clerke for ſ{d} P{r}cinct Munings Sawin, Choſen for ſexton Tho: Coollidge, and to be p{d} by two contributions as hath been formerly.

Voted that the monthly contrebution be continued for the Miniſtrey of the ſ{d} Congregation as it was the last year.

Voted. That there be a Contrebution on the firſt Thanksgiving day for to Repaire the old meeting houſe in ſaid Town, And we do deſire our Reverend Paſture M{r} Henry Gibbs to give seſonable notice of it to the s{d} Congregation.

[33]

Watertown May 24{th} 1715 Rec{d} of M{r} Robert Goddard Collecto{r} for the Easterly P{r}cinct in Watertown & by his Order, in full for my Salery for the year beginning Octob{r} 6{th} 1713 to Octob{r} the, 6. 1714. Rec{d} P{r} me
HENRY GIBBS.

Rec{d} alſo on the day of the Date above written of the p{r}ſon aboveſ{d} in full for two months salery, beginning the ſixt of Octob{r} 1714. Rec{d} P{r} me
HENRY GIBBS.

At a meeting of the Inhabitants of the Easterly Congregation in Watertown orderly warned and meet, the fift of October, 1715.

Voted and Chosen for a committe to warn meetings when their may be occation Deacon Barsham, Deacon Bond and M{r} Nathaniel Bright, Choſen for Clarke for ſd congregation Munings Sawin; Choſen Sexton Tho: Coolidge.

Voted that the monthly contrebution be ſtill continued on the Sabbath Day.

Voted that we will have a Contrebution the next Thanksgiving Day for the Repairing y{e} meeting houſe, and to be laid out by the former Committe.

[34]

At a meeting of the Easterly Congregation in Watertown Orderly warned & met together the 18{th} day of July 1715.

Voted & Choſen for Moderator Maj{r} Jonas Bond.

Voted that we will Choſe A comitte to Repreſent this Congregation, To wait on the Gen{ll} Court at their next ſeſſions, and to lay before ſd. Court how thire Orders & acts w{th} reſpect to the ſupport of the miniſtrey in Watertown are Slighted & contemned by the other Congregation. And the greater part of thoſe who are Chofen Town officers, whereby the Miniftrey do fail of their Juſt dues: And alſo to Addreſſ the ſaid Gen[ll] Court that in Caſe their cant be a dutifull complyance with the orders of Court and vote of the Town already made, That thire be a line of Diviſion made & ſettled between us under ſuch A Regulation as will tend moſt for peace and comfort for the futer.

Chofen for said Comitte for the ends aforeſ[d] Maj[r] Jonas Bond, Richard Coollidg, Samuel Livermore, Samuel Thatcher, William Shattuck, Nat[ll] Bright, Nathan Fiſke, Joſiah Goddard John Coollidg, Robart Goddard, and Henry Spring.

[35]

At a meeting of the Inhabitants of the Easterly Congregation in Watertown Orderly warned and met together September the, 4,[th] 1716. Robert Goddard was Chofen Moderator.

1 Voted that we will Chofe A Committe to treat with ſom man or men to be a conſtant & certaine help for the upholding of Preaching among us while M[r] Gibbs's Bodily elneſs Remaines upon him, or for ſuch time as they can agree for.

2 Voted, and Chofen for the comitte fore the ends aforeſ[d] the Deacons of the Church.

3. Voted, That we will have a free Contrebution on the third Sabbath of this P[r]ſent month for to help defray the charge of such as ſhall be procured to cary on Preaching among us

4 Voted that we do adjorn this meeting to the laſt monday of September Currant, at ſower of the Clock in the after noone, at this Place, to met againe to hear the Report of the comitte and conſider what is further to be don.

The above written votes wer paſt at ſaid meeting as atteſt
ROBERT GODDARD.

At a meeting of the Easterly Congregation in Watertown orderly warned & meet the 3[d] of October, 1716. Maj[r] Jonas Bond was Choſen moderator.

Voted, and Chofen for a comitte Maj[r] Jonas Bond, Deacon William Bond & M[r] Nat[ll] Bright, voted & chofen for Clerke Munnings Sawin, Choſen for Sexton Thomas Coollidg and to be pd. by two Contrebutions as hath been formerly.

Voted that the monthly Contrebution for the Miniſtrey be ſtill continued on y[e] Sabbath days.

Voted that ſuch as will be pleaſed to carry wood to M[r] Gibbs, do it on the firſt wedneſday of November next enſuing.

Voted, That we do defire Ebenezer Stone to take caer & provide faſtnings for the meeting-houfe windows, and to be paid his Reaſonable coſt out of the Contribution in Banke.

Voted, that we do defire y[e] aboveſ[d] Comitte to make inquiry into fom demand made by Joſeph Grant, for mending ſome glace for the meeting-houſe, and to make Report to the next meeting of what they find due.

[36]

At a meeting of the Easterly Congregation in Watertown Orderly warned and meet the 2'' of Octob'' 1717. M'' Nat'' Bright was Chosen Moderator.

Voted. and Chosen for a Committe, Maj'' Jonas Bond, Deacon William Bond & M'' Nat'' Bright.

Voted. And Chosen for Clerk Munnings Sawin, Chosen for sexton Thomas Coollidg, and to be paid by two Contrebutions, to be on the last Sabbath in Aprill next, and the last Sabbath in September next ensuing.

Voted That the monthly Contrebution be Continued for the Ministrey on the first Sabbath of every month during this year ensuing.

Voted. That we do desire Deacon William Bond & M'' Nat'' Bright to Invite Deacon Nathan Fiske & Deacon John Coollidg to sitt in the Deacons Pue.

And this meeting was Disolved by the Moderat'', orderly.

At a meeting of the Easterly Societie or Congregation in Watertown Orderly warned & meet the second Day of June, 1718. Voted and Chosen for Moderat'' M'' Nathanael Bright.

Voted And Chosen for A committe to take care to mend the Platform of the old meeting-house in s''. Town, Deacon Fiske and Deacon John Collidg, to procure & Provide materials and work men to do said worke sensonably as soone as may be, and to bring in a true account to the next meeting of s'' societie, and to be paid their Just Cost out of the money gathered for the end afores''

At a meeting of the East Congregation in Watertown Orderly warned and meet the 14''' of Aprill, 1719. M'' Nat'' Bright, was Chosen Moderator.

1 Voted, that we do lay down the monthly Contrebution for this presant year.

2 Voted, that we do desire the select-men would order the payment to the Rate for the Ministrey to be p'' Quarterly.

3 Voted, that we will have a free Contrebution Quarterly, or a subscription for to provide help to carry on the worke of the amongst us, which s''. Precinct shall Choose.

4. Voted, that we will have a free contrebution for the end afores'' and to begine the first Sabbath day in may next ensuing, and to be the Contrebutions for this p''esent year & to be quarterly.

5 Voted, that we will mend the fence of the Pasture Purchased for y'' Ministrey of the east Congregation,

6 Voted, That we desire M'' Joseph Coollidge to do the work about said Pasture and provide what fenceing stufe is wanting, and the Proprietors of s'' Pasture to se him paid for his cost & charges.

Said meeting is by a vote adjorn'' to the 29'''', of this Instant Aprill to five o'clock in the afternoon at the above s''d house.

At a meeting of the easterly Congregation by adjornment in Watertown the Twenty ninth day of Aprill one thousand seven hundred and nineteen.

[37]

Watertown may 4th 1719 At a meeting of the east Congregation in said Town, Orderly warned & meet.

Voted. That whereas one Article propofed in the warning of the Town meeting, at the Newe meetinghoufe on this day att three of the Clock in the afternoone, is, to fee what the Town will do in anfwer to an Addrefs made by fundrey Inhabitants, as to the Towns coming together in one Congregation in fome convenient time & place.

Wee chofe appoint & defire Maj^r Jonas Bond, Nathanael Bright, William Shattuck, Deacon William Bond, Deacon Nathan Fiske, Lt Richard Coollidg, Josiah Goddard, Jonathan Stone & Jofeph Mafon, to be a Committee to reprefent us of the east end Congregation att said Town meeting & in our name to enter a defent or Protest against the Towns Voting in fd affaire as not being the proper bufinefs of our Town Meetings and to declare y^t we esteem it repugnant to the act of settlement made & established by the great & Generall Court of this Province in the year, 1712. Relating to the Maintenace of ye Miniftry in the two Congregations of this Town, By virtue of which act, no major Vote of the Inhabitants can determine any thing obligatory in this matter, and withall to, Declare in our name, that if the other Congregation will pleas to Choofe & appoint a Committee to meet the aboves^d P^{r}sons whome we have Chofen & appointed to Reprefent our felves at any Convenient time & place, freely & calmly to Confult under o^r p^{r}sent Circumstances, about ye things that may promote ye Peace of the Town & the Interest of Religion Among us, which fo much depends upon a well grounded peace, we Redely Confent thereto, and heartily wish fuch a conference may be under Divine direction and obtaine a good Iffue. And that the Major part of the above named persons be rekoned a full committee for the East Congregation for ye ends above mentioned, and alfo upon any other occation of treating about fd. affaire & what shall be Confulted or proposed by sd. Committee to be laid before the easterly Congregation.

          Jonas Bond
          Nathaniel Bright
          Willam Shattuck
          William Bond
          Nathan Fiske
          Richard Coollidge
          Josiah Goddard
          Jonethan Stone
          Joseph Mafon

At a meeting of the Inhabitants of the Easterly Congregation in Watertown Orderly warned and meet the, 7th of October, 1719. Maj^r Bond was Choofen Moderator.

1 Voted, and Chofen for A comittee, Maj^r Jonas Bond, Deacon William Bond & Mr Nat${}^ll$ Bright.

2 Voted, and chosen Clark for sd. Congregation Munnings Sawin.

3 Voted, and Chosen for sexton Tho: Coollidg and to be p⁴ by two Contrebutions as formerly.

4 Voted, that we will have a free Contrebution on the next Thankgiving day to be Improved for the Repairing the Personage.

5 Voted, that we will have a Contrebution Quarterly on the Sabbath days for M{r} Gibbs as was the last year.

6 Voted, that on the second Tuisday of November next we appoint to Cart wood to M{r} Gibbs and to be gratis.

[38]

At a meeting of the Easterly Congregation in Waterfown Orderly warned and meet the 5{th} of October, 1720. Maj{r} Jonas Bond was Chosen Modera{tr} for sd meeting.

1 Voted, and Chosen for a Committee Maj{r} Jonas Bond esq{r} M{r} Nat{ll} Bright and Deacon William Bond. 2 Chosen for Clerk Munnings Sawin. 3 Chosen sexton Tho: Coollidge and to be paid by two Contrebutions for his service as formerly.

4 Voted, that their shall be a free Contrebution once A Quarter this P{r}sent year, Towards the Defraying the Charges in carrying on Preaching under M{r} Gibbs present Bodily illness.

5 Voted, That the second Tuisday of November next be appointed for carrying of Wood to the Rev{d} M{r} Gibbs for such as are free & willing so to do, and the wood that shall be so carried to be free & gratis & not accounted any part of the sallary.

6 Voted, That on the third Sabbath in this P{r}sent month their be a free Contrebution for the Raising of money to defray the Charge of some nessessary Repairs of the Ministerial place.

7 Voted, and Chosen for a committee to take care and see the worke done Serj{t} Josiah Goddard Ebenezer Stone and William Bond Jn{r} and to give an Account of the Charge to the Congregation when the worke is done.

At a meeting of the Inhabitants of the Easterly Congregation in Waterfown Orderly warned and meet the 14{th} of Octob{r} 1720. Voted & Chosen M{r} Nathanael Bright for Moderator.

Voted That we do Ajorne the aboves{d} meeting to the 21{st} day of this Instant October to three of the Clock in the afternoon, at Old meeting-house in sd. Town.

At a meeting of the Inhabitants of the Easterly Congregation in Watertown by Adjornment the 21{st} of October, 1720. M{r} Nat{ll} Bright was Chosen Moderator.

1 Voted, that we will Chose A committee to Address the Gen{ll} Court for a setled line or Boundary for each Precinct or Congregation in Watertown.

2 Voted, and Chosen A Comittee for the end afores{d} Maj{r} Jonas Bond Esq{r} M{r} Nath{l} Bright, Lieu{t} Ric: Coollidg, Deacon Nathan Fiske, M{r} Jon{th} Stone, Dea: Jn{o} Coollidg, M{r} Joseph Mason and M{r} Joseph Coollidge.

3 Voted, that they be a Comittee in our names & behalfe to address s{d} Court, that a Divisional line may be established, whereby

the Rattable estate of the Town may be equally parted between the two Congregations in the Town, The Town having acted in the same affaire Jan: 13th 1718/9. That fo each Congregation may be enabled comfortably to proceed in granting and Raifing money for their Respective Incidental Charges. The Salery for the Miniftrey to be Stil leveyed on ye whole Town, and equally divided according to the Order of the Great & Gen^{ll} Court bearing Date November the 4. 1712.

4 Voted, That we leave it with fd Comittee to Advife & confider what methods they may think best for Obtaining the ends afores^d.

To Munnings Sawin Clerk of the Easterly Congregation in Watertown, Whereas Sundrey of the Inhabitants of s^d Congregation have made known to us the fubfcribers who are the Committee to call meetings, That they defire ther might be A meeting warned for sd. Congregation to fee what methods are best to be taken to obtaine A setteled Precinct line between the Two Congregations in fd. Town.

These are therefore to defire you to Post up a warning for a Precinct or Congregation in ye words following.

Viz^t. The Inhabitants belonging to the Easterly Congregation are Desired to give a meeting at the Old meeting-houfe in fd Town on the fourteenth day of October Currant at three of the Clock in the after noon, to Confider, advife & act on fuch methods as may be thought Proper to obtaine a fettled Precinct line between the Two Congregations in fd. Town, That each Congregation may be better enabled to Raife money for Repaires, or other wife for their good & benefit, alfo to Raife money if need be for ye ends aforefd. By order of the Committee.

            Jonas Bond.
            Nat^{ll} Bright
            Willm Bond.

[39]

To Munnings Sawin Clerk of the Easterly Congregation in Watertown. You are hereby Ordered to post up an order on the next Sabbath day. vizt in the words following.

The Inhabitants of the Easterly Congregation in Watertown are hereby Ordered to meet at the old meeting houfe in fd Town, on the first wednesday of October next, at three of the Clock in the afternoon, To Chofe A committee, A clerk, and a sexton, and fuch other Bifnes as faid Congregation may then fee caufe to do. Watertown September. 30th 1721.

     JONAS BOND   ⎫
     NAT^{ll} BRIGHT   ⎬ Comittee.
     WILLIAM BOND ⎭

Perfuant to faid Order, I have Posted up the aboves^d Order according to the time, place and Bifnes therein mentioned.

    Munnings Sawin Clerk of sd Congregation.

At a meeting of the Easterly Congregation in Watertown, Orderly warned and meet the 4th of October, 1721. Coll^{ll} Jonas Bond esq^r was Chofen Moderator for s^d. meeting.

1 Voted, and Chofen for A committee, Jonas Bond esq^r Mr Nat^{ll} Bright and Dea: Willm Bond.

2 Voted and Chofen for Clerk Munnings Sawin, voted and Chofen for fexton Tho: Coollidge, and for his fervice to have two Contrebutions.

4 Voted, that we will have four Contrebutions Quarterly this enfuing year towards ye defraying the Charges of preaching in the aboves^d Congregation.

5 Voted, and agreed that all fuch that are of a willing mind to Carry wood gratis to our Rever^d pastor, Mr Gibbs on the last Tuisday of November next do then attend faid work.

At a meeting of ye Eaft Congregation in Watertown October the 13 1722

By Adjurnment from the third of f^d Octob^r which meeting was upon a defire to choofe and Incourage some perfon to take care of the Old meeting houfe as a fexton and to Defire and Appoint Some meet perfon to Officiate as a Clerk and to know the minds of ye Congregation as to Continue a quarterly Contribution &c

1 Thomas Coollidge was defired to take the care of the Meeting houfe, and that he should be rewarded by having two Contributions in the year, at Each half years end.

2 It was Agreed their S^{ld} be four Contributions free this year to be Improved so far as that will go towards the paying of Such as do preach among us under Mr Gibbs Confinement.

3 It was Agreed that the first tufday in Novemb^r next S^{ld} be the day for cuting & Carting of wood for Mr Gibbs, for Such as See caufe So to do, and to be free and not to be Accounted any part of his Sallery.

4 The form^r Committe are defired Still to Continue to call ye Congregation togeth^r when their is Occation for it.

5 Joseph Mafon is defired to be An Afsiftant to our prefent Clerk und^r his prefent illnefs and Indifpofition and to put on or take of the Precinct book as there may be need.

Hear Ends Congregational Affairs.

[40] Blank.

[41-43]

[Here follow the accounts of the assessors and the treasurer for the Easterly Precinct Affairs between the dates of March 14, 1733/4 and March 5, 1742/3. The Collector and Treasurer debit and credit accounts from 1734 to Feb. 28, 1742, having occupied the double pages 1 and 2 at the beginning of the book, preceding the general congregation affairs.—EDS.]

[44]

After the Town Was Divided and Precinct affairs ceased

Then the Town Voted this Book to be Improved p ye Treasurer in the Town Concerns

AND ACCORDINGLY
The Town Concerns begins Page 45
Which is over Leafe

[45 to 81]
[Here follow the accounts of the Treasurer of the Town Concerns between the dates of March 13, 1737/8, and June 18, 1792. At the reversed end of this book Precinct Affairs are continued. —Eds.]

[Precinct Affairs.]

[1]

Midd^x fs: To Mr Samuel Peirce Constable of the most Easterly Precinct in Watertowne, Greeting.

Application being this day made to me the Subscriber One of his Majesties Justices of the Peace within and for the s^d County of Midd^x By Jonas Bond Esqr and Ten other free holders and inhabitants within the Easterly Precinct in said Watertowne, Seting forth that there is great need of A Precinct meeting to be Called, (1) for to Choose A Clerk, Committe and all other Precinct Officers (2) to take Care for the Carrying on of Preaching in s^d Precinct, and to Come in to Some proper Method to proceed toward a full Settlement of the Gospel Ministrey in s^d Precinct (3) to agree how to raise Precinct meetings for the future.

These are therefore In his Maje^s Name to Will and require you the aboves^d Contables forthwith to Warne and give Notice to all the free holders and other Inhabitants Liveing within the bounds of the s^d Easterly Precinct at last Setled by Order of the Generall Court, Who are quallifyed according to Law to Vote in the affaires of s^d Precinct to meet at the Old Meeting house in s^d Precinct on Monday the Twenty third day of December Currant at Ten of the Clock in the forenoon: first after the Choice of A Moderator. To Choose A Precinct Clerk, Com^{tee} and all other Precinct Officers (2) To take Care for the Carrying on of Preaching in s^d Precinct, and to Come into Some proper Methods, to proceed toward, a full Settlement of the Gospel Ministrey in s^d Precinct (3) to Agree how to raise Precinct Meetings for the future,

And make Returne of your doings hereon Unto Jonas Bond Esqr one of the Principle Inhabitants of s^d Precinct at or before the Time prefixed for sd: meeting (for which this shall be your Sufficient Warrant) hereof you may not faile at your perrill &c.

Given Under my hand and Seale at Weston the Ninth day of December In the Tenth yeare of his Maje^s Reigne Anno-Domini 1723.   FRA: FULLAM Justice of Peace.

[2]

At a Gen[ll] Meeting of the free holders, and other Inhabitants of the Eafterly Precinct in Watertowne Regularly Warned (By Virtue of a Warrant from Francis Fullam Efq[r] one of his Maje[s] Juftices of the Peace for the County of Midd[x]) And Afsembled for the Choice of A Precinct Clerk and other Precinct officers and Such bufnefs as the Warrant Refered to

(1) Put to Vote and Chose Jonas Bond Efq[r] Moderator for s[d] Meeting.

(2) Put to Vote and Chose Dea: Jn[o] Coollidg Precinct Clerk.

(3) Put to Vote whether the Precinct will have five men to be A Com[tee] to manage the Prudentials of this Precinct and the Vote past in the affirmative.

(4) Put to Vote and Chose Jonas Bond Efqr: M[r] Nathanael Bright Cap[t] Abra[m] Browne M[r] Jn[o] Sterns & M[r] Henry Spring to be a Com[tee] for the ends above sd:

(5) Put to Vote & Choose Cor[t] Henry Bright, M[r] Natha[l] Harris and M[r] Jos: Coollidg for Afsefsors.

(6) Put to Vote and Chose for Collector M[r] Jona[th] Stone

(7) Put to Vote and Chofe for a Receiver for the Precinct Dea: Nathan Fifke

(8) Put to Vote and Chose for A Com[tee] to take Care the Pulpit be Supplyed for the prefent till the Precinct Can Come into a Settlement Dea: W[m] Bond Dea: Nathan Fifke and Dea: Jn[o] Coollidg

(9) Put to Vote whether the Precinct are Willing and agreed that the Method for the raifing of Precinct Meeting for the future shall be, by the Com[tee] or the Precinct Clerk in their Names Signing an Order directing it to the Conftable within s[d] Precinct to warne the Inhabitants to meet at place and Time appointed in Such Order and the Vote pafed in the Affirmative.

Mid[x] fs: Watertowne Janeuary 13th 1723/4

To Deacon John Coollidg Clerk of the Easterly Precinct in Watertowne you are hereby ordered to give out an order in the Name of the Com[tee] of s[d] Precinct directed to the Conftable dwelling within the bounds of sd: Precinct to be in the forme and for the ends following,

Midd[x] fs

To Sam[ll] Peirce Conftable of Watertowne Greeting, you are hereby Ordered and required to Warne all the freeholders and other Inhabitants dwelling within the bounds aud limits of the Eafterly Precinct of s[d] Towne to meet at the Old Meeting house in s[d] Towne on the first Munday of Febreuary next Comeing at one of the Clock in the after noone of s[d] day for the ends following.

1 That the Precinct may be informed of the Nomination the Church hath made at their meeting on the Tenth day of Janeuary Currant in Order to the Setling of A gofpel Minifter among us in s[d] Precinct.

2 That then the Precinct may proceed to the Choice & Selection of one out of the afores'd Nomination the Church hath made to be Setled in the worke of the Ministrey that we may Come to the injoyment of the Ordenances of Christ among us.

3 To Agree and determine what Incoragement to give to the Gentleman that may be Chosen both as to his Sallery & Settlement,

4 To Choose A Com'tee to treat with the perfon that may be Chofen with attefted Coppyes of the Votes that shall be made, hereof faile not and make returne of this order with your doings there in unto Some one of the Com'tee or Clerk before the time of s'd meeting by Order of the Com'tee Dated this 13th day of Janeuary Anno Domini 1723/4. J'no COOLLIDG Cler :

In obedience to this order I have Warned the freeholders and other Inhabitants to meet at time & place within mentioned according to the Tenoure of s'd Order. Jan'u 15 : 1723.
SAM'll PIERCE, Confiable
for Watertowne.

[3]

Febrewary the 3'd 1723/4 At a Meeting of the Eafterly Precinct in Watertowne being Orderly Warned and Mett

Voted 1 And Coronell Jonas Bond was Chosen Moderator of s'd Meeting.

Voted 2 And M'r Seth Storrer was Chosen to be the gospel Minifter for s'd Precinct Chosen by 56 Votes

Voted 3 To add 16 : £ : tot he 84 :£ : Ordered by the Gen'll Court for the Support of the Minifter in f'd Precinct yearly, Which makes up Said : 84£ : 100 :£ which Sum of one Hundred pounds to be M'r Seth Storrers yearly Sallery.

Voted 4 To give M'r Seth Storrer one Hundred pounds towards his Settlement And He wholly to Provide a Settlement for himfelf, Or to Procure the Tenement that the Rev'nd M'r Henry Gibbs last dwelt on and improved. And to Putt the buildings and fences in good repaires. And M'r Storrer to have the improvement thereof in Lieu of f'd 100 :£ : Which Services He pleases to accept off.

Voted 5 And Chosen Coro'n Jonas Bond, the three Deacons and Cap't Abraham Browne to be A Committe to Treat with M'r Storrer in Order to his Acceptance of Said Call.

Voted 6 The meeting to be Adjorned to the last Munday of Febrewary Current at one of the Clock in the after Noon to heare the returne of Said Committee.

At A Meeting of the Easterly Precinct in Watertowne on the last Munday in Febrewary by Adjornment 1723/4

Voted 1 To Choose A Com'tee of five men out of thofe in the Precinct who Neither they nor theire Predecefsors were out money in building the houseing and appurtenances where the Rev'd M'r John Bailye did live while he Lived in Watertowne.

Voted 2 And Chosen M'r Nath'll Harris M'r Edward Herington

Mr John Sternes Mr Sam^{ll} Peirce and Mr Ephraim Angier to be s^d Com^{tte} to Meet with the Proprietors of s^d Houseing and p^{r}mesis in Order to Project Some way that Said Tenement may become the Precincts and to make report to f^{ll} Precinct of theire doings thereon at theire next meeting by Adjornment

Voted 3 That this Meeting be Adjorned to the last Munday of March at One of the Clock in the afternoon of s^d day to have a fuller Anfwer from Mr Storrer and to heare the report of s^d Com^{tee}

At A Meeting of the Easterly Precinct in Watertowne by Adjornment on March the 30th 1724

Voted For A Com^{tee} to gather the money Subfcribed to repaire the Tenement the Revd Mr Henry Gibbs last dwelt on And to improve s^d money for the ends propofed, Mr Nathl Harris, Mr Edward Herington, Mr John Sternes, Mr Samuell Peirce and Mr Ephraim Angier.

Voted That the Com^{tee} that was Chofen to treat with Mr Storrer should waite on him againe to Se if he please to Cancel the Provifo in his Anfwer to the Church and Precinct.

Voted the meeting to be Adjorned to the last Munday of April next at 3 a Clock in the after noon of Said day.

[4]

At A Meeting of the East Precinct in Watertowne being Orderly warned & mett March the 30th 1724.

Voted 1 Coron^{ll} Jonas Bond was Chosen Moderator of s^d Meeting.

Voted 2 for a Precinct Com^{tee} for the yeare Enfuing Coron^{ll} Jonas Bond Mr Nat^{ll} Bright Leu^t Sam^{ll} Thacher, Mr Wm Shattuck, and Capt Abraham Browne.

Voted 3 for a Precinct Clerk John Coollidg.

Voted 4 for a Treafurer Serg^t Joseph Coollidg.

Voted 5 for Afsefsors Corn^t Henry Bright Serg^t Joseph Coollidg & Mr Nat^{ll} Harris.

Voted 6 for A Collector Mr Jno Hastings.

Voted 7 to take downe the uper Gallery in the Old meeting House and to improve the Stuft on the New Meeting house at the Schoolhouse hill.

Voted 8 To finifh the infide of the New meeting Houfe Excepting what room may be thought proper to build Pews on and to be managed by the prudence of a Com^{tee} now to be Chosen for that Purpose, And to be done by the money now to be granted for that End.

Voted 9 for Said Comi^{tee} Coron^{ll} Jonas Bond, Mr Nat^{ll} Bright, Dea: Nathan Fifke Mr Jno Sternes, Mr Thomas Larnard, Mr Jonath Stone, Mr Edw: Herington.

Voted 10 To raise Two Hundred pounds on the Precinct towards the finifhing the New Meeting House in s^d Precinct.

Voted 11 That the Afsefsors Shall make the invoice that the last Province Tax was made by, The Rule to Afsefs the Precinct for s^d money granted Excepting what may be proper to Very from it as to perticular perſons obſerveing the rules of Juſtice and Equity.

Voted 12 That the money granted be Collected and paid in unto the sᵈ Precinct Treaſurer at or before the laſt day of July next.

At A Meeting of the Eaſterly Precinct in Watertowne on the laſt Munday of Aprill 1724 by Adjornment.

Voted That Mʳ Storrers Anſwer to the Church and Precinct to be recorded in the Precinct Book of Records.

At a Meeting of the Comᵗᵉᵉ of the Eaſt Precinct in Watertowne june 22ᵐᵈ 1724

Ordered that the Precinct Clerk do forthwith give an order in Writeing to the Conſtable of sᵈ Precinct to warne all the free holders & other inhabitants dweling within the bounds of sᵈ Precinct who are quallifyed to Vote in Towne affairs to meet at the Old meeting houſe in sᵈ Precinct on the laſt Munday of june Currant at three of the Clock in the afternoon for the Ends following Viz:

1 To Se whether the Precinct will then agree upon a day for the ordination of Mʳ Seth Storer whome they have Called & invited to Settle among us, who hath alſo accepted of sᵈ Call

2 To agree upon a way & method to raiſe money for the defraying the Charge and Expence for the Entertaining yᵉ Revⁿᵈ Elders, & Meſsengers yᵗ may be ſent to to Carry on yᵉ work.

3 To Chouſe & impower A Comᵗᵉᵉ to take Care and provide a Suitable place to Entertaine the Elders & Meſsengers &c and all Suitable Entertainment for them, to be accountable to the Precinct when Called thereto what money they have Recᵈ & how they have improved the Same

Jonas Bond
Nathanael Bright
William Shattuck } Comᵗᵉᵉ for sᵈ Precinct
Samˡˡ Thacher
Abraham Browne

[5]

To the Church and Congregation in the Eaſtern Precinct in Watertowne.

Gentlemen,

I Thankfully acknowledge the reſpect you have Manifeſted to me in makeing Choice of, and inviting me to Settle with you in the work of the Sacred Miniſtrey.

I have taken the Same into moſt Serious Conſideration have aſked the Councill of heaven, and taken the advice of the moſt Suitable perſons to Conſult with on reference to Such an Affaire, who do advise me to Settle with you in this great and weighty work of the Miniſtery. And I find myself Inclined thereunto in having a proſpect in being inſtrumentall of promoteing the glory of God, the intereſt of Religion and the good of Souls among you.

I do therefore manefest my acceptance of the said Call upon thofe Conditions proposed Viz^t That together with my yearly Sallery I Should have the Use of the House and improvement of the Land which were lately in the Pofsefsion of the Revd Mr Henry Gibbs, as is Specified in your Vote, Hoping that if my Circumftances Should hereafter Call for more then they do at present in order to my Comfortable maintainance and Support in the Sacret Office you will Provide Suitable for me.

I Begg you prayers for me that God who is the Lord of the Harvest would make me a painfull faithfull and Sucefsfull Labourer in his Vineyard and that after I have preached to others I myself may not be a Castaway. I Commend you all to the divine Care and Conduct intreating that the God of Peace and Love would preferve Unity among you and add Continually to your Number and graces, And that ye may stand perfect and Compleat in all the Will of God, And that he would give you an inheritance among them that are Sanctified throu faith in Chrift Jesus. So prayes in all Humble maner

       Gentle^n your Affectionate friend
       and Humble fervant SETH STORER.

Cambridge March 27th 1724

Midd^x fs:

 To Mr Nat^{ll} Bright Conftable of Watertowne

 Sr Thefe are to will & require you forthwith to warne all the freeholders and other Inhabitants dwelling within the bounds of the Eafterly Precinct of s^d Towne who are quallifyed to Vote in Towne affaires to meet at the Old Meeting in s^d Precinct on the last Munday of june Currant at three of the Clock in the after Noone for the End following Viz^t:

 1 To See whether the Precinct will then agree upon a day for the Ordination of Mr Seth Storer whome they have Called and invited to Settle among us who hath alfo accepted of s^d invitation

 2 To agree upon a way and method to raife money for the defraying the Charge and Expense for Entertaining the Revnd Elders and Mefsengers that may be sent to for the Carrying on of Said work

 3 To Choose and impower a Com^{tee} to take Care and provide a Suitable place to Entertaine the Elders and Mefsengers &c and all Suitable Entertainment for them and to be accountable to s^d Precinct when Called thereto of what money they have recieved and how they have improved the Same, hereof faile not and make a true return of this Order and of your doings thereon to Some one of s^d Com^{tee} or Clerk of said Precinct Six houres at leaft before the Time of s^d meeting.

       Pr Order of s^d Com^{tee}
       Jn: Coollidg Cler:

Watertowne June the 23rd 1724

[6]

At a meeting of the Easterly Precinct in Watertowne on the last Munday of June 1724.

1 Coro[ll] Jonas Bond was Chosen Moderator of s[d] Meeting.
2 Voted to Agree on a day for the Ordination of M[r] Seth Storer.
3 Voted that the day for the Ordination of M[r] Seth Storer be the 4th Wednesday of July next.
4 Voted to Choose two men to travel the Precinct to propose to the Inhabitants to Se what they will give towards the Charge of the Ordination of M[r] Storer, And to take downe theire Names that will give and theire Sums and they that pay downe to Crofs theire Sums And to deliver what they Shall So receive to the following Com[tee] Mentioned underneath.
5 Thomas Bond and Ephraim Cutter jun[r] Chosen for s[d] two men.
6 Voted to Choose a Com[tee] to provide a place and Entertainment for said Affaire out of s[d] money
7 Chosen for S[d] Com[tte] Jn[o] Coollidg Serg[t] Jenifon M[r] Spring Serg[t] Stone M[r] Sternes Serg[t] Coollidg and M[r] Harris
8 Voted that S[d] Com[tee] to give accompt to S[d] Precinct of what money they receive and what they Expend when Called thereto

To M[r] Jn[o] Coollidg Clerk for the Easterly Precinct in Watertowne

S[r]

You are hereby Ordered forthwith to give an Order to Joseph Coollidg Treafurer or Receiver for s[d] Precinct to pay unto the Rev[d] M[r] Seth Storrer the Sum of Twenty pounds, And to Leu[t] Richard Coollidg the Sum of five pounds out of the forty Two pounds which was ordered by the Select men of s[d] Towne to be paid into S[d] Treafurer p[r] Conftable Samuel Peirce out of the Towne Rate Commited to him to Collect

Watertowne Sep[r]
24: 1724

Jonas Bond	
Natha[l] Bright	Precinct
W[m] Shattuck	Committe
Abra[m] Browne	

At a meeting of the Precincts Com[tte] Jan[y] the 5th 1724/5

M[r] Storrer being present it was then Agreed on that the Ministers that had preached after Decemb[r] the 4th 1723 and the Charge of theire Entertainment Should be paid out of the 84£: Sallery for the yeare 1724 the yeare Ending Dec: the 4th 1724 and the Residue of S[d] 84£ to be for M[r] Storer in full for his preaching in s[d] Precinct untill S[d] 4th day of Dec: 1724.

[7]

Middx fs

To M[r] Nathanael Bright Conftable of Watertowne,

S[r] Thefe are to Will and require you forthwith to warne all the freeholders and other Inhabitants who dwell in the Eafterly

Precinct in s^d Towne who are quallifyed to Vote in Towne Affaires to Meet at the New Meeting house in s^d Precinct on Munday the Eleventh day of Janewary Current at one of the Clock in the after noon of s^d day for the Ends following

(1) To Know the Precincts minde when they will meet at the New Meeting hons in s^d Precinct and make it the place of Pubblick Worship for ye future

(2) To Know the Precincts Minde how they would have the Old meeting house disposed of or Improved or any part of it.

(3) To Receive an Accompt from the Com^{tee} how they have improved the money already granted towards the finishing of the New Meeting house

(4) To See whether the Precinct will then grant money for the further finishing of s^d meeting house And the paying the Warnings of Precinct meetings: Hereof faile not and make Returne of this Order with your doings thereon unto Some one of the Com^{tee} or Clerk of s^d Precinct foure hours at least before the Time of s^d Meeting Dated the fifth day of Janewary in the Eleventh yeare of his Majesties Reigne Anno Domini 1724/5

       p^r Order of   } Jno Coollidg
       the Com^{tee} Cler:

At A Meeting of the Easterly Precinct in Watertowne on Munday the Eleventh of Janewary 1724/5

(1) A Vote passed and Cor^{ll} Jonas Bond was Chosen Moderator

(2) Voted to Meet at the New Meeting House on the first Sabbath day of Febreway next & then to make it the place of Publick Worship for the future

(3) Voted to take out of the old meeting House all that may be profitably improved in the New Meeting house next after the last Sabbath day in Janewary Currant

(4) To Raise Two Hundred pounds to pay what they are indebted for the New Meeting house and for the further finishing the Same and Sixteen pounds thereof to be part of Mr Storrers Sallery and for the paying for the Warning of Precinct Meetings and the makeing of Precinct Rates

(5) Voted that the former Com^{tee} imployed in building the New meeting house Should be the Com^{tee} to take out of the Old Meeting house and improve it in the New Meeting House what they think proper and Needfull, And to improve the Residue of s^d grant of 200^{lb} in further finishing of s^d house

[S]

Watertowne Janewary 18: 1724/5

To Deacon John Coollidg Clerk of the Easterly Precinct in Watertowne,

you Are hereby Ordered to deliver to the Assessors of s^d Precinct a Coppy of the grant of the Two Hundred pounds made by s^d Precinct at theire Meeting on the Eleventh day of Janewary

Curraat for the Ends therein Mentioned, And direct them to Afsefs the Same Spedily the money being now Wanted for the defraying of Debts already Contracted And for the further finifhing of the New Meeting House, Said Afsefsors are to Committ the Rate or Afsefsment when made with a Lawfull Warrant to Collect the Same unto Mr John Hastings the present Collector and to Issue and make up his Accompts at or before the first Munday of July Next Enfuing

JONAS BOND
NATHA^l BRIGHT } Com^{tee}
Wm SHATTUCK

Midd^x fs.

To Mr Nathanael Bright Conftable of Watertown

Sr Thefe are to will & require you forthwith to warn all the Freeholders and other Inhabitants who are Quallified to Vote in precinct Affairs who dwell in the Eafterly precinct to Meet at the New Meeting houfe in S^d precinct on the Third Monday of March Next Enfuing at Two of the Clock in the after Noone to choofe precinct officers for the year Currant. Alfo to know the minde of ye precinct how they would have ye remaind^r of ye old Meeting houfe Difpofed of which can not be profitably Improved in ye New: hereof fail not but make a true return of this ord^r and of Your doings thereon to Some one of ye Committee or Clerk of ye precinct four houres at Leaft before ye time of S^d Meeting Watertown Feb^r 16: 1724/5 Per od^r of ye Com^{tee}

JOHN COOLLIDGE Cler.

At a Meeting of the Easterly Precinct in Watertown on March the 15th 1724/5
1 Chosen for Moderator Col. Jonas Bond.
2 Voted to Choofe three Men to be a Standing Committe for the precinct for the Year.
3 Voted and Choofe for Said Com^{tee} Mr Nathanael Bright, Deacon William Bond and Coro^l Bond.
4. Voted and Chofen Clerk Joseph Mafon.
5. Voted and Chofen Treafurer Ser^t Joseph Coollidge
6. Voted and Chofen Afsefsors Cor^t Henry Bright Ser^t Joseph Coollidg & Mr Nathanael Harris.
7. Voted and Chofen Collector Mr Thomas Coollidg.
8. Voted and Chofen Sexton Mr Nathanael Sherman.
9. Voted y^t Said Sexton Shall have two Contributions in the year for his reward, vizt on the first Sabbath in September Next and on the firft Sabbath in March next
10. Voted to Difpose of ye whole remainder of ye old Meeting houfe and the whole Effects thereof to be improved in the further finifhing of ye New Meeting houfe, and if their be any overplufs of ye money Afsigned for that Ufe it Shall be in the money granted for finifhing Said Meeting houfe.

11. Voted that the Same Comm^tee that hath been improved in Mannaging the building of ye New Meeting houfe, Shall be the Comm^tee to Difpose of the Old Meeting houfe.

[9]

To Joseph Mafon Clerk of the Eafterly Precinct in Watertown

You are hereby ordred forthwith to give an order to Mr Joseph Coollidge precinct Treafurer To pay to the Reverend Mr Seth Storer the Sum of Sixteen pounds out of the Two hundred pound Rate granted Pr Said precinct on the Eleventh Day of January in the Year 1724/5 which Sixteen pounds is for the Compleating the Sallery According to Contract.

Watertown Feb^r 17th   Jonas Bond   } Precinct
    1725/6.   Nathanael Bright   } Com^tee

To Mr Joseph Coollidge Treafurer of ye East Precinct in Watertown

S^r

You are hereby ordred to pay to the Reverend Mr Seth Storer the fum of fixteen pounds Out of the Two hundred pound Rate granted Pr S^d Precinct on the Eleventh Day of January in the Year 1724/5 which S^d Sixteen pounds is for Compleating his Sallery According to Contract.

P^r order of ye Precinct Committe

Watertown Feb^r 21.   Joseph Mason Precinct Cler.
    1725/6.

Midd^x fs.

To Mr Jonas Bond Junr Conftable of Watertown Greeting.

S^r

You are hereby required forthwith to warne the Freeholders and oth^r Inhabitants within the Eafterly Precinct in S^d Town who are Quallifyed to Vote in Precinct Affaires to Meet at the Publick Meetinghoufe in S^d Precinct on ye fourteenth Day of March Next enfuing the Date hereof, at two of the clock in the afternoone of S^d day, for the ends following.

First. To choofe a Committee to mannage ye prudentials of S^d Precinct A Clerk and other precinct Officers which are proper to be chofen.

Secondly. To receive an Acc^t from the Committee wch were Imployed in finifhing the Meeting houfe, how far they have difpofed of the money already granted, Pr S^d Precinct for that End.

Thirdly. That the Precinct may then Mannifeft their Mindes if they fe caufe how and in what Method they will have the Vacant room und^r the gallireys in the Meeting houfe to be Improved.

Fourthly. To take effectual care that there be money raifed for the Minifters Sallery According to Contract, as alfo for others to whom money may be due from the Precinct.

Fifthly. To take care that the Saxftone may be Incourraged.
hereof fail not, but make return of this ord^r and Your Doings thereon to one of the Com^{tee} or Clerk of S^d Precinct at Leaft four hours before the time for S^d Meeting.

P^r ord^r of the Committee
JOSEPH MASON Cler.

Watertown Feb^r 21. 1725/6.

[10]

At a Meeting of the Inhabitants of the Eafterly Precinct in Watertown on the 14th Day of March 1725/6. for the Election of Precinct officers, And Such oth^r buifnefs as is Set forth in the Warnind of S^d Meeting.

Voted and Choofe for Moderator Jonas Bond Esqr.

Voted and Choofe for the Standing Comm^{tee} to Mannage the prudentials of the precinct this Psent Year. Jonas Bond Esqr Dea. Nathan Fiske & Dea John Coollidge.

Voted and Choofe for Precinct Clerk Mr Nathanael Harris.

Voted and Choofe for Precinct Treafurer (or Receivor) Mr Joseph Coollidge

Voted and Choofe for Afsefsors { Joseph Mafon / Mr Nathanael Harris / Mr Henery Bright.

Voted and Choofe for Collector Mr Edward Harrington.

Voted and Choofe for Saxton Mr Nathanael Shermon.

Voted for the Incourragment & reward of s^d Sexton, That there Should be Two Contributions in the Year for him, vizt the first Contribution to be on the first Sabbath Day in Septemb^r and the Second to be on the first Sabbath Day in March.

At s^d Meeting the Comm^{tee} Chofen for the finifhing the Meeting houfe, Laid their Acc^t before the Precinct of how much they had Difpofed of the Money Granted P^r y^e Precinct toward the finifhing of the Meeting houfe. The Acc^t Amounting to the Sum of £387=4=9. The s^d Acc^t was red to the Precinct. And Put to Vote whether the Precinct Do Axcept of Said Acc^t

And the Vote past in the Affirmative.

Put to Vote whether the Precinct will At this Meeting Manifest their Minds how, the Vacancy under the Gallerys shall be Improved.

The Vote past in the Negative.

Put to Vote whether the Precinct are willing to Allow the Precinct Afsefsors, for Making precinct Rates Two fhillings & fixpence Pr Day, and they Laying a fair Acc^t before the Precinct Comm^{tee} the Same be Allow'd. And the Vote paft in ye Affirmative.

Put to Vote whether the Precinct are willing to Allow Conftables three fhillings A Meeting for Warning precinct Meetings

The Vote paft in y^n Affirmative.

Put to Vote whether the Precinct are Willing to Allow the Sum of fourty Shillings to Mr John Haftings for Collecting the precinct

Rates Committed to him to Collect. The Vote paſt in the Affarmitive.

Put to Vote whether the precinct are Willing (and Do Now Grant) the Sum of Twenty five pounds to Pay ye Revd Mr Storer According to Contract and the Aſseſsors & Conſtables and others to whom Money May be due from s^d Precinct.

The Vote paſt in ye Affarmative.

Put to Vote whether the Precinct are Willing to Allow Mr Dan^{ll} Haſtings Ten ſhillings for ringin the bell from ye 1st Sabbath in Feb^r to ye 2^d in March, 1724/5.

And the Vote paſt in ye Affarmitive

[11]

To Nathaniel Harris Clerk of the Easterly Precinct in Watertown, You Are Hereby Ordered to Deliver to the Aſseſsors of Said Precinct A Coppy of the Grant of the Twenty five Pounds Granted by the Precinct aforeſaid Att there Meeting on the Fourteenth Day of March Last Past; For the Ends therein Mentioned and Direct them to Aſsess the Inhabitance of s^d Precinct as the Law Directs Spedily and to Commit the Rate or Aſsessment to Mr Edward Harrington the Present Collector for s^d Precinct With a Lawfull Warrent to Collect the ſame and to Issue and Make up his Accompts at or Before ye First Monday of Octo^{br} Next Inſueing.

Watertown July ye 11th 1726
JONAS BOND }
NATHAN FISKE } Com^{tee}

To M^r Joſeph Coollidge Treaſurer of ye East Precinct in Watertown

Sr You are Hereby Ordered to Pay to the Reverend Mr Seth Storer the Sum of Sixteen Pounds out of the Twenty five Pound Rate Granted Pr S^d Precinct on the Fourteenth Day of March Last Past which Sum of Sixteen Pounds is for the Compleating his Sallary According to Contract.

Alſo to Pay to Your ſelf the ſum of one Pound Six Shillings and three Pence.

To Corn^{tt} Henry Bright the Sum of One Pound Eleven Shillings and three Pence.

To Dea Joſeph Maſon the Sum of Five Shillings And to Nath^{ll} Harris the Sum of One Pound Eleven Shillings and three Pence which Sums Ware Reſpectively Allowed for Makeing of Precinct Rates.

To Mr John Hastings the Sum of Two Pounds Allowed him for Collecting of Precinct Rates Committed to him. To Mr Samuel Pirce Six Shillings for Warning Two Precinct meetings in the Year 1723. To Mr Nath^{ll} Bright Nine Shillings for Warning Three Precinct Meettings in the Year 1724. To Mr Jonas Bond Junr three Shillings for Warning one Precinct Meetting in the Year 1725. To Mr Daniel Haſtings the Sum of Ten Shillings for Ringing the Bell.

P^r order of the Precinct Com^{tee}

Watertown January the 17th 1726/7
NATH^{ll} HARRIS Cler.

Middlesx ss:
To M[r] Thomas Bond Constable of Watertown Greetting.
S[r]
You are hereby Required forthwith to Warn the Freeholders and other Inhabitance Within the Easterly Precinct in S[d] Town who are Qualified to Vote in Precinct affairs to Meet at the Publick Meeting house in s[d] Precinct on Monday the Thirteenth Day of March Next Insuing the Date hereof Att Two of the Clock in the afterNoon of s[d] Day for the Ends Following

Viz First to Choose a Precinct Committee to manage the Prudentialls of s[d] Precinct A Clerk and other Precinct officers Nefsary and Proper to be Chosen.

Secondly, that the Precinct May Confider (And if they Pleafe Conclude) How they will have the Vacant Room under the Galleries in S[d] Meetinghoufe Improved; and if it Should be agreed, and Concluded, to Build Pews Whether the Pews, Should be Built; By Perticular Perfons or by S[d] Precinct: and if it be there Minds S[d] Precinct Should Buld them as a Precinct, then to Take Care and Raife Money for the Same.

Thirdly to Take Effectuall Care that there be Money Raifed for the Ministers Sallary According to Contract and alfo for others to Whome Money May be Due from the Precinct, And Alfo to Raife Money for the Further Finishing S[d] Meeting houfe if there Shall be Occation.

Fourthly to Take Care that the Saxftone may be incoarriged. hereof fail Not but Make Return of this order and Your Doings thereon to one of the Committee or Clerk of s[d] Precinct at Least Four hours Before the Time for s[d] Meetting.

P[r] order of s[d] Committee.

Watertown Feb[ry] 27th   NATH[ll] HARRIS Cler.
1726/7

[12]

Att, A Meeting of the Inhabitance of the Easterly Precinct in Watertown. On Monday the 13th Day of March Anno Dom 1726/7 for the Election of Precinct Officers And Such Other Bufinefs as is Sett Forth in the Warning of Said Meetting.

Voted, And Chofe for Moderator Col[n] Jonas Bond Efqr.

Voted, and Chofe for a Standing Committee to Mannage the Prudentialls of f[d] Precinct For this Prefent Year L[t] Richard Coollidge M[r] Thomas Straith and Dea Nathan Fisk

Voted and Chofe for Said Precinct Clerk Nathaniel Harris

Voted and Chofe for s[d] Precinct Afsefsors - { M[r] Nathaniel Bright
{ M[r] Jofeph Holdin
{ M[r] John Straton

Voted and Chofe for s[d] Precinct Treafurer or Receiver M[r] Joseph Coollidge.

Voted and Chofe For Collector for f[d] Precinct for this Prefent Year M[r] Daniel Bond.

Voted and Chofe for Sexstone M[r] Nathaniel Shearmon.

Voted that there Should Be Two Contributions in this Prefent

Year for the Reward and Incourrigement of him the S[d] Sextone (Viz) one on the First Sabbath in September and the other on the First Sabbath in March.

Put to Vote Whether it Be the minds of the Precinct at this meetting, that the Vacant Room in the Meetting houfe under the Gallereis Should Be Improved with Pews; and that Perticuliar Perfons Should Build them under Such Regulations as the s[d] Precinct Shall agree upon; or by a Committee Appointed by s[d] Precinct for that Purpofe; and the Vote Paft in the affirmitive

Put to Vote Whether the Precinct will Now Choofe Five men for a Committee to Mannage that affair (Relating to or) Concerning the Building of Pews under the Gallerries in S[d] Meetting houfe and the Vote Pafsed in the affermitive.

Voted and Chose Ser[t] Joseph Coollidge, Enf[n] Jonathan Stone, Corn[tt] Henry Bright Ser[t] Ebenezer Stone & Nathaniel Harris for A Committee to Mannage that affair concerning the Pews haveing Refpect to Such Directions as they Shall hereafter Receive from s[d] Precinct

Voted that s[d] Committee Shall have Regard to what Perfons have Difburfted & have Bin Rated as to Reall & Personall Eftate for the Building of f[d] meeting houfe; and to have Regard to Perfons of Honnour and UfefallNefs in S[d] Precinct.

Voted that Whofoever Shall be admitted to Build Pews and they Shall Se Caufe to Difpofe of them or Leave them that the Precinct Paying the First Cost of Building the Pews Shall have them; and the Difpofsing of them again.

Put to Vote Whether the Precinct will Now att this Meetting Grant the sum of Twentifive Pounds to Pay the Reverend M[r] Storer according to Contract; and to Pay others to Whom Money may Be due from fd. Precinct: and for the Further Finishing the Meeting houfe under the Galleries; and the Vote Pafsed in the affermitive.

Putt to Vote Whether the Precinct will adjorn this meeting to the Second Monday of Aprill Next Infuing at two of the Clock in the afternoon of s[d] day to hear w[t] the Comt[ee] have done Relating to the Pews and then y[e] Vote Pafsed in the affermitive.

[13]

Att A Meeting, of the Inhabitance of the Easterly Precinct, in Watertown on Monday the 10th Day of Apprill, Anno Dom: 1727 by adjornment.

Put to Vote Whether the Report the Com[tee] have Made Concerning the Building of Pews in the Meettinghoufe, be acceptable to the Precinct, and the Vote Past in the Negative.

Put to Vote Whether the Precinct, will Now Choofe a Com[tee] to Draw a List of Forty Perfons, that thay Shall Think most Proper; to have Pews and Prefent to the Precinct for them, to Choofe Twenty out of, and the Vote Past in the Negative.

Put to Vote whether the Precinct, will Build Pews, at all, or No; Past in the Negative

Middlesex ss.
   To M{r} Ephraim, Cutter Jun{r} Constable of Watertown Greeting.
   S{r} You are Hereby Requiered Forthwith to Warn the Freeholders and other Inhabitance within s{d} Precinct in S{d} Town who are Qualified to Vote in Precinct Affairs to Meet At the Pnblick Meeting house in Said Precinct on Monday the Second Day of October Next Insuing the Date hereof at Two of the Clock in the Afternoon of S{d} Day for the Ends Following.
   Viz: (1) To No the Minds of the Precinct Whether they will Agree Upon Purchafing A More Convenient Place for A Perfonage or Ministeriall Place in s{d} Precinct.
   (2) To No the Minds of the Precinct if they Should Agree to Purchafe a more Convenient Ministeriall Place then whether the Precinct will be of the mind to sell the Prefent Ministeriall Place or any Part thereof to Pay Sd Purchafe.
   (3) To No if the Precinct Should Agree to Purchafe & Sel as aforefd if they will Choofe A Com{tee} and Impower fd Com{tee} to Manrage the affairs for and in Behalfe of fd Precinct.
   Hereof Fail Not But Make Return of this Order and Your Doings thereon to one of the Precinct Com{tee} or Clerk of s{d} Precinct At Least Four hours Before the Time of fd Meeting.
         P{r} Order of the Precinct Com{tee}
   Watertown Sept{m} the   NATH{ll} HARRIS Cler.
     18{th} 1727

At A Meeting of the Inhabitants of the Easterly Precinct in Watertown on Monday the Second Day of October Anno Dom 1727
   (1) Voted and Chofe for moderator Dea Nathan Fiske.
   (2) Put to Vote whether the Precinct will Purchafe a more Convenient Perfonage or Ministeriall Place for Sd Precinct & y{e} Vote Pafsed in the Affermitive.
   (3) Put Vote Whether it Be the minds of the Precinct to Sell all the Prefent Ministeriall Place (Excepting the Marfh) to pay s{d} Purchafe and the Vote Pafsed in the affermitive.
   (4) Put to Vote Whether it Be the Minds of the Precinct to Choofe A Committee to Mannage the Affair of Bying and Selling as aforefd and the Vote Pafsed in y{e} affermitive.
   (5) Put to Vote & Chofe for A Com{tee} Enfign Jonathan Stone, M{r} William Shattuck Serg{t} Jofeph Coollidge, Dea John Coollidge, and Quartermaster Thomass Larnard.
   (6) Put to Vote to no the Minds of the Precinct, if they will Impower the above sd Com{tw} to Sel ; all the Prefent Ministeriall Place Excepting the marsh, and to Purchafe a more Convenient Ministeriall Place for s{d} Precinct, Provided the Place s{d} Com{tee} Shall Purchafe Cost not above one Hundred Pounds more then they shall Sell the Prefent Ministeriall Place for Excepting the marfh, and y{e} vote Pafsed in the affermitive.

[14]
   To Nath{ll} Harris Clerk of the Easterly Precinct in Watertown. You are Hereby Requiered & Ordered to Deliver to y{e} Afsefsors

of s^d Precinct A Coppie of the Twenty-five Pounds; Granted by the Precinct Aforesd At there Meetting On the thirteenth Day of March Last Past for the Ends therein Mentioned; and Direct them to Afsess the Inhabitance of S^d Precinct as the Law Directs Speedily; & to Commit the Rate or afsefsment, to Mr Daniel Bond the Prefent Collecton for S^d Precinct; With a Lawfull Warrant to Collect the Same: & to Issue & Make Up his Accompt with m^r Jofeph Coollidge Precinct Treafurer or his Successor in S^d Office at or Before the First Day of December Next Infuing.

Watertown, October
the 14th 1727.
$\left. \begin{array}{l} \text{Thomas Strait} \\ \text{Richard Coollidge} \end{array} \right\}$ Com^tee

Middlefx

To Mr Joseph Coollidge Treafurer of the East Precinct in Watertown.

Sr You are hereby Ordered to Pay to the Reverend Mr Seth Storer the Sum of Sixteen Pounds out of the Twentyfive Pounds Rate Granted Pr S^d Precinct on the Thirteenth Day of March Anno Dom 1726/7 which is for the Compleating his Sallery According to Contract.

Alfo to Pay to Mr Jofhua Grant Junr the Sum of Four Pounds and one Shilling. Allowed to him for Mending the Glace on the Meettinghoufe in Sd Precinct.

Alfo to pay to Mr. Thomas Bond the Sum of Three Shillings for Warning one Precinct Meetting in the Year 1726.

Alfo to Pay to Mr Ephraim Cutter Junr the Sum of Six Shillings for warning Two Precinct Meeting in the Year 1727.

Alfo to Pay to Mr John Straton the Sum of Ten Shillings for making A Precinct Ra'

Alfo to Pay to Mr Nathaniel Bright the Sum of Ten Shillings for Making a Precinct Rate.

March the 11th 1727/8
⅌ Order of s^d Precinct Com^tee.
Nath^ll Harris Cler.

Middlefex fs

To Mr Ephraim Cutter Conftable of Watertown, Greeting.

Sr You are Requiered hereby Forthwith To Warn the Freeholders and Other Inhabitance Within the Easterly Precinct in S^d Town Who Are Quallified to Vote in Precinct Affairs To Meet At the Publick Meettinghouse in S^d Precinct On Monday the Eleventh Day of March Next Infuing the Date hereof At Two of the Clock in the Afternoon of Said Day for the Ends Following.

Viz First. To Choofe A Precinct Committee To Mannage the Prudentialls of s^d Precinct, A Clerk and other Officers Nefsasery & Propper to be Chofen.

Secondly, to Take Effectuall Care That there be Money Raifed for the Ministers Sallary According to Contract and alfo for others to Whom Money May Due from the Precinct.

Thirdly. To hear the Com^tees Accompt that was Chofen for the Building & Finishing the Meetinghoufe, on Scoolhous hill, And if it be Needfull to Make Some Additionall Grants of Money for the Further Finishing of the s⁴ Meetinghouse.

Fourthly, to Take Care & Agree with the Sexton that May be Chose for s⁴ Precinct.

Hereof Fail Not But Make Return of this Order & Your Doings thereon to one of the Com^tee or Clerk of s⁴ Precinct at Least Four hour Before the Time for sd meeting.

Pr Order of s⁴ Precinct Com^tee

Watertown February the 26th Nath^ll Harris Cler.
1727/8.

[15]

Att A Meetting of the Freeholders & Other Inhabitance in the Easterly Precinct in Watertown, the 11th Day of March Anno Dom 1727/8 for the Election of Precinct Officers & Such Other Buisnefs as in Set Forth in the Warning of s⁴ Meetting.

(1) Voted, and Chofe Deacon Nathan Fisk Moderator.

(2) Voted, and Chofe for A Standing Com^tee to Mannage the Prudentialls of s⁴ Precinct for this Prefent Year Dea Jofeph Mafon Mr Thomas Bond, and Serg^t Samuel Janifon.

(3) Voted, and Chofe for s⁴ Precinct Clerk Nathaniel Harris.

(4) Voted and Chofe for sd Precinct Treafurer or Reciever Mr Jofeph Coollidge.

(5) Voted and Chofe for s⁴ Precinct Afsefsors { Nathaniel Bright. Lt Richard Coolidge. Nath^ll Harris.

(6) Voted and Chofe for Collector for s⁴ Precinct for this Prefent Year Jonathan Stone Junr.

(7) Voted, and Chofe for Saxton for this Prefent Year Mr Nath^ll Shearmon.

(8) Voted, and Granted the sum of Twenty Pounds To Pay the Revd Mr Storer According to Contract & to Pay others to Whom Money May be due from s⁴ Precinct.

(9) Voted & Excepted the Committees Accompt; that was Chofen for the Building & Furnishing the Meetinghoufe on Scoolhous hill So far as it is Finished.

(10) Voted & Granted the sum of Ten Pounds Two Shillings and Nine Pence to Ballance accompts with s⁴ Committee for Building and Finishing s⁴ Meetting houfe Together with the Arrearages that are in Collector Daniel Bonds Hands, and the arrearages in Collector John Hastingses Hand (Excepting, Seven Pounds Eighteen Shillings and Five Pence w^h is not At Prefent Likely to be Collected.

(11) Voted & Granted the Sum of Five Pounds to Whitwash Point and Further Finish s⁴ meetting houfe.

(12) Voted to Pay the Sexton by Two Contrabutions (Viz) one on the First Sabath in September Next and the other on the First Sabath in March Next.

[16]

To Nathaniel Harris Clerk of the Easterly Precinct in Watertown.

You are hereby Ordered Seasonably to Give out an order to the Constables Dwelling Within the Limits of s^d Precinct to Warn the Free holders And Other Inhabitance Who Are quallified to Vote in Precinct Affairs to Meet at the Publick Meettinghouse in s^d Precinct on the Tenth Day of June Next Insuing the Date hereof Att Eight of the Clock in the forenoon of s^d Day for the Ends Following.

(1) To hear the Report of the Com^{tee} that Ware Appointed by the Precinct to Make Sale of the Minnisterial Place that the Revd Mr Gibbs Lived in & also to Purchase a More Convenient Place in Lew thereof for to be A Minnisteriall Place.

(2) To Know the Minds of the Precinct Whether the Reverend Mr Storers Posfession of the New Ministerial Place (Lately Bought of Dea: Joseph Coolidge of Cambridge and Mr Daniel Hastings of Watertown) Dureing the Time of his Being the Precincts Minister Should be Recorded on the Precincts Records & to be in Lew of the Posfession which he had (by Agreement at his Settlement) of the Ministerial Place Lately Sold.

(3) To Know the Mind of the Precinct Whether they Will Make A Sutable Convenient Addition to the Ministerial house.

(4) To Know the Mind of the Precinct Whether they Esteem the Votes that Past at A Meetting of s^d Precinct by Adjornment on the Tenth Day of Aprill 1727 Referring to the Pews Ware Good and Reguller.

Watertown May the 27th 1728.

SAMUEL JENIſON,
THOMAS BOND,
JOſEPH MAſON.
} East Precinct Com^{tee}

Middlefex fs. To Mr Joseph Harrington Constable of Watertown Greetting. Sr You are hereby Requiered forthwith to Warn the Free holders & other Inhabitance Within the Easterly Precinct in s^d Town Who Are Quallified to Vote in Precinct Affairs to Meet at the Publick Meetting house in s^d Precinct on Monday the Tenth Day of June Next Infuing the Date hereof Att Eight of the Clock in the fore noon of s^d Day for the Ends Following.

(1) To hear the Report of the Committee that Ware Appointed by the Precinct to Make Sale of the Ministeriall Place that the Revd Mr Gibbs Liv^d in and also to Purchase A More Convenient Place in Lew thereof to Be A Ministeriall Place.

(2) To Know the Minds of the Precinct Whether the Rever^d Mr Storer Poſsestion of the New Ministeriall Place Lately Bought of Dea Joseph Coollidge of Cambridge and Mr Daniel Hastings of Watertown Dureing the Time of his Being the Precincts Minister Should be Recorded on the Precincts Records & to be in Lew of the Poſsestion which he had by agreement At his Settlement of the Ministeriall Place Latly Sold.

(3) To Know the Minds of the Precinct Whether thay will Make a Sutable Convenient Adition to the Ministeriall house.

(4) To Know the Minds of the Precinct Whether they Esteem the Votes that Pafsed at a meetiing of s^d Precint P^r adjornment on the Tenth Day of Aprill 1727 Refering To the Pews Ware Good & Reguliar.

Hereof Fail Not But Make Return of this order & of Your Doings thereon to one of the Comm^tee or Clerk of s^d Precinct at Least Four hours Before the Time for s^d Meetting.

Pr Order of the Com^tee

Watertown May ye 30th 1728.   NATH^ll HARRIS Cler.

[17]

Att a Meetting of the Freeholders and Other Inhabitance of the Easterly Precinct in Watertown the Tenth Day of June Anno Dom 1728.

(1) Voted & Chofe For a Moderator Dea. Nathan Fisk.

(2) Voted & Accepted the Report the Com^tee Made that Ware appointed by the Precinct To Make Sale of the Ministeriall Place that the Revd Mr Gibbs Liv^d in and alfo to Purchafe A more Convenient One in Lew thereof, the sd Com^tee Reported as Followeth, that thay had Purchafed of Daniel Hastings late of Watertow^n and of Dea Jofeph Coollidge of Cambridge A Teniment in Watertown afore s^d Where Daniel Hastings Lately Dwelt Containing about Twenty one Acres of Land with the Buildings thereon, For the Sum of Four Hundred & Fifty Pounds & had Recieved a Deed of s^d Daniel Hastings of Two third Parts of s^d Place and a Deed of one third Part of s^d Place of Dea Jofeph Coollidge.

And, that they had Alfo Sold the Ministeriall Place that the Revd Mr Gibbs Liv^d in Excepting the Marfh to Doct^r Richard Checkley of Boston for the Sum of Three hundred & Fifty Pounds and had Given him a Deed thereof.

(3) Voted & Allowed the Com^tee the Sum of one Pound Five Shillings & Ten Pence for Writings in & about the Purchafing of the New Ministeriall Place.

(4) Put to Vote Whether the Precinct will allow s^d Com^tee the Sum of Seven Shillings and Six Pence for Writings in the Sale of the Former Ministeriall Place, Past in ye Negative.

(5) Voted & allowed Mr William Shattuck the Sum of Fifteen Shillings for Putting ye Sale of the Former Ministeriall Place into the Publick News Letter Three Times 5^s Each Time.

(6) Voted that the Rever^d Mr Storer Should have the Pofseftion of the New Ministeriall Place Lately Bought of Mr Daniell Hastings & Dea Jofeph Coollidge Dureing the Time of his Being the Precincts Minister in Lew of the Pofseftion which he had of the Ministeriall Place Lately Sold which he had by agreement at his Settlement.

(7) Voted that the Precinct Will Make A Sutable Adition to the New Ministeriall Houfe.

(8) Put to Vote Whether it Be the Mind of the Precinct that the Addition to the Ministeriall houfe y^t was Latly Bought, Should be An End (with A Cellar Under it) Twenty four Feet in Lenth

and Eighteen feet in Breadth Faceing Easterly well Finished with a Chemney at the North End, and alfo to Raife the Leanter End to the height of the Rest of the houfe, and the Vote Pafsed in the Affermative.

(9) Put to Vote Whether the Precinct Will Choofe a Com^{tee} to Build & Finifh s^d adition, and the Vote Paft in the Affermative.

(10) Voted And Chofe for a Com^{tee} to Mannage the affair of Building & Finifhing the Adition to the Ministeriall houfe Lately Bought Lt Richard Coollidg Corn^{tt} Henry Bright & Serg^t Jonas Bond.

(11) Voted that it is the Minds of the Precinct that this Com^{tee} Acquaint the Proprietors Com^{tee} of the Ocation for Money to Make the adition to the Ministeriall houfe.

(12) Put to Vote Whether the Precinct Esteem the Votes that Past at a Meetting of s^d Precinct by adjornment on the Tenth Day of Aprill 1727 Refering to the Pews ware Good & Regaliar, and the Vote Past in the Negative.

[18]
To Nath^{ll} Harris Clerk of the Easterly Precinct in Watertown.

You are hereby Ordered to Diliver (or Show) to the afsefsors of s^d Precinct A Copy of the Grants of Money Made by s^d Precinct at their Meetting on the Eleventh Day of March Last Past for the Ends therein Mentioned And Direct them Speedily to Afsefs the inhabitance of s^d Precinct As the Law Directs And to Committ the Rate or Afsefsment to Mr Jonathan Stone Junr the Prefent Collector for s^d Precinct With A Lawfull Warrent to Collect the Same & to Pay in to the Precinct Treafurer Lt Jofeph Coollidge or to his Succefsor in s^d Office So as to Ifue & Make up an account of the Whole of s^d Afsefsment At or Before the Last Day or October Next Insuing ye Date Hereof.

SAMUEL JENIfON
THOMAS BOND
JOfEPH MAfON

} Com^{ee} of the East Precinct in Watertown.

Watertown June the 12th 1728

To Nath^{ll} Harris Clerk of the East Precinct in Watertown. You are hereby Ordered Forthwith to Give An Order to Mr Jofeph Coollidge Treafurer of said Precinct To Pay out of the Grants of s^d Precinct Made the 11th Day of March Last Past & Committed To Mr Jonathan Stone Junr Collector to Collect Viz. To the Reverend Mr Seth Storer the Sum of Sixteen Pounds which is to Compleat his Sallary According to Contract.

To the Com^{tee} for Building & Finishing the Meetting houfe in s^d Precinct or their Order the Sum of Ten Pounds Two fhillings & Nine Pence To Ballance s^d Com^{tees} Accompts And To s^d Com^{tee} the Sum of Five Pounds w^h was Granted to Whitewash Point And further Finish s^d Meetting houfe.

To Conftable Ephraim Cutter the Sum of Three Shillings for Warning one Precinct Meetting.

To Joseph Harrington Conftable the Sum of Three Shillings for Warning one Precinct Meeting.

To Lt Richard Coollidge the Sum of Eight Shillings & Nine Pence To Mr Nath^ll Bright the Sum of Eight Shillings & Nine Pence and To Nath^ll Harris the sum of Eight Shillings & Nine Pence it Being for their Making the Last Precinct Rate.

Watertown January 27th 1728/9   THOMAS BOND ⎱ Precinct
JOSEPH MASON ⎰ Com^{tee}

To Mr Joseph Coollidge Treafurer of the Easterly Precinct in Watertown.

Sr You Are Hereby Ordered to Pay to the Reverend Mr Seth Storer the Sum of Sixteen Pounds (: out of the Grants of Money Granted the 11th Day of March Last Past & Commited to Mr Jonathan Stone Collector to Collect) which is to Compleat his Sallary According to Contract.

To the Committee for Building & Finishing the Meetting houfe in s^d Precinct the Sum of Ten Pounds Two Shillings and Nine Pence to Ballance s^d Com^{tee} Accompts :— And to s^d Com^{tee} the Sum of Five Pounds which was Granted to Whitewash Point and Further Finish s^d Meetinghoufe.

To Conftable Ephra Cutter the Sum of Three Shillings for Warning one Precinct Meetting.

To Constable Joseph Harrington the Sum of Three Shillings for Warning one Precinct Meeting.

To Lt Richard Coollidge the Sum of Eight Shillings and Nine Pence To Mr Nath^ll Bright the Sum of Eight Shillings & Nine Pence and to Nath^ll Harris the Sum of Eight Shillings and Nine Pence it Being for their makeing the Last Precinct Rate p order of s^d Precinct Com^{tee}.   NATH^ll HARRIS Clerk.

[19]

Watertown Feb: 29th 1728/9

To Nathaniel Harris Clerk of the Easterly Precinct in Watertown.

You are Hereby Ordered to Write An Order or Warrant & Direct it to Mr Joseph Harrington Conftable for s^d Towne Who dwells Within s^d Precinct in the Words Following.

You are Hereby Ordered & Requiered Forthwith to Warn the Freeholders and Other Inhabitants Within the Easterly Precinct in Watertown Who Are Quallified According to Law to Vote in Precinct Affairs to Meet Att the Publick Meetting houfe in s^d Precinct On Thirsday the 6th Day of March Next at one of the Clock in the Afternoon of s^d Day for the Ends Following.

First, To Choofe Such Precinct Officers as by Law Are Requiered to be Chofen in the Month of March.

Secondly to hear the Propofalls of the Com^{tee} (Who ware Chofen and Impowered to Erect A New Addition to the Minifteriall houfe) for the makeing the Addition to the Minifteriall houfe More Convenient and accommodateing And to Know the

Minds of the Precinct Whether they Will Alter the Former Scheme they Layed for s^d Addition and Come into A New Scheme for the Better Accomodateing & Makeing and making the Ministeriall houſe More Convenient.

Thirdly to hear the Pettition of Sundry of the Inhabitance of f^d Precinct with Reſpect to the Vacant Room Under the Gallaries And on Both Sids the Pullpitt in the Meettinghouſe Above s^d & to Know the Minds of the Precinct on s^d Affair

Fourthly to Grant Such a Sum of Money as is Sofitient to Compleat the Reverend Mr Seth Storer Sallary According to Contract & to Pay Such Perſons as ye Precinct Are Indebted to.

You Are Alſo Required to Notifie Such Perſons as the Precinct Are Indebted to to Bring in An Accompt of their Credit to the Precinct Com^{tee} on Thursday the Forth Day of March Next at four of the Clock in the Afternoon of Said Day at the houſe of Mr Thomas Bonds.

Sam^{ll} Janiſon
Thomas Bond
Joſeph Maſon
Precinct Com^{tee}

Middleſx : ſs.

To M^r Joſeph Harrington Constable of Watertown Greeting Sr You Hereby Requiered forthwith to Warn the Freeholders and Other Inhabitance with in the Easterly Precinct in Watertown who Are Quallified to Vote in Precinct Affairs to Meet at the Publick Meetting houſe in s^d Precinct on Thursday the Sixth Day of March Next at one of the Clock in the Afternoon of s^d Day for the Ends Following (1) to Chooſe Such Precinct Officers as by Law are Required to be Choſen in the Month of March (2) To hear the Propoſalls of ye Comm^{tee} (Who Ware Choſen & Impowered to Erect a New Addition to the Ministeriall house) for the Makeing the Addition to the ministeriall houſe more Convenient and Accommodateing and to Know the Minds of the Precinct Whether they will Alter the Former Scheme Laid for ſ^d Addition and Come into a New Scheme for the Better Accommodateing & Makeing the Ministeriall houſe more Convenient (3) To Grant Such a Sum of money as is Sofitient to Compleat the Revend Mr Seth Storers Sallery according to Contract and to Pay others that the Precinct are Indebted to : (4) To hear the Petition of Sundry of the Inhabitance of s^d Precinct With Reſpect to the Vacant Room under the Gallarys & on Both ſ^d the Pulpit in ye meeting houſe aboveſ^d & to Know the mind of the Precinct on ſ^d affair. You are alſo Requiered to Notifie Such Persons as ye Precinct are Indebted to to Bring in an Accompt of their Credits to the Precinct Com^{tee} on Thirsday the Forth of march Next at the houſe of Mr Thomas Bonds at Four of the Clock in the afternoon of s^d Day. Hereof

[20]

Hearof Fail Not But Make Return of this Order And Your Doings Thereon to one of the Comm^tee or Clerk of s^d Precinct at Least four hours Before the Time of s^d Meeting.

1^r Order of the Comm^tee

Watertown Feb: the NATH^ll HARRIS Clerk.
19th 1728/9

Att A meeting of the Freeholders & Other Inhabitance of the Easterly Precinct in Watertown Who ware Quallified to Vote in Precinct Affaires on the Sixth Day of March Anno Dom: 1728/9.

(1) Voted and Chofe for moderator Cornit Henry Bright

(2) Voted and Chofe for a Standing Com^tee to Mannage the Prudentialls for S^d Precinct for this Prefent Year Mr Samuel Pirce Mr John Stearns & Mr Jonas Bond.

(3) Voted and Chofe for Precinct Clerk Nath^ll Harris.

(4) Voted and Chofe for Precinct Treafurer or Reciver Lt Joseph Coollidge.

(5) Voted and Chofe for afsefsors for this Prefent Year { Jofeph Holden, Ebenezer Goddard, Henry Bond.

(6) Voted and Chofe for Collector for this Prefent Year Mr Thomas Coollidge.

Put to Vote Whether the Precinct will Choofe another Collector the Vote Pafsed in the Negative.

(7) Voted and Chofe for Saxton for this Prefent Year Mr Nath^ll Shearmon.

(8) Voted and Granted the Sum of Twenty Pounds to Pay the Revd Mr Storer to Compleat his Sallery according to Contract: and to Pay Others to Whom money may be Due from s^d Precinct.

(9) Voted that the Precinct will Come into the Propofalls of the Com^tee appointed for the Erecting an addition to the Minifteriall Houfe: the s^d Propofalls Being as Followeth,

Watertown March the 5th 1728/9

Viz: That the Frame for the addition to the Miniftereall houfe be of the Following Dementions (viz) 25 feet in Length & 24 feet in Wedth the Posts be 16 Feet in Leuth the Chemney to Stand on the Weft Side of the Building & to have an entry Way of Seven Feet Wide Betwixt the Old Building and the New: for the accomodating the Stareway into ye Chamber, And Further it is Propofed that the Roof on the Front of the Old Building be Raifed So as to Conform to the New Building or addition (which will make a Very Hanfom and Commodious Front Both East and South, and Further that the Leantor or Kichen that is to be Raifed be Raifed to Such a heigth as to Conform to the Other Parts of the Building and to accommodate the Chamber Over the Kichen that their be Built a Small Chemney in s^d Chamber: and that the Whole be well Finifhed in the Moft Prudent Way and Manner With all Speed.

(10) Putt to Vote Whether the Precinct will act any thing at this meetting Relateing to the Improveing the Vacant Room Under the Gallerys and on Both fids the Pulpitt in the Meettinghoufe in s^d Precinct & the Vote Pafsed in the Affermative.

[21]

(11) Put to Vote Whether the Precinct Will Improve s^d Vacant Room With Pews and the Vote Pafsed in the Affermative.

(12) Put to Vote Whether the Precinct Will Adjorn this Meetting to Friday the 14th of March Current at Two of the Clock in the afternoon of s^d Day and the Vote Pasted in the Affermative.

Att A Meetting of the Easterly Precinct in Watertown the 14th of March Anno Dom 1728/9 by adjornment at Two of ye Clock in ye afternoon of s^d day.

(1) Fut to Vote Whether the Precinct Will Erect & build A Pew for the Reverend Mr Storer (Where he Shall Choofe the Same) & for his Succefsors in the Ministry and the Vote Pafsed in the Affermitive.

(2) Put to Vote Whether the Precinct as a Precinct Will Build Pews in the Remaining Vacancy under the Gallarys & on Each Side of the Pulpitt (Convenient Allyes Excepted) and Difpofe of them as they Shall Think Fitt : the Vote Paft in ye Negative.

(3) Put to Vote Whether it Be the Minds of the Precinct to Choofe A Com^{tee} of Five Men to Difpofe of s^d Vacant Room Under the Callarys & on Each fide of the Pulpitt (Convenient Alley Room Excepted as aforefaid) Pews to Perticular Perfons they the f^d Perfons Building the Same; under fuch Reftrictions & Limitations as the Precinct Shall Think Proper the Vote Pafed in ye affermative.

(4) Put to Vote Whether f^d Com^{tee} in the Difpofalls of s^d Room Shall have Due and Strict Regard to mens Reall & Perfonall Eftates w^h they now Pofsefs in Fee Simple Within the Bounds & Limits of s^d Precinct the Vote Pafed in ye affermative.

(5) Put to Vote Whether the s^d Com^{tee} Shall have A fortnight to Difpofe of the s^d Room to Perfons tht the Com^{tee} Shall Think they Belong to under the afores^d Limitations and that if the Perfons to Whom Pews are offered, Shall not See Caufe to Except of the Same Within a Week after they are Offered that the Com^{tee} Shall Give them to Perfons to Whom they Mextly Belong to and the Vote Pafsed in the Affermative.

(6) Put to Vote Whether the Perfons that Shall Except of the Refpective Placess Offered them Shall be Obliged to Build their Pews Within One Quarter of a Year and Whether if they Shall Neglect to Build them Within s^d Term the s^d Room and the Difpofall thereof shall Return to the Precinct Again the Vote Pafed in the Affermative.

(7) Put to Vote Whether that if Perfons that have Pews Shall fel & Dipofe of their Estates in s^d Precinct their Pews Shall Return to the Precinct the Vote Past in ye Affermative.

(8) Voted that thofe Perfons that Accept of A Pew & Build the Same Shall be Obliged to Set in the Same Perfonally.

(9) Voted & Chofe Five men to be a Com[tee] to manage the affair of s[d] Pews (Viz) Quat[r] Thomas Larned Cor[l] Henry Bright Jonathan Stone Jun[r] Edward Harrington and Jofeph Holding.

(10) Voted & Chofe M[r] Oliver Livermore Collector for y[e] year Infuing in Thomas Coollidgs ftead

(11) Voted & Granted the fum of Three Pounds to Build y[e] Rev[d] M[r] Storers Pew.

[22]

To Nath[ll] Harris Clerk of the Easterly Precinct in Watertown You are Hereby Ordered to Give Out An Order to the Constable Within s[d] Precinct to Warn the Freeholders and Other Inhabitance Within s[d] Precinct Who Are Quallified to Vote in Precinct Affars to Meett Att the Publict Meetting houfe in s[d] Precinct On Monday the 14th of Aprill Current At one of the Clock in the Afternoon of f[d] Day for the Ends Following.

(Viz) 1 To Hear the Pettitions of Sundry of the Inhabitance of s[d] Precinct Concerning the Vacant Room in the Meetting in s[d] Precinct Under the Gallaries & On Each side of the Pulpitt that hath lately Bin Lotted into Pew Lotts; the Pettitioners Being the Perfons to Whom Pew Lotts Ware allotted to.

(2) For the Precinct to Proceed & Difpofe of the afores[d] Vacant Room as they Shall Apprehend Will Conduce Most to the Peace and Comfort of s[d] Precinct if they Pleafe.

Watertown Aprill the
4th 1729

JOHN STEARNS
SAM[ll] PIRCE } Precinct Com[tee]
JONAS BOND

Middfx fs To M[r] Jofiah Perrey Conftable of Watertown Greeting. S[r] You are hereby Required Forthwith to Warn the Freeholders and Other Inhabitance Within the Easterly Precinct in Watertown Who are Quallified to Vote in s[d] Precinct Affairs to meet att the Publict Meetting houfe in Said Precinct On Monday the 14th of Aprill Current At one of the Clock in the Afternoon of s[d] Day for the Ends Following (Viz)

(1[ft]) For the Precinct to hear the Pettition of Sundry of the Inhabitance of s[d] Precinct Concerning the Vacant Room in the Meetting houfe in s[d] Precinct Under the Gallaries & on Each fide of the Pulpitt, that hath Lately Bin Lotted into Pew Lotts the Pettitioners Being the Perfons to Whom Pew Lotts Ware Allotted to.

(2) For the Precinct to Proceed & Difpofe of the afores[d] Vacant Room as they Shall apprehend will Conduce most to the Comfort & Peace of s[d] Precinct if they Pleafe. Hereof Fail Not But make Return of this Order & Your Doings thereon to one of the Com[tee] or Clerk of s[d] Precinct At Least Four hours Before the Time of s[d] Meetting.

Watertown Aprill the
4th 1719.

₽ Order of the Com[tee]
NATH[ll] HARRIS, Cler[k].

Watertown Aprill the 14th 1729.

Att A metting of the Freeholders & Other Inhabitance within the Easterly Precinct in Watertown Who Ware Quallified to Vote in Precinct affairs.

(1) Voted & Chofe for Moderator for s^d Meetting Cornitt Henry Bright.

(2) Voted that Whereas Jonathan Stone Junr Edward Harrington & Oliver Livermore have Bin at Cost and Charge in Laying a Platform for Three Pews in the Meetting houfe in s^d Precinct that if the s^d Precinct Should Build Pews thereon as a Precinct or that s^d Platform Should be Difpofed of to any Other Perfons that they shall have Reafonable Pay for What they have Expended On s^d three Pew Lotts.

Put to Vote and Voted that the Precinct will adjorn this meetting to Monday the 21st Inftant at one of the Clock in the afternoon of s^d Day.

[23]

At A Meetting of the Freeholders & Other Inhabitance of the Easterly Precinct in Watertown on the Twentyfirst Day of Aprill Anno Dom 1729 by adjornm^{ent}.

Put to Vote Whether the Precinct Will Choofe A Com^{tee} of Three or five men to Search the Lists of Rates and Find thofe Perfons that have Paid most to ye Building the Meetting houfe in s^d Precinct; and that thofe Perfons Shall Draw Pews Succesively According to w^t they have Paid; Allowing But Two heads or Polls to Any (one) Estate. Where it Happens that there is more; and Where the Fathers are Difcafed their Children or Nattural heirs to Draw according to What the Fathers have Paid or Caufe to Be Paid or their Estates have Paid Since their Deceafe. And the Vote Past in the Affermative.

Put to Vote Whether the Precinct Will Choofe A Com^{tee} of Five men to Search the Lists of Rates upon the affair of the Pews as afores^d and Any three of them Agreeing to be Difcisive and the Vote Passed in the Affermative.

Voted and Chofe For A Com^{tee} to Search the Lists of Rates Concerning the Drawing of Pews as afors^d Cor^t Henry Bright Dea Jofeph Mason Nath^{ll} Harris Mr Samuel Pirce and Lt Jofeph Coollidge.

Put to Vote Whether the Precinct are of the Mind that after the above Said Com^{tee} have Searhed the Lists of Rates afores^d, and Found out thofe Perfons Who Are the highest in s^d Lists Who According to the Vote of the Precinct are to Draw the Pew Lotts, that if any of s^d Perfons Shall not Accept of a Pew Lot that the Com^{tee} Shall then Offer them, that then the Lot or Lotts so Refufed, to be Offered by s^d Com^{tee} to the Next Highest Perfons Successively as they Stand in s^d Rates; and that A Plan of the Pew Lotts be Drawn by s^d Com^{tee} and that Every Perfon that Accepts of a Pew Lott Shall fet his Name in the Spot he Shall Choofe and that Every Perfon that Accepts of a Pew Lot Shall be Obliged to Build his Pew Within three Months at Furthest from the Date hereof, or Forfit his Pew Lot to the Hands of the Precinct again to be Disposed of by the above s[d] Com[tee] as if s[d] Persons had Refused; and that Every Person that Accepts of a Pew Lot and Builds a Pew Shall be Obliged to set Personally therein, And if any Person   Persons Shall See Cause to Dispose of his or their Pew that the Precinct Shall have the Refusall Paying the Prime Cost.

And that after the Com[tee] have Compleated the Plan above s[d] according to the Votes of the Precinct that Said Plan Be Recorded in the Precinct Book of Records, as a Finall Settlement of s[d] Pew Lotts; the Vote Past in the affermative.

Put to Vote and voted that the Negative Votes that have Pased at this Meeting Shall not Be Recorded in the Precinct Book of Records.

[24]

To Nath[ll] Harris Clerk of the Easterly Precinct in Watertown You are hereby Ordered to Give out An order to Josiah Perry Constable to Warn the Freeholders & Other Inhabitance who are Quallified to Vote in Precinct Affairs according to Law: to meet At the Publict Meetting house in s[d] Precinct on the 5th Day of May Next at Two of the Clock in the afternoon of s[d] Day for the Ends Following,

(1) For the Precinct to Choose A Com[tee] of Five Men & Impower them to go through with the Service Relating to the Dispofall of the Pew Lotts in the meetting house in s[d] Precinct which the Com[tee] that was Chosen by the Precinct Att their Meetting on the 21st of Aprill Current by adjornment Declined to Perform and go through with.

(2) That Whereas the Precinct at their meetting afores[d] Voted that their Com[tee] Should Scearch the Lists of Rates for Building the Meettinghouse and that Persons Should Draw Pews according to w[t] they have Paid: that the Precinct would manifest w[t] Perticular Rates they will have their Com[tee] Scearch for their Rule to Act by, that their by they may Prevent Conterary Opinions in their Com[tee] And Whereas by s[d] Vote the Children of Deceased Fathers were to Draw Pews According to w[t] their Fatheirs have Paid: that if s[d] Children Should not agree when a Pew Lot is Offered within a week after s[d] Offer is made then s[d] Pew Lot to Return to the Precinct Again for their Com[tee] to Dispose of to one of s[d] Children which they shall Think ought In Justice to have the Same.

(3) For the Precinct to hear M[r] Jonathan Stone Jun[r] Accompt and M[r] Edward Harringtons and M[r] Olliver Livermors for Laying the Platform for Three Pews in the meetting house and for the Precinct to Take Care how they shall be Paid and order the Constable to Notifie M[r] Jonathan Stone M[r] Edward Harrington & M[r] Olliver Livermore to Bring in there accompts to y[e] Precinct at s[d] Meetting.

Watertown Aprill 28th 1729:   JOHN STEARNS } Precinct
                                  JONAS BOND   } Com[tee]

Middlesx fs

To Mr Josiah Perry Constable of Watertown Greetting. Sr You are Hereby Requiered Forthwith to Warn the Freeholders and Other Inhabitance of the Easterly Precinct in Watertown Who Are Quallified to Vote in Precinct Affairs to Meett at the Publict Meetting house in s^d Precinct On Monday the 5th Day of May Next at Two of the Clock in the Afternoon of s^d Day for the Ends Following.

(1) For the Precinct to Chofe a Com^{tee} of Five Men and Impower them to go through with the Service Relating to the Difpofall of the Pew Lotts in the meetting house in s^d Precinct w^h the Com^{tee} that was Chofen at the meetting of the Precinct the 21st of Aprill Current by adjornment. Declined to Perform and go through with.

(2) That Whereas the Precinct Voted At their Meetting afores^d that their Com^{tee} Should search the Lists of Rates and thofe that stood Highest in s^d Lists and had Paid Paid most to the Building the meetting house should Draw Pews Successively according to w^t they have Paid, that the Precinct may Mennafest w^t Perticuliar Lists of Rates they would have their Com^{te} Search for their Rule to Act by that thereby they may Prevent Conterary Opinions in their Com^{tee} and whereas by s^d Vote the Children of Deceafed Fathers Should Draw Pews According to w^t their Fathers have Paid that if s^d children should not agree within a Weak after they have the offer of a Pew Lot and Except of the Same y^t s^d Pew Lot to Return to the Precinct again for their Com^{tee} to Difpofe of it to one of s^d Children w^h they shall Think ought in Justice to have the same.

(3) for the Precinct to hear Mr Jonathan Stone Junr Mr Edward Harringtons & Mr Oliver Livermors accompt for laying a Platform for three Pew Lotts & to Take Care how they shall be Paid for ye fame. You are also to notifie s^d Jonathan Stone, Edward Harrington & Oliver Livermore to Lay their accompts Before the Precinct at s^d meetting, hearof fail not But make Return of this order and your Doings thereon to one of the Com^{tee} or Clerk of s^d Precinct at Least four hours Before the Time of s^d meetting.

P order of the Com^{tee} NATH^{ll} HARRIS Clerk.
Watertown Aprill 28th, 1729.

[25]

Att A Meetting of the Freeholders & other Inhabitance of the Easterly Precinct in Watertown May the 5th anno Dom 1729 Who were Quallified to Vote in Precinct affairs.

(1) Voted and Chofe for Moderator Mr Thomas Strait.

(2) Put to Vote Whether the Precinct Will Act upon the Warrant by w^h this meetting was Warned and the Vote Past in the Affermative.

(3) Put to Vote Whether the Precinct will Act upon the First Article in the Warrent of this Meetting and the Vote Past in the Affermative.

Rachel Goffe / Eliza Abney	W^m + Door	Joseph Batson	Abra^m Brown
Gregory Stone			

Is This Alley to be

East Precinct in Watertown,
June the 17th 1729.

These Persons Whose Names are on this Plan and Pr'sent in the Townsh'p Pew Spotts are these Persons that have Applyed of the Township Pew Spotts to which they have affixed there Sevarall Names Agreeable & Conformable to the Vote of the Precinct above s'd for Settling s'd Pew Spotts

In testifi'd Under Our Hands this Day and Date above s'd ———

) time Inches.

Thomas Lynne
Henry Bright } Comm̄:ᵗᵉᵉ
Joseph Appleton
John Hastings

Three feet Alley

Jonas Bonds

Joshua Bigelow

East Door

John Horton

Gallery Stairs

(4) Voted and Chofe for a Com^tee to go through wth the Service Relating to the Difpofall of the Pew Lotts in the meetting houfe in s^d Precinct as Set Forth in the first article in the Warrent for s^d meetting Deacon Jofeph Mafon Cor^l Henry Bright Ser^t Jonas Bond Serg^t John Haſtings and Qua^tr Maſter Thomas Larnard.

(5) Put to Vote Whether the aforesd Com^tee Shall Search all the Lists of Rates that they Can Find for their Rule to Act by and the Vote Past in the Negative.

(6) Put to Vote Whether the Com^tee afores^d Shall Search the List of Rates for Building the Meetting houfe that was Com^ted to Conſtable William Shattuck and the Two Lists of Rates Committed to Collector John Haſtings to Collect: for their Rule to Act by and the Vote Paſt in the affermative.

(7) Put to Vote Whether the Precinct will act on that Part of the Second Article in s^d Warrent Relating to the Children of Deceafed Fathers and the Vote Past in the Negative.

(8) Put to Vote & Voted that thofe Perfons that May have thofe Platforms Allotted to them; that Mr Jonathan Stone Junr Mr Edward Harrington and Mr Oliver Livermore Layed upon three Pew Lotts for three Pews in the meettinghoufe: Shall Pay them (viz Jonathan Stone Edward Harrington and Oliver Livermore) Reafonably; According to the Vote of the Precinct.

To Nathaniel Harris Clerk of the Easterly Precinct in Watertown. You are Hereby Ordered to Diliver (or fhow) to the Afseſsors of s^d Precinct A Coppy of the Grants of Money Made by s^d Precinct At there Meetting on the fixth Day of March Last Paſt for the Ends therein Mentioned & Direct them Speedily to Afsefs the Inhabitance of s^d Precinct as the Law Directs and to Committ the Rate or Afsefsment to Mr Oliver Livermore the Prefent Collector for s^d Precinct With A Lawfull Warrent to Collect the fame, and to Pay into the Precinct Treafurer Lt Jofeph Coollidge or his fucceffor in s^d Office So as to Iſue and Make up An Accompt of the Whole of s^d Afsefsment Att or Before the Fourth Day of December Next Infuing the Date Hereof

Watertown November the
8^h 1729

Sam^ll Pearce
John Stearns
Jonas Bond
} Precinct Comm^t.

[26] [Plan of seats in meeting house.]

[27]

To Nath^ll Harris Clerk of the Easterly Precinct in Watertown. You Are hereby Ordered to Give Out An Order Forthwith to Lt Jofeph Coollidge Treafurer for s^d Precinct to Pay out of the Grants of Money Made by s^d Precinct the fixth Day of March Last Past and Committed to Mr Oliver Livermore Collector to Collect.

To the Reverd Mr Seth Storer the Sum of Sixteen Pounds to Compleat his Sallary According to Contract.

To Mr Jofeph Hedding Mr Ebenezer Goddard & Mr Henry Bond One Pound Six Shillings And Three Pence (viz) the Sum of Eight Shillings and Nine Pence Each of them for Makeing one Precinct Rate.

To M^r Joſeph Harrington for Warning one Precinct Meetting three Shillings.

To M^r Joſiah Perry the Sum of Six Shillings for Warning Two Precinct Meetings.

To Mr Edward Harrington the Sum of One Pound & Ten Shillings in Part for Building the Reverd Mr Storers Pew.

To the Heirs of Thomas Larned Deceaſd; the Sum of One Pound & Ten Shillings in Part for the Building the Reverd Mr Storers Pew.

To M^r Joſhua Grant Junr the Sum of Two Pounds Four Shillings & Nine Pence for Mending the Glaſs on the Meetting houſe in s^d Precinct.

Alſo to Pay to M^r Joſhua Grant the Sum of one Pound Two Shillings & Seven Pence out of the Grant of Money made by s^d Precinct on the 11th Day of March annoque Dom 1727/8 w^h was Committed to Mr Jonathan Stone to Collect.

Watertown January the 6th
1729/30

JOHN STEARNS } Precinct
JONAS BOND   } Com^{tee}
SAM^{ll} PIRCE }

To L^t Joſeph Coollidge Treaſurer for the East Precinct in Watertown Sr You are Hereby Ordered to Pay to the Reverd Mr Seth Storer the Sum of Sixteen Pounds (out of the Grants of Money Granted the 6th Day of March Last Past and Committ^d to Mr Oliver Livermore Precinct Collector to Collect) w^h is to Compleat his Sallary According to Contract.

To M^r Joſeph Holding the ſum of Eight ſhillings and Nine Pence: to Mr Ebenezer Goddard the ſum of Eight Shillings & nine Pence & Alſo to Mr Henry Bond the Sum of eight Shillings & nine Pence for making One Precinct Rate.

To M^r Joſeph Harrington the ſum of Three ſhillings for Warning one Precinct Meeting.

To M^r Joſiah Perry the Sum of Six Shillings for Warning Two Precinct Meettings.

To Mr Edward Harrington the ſum of one Pound & Ten in Part for Building the Reverd Mr Storers Pew.

To the Heirs of Thomas Larnard Deceaſed the ſum of One Pound & Ten Shillings in Part for Building the Reverd Mr Storers Pew.

To M^r Joſhua Grant Junr the ſum of Two Pounds four Shillings and nine Pence for Mending the glaſs on the Meetting houſe in s^d Precinct alſo to Pay to M^r Joſhua Grant the Sum of One Pound Two Shillings & Seven Pence out of the Grant of Money Made by s^d Precinct on the 11th Day of march anno Dom 1727/8 w^h was Committed to Mr Jonathan Stone to Collect.

Watertown January the 6th
1729/30

p Order of the Precinct
Com^{tee} NATH^{ll} HARRIS Cler.

[28]

To Nath{ll} Harris Clerk of the Easterly Precinct in Watertown. You Are Hereby Ordered to Give out An Order Forthwith to M{r} Josiah Perry Constable of s{d} Watertown to Warn the Freeholders and Other Inhabitance in s{d} Precinct Who Are Quallified to Vote in Precinct Affairs to Meet at the Publict Meettinghouse in s{d} Precinct on Fryday the Sixth Day of March Next at one of the Clock in the afternoon of s{d} Day for the Ends Following.

Viz First, To Choose a Precinct Committee A Precinct Clerk Afsefsors & other Precinct Officers Nefsafary to be Chosen as the Law Directs, & Requiers:

Secondly, To Grant A sofitient sum of money to Pay the Rev{d} M{r} Storer According to Contract & to Pay others to Whom Money may be Due from s{d} Precinct.

Thirdly, For the Precinct to hear the Pettition of Sam{ll} Barnerd John Orms and Sundry Others of the Inhabitance of s{d} Precinct, Relateing to the Seatting the Meeting house in s{d} Precinct and Repairing of Glase in s{d} Meettinghouse and that the Precinct May Act thereupon as they fhall fee Meett.

Dated att Watertown afore the 20{th} Day of February Anno Dom 1729/30

          JOHN STEARNS
          SAM{ll} PIRCE } Precinct Com{tee}
          JONAS BOND

To Nath{n} Harris Clerk of the Easterly Precinct in Watertown. You Are Hereby Ordered to Give out An Order Forthwith to L{t} Joseph Coollidge Treasurer of s{d} Precinct to Pay to M{r} Joshua Grant Jun{r} the sum of Fourteen shillings Out of the Grants of Money Made by s{d} Precinct the 11{th} Day of March 1727/8 and Committed to M{r} Jonathan Stone Collector to Collect; for mending Glase in the meettinghouse in s{d} Precinct.

Watertown March the 6{th}   JOHN STEARNS
1729/30   JONAS BOND } Precinct Com{tee}
                              SAM{ll} PIRCE

To L{t} Joseph Coollidge Treasurer of the Easterly Precinct in Watertown, S{r} You are hereby Ordered to Pay to M{r} Joshua Grant Jun{r} the sum of Fourteen shilling out of the Grants of Money Made by s{d} Precinct on the 11{th} Day March 1727/8 and Committed to M{r} Jon{a} Stone Jun{r} Collector for s{d} Precinct to Collect: it Being for mending Glase in the Meetting house in s{d} Precinct.

Watertown March the 6{th} 1729/30

                  p Order of the Precinct Com{tee}
                          NATH{ll} HARRIS Cler

Middfx fs.

To M{r} Josiah Perry Constable of Watertown Greetting. S{r} You are hereby Ordered Forthwith to Warn the Freeholders and other Inhabitance Within the Easterly Precinct in Watertown afores{d} who are Quallified according to Law to Vote in Precinct affairs to meett at the Publict meettinghoufe in s[d] Precinct on Fryday the Sixth Day of March Next at one of the Clock in the afternoon of s[d] Day for the Ends Following (viz): 1: to Choofe a Precinct Com[tee] A Precinct Clerk Afsefsors & other Precinct Officers Nefsafary to be Chofen as by Law Requiered. (2.) To Grant A Sofitient Sum of Money to Pay the Reverd M[r] Storer According to Contract & to Pay others to Whom money may be Due from s[d] Precinct. (3) for the Precinct to hear the Petition of Sam[l] Bernard John Orms & Sundry others of the Inhabitance of s[d] Precinct Relateing to the feating the meettinghoufe in s[d] Precinct & for the maintaining Glafe in s[d] meettinghoufe in s[d] Precinct y[t] s[d] Precinct may act thereupon as they Shall See meet:

Hereof Fail not But make Return of this Order & your Doings thereon to one of the Com[tee] or Clerk of s[d] Precinct at Least Four hours Before the Time of s[d] meetting p order of the Precinct Com[tee] NATH[ll] HARRIS Clerk.

Watertown February the 21st 1729/30

[29]

Att A Meetting of the Easterly Precinct in Wattertown the 6th Day of March Anno Domini 1729/30

(1) Voted and Chofe for Moderator for s[d] Meetting Dea Jofeph Mafon.

(2) Voted and Chofe for a Standing Com[tee] for the Infuing year M[r] Oliver Livermore M[r] Samuel Brown and M[r] Jonas Bond.

(3) Voted and Chofe for Clark for f[d] Precinct for the year Infuing Nath[ll] Harris.

For Precinct Treafurer was Chofen Jofeph Coollidge

(4) For Afsefsors for the year Infuing } Ebenezer Goddard
Nath[ll] Bright
Jofeph Holding.

(5) Voted and Chofe for Collector for the Year Infuing M[r] Ebenezer Cheury.

(6) Voted and Chofe for fexton M[r] Ebenezer Hastings.

(7) Voted that the fexton fhould be Payed by Two Free Contributions: viz: the First on the First Sabath in September and the fecond on the First Sabath in March.

(8) Voted and Granted the fum of Twenty Pounds to Pay the Revd M[r] Storer according to contract and to Pay others to Whom Money May be Due from s[d] Precinct.

(9) Put to Vote Whether the Precinct Will Act on the Pettition of Sam[ll] Barnard John Orms and others Relating to the feating the meettinghoufe and Repairing Glafe and the Vote Past in the Negative.

To Nath[ll] Harris Clerk of the Easterly Precinct in Watertown. You are Hereby Required to Give out an order Forthwith to M[r] Ebenezer Stone Conftable of Watertown aforef[d] to Warn the Freeholders & other Inhabitants Within the Easterly s[d] Precinct who are Quallified to Vote in Precinct affairs to Meet at the Publict Meettinghoufe in s[d] Precinct on Monday the 10th Day of August

Current at Two of the Clock in the afternoon of s⁴ Day for the Ends Following.

Viz) First To Know the Minds of the Precinct Whether they will Releafe their Com⁴ᵉᵉ that Was Chofen to make the addition to the ministeriall houfe & Choofe a New Com⁴ᵉᵉ to Proceed in s⁴ Work & Finish s⁴ Houfe.

Secondly, to Know the minds of s⁴ Precinct whether they will grant a sum of money for Mannageing s⁴ work & Finishing s⁴ Ministerial Houfe & how much they will Grant.

Thirdly, to hear the Return of the Com⁴ᵉᵉ Chofen to fell the Former Ministeriall Place and to Purchase the Prefent Ministeriall Place & how they Will Reward them for s⁴ fervice & Whether the Precinct Will Grant Money for that Purpofe:

Alfo to Notifie the Com⁴ᵉᵉ Chofen to Make the addition to the Ministeriall Houfe to Bring in there Accomps of wᵗ they have Done Relateing to s⁴ Houfe.

      OLIVER LIVERMORE } Precinct
      SAMˡˡ BROWN   } Com⁴ᵉᵉ

Watertown August the 3ᵈ 1730

[30]

Middlſſs

To Mʳ Ebenezer Stone, Conftable of Watertown Greetting, Sʳ You are Hereby Requiered Forthwith to Warn the Freeholders & other Inhabitance Within the Easterly Precinct of Watertown aforeſᵈ Who Are Quallified to Vote in Precinct Affairs to Meet At the Publict Meetting houfe in s⁴ Precinct On Monday the 10ᵗʰ Current, at Two of the Clock in the afternoon of s⁴ Day for the Ends Following.

First to Know the Minds of the Precinct Whether they Will Releafe their Com⁴ᵉᵉ that was Chofen to Make the Addition to the Ministeriall houfe, & Choofe a new Com⁴ᵉᵉ to Proceed in s⁴ Work and Finish s⁴ houfe.

Secondly to Know the Minds of s⁴ Precinct Whether they Will Grant A fum of Money for the Mannageing s⁴ Work & Finishing s⁴ Ministeriall houfe and how much they will Grant.

Thirdly to hear the Return of the Com⁴ᵉᵉ Chofen to fell the Former Ministeriall Place And to Purchase the Prefent Ministeriall Place, and how they will Reward them for fᵈ fervice; and Whether s⁴ Precinct Will Grant Money for that Purpofe.

Alfo You Are hereby Ordered to Notifie Lᵗ Richard Coollidge, Corᵗ Henry Bright, & Serᵗ Jonas Bond Who Ware A Com⁴ᵉᵉ Chofen for to Make the addition to the Ministeriall houfe, to Bring in An Accompt to the Precinct of their Proceedings in that affair.

Hereof Fail Not but make Return of this Order with your Proceedings thereon to one of the Precinct Comᵗ ᵉ or Clerk of fᵈ Precinct at Least Four hours Before yʳ Time of s⁴ Meetting.

      p Order of the Precinct Comᵗ ᵉ

Watertown August the 3ᵈ 1730   NATHˡ HARRIS Cler.

Att A Meetting of the Inhabitance of the Easterly Precinct in Watertown, the Tenth Day of August Annoque Dom 1730

(1) Voted & Chofe for Moderator for 1ᵈ Meeting Dea Joseph Mafon.

(2) Put to Vote and Voted that the Precinct Will Release their Com^{tee} Chofen to Make the Addition to the Ministerial Houfe.

(3) Put to Vote & Voted that the Precinct Will Chofe a New Com^{tee} to Proceed in fd Work and to Finish fᵈ Ministeriall houfe.

(4) Put to Vote Whether it be the Minds of the Precinct to Chofe three Men for a Com^{tee} for that Purpofe and the Vote Past in the Affermative.

(5) Voted and Chofe for fᵈ Com^{tee} Dea: Nathan Fisk Mʳ Oliver Livermore & Nath^{ll} Harris.

(6) Put to Vote Whether the Precinct Will At this Meetting Grant A fum of Money for to Finish the Ministeriall houfe & the Vote Past in yᵉ affermative.

(7) Put to Vote Whether the Precinct Will adjorn this Meetting And the Remaining Buisnefs of the fame to FryDay Next At Five of the Clock in the afternoon of sᵈ Day : and their New Com^{tee} in the Mean Time to View the Materialls of sᵈ Ministeriall houfe & Report to the Precinct at their adjornment wᵗ they Are apprehenfive will be Needfull for the Finishing fᵈ Ministeriall houfe And the Vote Past in the Affermative.

[31]

Att A Meeting of the Easterly Precinct of the Easterly Precinct in Watertown the 14th of August Annoque Dom 1730 by adjornment.

Put to Vote Whether the Precinct Will Grant the fum of Two Hundred Pounds to Pay the Arrearages : and for the Finishing the Ministeriall houfe in sᵈ Precinct And the Vote Past in the Affermative.

Voted that the afsefsors for fᵈ Precinct be Directed in there Warrent to the Collector to Order that the sᵈ Sum of Two Hundred Pounds to be Collected & Payed in to the Precinct Treafurer by the First Monday of October Next Infuing. And that there Com^{tee} Chofen for the Finishing fᵈ Ministeriall houfe be Impowered to Draw tᵈ Money Out of the Treafury as fhall be Needfull for the Finishing sᵈ Ministeriall houfe and Paying the arrearages.

Put to Vote Whether the Precinct Will at this Meetting Act Any thing Upon the Third Article of the Warning of fᵈ Meetting And the Vote Past in the Negative.

Watertown, August the 17th 1730

To Nath^{ll} Harris Clerk of the Easterly Precinct in Watertown aforesd. You are Herby Ordered Forthwith to Give to the Afsefsors for tᵈ Precinct A Coppie of the Grant of Money Made by fᵈ Precinct the 6th Day of March Last Past, also a Coppie of the Grant of Money made by tᵈ Precinct the 14th of August Current & Direct them fpeedily to afsefs the fame upon the Inhabitance and

Ratable Estates in f'd Precinct as the Law Directs; and to Committ the ſd Rate or aſseſsment to Mr Ebenezer Chenry Precinct Collector With A Lawfull Warrent to Collect the ſame, and to Pay in to Leut Joſeph Coollidg or his ſucceſſor in ſd Office ſo as to Iſsue and make up an accompt of the Whole of ſd aſseſsments at or Before the First Monday of October Next Inſuing.

JONAS BOND
OLIVER LIVERMORE } Precinct Comtee
SAMll BROWN

To Nathll Harris Clerk of the Easterly Precinct in Watertown. You are Hereby Ordered to Give out an order to Mr Ebenezer Stone Conſtable of Watertown To Warn the Freeholders and Other Inhabitants in the Easterly Precinct in Watertown Who Are Quallified to Vote in Precinct Affairs to meet att the Publict Meettinghouſe in the ſd Precinct On Fryday the Twelfth Day of march Next at one of the Clock in the afternoon on ſd Day for the Ends Following.

First to Chooſe a Precinct Comtee Clerk and Other Precinct Officers Nefsaſary to be Choſen in the Month of march.

Secondly, that the Precinct may Grant a ſofitient ſum of money to Pay the Revd Mr Seth Storrer according to Contract and to Pay other to Whom Money may be Due from ſd Precinct.

Thirdly to Chooſe A Saxton and Take Care how he ſhall be Rewarded for his Labour.

Fourthly to Know the mind of the Precinct whether they will Take any Further Care to Preſerve the Glaſs in the meetting houſe and whether it be there minds to make ſhutters or Barrs to Preſerve the ſame and if it be there minds to Do any thing Further to Preſerve ſaid Glaſs to Grant money for the Preforming the ſame.

and alſo to Notifie the Precinct Credditors to bring in there accompts to the Comtee at the houſe of Mr Larnerds on the Fifth Day of march Next at Four of the Clock in the afternoon of ſd Day.

Watertown Feb : 22 : 1730/31 : OLIVER LIVERMORE
SAMll BROWN } Comtee
JONAS BOND

[32]

To Nathll Harris Clerk of the Easterly Precinct in Watertown. You are Hereby Ordered to Give out An Order to Lt Joſeph Coollidge Treaſurer of the Easterly Precinct in Watertown To Pay out of the Grants of money made by the Precinct on the ſixth Day of March Last Past and Committed to Mr Ebenezer Chenry Collector to Collect ſd Grant Being Twenty Pounds.

To the Revd Mr Seth Storer the ſum of ſixteen Pounds to Compleat his Sallary According to Contract.

To Mr Ebenezer Goddard the ſum of Fifteen ſhillings. To Mr Joſeph Holding the ſum of Fifteen ſhillings. to Mr Nathll Bright the ſum of Fiſten ſhillings for making Precinct Rates.

To M{r} Ebenezer Stone the fum of fix fhillings for Warning Two Precinct Meetings.

To M{r} Ephraim Cutter Jun{r} the fum of one Pound and Nine fhillings for mending Glafs in the meeting houfe it Being in Part : &

Watertown March the 5{th} 1730/31

OLIVER LIVERMORE
SAM{ll} BROWN
JONAS BOND
} Precinct Com{tee}

To L{t} Jofeph Coollidge Treafurer of the Easterly Precinct in Watertown, S{r} Your are Hereby Ordered to Pay out of the Twenty Pound Grant of money made by the Precinct afores{d} on the fixth Day of march Last Past and Committ{d} to M{r} Ebenezer Chenry Collector to Collect.

Unto the Reverend M{r} Seth Storer the fum of fixteen Pounds to Compleat his Sallary According to Contract.

To M{r} Ebenezer Goddard the fum of £0-15-0 To M{r} Nath{ll} Bright the fum of £0 15-0. To M{r} Jofeph Holding the fum of £0:15:0: for making Precinct Rates.

To M{r} Ebenezer Stone the fum of fix fhillings for Warning Two Precinct meetings.

To M{r} Ephraim Cutter Jun{r} the fum of One Pound and Nine fhillings for mending Glafs in the meetting houfe in s{d} Precinct: it Being in Part &c :

Watertown March the fixth 1730/31
p Order of the Com{tee} of f{d} Precinct.

NATH{ll} HARRIS Clerk

Middlx fs To M{r} Ebenezer Stone Conftable of Watertown, Greetting. S{r} You are Hereby Ordered and Required Forthwith to warn the Freeholders and other inhabitants within the Easterly Precinct in Watertown Who are Qualified according to Law to Vote in Precinct affairs to meet at the Publict meeting houfe Within the f{d} Precinct on Fryday the Twelfth Day of march Next at one of the Clock in the afternoon of f{d} Day for the Ends Following.

First to Choofe A Precinct Com{tee} Clerk & other officers Nefsafary to be Chofen in the month of March.

Secondly for the Precinct to Grant a fofitient fum of money to Pay the Revd M{r} Seth Storrer According to Contract and to Pay others to Whom money may be Due from f{d} Precinct.

Thirdly to Choofe a fexton and to Take Care how he fhall be Rewarded.

Forthly, to Know the minds of the Precinct Whether they will Take any Further Care to Preferve the Glafs on the meetting houfe in f{d} Precinct: and Whether it be there mind to make Barrs or fhuters to the Windows to Preferve the fame : and if it fhould be there minds to Do Any thing Further to Preferve f{d} Glafs to Grant money to Perform the fame.

You are alfo to Notifie the Precinct Creditors to Bring in there accompts to the Precinct Com{tee} at the houfe of M{r} Larnerds on the Fifth Day of march Next at Four of the Clock in the afternoon of f{d} Day : Hereof Fail Not But make Return of this order &

your Doing thereon to on of the Precinct Com^te or to the Clerk of f^d Precinct at Leaft four Hour Before the Time of f^d meetting Watertown February the 22^d 1730/31

p^r Order of the Precinct Com^te
Nath^ll Harris Cler.

[33]

Att A Meetting of the Freeholders and other Inhabitants of the Easterly Precinct in Watertown the Twelfth Day of march : 1730/31 :

(1) Voted and Chofe for Modderator for faid Meetting Dea John Coollidge.

(2) Voted & Chofe for a Standing Com^tee to mannage the Prudentialls for faid Precinct the Infuing Year : Mr Jofiah Perry Lt Jofeph Coollidge and Mr Jofeph Child.

(3) Voted and Chofe for there Clerk Nath^ll Harris.

(4) Voted and Chofe for Precinct Treafurer & Reciver Nath^ll Harris.

(5) Voted and Chofe for Afsefors for the Infuing Year } Samuel Brown, Oliver Livermore, Ebenezer Goddard.

(6) Voted and Chofe for Precinct Collector James Barnard.

(7) Voted and Chofe for fexton Ebenezer Haftings.

(8) Voted to Pay f^d fexton by Two Contributions as Ufuall.

(9) Voted and Granted the fum of Thirty fhillings to Mr Edward Harrington and Mrs Mary Larned in Full with what they Have Had for Building the Ministeriall Pew :

(10) Voted & Granted the fum of Four Pounds Twelve fhillings and Ten penfe to Pay Precinct Credditors (viz) for Ephraim Cutter Junr feventeen fhillings for John Brown four fhillings for Isaac Child Ten fhillings : for the Com^tee Mr Oliver Livermore Mr Sam^ll Brown and Mr Jonas Bond : the fum of Ten fhillings it being for Hanging the Bell in the Publick meetting houfe. for Mr Willm Shattuck the fum of Fifteen fhillings : for the Com^tee Imployed in the fale of the Old Ministeriall Place the fum of feven fhillings & fix pence, for Jofiah Perry three fhillings for Warning one Precinct meetting. for Dea John Coollidge Twenty fhillings for fervice in the Purchafs of the Prefent Ministeriall Place. for Benjamin Haftings the fum of fix fhillings.

(11) Voted and Granted the fum of fixteen Pounds to Pay the Reverd Mr Storer to Compleat his falary according to Contract :

(12) Voted and Granted four Pounds to Pay others to Whom money may be Due from faid Precinct.

(13) Voted And Granted the fum of Ten Pounds to Procure Barrs to Preferve the Glafs on the Meetting Houfe and for the Further Mending of the f^d Glafs &c.

Watertown March the 19th 1730/31

To Nath^ll Harris Clerk of the Easterly Precinct in Watertown You are Hereby Ordered Forthwith to Give to the Afsefors of s^d Precinct A Copie of the Grants of money Made by s^d Precinct on the Twelfth Day of this Inftant March and Direct them Speedily to afsefs the fame on the Inhabitants of f[l] Precinct as the Law Directs and to Committ the Rate or Afsefsments to M[r] James Barnard Collector for f[l] Precinct with a Law full Warrent to Collect the fame and to Pay in to Nath[ll] Harris Treafurer for f[l] Precinct or his fuccefsor in f[l] office the Whole of the f[l] afsefsments at or Before the First Monday of June Next Infuing.

        Josiah Perry } Precinct
        Joseph Coollidg } Com[tee]
        Joseph Child }

[34]

  To Nath[ll] Harris Clerk of the Eafterly Precinct in Watertown. You are Hereby Ordered to Give Out An Order to M[r] Samuel Thacher Conftable of Watertown afores[d] Within f[l] Precinct to Warn the Freeholders and other Inhabitance Within f[l] Precinct Who Are Quallified to Vote in Precinct affairs to meett att the Publict Meetting houfe in f[l] Precinct On Monday the 24th Day of May at one of the Clock in the afternoon of s[d] day for the Ends Following.

 (viz) First To Know the Mind of the Precinct Whether they are Willing the Town fhould be Divided by the Prefent Precinct Line, if fd Vote Pafses in the Negative then,

 Secondly, Whether they Are Willing the Town fhould be Divided by fome Other Line that may be Projected and for the Precinct to Act and Do any other Thing or Things that they May think Needfull and Prudent Relating to f[l] Affair.

        Josiah Perry } Precinct
Watertown May the 18th 1731 Joseph Coollidg } Com[tee]

Middfx fs

 To M[r] Sam[ll] Thacher Conftable for the Easterly Precinct in Watertown,

 S[r] You Are Hereby Requiered Forthwith to Warn the Freeholders and Other Inhabitants Within the Easterly Precinct in Watertown Who Are Quallified to Vote in Precinct Affairs to Meet at the Publict Meetting houfe in f[l] Precinct on Monday the 24th Day of May Current at One of the Clock in the Afternoon On f[l] Day for the Ends Following (Viz),

 (1) To Know the Minds of the Precinct Whether thay Are Willing the Town fhould be Divided by the Prefent Precinct Line, and if faid Vote Pafses in the Negative then,

 (2) Whether they Are Willing the Town fhould be Divided by fome Other Line that May be Projected, and for the Precinct to Act and Do any other thing or things y[t] they may Think Needfull and Prudent Relateing to faid affair.

 Hereof Fail Not But Make Return of this Order and your Doings thereon to one of the Precinct Com[tee] or to the Precinct Clerk at Least Four Hours Before the Time of f[d] meetting,

     p Order of the Precinct Com[tee]
Watertown May the 18th 1731 Nath[ll] Harris Cler.

Att A Meeting of the Freeholders and Other Inhabitants of the Easterly Precinct in Watertown, Who Are Quallified to Vote in Precinct affairs the 24th Day of may 1731.

(1) Voted and Chofe for Moderator for f[d] meeting Dea John Coollidge.

(2) Putt to Vote Whether the Precinct Are Willing that the Town fhould be Divided by the Present Precinct Line, and the Vote Pafsed in the Negative.

(3) Put to Vote Whether the Precinct are of the Mind that the Town fhould be Divided by fome other Line (then the Prefent Line) that may Hereafter be Projected, and the Vote Pafsed in the affermative.

(4) Put to Vote Whether it be the Mind of the Precinct that the Town fhould be Divided the East Part to Have Half the Land Contained in the Town and the Vote Pafsed in the Negative.

(5) Put to Vote Whether the Precinct will Chofe a Com[tee] of three men to Project fome Convenient Line and make Report thereof to the Precinct at the adjornment of this meeting, and the Vote Paft in the affermative.

(6) Voted and Chofe for a Com[tee] to Project and Report as affores[d] Dea Nath[n] Fisk Dea Jofeph Mafon and Dea John Coollidge.

(7) Put to Vote Whether the Precinct will adjorn this meeting to thursday the 27th Current at Four of the Clock in the afternoon of f[d] Day and the Vote Past in y[e] affermative.

[35]

Att A Meeting of the Inhabitants of the Easterly Precinct of Watertown the 27th Day of May Annoque Domini 1731 by adjornment.

(1) Put to Vote Whether it be the mind of the Precinct that the Dividing Line Between the East Part of the Town and the West Part fhould the Westerly Line of the First Divident fo Runing upon a Strait Line With that Divident Line Southerly to Charles River; and alfo Northerly to Cambridge Line and the Vote Past in the affermative.

(2) Put to Vote Whether it be the mind of the Precinct to Choofe three men a Com[tee] to addrefs the Great and Generall Court in their Behalf that (if the Hon[rd] Court fe Reafon to Divide Watertown into Two Diftinct Townfhips) the above mentioned and Voted Line may be the Dividing Line and the Vote Past in the Affermative.

(3) Voted and Chofe for there Com[tee] to addrefs the Generall Court as aforesd Dea, Nathan Fisk Dea, John Coollidge & Dea Jofeph Mafon.

(4) Put to Vote Whether it be the Mind of the Precinct; that (in Case the Great and Generall Court fhould fee Reafon to Divide the Town of Watertown into Two Diftinct Towns) that there affores[d] Com[tee] addrefs the Court that Each Part be Obliged to Pay there Respective Proportion and Rateable Part to the Maintaining the Great Bridge Over Charles River in Watertown affores[t] for the Future, and the Vote Past in the affermative.

(5) Put to Vote Whether it be the Mind of the Precinct that if the Town fhould be Devided as afforef¹; that Each Part fhould be Obliged to Pay there Refpective Parts of the Towns Debts that are alredy Contracted, and the Vote Paft in the Affermative.

(6) Voted that Each Part as afore f¹ be Obliged to Pay and Do there Proportionable Parts to the Maintainance and fupport of Any Poor Perfon or Perfons that Have Heretofore Moved out of the Town of Watertown, if it fhould fo Happen that they fhould Hereafter Become a Charge to Watertown by Reafon of there Being Duly Warned out of other Towns Where they may Now Live.

Middlfx fs

To Mr Samuel Thacher Conftable of Watertown Greetting. Sr You are Hereby Ordered & Requiered Forthwith to Warn the Freeholders and Other Inhabitance of the Easterly Precinct in Watertown Who Are Qualified to Vote in Precinct Affairs (according to Law) to meet at the Publict meetting houfe in f¹ Precinct On Monday the 13th of March Next Infuing at one of the Clock in the afternoon of f¹ Day for the Ends Following.

First to Chofe a Precinct Com^{tee} Clerk & other Precinct Officers Nefsafary to be Chofen in the Month of March.

(2) For the Precinct to Grant a fofitient fum of money to Pay the Reverd Mr Seth Storer according to Contract & to Pay others to Whom Money may be Due from f¹ Precinct.

(3) To Chofe A fexton and to Take Care how he fhall be Paid.

(4) To Know the Minds of the Precinct Whether they will feat there Meetting houfe under fuch Rules & Regulations as they agree upon.

(5) For the Precinct to hear the accompts of their First Com^{tee} Chofen by the Precinct to make the addition to the ministeriall houfe in s^d Precinct and that the Precinct may act there upon and with Relation thereunto as they fhall fee meet: Hereof Fail Not but make Return of this order & your Doing thereon unto one of the Com^{tee} or Clerk of f¹ Precinct at Least four hours Before the Time of f¹ meeting.

p^r order of the Com^{tee}. NATH^{ll} HARRIS, Cler.

Feb: 21st: 1731/2

[36]

Att A Meetting of the Inhabitance of the Easterly Precinct in Watertown the 13th Day of March Annoque Domini 1731/2.

(1) Voted and Chofe for Moderator for f¹ Meetting Dea Nathan Fisk.

(2) Voted & Chofe for a Standing Com^{tee} to Manaage the Prudentialls for s^d Precinct for the Infuing Year John Hastings Wm Williams & Oliver Livermore.

(3) Voted and Chofe for Precinct Cler Nath^{ll} Harris.

(4) Voted and Chofe for Precinct Treafurer Nath^{ll} Harris.

(5) Voted and Chofe for Precinct Afsefsors } Nath^{ll} Harris.
        for ye Infuing Year   } Samuel Brown
                                                  } Henry Bond

(6) Voted and Chofe for Collector for the Infuing Year Nath'll Clark.

(7) Voted & Chofe for fexton Eben' Hastings.

(8) Voted that the fexton fhould be Paid by Two Contributions as Ufuall.

(9) Voted & Granted the fum of Twenty Pounds to Pay the Rev'd M' Seth Storer according to Contract and to Pay others to Whom Money may be Due from f'l Precinct.

(10) Put to Vote Whether it Be the Mind of the Precinct to feat there meettinghoufe under fuch Rules & Regulations as they fhall agree upon and the Vote Past in y" affermative

(11) Put to Vote Whether it be the mind of the Precinct to Chofe A Com'tee to feat there meeting houfe as aforef'd and the Vote Past in the Affermative.

(12) Voted that the Precinct Will Chofe a Com'tee of Five men to feat the f'd meetting houfe.

(13) Voted & adjorned this meetting & the Remaining Bufinefs thereof to Monday the 20'th of March Inftant at Two of the Clock in the afternoon of f'd Day.

Att A Meetting of the Inhabitants of the Easterly Precinct of Watertown on the 20'th Day of March Annoque Domini 1731/2 by adjornment.

(1) Put to Vote Whether it be the Mind of the Precinct that the Third feat Below in the Body of feats and the Fore feat in the Front Gallarys fhould be Equill in Dignity and the Vote Past in the Affermative.

(2) Voted that the Forth feat Below as aforesd and the Fore feats in the Side Gallaries fhould be Equill in Dignity.

(3) Voted that it is the mind of the Precinct that there Com'tee in feating the meetting houfe fhall have Due Regard to Age: and to Perfons Reall & Perfonall Estate in the Last Invice, Haveing Refpect to but one Head or Poll to One Estate.

(4) Voted and Chofe for A Com'te to feat the f'd Meettinghoufe Dea Nathan Fisk Dea John Coollidge Dea Jofeph Mafon, M' John Hastings & M' Oliver Livermore.

(5) Voted that it is the Mind of the Precinct that the Boys under 14 year of age fhall fet in the Hind feats under the Pews in the Galleries on the Men fide; and that the Girls under foreteen year of age fet in the hind feat under the Pews in the Gallaries on y' womens fide.

(6) Put to Vote Whether the Precinct Will Accept of the Accompt of there First Com'tee Chofen to make the addition to the ministeriall houfe in f'd Precinct, & the Vote Past in the affermative.

[37]

Middfx f's: To M' Jofeph Holding Conftable of Watertown Greetting, S' You are Hereby Ordered & Requiered forthwith to Warn the Freeholders & other Inhabitance Within the Easterly Precinct of Watertown afores'd Who are Quallified to Vote in Precinct affairs To meet at the Publict meetting houfe in f'd Precinct on Monday the 24th Day of Aprill Current at Five of the Clock in the afternoon of f'd Day for the Ends following.

Viz First To Know the Mind of the Precinct Whether they will Grant a fofitient fum of Money to finish the Ministeriall houfe in f'd Precinct.

Secondly, To Know the Mind of the Precinct Whether they will Do any thing about the Meetting houfe in f'd Precinct that fo People may in Durty feafons Get to and go into f'd meetting houfe without Being Expofed to Wade in Mudd & Water: and alfo Whether they Will Provide fome More Conveniencys for to go up to the Bell in f'd Meetting houfe & if it be the Mind of the Precinct to Do any thing in thefe Refpects then to Grant money to Defray the Charges of the fame.

Thirdly, For the Precinct to hear the Report of the Com[tee] Chofen by the Precinct to feat there meetting houfe.

Forthly For the Precinct to agree upon fome Certain Place for the Hearfe Cloath to be Keept in.

Hereof Fail Not but make Return of this Order & your Doings therein to one of the Precinct Com[tee] or Clerk of f'd precinct at Leaft four hour Before the Time of f'd meetting.

Watertown aprill the 15th 1732
p[r] Order of the Precinct Com[tee]
NATH[ll] HARRIS Cler.

Att A Meetting of the Inhabitance of the Easterly Precinct in Watertown the 24th Day of aprill Anno Dom 1732 Being Regularly Warned &c.

(1) Voted & Chofe for moderator Nath[ll] Harris.

(2) Put to Vote Whether it be the mind of the Precinct to Grant any fum of money to Finish the Ministeriall houfe in f'd Precinct and the Vote Past in the affermative.

(3) Voted and Granted the fum of Eighty Pounds to Finish the Ministeriall houfe in f'd Precinct and to make a Yard about f'd houfe.

(4) Voted that the Deacons Wives fhould fet in the Fore feat in the Body of feats Below.

(5) Voted that the Hearfe Cloath fhould be Keept at the houfe of M[r] John Hastings.

Middlefex fs To M[r] Jofeph Holding Conftable for Watertown Greetting &c.

S[r] You are hereby Ordered & Required forthwith to Warn the Freeholders and other Inhabitants of the Easterly Precinct in Watertown Who are Quallified according to Law to Vote in Precinct affairs to meet at the Publict Meetting in f'd Precinct on monday the 12th Day of March Next at Two of the Clock in the afternoon on f'd Day for the Ends Following,

(1) To Choofe a Precinct Com[tee] Clerk & other Precinct officers Nefsary to be Chofen in the Month of March.

(2) for the Precinct to Grant a fofitient fum of money to Pay the Reverd M[r] Storrer according to Contract and to Pay others to Whom money may be Due from f'd Precinct.

(3) To Choose a sexton and to Take Care how he Will be Paid,

[38]

(4) To Know the Minds of the Precinct Whether they Will sink some Rates of severall Persons in the Lists of Rates in severall of the Late Collectors Hands.

(5) To Know the Mind of the Precinct Whether they Will Do any thing about the meeting house in s'd Precinct for the more Comfortable Passing into s'd Meettinghouse in Wet and Durty seasons and Whether they Will Provide any more Conveniencys to Git up to the Bell in s'd Meettinghouse.

You are also Requiered to Notifie the Precinct Credditors to Bring in there Creddits to the Precinct Com'tee at the house of M'rs Mary Larnard Inholder at four of the Clock in the afternoon on Fryday the Ninth Day of March Next Insuing.

Hereof Fail Not But Make Return of this order and Your Doings thereon at Least four hour before the Time of s'd Meeting to one of the Precinct Com'tee or Clerk of s'd Precinct.

February 8th 1732/3 Per Order of the Precinct Com'tee.

NATH'l HARRIS Cler.

Att A Meeting of the Freeholders and other Inhabitance of the Easterly Precinct in Watertown on Monday the 12th Day of March Annoque Domini 1732/3.

(1) Voted and Chose for moderator for s'd Meeting Nath'l Harris.

(2) Voted and Chose for Precinct Com'tee, to Mannage the Prudenshalls of s'd Precinct for the Year Insuing { Jonathan Brown, John Hastings, Eben'r Stone.

(3) Voted and Chose for Clerk of s'd Precinct Nath'l Harris

(4) Voted and Chose for Precinct Treasurer Nath'l Harris

(5) Voted and Chose for Precinct Assessors { Eben'r Goddard Samuel Brown Henry Bond

(6) Voted and Chose for Precinct Collector Samuel Stratton.

(7) Voted and Chose for sexton   Ebenezer Hastings

(8) Voted that the sexton be Paid by two Contributions as Usiall.

(10) Put to Vote Whether the Precinct are Willing to sink Thomas Reads Rate amounting to the sum of £o: 15s: 8 in the £220 Precinct Rate Committed to M'r Ebenezer Cheury to Collect, and the Vote Past in the affermative:

(11) Put to Vote Whether the Precinct Are Willing to Sink Allexander Maccoys Rate being £o: 2: o: the Wid'w Elizabeth Dixes Rate Being £o: 1: 1: Samuel Hancoks Rate Being £o: o: 1: and John Kings Rate: Being £o: 1: 5: all Being in the List of Rates Committed to M'r Edward Harrington to Collect: and the Vote Passed in the affermative.

(12) Put to Vote Whether the Precinct Will Allow M'r E'lwad Harrington the sum of Twenty shillings for Gathering 25'l and the Vote Passed in the Negative.

(13) Put to Vote Whether the Precinct Will allow Ebenezer Chenry the sum of £1 : 5 : 0 for Gathering £220 : 0 : 0 : and the Vote Passed in the affermative.

(14) Put to Vote Whether the Precinct Will allow Mr Edward Harrington five shillings for Gathering £25 : 0 : 0 : and the Vote Past in the Negative.

[39]   (15

(15) Put to Vote Whether Precinct Will sink Nath^{ll} Stratons Rate Being £0 : 4 : 10 : John Orms Rate Being £0 : 8 : 7 : Allexander Maccoys Rate Being £0 : 3 : 4 : Joseph Shattucks Rate Being £0 : 4 : 6 : Thomas Hills Being £0 : 3 : 3 all in the List of Rates Commite^d to Jonathan Stone Junr Late of Watertown Deceased, and the Vote Past in the affermative,

(16) Put to Vote Whether the Precinct Will Grant the sum of Thirty Pounds to Pay the Revnd Mr Seth Storrer according to Contract and to Pay others to Whom money may be Due from the Precinct. and the Vote Passed in the affermative.

(17) Put to Vote to Know the mind of the Precinct Whether they will Do any thing about the meetinghouse in f^d Precinct for the more Comfortable Passing into the Meetting house in Wet and Durty seasons and also Provide some conveniency to get up to the Bell and the Vote Past in the affermative.

(18) Voted that the standing Committy for the Precinct for the Present year be a Committy to Do What they shall Think Proper about the meetting house, for the more Comfortable Passing into f^d meetting house in Wet and Dirty seasons, and also for the more Convenient Gitting up to the Bell on 1^d meettinghouse.

Watertown Aprill the 11th 1733

To Nath^{ll} Harris Cler of the Easterly Precinct in Watertown, You are hereby ordered to Give to the assesors for f^d Precinct a Copie of the Grant of Money made by f^d Precinct on the 12th Day of March Last Past and Direct them speedily to assess the same and to Committ there Rate or assessment to Mr Samuel Stratton Collecttor to Collect With a Lawfull Warrent to Collect the same and Order him to Pay in the Whole of his Collections to Nath^{ll} Harris Precinct Treasurer or his successor in f^d office : and to Issue and make up an accompt of the Whole of his Collections at or Before the First Day of July Next Insuing.

Eben^r Stone ⎱ Precinct
Jon^a Brown ⎰ Com^{teo}

To Nath^n Harris Clerk of the East Precinct in Watertown. You are hereby Ordered Forthwith to Give out An Order to Mr Benjamin Whitney Constable of Watertown and Order him therein to Warn the Freeholders and other Inhabitants of the Easterly Precinct in Watertown who are Quallified to Vote in Precinct affairs to meett at the Publict Meetting house in f^d Precinct on Monday the 11th Day of March Next at one of the Clock in the afternoon on f^d Day for the Ends Following viz.

(1) To Choose a Precinct Com^tee Clerk and all other Precinct Officers Nefsasary to Chofen in the Month of March.

(2) For the Precinct to Grant a fuficient fum of Money to Pay the Reved Mr Seth Storer according to Contract and to Pay others to whom Money may Due from f^d Precinct alfo to Know the minds of the Precinct Whether they will Grant an additionall fum of money to the Revend Mr Storer fallary.

(3) For the Precinct to Choofe a fexton and to Take Care how he may be Paid :

(4) To Hear the Precinct Treafurs accompt &c.

> Jonath^n Brown
> John Hastings
> Eben^r Stone
> } Precinct Com^tee

[40]

At a Meetting of the Freeholders and other Inhabitants of the Easterly Precinct in Watertown on Monday the 11th of March : A : D : 1733/4

1) Voted and Chofe for Moderator for f^d meetting Dea Nathan Fisk.

2) Voted and Chofe for the Precinct Com^tee to mannage the Prudentialls for the Precinct the Infuing Year (Dea Nathan Fisk. Enf^n Jon^a Stone. Dea John Coollidge.

3) Voted and Chofe for Precinct Clerk Nath^ll Harris.

4) Voted and Chofe for Precinct Treafurer Nath^ll Harris.

5) Voted & Chofe for afsefsors } Samuel Warrin, Samuel Brown, Thomas Bisco :

6) Voted and Chofe for Collector John Whitney.

7) Voted and Chofe for fexton Ebenezer Hastings.

8) Put to Vote Whether it be the mind of the Precinct to Pay the fexton by Two Contributions one on the First Sabath in September and the other on the First fabath on March and the Vote Past in the affermative.

9) Voted and Granted the fum of Twenty Pounds to Pay the Revend Mr Seth Storer According to Contract and to Pay others to Whom Money may be Due from f^t Precinct.

10) Put to Vote Whether it be the mind of the Precinct to make an addition to the Revend Mr Storers fallary and the Vote Past in the affermative.

11) Put to Vote Whether it be the mind of the Precinct to add Forty Pounds to the Revend Mr Storers fallary for this Prefent year (and to Grant the fame) and the Vote Past in the affermative :

12) Voted that the Precinct will finck John Phillips Rate in Daniel Bonds List of Rates Being £o-2-5 : and Alexander Maccoys Rate Being £o :2 :0.

Middlefex fs. Watertown February the 15th 1734/5.

To Mr John Sawin of Watertown in the County of Middlefex and one of the Conftables of f^t Watertown Greetting.

You are Hereby Ordered And Required Forthwith to Warn the Freeholders and Other Inhabitance of the Easterly Precinct in Watertown Who Are Quallified to Vote in Precinct affairs to meet at the Publict meeting houfe in 1ᵈ Precinct on Thursday the fixth Day of March Next at Two of the Ciock in the afternoon for the Ends Following (viz),

First To Choofe Precinct offices as the Law Directs,
Secondly to Grant money to Pay the Precinct Creddittor.
Thirdly to Grant fixteen Pounds wᶜʰ makes up the fallary of the Revend Mʳ Storer for the year according to Contract.
Fourthly to Know the Precincts mind wᵗ addition they will make to Revend Mʳ Storrers fallary for the year Current.
Fiftly to Choof a fexton.
Alfo to notifie the Precinct Credditors to Bring in their accompts to the Precinct Comᵗᶜᵉ on the aforefd fixth Day of March at one of the Clock in the afternoon at the abovefᵈ meeting houfe.

 pʳ Order of the Precinct Comᵗᶜᵉ
 NATHˡˡ HARRIS Cler

[41]

Att A Meetting of the Freeholders and Other Inhabitants of the Easterly Precinct in Watertown on Thirsday the fixth Day of march Annoque Domini 1734/5.

1) Voted & Chofe for Moderator for fᵈ Meeting Jofeph Mafon Efqr
2) Voted and Chofe for a ftanding Comᵗᵉᵉ ⎫ Jonas Bond,
 to mannage the Prudentialls for fᵈ ⎬ Wᵐ Williams,
 Precinct the Infuing Year ⎭ Oliver Livermore.
3) Voted & Chofe for Precinct Cler Jofeph Mafon Efqr
4) Voted & Chofe for Precinct Treafurer Jofeph Mafon Efqr :
 ⎫ Henry Bond,
5) Voted & Chofe for Precinct afsefsors ⎬ Samˡˡ Brown,
 ⎭ Nathˡˡ Bright,
6) Voted & Chofe for Precinct Collector John Coollidge Junʳ,
7) Voted & Chofe for fexton Ebenezer Hastings.
8) Voted and Granted the fum of fix Pounds to Pay Precinct Credditors, for Mending of the Glafs on the meeting houfe in fᵈ Precinct and for to Purchafe a Fram to fet the hour Glafs in.
9) Voted and Granted the fum of fixteen Pounds to Compleat the Revend Mʳ Storers falary according to Contract,
10) Voted and Granted the fum of Forty Pounds as an addition to the Revnd Mʳ Storers falary for the Year Current,
11) Voted to Pay the fexton by Two Contributions as Ufiall,

 Watertown October 20ᵗʰ 1735.
To Joseph Mason Clerk of yᵉ Easterly Precinct in fᵈ Town.

You are hereby ordred to give to the Afsefsors of fᵈ Precinct A Copy of yᵉ Grants of Money made by the Inhabitants of sᵈ Precinct on the fixth day of March laft paft. And direct them fpeedily to Afsefs the fame on the Inhabitants &c. of faid Precinct, And Commit the Afsefment to Mʳ John Coollidge Junʳ Collector for ſaid Precinct with a Lawfull Warrant to Levy and Collect the ſame and Order him to pay in the whole of his Collections to Joseph Mason Treaſurer for ſᵈ Precinct or to his Succeſsor in ſaid Office And to Iſu and make up an Accᵗ of the whole of his Collection At or upon the first day of December Next Enſuing.

        JONAS BOND } Precinct
        OLIVER LIVERMORE } Comᵗᵗᵉ

[42]

To Joseph Mason Clerk of yᵉ Eaſt Precinct in Watertown,

You are hereby Ordred and Directed forthwith to give out a Notification to Mʳ John Bright one of yᵘ Conſtables of Watertown aforeſᵈ And order him therein to Warn the Freeholders and other Inhabitants in ſᵈ Precinct who are Quallified to Vote in Precinct Affairs to Meet at yᵉ Publick Meeting houſe in ſᵈ Precinct on Munday the Eighth day of March Next at one of yᵉ Clock in the Afternoon of ſᵈ day for the Ends following.

 1. To Choſe a Committee a Clerk Treaſurer and all other Precinct Officers Neceſary to be choſen in the Month of March.

 2. To Grant Money to pay and Satisfye the Revᵈ Mʳ Storer According to Contract, And All other Perſons to whom yᵉ Precinct is indebted.

 3. To know the Mind of the Precinct what ſum they will Grant as an Addition to the Revᵈ Mʳ S. Storers Sallery for the preſent Year.

 4. To Choſe a Sexton & to take care how he may be paid.

 5. To know the Mind of the Precinct whether they will Appoint a Perſon to take the whole care of the Mending of the Meeting houſe Glaſs as there ſhall be Ocation and to be paid by the Precinct.

And ordʳ the ſᵈ Conſtable to Notify the Perſons to whom the Precinct is Indebted to bring in their Accᵗˢ to the Comᵗᵗᵉ at ſᵈ Meeting at one of yᵉ Clock.

        JONAS BOND } Precinct
Watertown Febʳ 13. 1735/6. OLIVER LIVERMORE } Commᵗᵉᵉ

Middˣ. ſs. To Mʳ John Bright Conſtable of Watertown in ſd County Greeting.

You are hereby ordred and required forthwith to Warn the Freeholdʳˢ & other Inhabitants in the Easterly Precinct of ſᵈ Town who are Quallifyed to Vote in Precinct Affairs to Meet at yᵉ Publick Meeting houſe in ſᵈ Precinct on Munday the Eighth Day of March Next at one of yᵉ Clock in yᵉ Afternoon of ſᵈ Day for yᵉ Ends following vizᵗ.

 1. To Choſe a Committee a Clerk & other Precinct officers Neceſsary to be choſen in the Month of March.

 2. To Grant Money to pay yᵉ Revᵈ Mʳ Seth Storer According to Contract and all other Perſons to whom yᵉ Precinct is Indebted.

 3. To Know yᵉ Mind of yᵉ Precinct what ſume of Money they will Grant as an Addition to yᵉ Revᵈ Mʳ Storers Salery for this Pſent Year.

4. To Chofe a faxton and to take care how to pay him.

5. To know the Mind of ye Precinct whether they will Appoint Any Perfon to take the whole care of ye Mending the Meeting houfe Glafs as there fhall be Ocation and to be paid by ye Precinct.

And Notify fuch Perfons to whom ye Precinct is Indebted to bring in their Acc^t to ye Committee at f^d Meeting at one of ye Clock.

Hereof fail not and Make return of this Ord^r to ye Com^te or Precinct Clerk seafonably before the time Appointed for f^d Meeting, Dated in Watertown the 13 Day of Feb^r A.D. 1735/6.

p^r order of the Precinct Comm^tee

JOSEPH MASON Pre^t Clerk

[43]

At a General Meeting of the Freeholders and other Inhabitants of the Eafterly Precinct in Watertown on Munday the 8th Day of March 1735/6

Voted and chofe Joseph Mason Esqr Moderator for f^d Meeting.

Voted and chofe for a Com^tee to Manage ye Prudentials of y^o Precinct { Dea: Jno Coollidge, Mr Jonas Bond, Mr Ebenz Stone,

Voted and chofe Joseph Mason Esqr Precinct Clerk,

Voted and Chofe Joseph Mason Esqr Precinct Treafurer.

Voted and chofe for Afsefsors { Henry Bond, John Coollidge Junr, Ebenez^r Goddard,

Voted and Chofe Nathanael Coollidge Precinct Colletor.

Voted and Chofe Ebenez^r Haftings faxton, And to be paid as Ufully.

Voted and Granted ye fum of fixteen Pounds to pay ye Revd Mr Seth Storer According to Contract.

Voted and Granted to Mr Wm Williams fix fhillings & fix pence.

Voted and Granted to Jonas Coollidge to fatisfy his Acc^t ye Sum of Three pounds three fhillings and fix pence.

Voted and Granted the fum of four pounds to mend the Glafs on ye Meeting house; & to pay ye Afsefsors this pfent Year.

Voted and Granted the fum of fifty Pounds at an Addition to the Revd Mr Storers falery for the Prefent Year.

Voted and Granted ye fum of Twenty fhillings to purchase a Book to keep ye Treafurers Acc^ts in.

The Vote was put whether it is the mind of ye Precinct to Appoint any Perfon to take ye whole care of ye Mending of ye Meeting houfe Glafs as there fhall be Ocation. And ye Vote paft on the Negative.

Watertown Sepr 17th 1736.

To Joseph Mason Esqr Clerk of ye Easterly Precinct in fd Town.

You are hereby Ordered to give the Afsefsors of f^d Precinct a Copy of the Grants of Money Made by ye Inhabitants of f^d Precinct at their Meeting on the Eighth Day of March Laft past, and Direct them Speedly to Afsefs the fame on the Ratable Inhabitants & Estates of f^d Precinct & Committ the Afsefm^t to ye Collector of f^d Precinct with a Lawfull Warrant to Levy and Collect the fame and to pay in the whole of his Collection to Your felf Treafurer for f^d Precinct or to your Succefsor in f^d Office & to make up An Acc^t of the whole of f^d Afsefm^t at or upon the firft day of Decemb^r Next.

                        JOHN COOLLIDGE ⎫
Which was Done p   JONAS BOND   ⎬ Com^tee
  J: Mafon Clerk   EBENEZER STONE⎭

[44]

Midd^x fs. To Mr Nathaniel Coollidge Collector for ye East Precinct in Watertown.

You are hereby Defired to Notify the Freehold^rs and oth^r Inhabitants in f^d Precinct who are Qualifyed to Vote in Precinct Affairs To meet at the Publick Meeting houfe in faid Precinct on Munday the Twenty Eigth day of March Currant at Two of ye Clock in the Afternoon for the Ends following vizt

To Chofe a Committee to manage ye prudentials of f^d Precinct ye Pfent Year.

To Chofe a Clerk A Treafurer and all other Precinct Officers Necefsary to be Chofen in March.

To Chofe a Sexton; and take care how he Shall be paid.

To Grant Money to pay the Revd Mr Seth Storer According to Contract.

To Grant Money to pay Such as the Precinct are Indebted to. And to Defray other Necefsary Charges y^t may Arife in the Precinct.

To know the mind of the Precinct what Sum of money they will Grant As An Addition to the Revd Mr Storers Salery, for ye prefent Year.

To know the mind of the Precinct whether they will Grant a Sutable Sum of Money to be Improved in the repairing the fences belonging to the Minifterial place in this Precinct.

To Chofe a Com^tee to Improve ye money y^t may be granted for f^d end.

To hear the Acc^ts of the Com^tee who were chofen to finifh the Minifteral house, how they have proceeded in y^t Affair.

Hereof fail not and make return of this Notification and Your Doings thereon feafonably to ye Precinct Clerk before the time Appointed herein for f^d Meeting.

Dated at Watertown the 19th Day of March A.D. 1736/7.
        p^r order of the Precinct Committee.
                  JOSEPH MASON Prec^t Clerk.

At a Meeting of the Inhabitants of the Eafterly Precinct in Watertown Regurely Afsembled on the 28^t Day of March 1737.

Voted and Chofe Joseph Mason Moderator of f^d Meeting.

Voted and Chofe Joseph Mason Deacon John Coollidge & Capt Joseph Coollidge to be a Committee to manage ye prudentials of ye Precinct ye Pfent Year.

Voted and Chofe Joseph Mason Precinct Clerk.
Voted and Chofe Joseph Mason Precinct Treafurer.
Voted and Chofe Deacon John Coollidge Joseph Mason & Capt Joseph Coollidge Afsefsors. (who were Sworn by Justice Harris at f^d Meeting.)
Voted and Chofe David Sanger Collector for ye Precinct.
Voted and Chofe Ebenezer Hastings Sexton. Voted that there S^{ld} be two Contributions as ufal to pay the Sexton.
Voted and Granted the Sum of Sixteen pounds to pay ye Revd Mr Storer according to Contract.
Voted and Granted ye Sum of Twenty eight fhillings to pay Capt Joseph Coollidge his Acc^t.
Voted and Granted ye Sum of Twenty three Shillings & 4^d to pay Ep^m Cutters Acc^t for mending the Meeting houf Glafs.
Voted and Granted the Sum of Twenty two Shillings & 8^d to pay Jonas Coollidge for aladd^r for ye Ministeral houfe.
Voted and Granted 3/6 to pay Jofiah Perry for a lok.
Voted and Granted 3/ to pay John Bright for warning one meeting. And 3/ to pay Nathl Coollidge for warning this Meeting.
Voted and Granted Six pounds for Necefsary Charges y^t may Arife in ye Precinct,
Voted and Granted the Sum of fifty Pounds As An Addition to ye Revd Mr Storers Salery for this Pfent Year.
Voted and Granted ye Sum of Twenty pounds to be Improved in repairing the fences belonging to ye Ministeral place.
Voted and chofe Joseph Mafon Dea John Coollidge & Capt Joseph Coollidge to be A Com^{tee} to Improve fd money for fd Ends.
The Committee for finifhing ye Ministeral Houfe laid y^r Acc^t before ye Precinct.
Voted their Acceptance of f^d Acc^t & Voted and Granted ye Sum of Eight fhillings & Six pence Ballance Due to f^d Committee.

[45]

Midd^{ll} fs. To Mr John Stowel Conftable of Watertown in f^d County Greeting.

You are hereby required to Warn the Freehold^{rs} and other Inhabitants in the Eafterly Precinct of f^d Town who are Quallifyed to Vote in Precinct Affairs to meet at ye Publick Meeting houfe in the f^d Precinct on Munday the fifth day of Decemb^r Next at one of ye Clock in the Afternoon for ye Ends following vizt

To know the Mind of ye Inhab^{ts} of f^d Precinct, whether they are willing (for ye Sake of peace in the Town) that ye Town of Watertown S^{ld} be Divided and made two Seperat Townfhips Upon the following Conditions vizt

That the f^d Town be Divided into Two Townfhips, and the Dividing Line to be as the Precinct Line Now is.

That the Great Bridge over Charles River in f^d Town be maintained by Each Town in proportion as they Shall be Set in the Province Tax.

That the poor who at prefent are Maintained by the Town be maintained by Each Town in proportion to their Province Tax, and if any Perfon gone out of Town S[d] be returned to Watertown and become a Charge that they be maintained by Each Town in like proportion as AforeS[d].

That the Towns Stock of Arms and Ammunition be Divided in Equal proportion between Each Town.

That Watertowns part of y[e] Two Thoufand Acres of Land Granted by the General Court to them and Wefton Be divided in Equal halves as to Quantity & Quallity between the two Towns when Divided.

That the Intereft of Watertowns part of y[e] fixty thoufand pound Loan be Divided to Each Town According to their Province Tax.

That the Books and records of y[e] Town of Watertown be Delivered up to a Com[te] of y[e] Eaft Town who may be Chofen and Appointed to receive the Same.

That the Debts of y[e] Town be paid by Each Town in proportion to y[r] Province Tax.

That if any Money upon Ballanceing the Treafurey Acc[t] remain in the Treafurey it be Divided between the Towns in like proportion as aforef[d].

That the Publick Ways in the Town from Mafterfs Brook to Cambridge, line be Stated and Settled as to their Courfe and wydth as the Court of General Sefsions of y[e] peace Agreeable to the reporte that be made by their Committee for that purpose Appointed Shall be pleafed to Ord[r], And if any Lands Now Lying as Ways or reputed as Such Shall not be included in the Ways when Stated as Afore[d] the Same Shall be to and for the Sole Ufe & benefit and at the Difpofal of the Town where in the Same Shall Ly: Provided however that if the Sale of any of the Lands afores[d] y[t] have been Difpofed of by the Towns Com[tee] (not included in the ways when Stated as Aforef[d]) Shall remain good And Valled to the Perfons who have Purchafed y[e] Same, Alfo y[t] Each Town Shall have the Benefit of the proceeds of y[e] Sale of Such of y[e] Land afores[d] as Ly within y[e] Same.

That if the f[d] Ways when Stated as Afores[d] Shall Include any Land belonging to any Perticular Perfon the owner of Such Land Shall have Meet recompence made him by the Town wherein the Same Lyes. Hereof fail not and make feafonable Return of this Warrant and Your Doings thereon to the Precinct Com[tee] or Clerk before the Time Appointed for f[d] Meeting. Dated at Watertown the 29th Day of Novemb[r] A.D. 1737.

y[r] Order of the Precinct Committee

JOSEPH MASON Precinct Cler.

[46]

At a Meeting of the Freehold[rs] and other Inhabit[ts] of ye Eafterly Precinct in Watertown Regularly Convend on the 5th Day of Decemb[r] 1737.

Voted and Chofe Joseph Joseph Mason Esq[r] Moderator of f[d] Meeting.

Whereas Sundry Unhapy Differances have Arifen in Watertown for the peaceable putting and End to the Same; it is tho^t that Dividing the Town into Two Townfhips May be very Conducive. And in hopes of Obtaining the Valuable Blefsing of peace,

The following Vote was put. vizt Whether it is the Mind of the Precinct (the Weft Precinct in f^d Town Petitioning ye General Court therefor) that the Town of Watertown be Divided into Two Townships On the Conditions and provifions following Namely

(1) That the Dividing Line be as the Precinct Line Now is.

(2) That Watertowns part of ye Charge of ye repairs & rebuilding of ye Great Bridge over Charles River in f^d Town be borne by Each Town in Proportion as they Shall be Set in the Province Tax.

(3) That the poor who at prefent are maintained by the Town be maintained by Each Town in Proportion to y^r Province Tax, and if any perfons gone out of Town Shall be returned to Watertown and become a Charge, that they be maintained by Each Town in Like proportion as aforef^d.

(4) That the Towns Stock of Arms and Ammunition be divided in Equal Proportion between Each Town. (5) That Watertowns Part of the Two Thoufand Acres of Land Granted by ye General Court to them and Wefton Be Divided in Equal halves as to Quantity and Quality between the Two Towns When Divided. (6) That the Intereft of Watertowns part of the Sixty Thoufand pounds Loan be Divided to Each Town in proportion to y^r Precinct Tax (7) That the Books records and papers belonging to the Town of Watertown be Delivred up to A Com^{tee} of the Eaft Town who may be Chofen and Appointed to receive ye Same (8) That the Debts of the town be paide by Each Town in proportion to y^o Province Tax. (9) That if any Money upon Ballanceing the Treafurers Acc^{ts} remain in the Treafury it be Divided between the Towns in Like Proportion as aforef^d.

(10) That the Publick Ways in the Town from Mafters Brook to Cambridge line be Stated and Settled as to their Corfe and Wydth as the Court of General Sefsions of the peace Agreeable to the report that may be made by y^r Committee for that purpofe already Appointed Shal Order, And if any Land Now Lying as ways or reputed as Such Shall Not be inCluded in the Ways so Stated, the Same Shall be to and for the only Ufe and benefit and At the Dispofe of the Town wherein the Same Shall Ly.

Provided that the Sale of any of ye f^d Lands already Dispofed of by ye Towns Com^{tee} (which Shall not be included in the ways when Stated as aforef^d) Shall remain good And Valled to the Purchefer of the Same, Alfo that Each Town Shall have the Benefit of the proceeds of ye Sale of Such of the Lands before mentioned as ly within the Same. And if the Ways Stated as Aforef^d Shall Include any Lands belonging to Any Perticuler Perfon the owner of Such Land Shall have Meet recompence made him by the Town wherein the Same Lye.

And the Vote Past in the Affirmative

Year Ends Precinct Affairs

The End of Precincts.
Decr 1737.

[47] Blank

[48] Entries of certificates from the Minifter of ye C^{hch} of England.

To y^o Town treafurer of Watertown.

This may certify that Mr Josiah Stowel of Watertown in the County of Middlefex is a profest Member of the Church of England and Hath Submitted himfelf to me as his Minifter in Chrift Church in Boston where he has attended the worfhip of God for a confiderable time.

       TIMOTHY CUTLER
Boston Sepr 7th 1754. JOHN BAKER   } Church
Rec^d the 23^d of Sepr ALEX^r CHAMBERLAIN } Wardens

To the Town treasurer of Watertown

This may certify that Mr Elijah Bond of Watertown in the County of Middlefex is a Profeft Member of the Church of England & hath Submitted himfelf to me as his Minifter in Chrift Church in Boston, where he has attended the worfhip of God for a Confiderable time.

       TIMOTHY CUTLER
Boston Sepr 30. 1754. JOHN BAKER   } Church
Rec^d Octob^r 7. 1754. ALEX^r CHAMBERLAIN } Wardens

To the Town Treafurer of Watertown

This may certify that Mr Josiah Bright of Watertown in the County of Midd^x is a Profeft Member of the Church of England and hath Submitted himfelf to me as his Minifter in Christ Church in Boston where he has attended the worship of God for a Confiderable time

       TIMOTHY CUTLER
Boston Sepr 30th 1754. JOHN BAKER   } Church
Rec^d October 7th 1754. ALEX^r CHAMBERLAIN } Wardens

Boston October 7th 1754.

This may Certify all whom it may Concern that Mrs Elizebeth Vila of Watertown in the County of Midd^x and Province of ye Mafsachufetts Bay in New England is a proflefsed Member and Communicant of ye Church of England and ufually & frequently attends the Publick Worfhip of God on ye Lords Days at a Church of England in Boston in the Province aforef^d Called Kings Chapel   H CANER Minister &
     Teft JAMES FORBIS } Wardens
       JOHN BOX } of f^d Chapel

To Mr Jofeph Mafon Treafurer of the
  Town of Watertown aforef^d.

This may Certify that Mr John Coollidge of Watertown is a profeft member of the Church of England and for many years has Attended the Publick Worship of God in Christ Church Boston where I y[e] Subscriber am a Minister and has Subjected himself to me as his Minister.

                TIMOTHY CUTLER
                JOHN BAKER   ) Church
Boston, Oct[r] 5, 1754.   ALLEX[r] CHAMBERLAIN) Wardens
  To the Clerk and Treasurer of y[e]
      Town of Watertown

[49]

  M[r] James Baily of Watertown hath for many years been a Profest Member of the Church of England According to the Records of Christ Church in Boston whereof I am Minister. His Daughter Elizebeth was Baptized October 10th 1731 and before and ever since that time he has been a Profest Churchman and for a Long time has Usualy & frequently attended the Publick Worship of God in Christ Church as a Parishioner of it.

                TIMOTHY CUTLER
                JOHN BAKER   ) Church
Boston Octo[r] 1. 1754.   ALEX[r] CHAMBERLAIN) Wardens
  To the Clerk and Treasurer of Watertown

  This may Certify that M[r] William Goding of Watertown is a Profest Member of the Church of England, and has Subjected himself to me the Subscriber as Minister of Christ Church in Boston.

                TIMOTHY CUTLER
                JOHN BAKER   ) Church
Boston Octo[r] 5. 1754   ALEX[r] CHAMBERLAIN) Wardens
  To y[e] Clerk & Treasurer of y[e] Town of Watertown.

      To the Town Treasurer of Watertown

  This to Certify that Silas Bright of your Town is a Profest Member of y[e] Church of England, and has Submitted himself to me as his Minister where He has Attended the Publick Worship of God for two months past.

                TIMOTHY CUTLER
                ALEX[r] CHAMBERLAIN) Church
Watertown Octo[r] 23. 1754   JOHN BAKER   ) Wardens

  This may Certify that M[r] Jonathan Brown jun[r] and M[r] Jonas Bond jun[r] both of Watertown are Profest Members of y[e] Church of England and for Several months past have frequented the Worship of God in Christ Church Boston and have submitted themselves to me the Subscriber as Minister of s[d] Church.

                TIMOTHY CUTLER
                JOHN BAKER   ) Church
Boston Sep[r] 14. 1754.   ALEX[r] CHAMBERLAIN) Wardens.
  To M[r] Joseph Mason, Town Treasurer of Watertown.

  This may Certify that Sam[l] Stratton of Watertown is a profest member of y[e] Church of England and hath Attended the Publick Worship of God in Christ Church Boston ever since May Last.

                TIMOTHY CUTLER
                JOHN BAKER   ) Church
Boston Sep[r] 14, 1754   ALEX[r] CHAMBERLAIN) Wardens.

The three following Order of Seatings in the Meetinghouse are inserted papers taken from the Town Clerk's file of Original Papers.—EDS.

[50]

The Report of the Com^tee chosen to Seat the meeting house in East Precinct in Watertown. The Ord^r of Seating in as follows.

Seated in the first Seat below
Mr Wm Shattuck
Mr Tho : Straight
Mr Henry Spring
Mr Simon Tayntor
Mr Tho : Traine
Mr Zec Cutting
Mr Eph^m Cutter

in the 2^d Seat
Mr David Stone
Mr Tho : Coollidge
Mr And^w White
Lt Joseph Coollidge
Mr John Kimbal
Mr Saml Pierce
Mr John Cunningham

3^d Seat
Lt John Fiske
Mr Tho : Bond
Mr Joseph Child
Mr John Holland
Mr Joseph Harrington
Mr Richd Clark
Mr Daniel Bond

4th Seat
Mr Joseph Bright
Mr Stephen Cooke
Mr Benjn Whitney
Mr Saml Parry
Mr Saml Warrin
Mr Eph^m Cutter Junr
Mr Joshua Grant

5
Mr John Ormes
Mr Wm Williams
Mr Joseph Holdin
Mr David Sanger
Mr Jona^n Benjamin
Mr Wm Goddin
Mr Isaac Church

6 Seat
Mr Nathl Clark
M^r Eb : Haftings
Mr Geo : Cutting
Mr John Beers
Mr Theo : Grover
Mr John Tayntor
Mr Tim^y Harris

7 Seat
Mr Nathl Stearns
Mr John Coollidge
Mr Benjn Chadwick
Mr Joshua Warrin
Mr John Stearns
Mr Henry Goddins

Fore Seat in the front Galy
Mr Oliver Livermore
Mr Nathl Harris
Mr Nathl Bright
Mr John Haftings
Mr John Stonel
Mr Saml Brown
Mr Danl Whitney

fore Seat in ye Side Galy
Mr Josiah Perry
M^r Eb : Stone
Mr John Bright
Mr John Bond
Mr Benjn Haftings
Mr John Maddocks
Mr Nathl Norcrofs
Mr And^w White Junr
Mr Nathl Bond
Mr Saml Hager
Mr Henry Spring Junr
Mr Saml Stratton
Mr John Whitney
Mr Henry Bond
Mr Soloman Stoddard
Mr Jona^n Bemis

Front 2^d Seat
Mr John Brown
Mr Nathl Coollidge
Mr Simon Coollidge
Mr Joshua Learned
Mr Saml Clark
Mr Edm^d Dix
Mr Saml Dix

Front Gallery Pew
Mr John Reed
Mr Josiah Reed
Mr Jona^n Learned
Mr David Learned
Mr Isaac Holdin
Mr Wm Goddin
Mr Tho : Bishop

Side Gallery Pew Mr Eb: Eddy Mr Joſiah Livermore Mr Jonas Coollidge Mr Nathl Haſtings Mr Edmd Livermore Mr Henry Fiske Mr Danl Fiske Mr Joseph Allen Mr Jonan Perry Mr Wm Murch	4 Seat All ye Wives of thoſe Seated in ye fourth Seat & ye Widow Abigail Grant
In the firſt Seat below on ye Womens Side Widow Penneman Widow Convers Widow Bond & ye Gentlems wives yt are Seated in ye fore Seat	5 Seat the Wives of thoſe Seated in 5 Seat on ye men Side
	6 Seat In the Same Ordr
	And ye Same Ordr in ye 7th Seat
2d Seat Mr Chary Stone Widw Cheury Widow Stratton And the wives of thoſe Gen- tlemen Seated in ye Second Seat mens Side	Fore Seat in ye front Gallery on ye Womens Side Ye Wives of thoſe Gentlemn Seat in the fore Seat mens front
	Fore Seat on ye Side Gallery on ye Womens Side Mrs Martha Coollidge And ye Wives of thoſe Seated In the fore Seat on ye oppoſite Gallery
3d Seat Widow Mary Haſtings Widow Elizh Benjamin Widow Mary Grant And ye Wives of thoſe Seated in ye 3d Seat	NATHAN FISKE JOHN COOLLIDG JOSEPH MASON } Comtee JOHN HASTINGS OLIVER LIVERMORE

Watertown April 24: 1732

[31]

The Report of the Comtee Choſen to Seat the Meeting House in Watertown, the Order of Seeting is as follows.

Seated in the firſt Seat below. Mr Thomas Stright Mr Henry Spring Nathl Harris Eſqr Mr John Hunt Doctr Joſiah Convarse Mr Oliver Livermore Captn Thomas Homans Captn Joſeph Coollidg John Kimball	3d Seat Mr Isaac Church Mr James Baley Mr Stephen Cooke Mr John Whitney En. Ebenezer Stone Mr Joseph Bright Mr John Coollidge Jr Mr Daniel Bond
In the 2d Seat Mr David Stone Mr Andrew White Mr Richard Clark Leut John Fiske Mr Joſeph Harrington Mr John Haſtings Mr Joſeph Child Mr William Gooding	4th Seat Mr Ebenezar Thornton Mr Joſiah Perry Mr Saml Perry Mr Jacob Parker Mr Nathll Norcrofs Mr John Bond Mr Henry Spring Junr Mr Walter Beath

5th Seat
M⁽ʳ⁾ John Bell
M⁽ʳ⁾ John Becks
M⁽ʳ⁾ Jonᵃ Benjamin
M⁽ʳ⁾ Samᵘˡ Warrin
M⁽ʳ⁾ Ebenʳ Hastings
M⁽ʳ⁾ David Sangar
M⁽ʳ⁾ Joseph Whitney
M⁽ʳ⁾ William Goding Juʳ

the Sixth Seat Below
M⁽ʳ⁾ Edmond Livermore
M⁽ʳ⁾ Benjamin Whitney
M⁽ʳ⁾ Henery Goding
M⁽ʳ⁾ Nathˡˡ Bond
M⁽ʳ⁾ Joshua Warrin
M⁽ʳ⁾ Joſeph Stearns
M⁽ʳ⁾ Samˡˡ Nutting

7th Seat
M⁽ʳ⁾ Nathˡˡ Stearns
M⁽ʳ⁾ John Stearns
M⁽ʳ⁾ Iſaac Holding
M⁽ʳ⁾ Samˡˡ Stovell

Side Gallery Pew
M⁽ʳ⁾ Nathˡ Stone
M⁽ʳ⁾ Samˡˡ Child
M⁽ʳ⁾ James Dix
M⁽ʳ⁾ Joseph Maſon Jʳ
M⁽ʳ⁾ David Livermore
M⁽ʳ⁾ James Hacklton
M⁽ʳ⁾ Isreal Meed
M⁽ʳ⁾ Phinias Holding
M⁽ʳ⁾ John Gleason
M⁽ʳ⁾ Richard King
M⁽ʳ⁾ Nathan Parrey

Front Pew
M⁽ʳ⁾ Samˡˡ Warrin Jʳ
M⁽ʳ⁾ Thomas Stovell
M⁽ʳ⁾ Josiah Stovell
M⁽ʳ⁾ David Gleason

In the first Seat Below on the
Womens Side
Widow Rebecak Train
And yᵉ Gentlemens Wives that
are Seated in the fore Seat

2d Seat
Widow Mary Grant
And the wives of those Gen-
tlmen Seated in the Seckond
Seat

3d Seat
M⁽ʳˢ⁾ Martha Coollidge
And the Wives of those Gen-
tlmen Seated in the third
Seat

4th Seat
Widow Elizabeth Cutting
And the Wives of those Gen-
tlmen Seated in yᵉ forth Seat

fore Seate in yᵉ front Gallry
M⁽ʳ⁾ Daniel Whitney
M⁽ʳ⁾ John Stovell
M⁽ʳ⁾ John Bright
M⁽ʳ⁾ John Taintor
M⁽ʳ⁾ Jonᵃ Bemis
M⁽ʳ⁾ Joſeph Willington
M⁽ʳ⁾ Benjimin Haſtings
M⁽ʳ⁾ Andrew White Junʳ

fore Seat Side Gallery
M⁽ʳ⁾ Samˡˡ Hager
M⁽ʳ⁾ Henry Bond
M⁽ʳ⁾ Thomas Saltmarsh
M⁽ʳ⁾ John Brown
M⁽ʳ⁾ Crifterpher Grant
David Learued
Jonᵃ Church
M⁽ʳ⁾ Simon Coollidge
M⁽ʳ⁾ Samˡˡ Stratton
M⁽ʳ⁾ Joshua Learned
M⁽ʳ⁾ Samˡˡ Fiske
M⁽ʳ⁾ Amos Bond
M⁽ʳ⁾ Nathˡˡ Bright
M⁽ʳ⁾ David Coollidge
M⁽ʳ⁾ Samˡˡ Prentice
M⁽ʳ⁾ John Velah

Front 2d Seat
M⁽ʳ⁾ Jonathan Child
M⁽ʳ⁾ Stephen Sawin
M⁽ʳ⁾ Isaac Sanderſon
M⁽ʳ⁾ William Lawrence
M⁽ʳ⁾ Samˡˡ Cooke
M⁽ʳ⁾ Samˡˡ Whitney
M⁽ʳ⁾ James Grimes
M⁽ʳ⁾ Joſiah Perry Junʳ

And the Gentlemens Wives
Seated in the other Seats in
the Same order

OLIVER LIVERMORE ⎫
JOHN TAYNTER   ⎬ Comᵗᵉ
JONATHAN CHURCH ⎪
HENRY BOND   ⎭

Watertown June yᵉ 15ᵗʰ 1741.

[52] Blank.

[53]

Watertown June 10th 1748

We the Subscribers being a committee appointed by the town of Watertown at a General town meeting on the sixteenth of January last in order to Seat the meeting houfe have Seated it as follows (viz)

In the fore Seat below
 Doct Josiah Convers
 Mr John Kimball
 Mr Richard Clark
 Mr James Bailey
 Mr Joseph Harrington
 Mr Joseph Child
 Mr Stephen Coock
 Mr John Bright

In the Second Seat below
 Capt John Tainter
  Henry Spring Junr
  John Whitney
  Andrew White
 En. Ebenzr Stone
  Joseph Bright
  Saml Hagar
  Benja Hastings

In the third Seat below
 Ebenzr Thorington
 Thomas Saltmarsh
 Saml Parry
 Saml Warrin
 Josiah Perry
 John Coollidge Jr
 Joseph Whitney
 Saml Nutting

In the fore Seat in the front
 Sam Fisk
 Nathl Harrington
 Nathl Bright
 Amos Bond
 Jonas Coollidge
 William Coollidge
 David Larnard
 Wd Elizabeth Larnard

In the forth Seat below
 David Coollidge
 David Sangar
 Sam Prentice
 Saml Stratton
 William Godding
 Henry Godding
 Joseph Stearns
 Siman Coollidge
 Criftopher Grnt

In the fore Seat in the long Gallirey
 Jona Stone Junr
 Jona Brown Junr
 Nathl Stone
 Seth Hastings
 Nathan Perry
 Edmund Foul
 James Dix
 Smith Prentice
 Saml Coock
 David Livermore
 Bezalal Larnard
 Saml Whitney
 Jona Stone tartus
 Jacob Calwell

In the fifth Seat below
 John Vela
 Joshua Warring
 Henry Bond
 Jona Child
 Saml Child
 Uriah Clark
 Saml Warring Junr
 William Lee
 John Clark

In the Second Seat in ye front
 Isaac Sanderfon
 Josiah Stowell
 Henry Larnard
 John Young
 Will Gamage
 Benja Whitney
 Isreal Mead
 Henry Spring tartus

In the hind Seat in Ce Large Gallirey
 Joseph Hastings
 Nehemiah Mason
 Sam Coollidge
 Phenihas Hoden
 Elias Mason
 Nathan Stone
 Eliha Coollidge
 Eprora Warrin
 Pearce Jone Junr
 John Gra
 Eben Stone Junr

In the hind Seat in yᵉ front
Daniel Pierce
Jabez Harrington
Joseph Chiles Junʳ
Stephen Stearns
John McCollifter
Charles McCollifter

These Persons who have Wives their Wives are placed in the Oppifite Seats to their Hufbands in the Womens Seats

Nathˡ Bright
Jonathan Bemis
Daniel Whitney
Andrew White
Thoˢ Saltmarfh
Comᵗᵉᵉ

[54] Blank.

[55]

To the Freeholders & other Inhabitants of Watertown afsembled at their annual meeting March 2ᵈ 1746/7

Gentlemen, Whereas by Reafon of the finking Value of our Paper Currency, the Sums of money annually granted for my Support in the Work of the Miniftry, together with all the Advantages I make by the Miniftry, have for many Years paft, fallen very much fhort of being fufficient to defray the necefsary Charges of my Family: I do hereby requeft you to take the fame into your ferious Confideration, & to do what you may in your Wifdom and Goodnefs, think proper to be further done for the Support of a Gofpel Minifter, who is
    Your Affectionate & faithful Paftor
            SETH STORER.

Watertown March 2ᵈ, 1746/7
To the Moderator of faid meeting to be Communicated.

[56 & 57]

  Plan of Watertown Meeting House Lore floor.
   See Town Records 1755. Book V, p. 134

[58]

At a General Town Meeting of the Freeholders & other Inhabitants of Watertown qualified to vote in Town affairs regularly afsembled at the Publick Meeting house on Monday the second Day of June AD 1755. By Adjournment.

Put to vote whether it is the mind of the Town that those Persons who injoyᵈ Pews in the former Meeting house should have Pews in the present Meeting house in the same places where their Pews were in sᵈ former Meeting house under the regulations and upon the Terms other Pews shall be difposᵈ of. And the Vote past in the Negative.

Put to vote whether it be the mind of the Town that the Pews should be settled upon Real & Personal Estate and one Head, And the Vote past in the Affirmative.

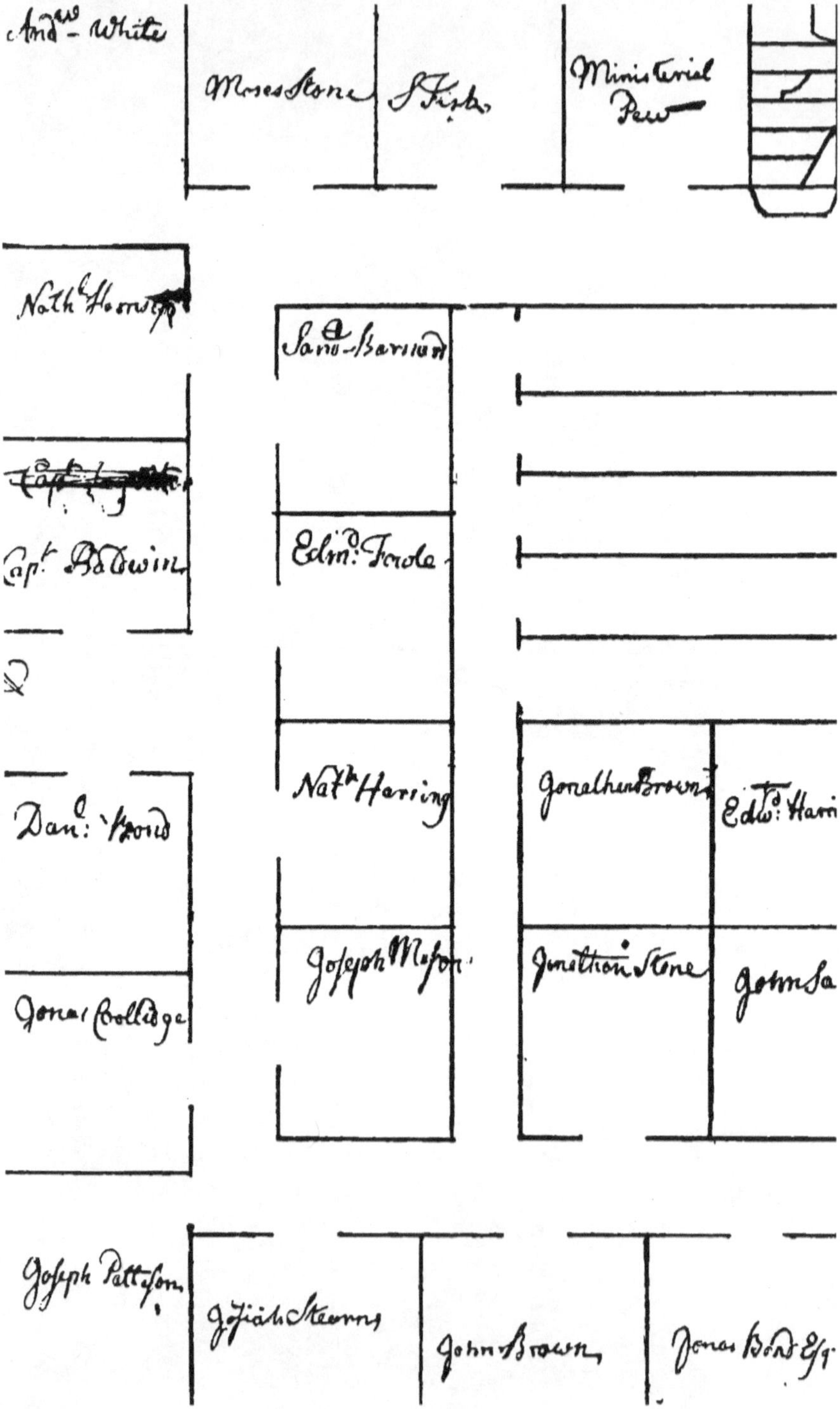
Andw White
Moses Stone
S Fisk
Ministerial Pew
Saml Barnard
Capt Baldwin
Edmd Fowle
Nath Haring
Jonathan Brown
Edwd Harri
Danl Bond
Joseph Mason
Jonathan Stone
John Sa
Jonas Coolidge
Joseph Patterson
Josiah Stearns
John Brown
Jonas Bond Esq

	Henry Spring		Sam: Benjamin
W. Bright	John Cook		Cap.t Tainter
	John Whitney	Nath: Stone	
Joseph Harrington	John Coll	E: Goddard	

Door

Put to vote whether it is the mind of the Town that the Valuation by which the Rate was made for building the Meeting house be the Rule by which the Pews shall be despos'd of, And the Vote past in the Affirmative.

Voted that the Persons to whom the Pews shall be granted or who shall draw the Pews, personally set in them usually with their Families or s'd Pews shall revert to the Town.

Voted that when any Persons shall see cause to sell their Pews the Town shall have the refusal of s'd Pews paying the Money rais'd on s'd Pews.

Voted that if any Persons sell their Estates and move out of Town their Pews shall revert to the Town. The Town paying or reimbursting to them the money paid by them for s'd Pews.

[59]

Voted that those Persons who are reputed Members of the Church of England have a chance for drawing Pews and enjoy the Pews they shall draw as long as they pay their proportion to the Meeting house & Support of the Minister in this Town. Which if they refuse to do s'd Pews shall revert to the Town for the Town to dispose of as they shall see fit.

Voted that the Afsefsors be the Committee to make the Adjustment of the Charge to be laid upon the Pews, And to offer the Pews to Persons according to their pay, the highest payer first and so on succefsively.

L't Edward Harrington's Pew Afsefs'. £25-4-11 Old Tenor
A true Copy from Records
      Nath'l R. Whitney, Town Clerk.
Watertown Dec'r 23'd 1793.
       See Bk. V. p 134.

I am of Opinion that Edward Harrington did not convey his Pew in Watertown Meeting House to his Sons by his deed of Gift of his Real Eftate to them in his life time, And that the fame Pew by his Death Defcended to his Heirs at law.

[Record Book of the Pastors.
1686 to 1819.]

---

[i]   John Balye's Booke
              Pretium 0—6—8 Dublin Dec: 29. 1668:
              By the Gift of Mrs Sufannah Baily.
              becoms Henry Gibb's Booke Nov. 24, 1698

[ii]
          An Account of all ye Mariages I folemnized in New E
      ye first of which was on ye 10th of Auguft 1686 &c And fo
      ye reft as you find y^m putt down
              The Church Book
          containing various Matter's,
            " Which we from former Registers
            " Of Antient Times have known,
            " And our Forefather's pious Care
            " To us has handed down.
            " That Generations yet to come
            " Should to their yet unborn Heirs
            " Religiously transmit the fame
            " And they again to their's."

[iii]
    Upon Aug. 10: 1686. I married in my own houfe in Watertown (it was ye firft time) Rich. Norcrofs, & Rofe Woodward in y^r parents full confent being legally publifhed
    This was returned by Mr Bond at Cambridge Oct. 19. 86.
    Upon January ye 4th 1686/7 I maryed at Watertown Mill Samuel Haftings (ye fon of Thomas Haftings ye deacon of ye church in Watertown) & Lidia church, ye daughter of mr Caleb Church, wth y^r parents full confent being legally published
    Upon ye 1st of February 1686/7 I maryed in my own houfe in watertown Solomon Johnfon widower of Sudbury, & Hannah Grefte of Natomy being legally publifhed
    Upon ye 11th of March 1686/7 I maryed Abraham Prenfe & Ifsabell Whitherfpoon in my Brothers houfe in Bofton being legally publifhed
    Upon ye 25th of March 1687 I maryed Danyell Benjamin (ye fone of John Benjamin) & Elizabeth Brown (ye daughter of Jon. Brown) both of Watertown, in my houfe they being legally publifhed, & y^r parents fully confenting

Upon y 25th of March 1687 at my houfe in Watertown I maryed James Begalow (ye fon of John Begalow Serg*t*) & Patience Brown (ye daughter of Jon. Brown) wth their Parents full confent, y being legally publifhed

Upon ye 31th of March 1687 at my houfe in Watertown I maryed William Hager) ye fone of widdow Hager) & Sarah Benjamin (ye daughter of John Benjamin) wth their parents full confent, ye being legally publifhed

Upon ye 31 of March 1687 at my houfe in Watertown I maryed Benjamin Whitney (ye fon of John Whitney) & Abigail Hager (ye daughter of widdow Hager) wth yr parents confent, ye being legally publifhed

Upon ye 5th of May 1687 at my houfe in Watertown I maryed Jofeph Allen (ye fon of John Allen of Sudbury) & Abigaill Myrieck (ye daughter of John Miriack, of charlftown, wth their parents confent, being legally publifhed

Upon ye 24th of May 1687 I maryed near ye Mill bridge in Bofton Edward Taylor Juniour (his Father lodged at Mr W. Gibbins) & Rebekah Humphreys (who came lately from Antigo, but her Mother fully confenting her father witnefsing it) be'g Licenfed

[iv]

Upon ye 25th of May 1687 I maryed in my Brothers houfe in Bofton William Clargett, & Mary Neggres, both of ym dwelling in Mr Jo. Adams houfe in Boston, they being Licenfed &c i—e. ye having a fpeciall Licence

Upon ye 25th of May 1687 I maryed in ye Almfhoufe on ye common in Bofton James Cornifh Juniorr, & Mary Kay ye daughter of Thomas Kay ye being legally publifhed

All thefe Eleven laft were returned to ye Court at Cambridge by Mr William Bond Seni*r* Juftice of peace, this 7th day of June 1687.

Upon ye 20th of June 1687 I maryed in my houfe at Watertown Nathanaell Norcrofse (ye fon of Richard Norcrofse) & Mehetabell Hager (ye daughter of Widdow Hager) both of Watertown wth ye full confent of their parents ye being legally publifhed

Upon ye 4th of July 1687 I maryed in ye houfe of Goody Mefsenger in Bofton Richard Leekey, & Ann Greenfield he having a fpeciall Lycence

Upon ye 4th of July 1687 I maryed Ebenezer Mefsenger & Rofe Collins both of Bofton (in his Mothers houfe) wth ye confent of friends, ye being legally publifhed

Upon ye 11th of Auguft 1687 I maryed in my houfe at Watertown Eliezer Whitney (ye fon of Thomas Whitney of Watertown) now living in Sudbury, & Dorothy Rofse ye daughter of James Rofse of Sudbury wth ye confent of parents, being legally publifhed

Upon ye 17th of Auguft 1687 I maryed in my houfe at Watertown Thomas Fenton & Elizabeth Bafset both of Bofton, being legally publifhed (I having their cirtificutt) & friends confenting

All thefe 5 laft couples were returned to ye Quarter fefsions at Charlftown by William Bond Senio*r* Juftice of peace this 6 day of September 1687

As for any other Mariages y^t may afterwards be you may look for them on ye 2 page, All thefe hitherto being faithfully returned as above faid

[1] [This page occupied by meditations upon Bible texts.]

[2] Mariages Solemized by me, whilft I lived in Watertown

1687

Upon ye 18th of October 1687 I maryed in my houfe at Watertown William Feris, Taylor of Watertown & Abigaill Avered widdow of dedham being publifhed according to law

Upon ye 3^d of November 1687 I maryed in my houfe John Garfield of Watertown, & Deborah Holman of Cambridge, wth ye confent of parents, they being publifhed according to law

Upon ye 22^d of November 1687 I maryed Peter Barbour, taylor, & coufin Sarah Willy in her chamber in Bofton, parents confenting ye having a fpecial Lycenfe

Upon ye 24th of November 1687 I maryed Jofeph Winfhipp ye fon of Lt. Edward Winfhipp of Natomys, & Sarah Harrington ye daughter of Robert Harrington of Watertown in his houfe wth ye confent of Friends, ye being publifhed according to law

All thefe 4 laft couples were returned to ye Court at Cambridge by Mr William Bond Juftice of Peace this 6th day of December 1687

Upon ye 15 of December 1687 I maryed in my houfe George Blanchard & Sarah Baffett both of charlftown with ye confent of Friends ye being publifhed according to law

Upon ye 2^d of January 1687 I maryed in my houfe Nathanaell Coolidge (ye fon of Nathanaell Coolidge) & Lidia Jones (ye daughter of Jofiah Jones) both of Watertown, wth ye confent of Friends, ye being publifhed according to law

Thefe 2 laft Mariages were returned to ye Court at Charlftown by Mr William Bond Juftice of peace this 6th day of March 1687/8

Upon ye 10th of Aprill 1688 I maryed in my houfe in Watertown John Whitney (ye fon of Jonathan Whitney) & Mary Hapgood (ye daughter of Shadrach Hapgood) both of Sherborn, wth ye confent of friends, ye being publifhed according to law

Upon ye 26th of Aprill 1688 I maryed in my houfe in Watertown James Smith & Prudence Harrifon widdow, both of Bofton, having a fpeciall Lycence

Upon ye 30th of May 1688 I maryed in my houfe in Watertown Thomas Woodward of Muddy river & Tryphena Fairfield of wth ye confent of friends being publifhed according to law

[3]

Marriages folemnifed by me whilft I lived in Watertown

N. E. 1688.

Thefe 3 laft Marriages were returned to ye Court at Cambridge by Mr William Bond Juftice of ye peace this 5th day of June 1688

Upon ye 24th of Auguft 1688 I maryed in my houfe in Watertown Jonatan Fairbanks of Lancaster & Mary Haward of Concord wth ye consent of Friends ye being published according to law.

This last Marriage were returned to ye Court at Charlestown by Mr William Bond Justice of peace ye 4th of September 1688.

Upon ye 19th of September 1688 I maryed in my house at Watertown Thomas Knop & Mary Grout of Sudbury wth ye consent of friends ye being published according to law

Upon y^t 26th of September 1688 I maryed in my house at Watertown Richard Blofse of Watertown & Ann Cutler of Cambridge Farmes wth ye consent of Friends, ye being published according to law.

Upon ye 7th of November 1688 I maryed in my house at Watertown Joseph Harrington & Joanna Mixer both of Watertown with ye consent of Friends, ye being published according to law

These 3 last Marriages were returned to ye Court at Cambridge by Mr William Bond Senr Justice of peace ye 4th of December 1688

Upon ye 21st of February 1688/9 I maryed in my house at Watertown Ephraim Rife of Sudbury & Hannah Livermore of watertown wth ye consent of Friends, ye being published according to law

This Single mariage were returned to ye court at Charlestown by Mr W. Bond Justice, the 5th of March 1688/9

Upon ye 13th of March 1688/9 I maryed in my house at Watertown Abraham Watson & Mary Butterfield both of Cambridge with ye consent of Friends, ye being published according to law.

Upon ye 20th of March 1688/9 I maryed in my house at Watertown Joseph Pearse juni^r & Ruth Holland both of Watertown wth ye consent of friends, being published according to law

Upon ye 5th of Aprill 1689 I maryed in my house at Watertown John Earl of Boston (a seaman) & Mary Lawrence (ye daughter of George Lawrence of Watertown, but she now living in Boston) with ye consent of Friends, ye being published according to law—

[4]

Marriages solemnized by me in Watertown.

1689.

Upon ye 26th of September 1689 I maryed in my house at Watertown Benjamin Flagg & Experience Child wth ye consent of Freinds ye being published according to law

Upon ye 31st of December 1689 I maryed in my house at Watertown William Ward & Abigail Spring both of Cambridge village, wth ye consent of Friends, ye being published according to law y Deputy Governour Danforth was present

Upon ye 8th of January 1689/90 I maryed in my house at Watertown John Mofse, & Elizabeth Gooding (ye daughter of Gregory Cooke wife by a former husband) wth ye consent of Friends, y being published according to law

There is now an end of my Marrying. N. E being in some measure restored to its old way, for w^ I desire heartily to bless g^d—the Magistrats now marry, its very well, Vale conjugium,

Upon y̆e 22th of December 1690 I maryed in my houſe at Watertown Alexander Bulman & Margarett Taylor with ye conſent of Friends ye being publiſhed according to law

This next above mentioned couple I were much adoe prevailed wth to marye them, ptly for my own ſake, bsc I wid not give offence (tho I hope I ſhall not) & ptly for their ſake, bec its good doing what is done on a good foundation & wth Authority. I was much importuned by friends, ſhe is one of my Ireland friends, & was once my ſervt, it hath been practiſed, I leave it wth gd, oh yt I was maryed to J. X.

Upon ye 5th of March 1690/1 I maryed in my houſe (i. e. in my study at Watertown) Peter Allen & Mary Smethurſt wth yo conſent of Friends ye being publiſhed according to law

This above couple were my countrey Folk who by their Importunity prevailed wth me I am not forbidden to marry, yefore I do it only on ſpeciall occaſions

[5]

Mariages Solemnized by me in Boſton, in N. E.

1692

There was by ye Generall Aſsembly ſitting in October & November 1692 an order made for Miniſters marying as well as Juſtices of the peace. wch hath encouraged me to do it at ye importunity of Friends

Upon ye 8th of November 1692 I maryed Joſhua Corniſh & Suſanah Bennet both of Boſton (at her fathers houſe) with ye conſent of Friends, ye being publiſhed according to law.

This above named Mariage was returned & recorded ye 21st of Feb. 1692/3 by Mr Webb ye Tn. Clarke, Mr Wilkins went to him

Upon ye 9th of May 1693 I maryed in my houſe in Boſton Simon Taintor & Joanna Stone both of Watertown with ye conſent of Friends ye being publiſhed according to law

Muning Sawin was ye Clark, & teſtifyed it publickly.

This above named mariage was recorded in ye later end of May or begining of June 1693 by Mr Webb, Mr Wilkins went wth it to him, I gave him 3 black doggs

Upon ye 14th of September 1693 I maryed (in Capt. Leggs houſe) Capt John Barrett & Sabella Legg both of Boſton with ye conſent of Friends ye being publiſhed according to law

This next above named mariage was recorded ye 4th of October 1693 by Mr Webb, I went wth it myſelf & payd him.

Upon ye 5th of October 1693 I maryed in my houſe John Child & Hannah French both of Watertown wth ye conſent of Friends ye being publiſhed according to law

Upon ye 19th of October 1693 I maryed in Capt. Checkly's John Adams & Hannah Checkley both of Boſton wth ye conſent of Friends ye being publiſhed according to law

The 2 above mentioned mariages was recorded by Mr Webb ye 20th of October 1693, I delivered ym myſelf unto him

Upon ye 16th of November 1693 I maryed in my houſe in Boſton

Samuel Capen & Ann Stone both of Doracefter (tho fhe belongs to Watertown) wth ye content of Friends y^n being publifhed according to law

This above mentioned mariage was given to Mr Webb to be recorded by Mr Wilkins y^n 12th of December 1693 wth ye money due to him for fo doing

[6]

Mariages folemnized by me in Bofton in N. E. 93. 94.

Upon y^n 13th of December 1693 I maryed in my houfe in Bofton Daniel Collins & Rebekah Clemens both of Bofton w^t y^n confent of Friends y^n being publifhed according to law

This above mentioned mariage was given to Mr Webb to be recorded by Mr Wilkins ye 5th of January 1693/4

Upon y^n 26 of April 1694 I maryed in my houfe in Bofton William Brown Efq of Salem, & Sifter Rebekah Bailey in Bofton, ye being publifhed according to law, wth ye confent of friends

Upon ye 17th of May 1694 I maryed in Bofton Jabez Beers & Elizabeth Barber both of Watertown wth y^n confent of Friends y^n being publifhed according to law.

Deacon Allen was prefent.

Thefe 2 above mentioned mariages was given by Mr Wilkins to Mr Webb to be recorded ye 18th of May 1694.

Upon y^n 29th of May 1694 I maryed in my houfe in Bofton Mathew Poole & Sarah Blake of Bofton y^n being publifhed according to law

This above mentioned mariage was given by Mr Wilkins to Mr Webb to be recorded ye 13th of June 1694.

Upon y^n 3^d of July 1694 I maryed in my houfe in Bofton Thomas Gray of Plymouth, & Anne Little of Marfhfield with y^n confent of Friends they being publifhed according to law

This above mentioned mariage was given by M^r wilkins to Mr Webb to be recorded y^n 24th of July 1694

Upon y^n 9th of Auguft 1694 I maryed Francis Threfher & Elizabeth Hicks both of Bofton (widow in her houfe in Bofton) y^n being publifhed according to law.

This above mentioned marriage was given by M^r wilkins to Mr Webb to be recorded ye 29th of Auguft 1694

Upon y^n 11th of Auguft 1694 I maryed in my houfe in Bofton a couple of Negros, ye mans name was George, living wth Sam. Gray, y^n womans name was Hager living wth Mrs Sweet, al y^t belonged to y^m gave y^m free & full confent, y^n were not publifhed, for fuch ufe not to be as ye fay

This mariage was given by Mr Wilkins to Mr Webb to be recorded y^n 16th of January 1694/5

[7]

Mariages Solemnized by me in Bofton in N. E.-94-& 95-

Upon y^n 15th of September 1694 I maryed in my houfe in Bofton Benjamin Watfon & Ann Due both of Bofton wth y^n confent of Friends ye being publifhed according to law

This above mentioned mariage was given by M{r} Wilkins to M{r} Webb to be recorded y{e} 18{th} of Oct. 1694

Upon y{e} 28 of November 1694 I maryed in M{r} Peter Butlers houfe M{r} George Jafferyes of Pifcataqua & Mrs. Anna Porter of Bofton they being publifhed according to law

This above mentioned mariage was given by M{r} Wilkins to M{r} Webb to be recorded by him y{e} 18{th} of January 1694/5

Upon y{e} 7{th} of February 1694/5 I maryed in M{r} Chriftophers houfe in Bofton John Wiett & Hannah Garratt both of Bofton y{e} being publifhed according to law

This above mentioned mariage was given by M{r} Wilkins to M{r} Webb to be recorded by him y{e} 14{th} of March 1694/5

Upon y{e} 4 of Aprill 1695 I maryed in my houfe M{r} Robert Fitzhugh & M{rs} Hannah Man both of Bofton y{e} being publifhed according to law

This above mentioned mariage was given by M{r} Wilkins to M{r} Webb to be recorded by him y{e} 23 of April 1695

Upon y{e} 2{d} of May 1695 I maryed in my houfe in Bofton Robert Hanna & Hannah Maefon both of Bofton y{e} being publifhed according to law

This above mentioned mariage was given by M{r} Wilkins to M{r} Webb to be recorded by him y{e} 11{th} of June 1695

Upon y{e} 10{th} of June 1695 I maryed in my houfe in Bofton William Briggs & Rebekah Dyer both of Bofton, being publifhed accordng to law

Upon y{e} 27{th} of June 1695 I maryed in old M{r} Pembertons houfe M{r} Jonathen Elliston & Mis Elizabeth Wisondonk both of Bofton, y{e} being publifhed according to law

Thefe 2 above mentioned mariages was given by M{r} Wilkins to M{r} Webb to be recorded by him y{e} Firft of July 1695

Upon y{e} 26{th} of July 1693 I maryed in my houfe in Bofton Richard Thomas & Mary Mafon both of Bofton y{e} being publifhed according to law

This above mentioned Mariage was given by M{r} Wilkins to Capt. Savage to be recorded by him (whofe work it is at prefent) y{e} 22 of Auguft 1695

Upon y{e} 15{th} of Auguft 1695 I maryed a couple of M{r} Gibbins Negros in his houfe viz Toby & Jane, y{e} confented to it, & there were many witnefses

[8]

Mariages Solemnized by me in Bofton in N. E. 1695 1696-

Upon y{e} 25 of October 1695 I maryed in my houfe in Bofton Humphrey Richards & Sufanna Wakefield both of Bofton with y{e} confent of Friends, y{e} being publifhed according to law

Upon y{e} 11{th} of December 1695 I maryed in my houfe in Bofton Nathanael Pitman & Mary George both of Bofton w{th} y{e} confent of Friends y{e} being publifhed according to law

Thefe 2 above mentioned Mariages given by M{r} Wilkins to Capt. Ephraim Savage to be recorded by him y{e} 26{th} of December 1695

Upon y ͤ 4 th of February 1695/6 I maryed in my houſe in Boſton Elias Maverick & Sarah Smith both of this town y ͤ being publiſhed according to law

Upon y ͤ 13 th of February 1695/6 I maryed in old M ͬ Pembertons Houſe Major Read Elding & Hannah Pemberton of Boſton y ͤ being Legally publiſhed

Upon y ͤ 9 th of April 1696 I maryed in my houſe in Boſton Thomas Stevens & Sarah Place both of Boſton being legally publiſhed

Upon y ͬ 9 th of April 1696 I maryed in my houſe in Boſton William Hannah of Boſton & Martha Clark of Roxbury y ͤ being legally publiſhed

Theſe 4 above mentioned mariages was given by myſelf to Capt. Ephraim Savage to be recorded by him y ͤ 11 th of Aprill 1696

Upon y ͤ 24 th of March 1697 I maryed in Capt. Legs houſe Samuel Weaver & Eliz Cravath both of Boſton, being legally publiſhed

This above mentioned mariage was given by myſelf into y ͤ hand of M ͬ William Grays (to whom now it appertains) to record it viz this 31 of May 1697 w ͪͫ I dined at M ͬ Isaac Tay's

Upon y ͤ 29 of July 1697 I maryed at y ͤ Bowling Green Joſeph Royall & Eliz Coleman both of Boſton being legally publiſhed

[9]   [Record of those who owned y ͤ Covenant.]

1724/5.	January. 27.	Oliver Livermore
	Feb. 14.	Jonathan Stone Jun ͬ
	21.	George Lawrence Jun ͬ
	March. 7.	Joſhua Warren Jun ͬ
	28.	Nath ll Bond & Ann Bond
	April. 25.	Hephzibah Bond
	July. 18.	Ebenezer Chenery & Ruth his wife, Sam ll Hager & Hannah his wife
	Nov. 14.	Hannah Stone
1725/6.	Feb. 6.	Daniel Haſtings & Sarah his wife
	March. 27.	Jabez Stratton & Tabitha his wife
	May 1.	Jon th Harrington
	Aug. 21.	Isaac Barnard
	Sept. 11.	Samuel Jenniſon Jun ͬ
1726/7	Jan. 15.	Samuel Benjamin & Mary his wife
1727.	April 9.	Edward Jackſon & Abigail his wife
	Nov. 5.	Charles Chadwick & Sarah his wife
	19.	Hannah Cutler made publick Confeſsion of her sin & owned y ͤ Covenant.
	Dec. 3.	John Dix, Samuel Dix & Mary Dix
	31.	Simon Coolidge owned y ͤ Covenant, and Caleb Benjamin & Abigail his wife made publick Confeſsion
1727/8.	Jan. 14.	Caleb Benjamin, Suſanna Benjamin, Abigail Benjamin & Abigail Dix
	Feb. 11.	Judith Sawin
1728.	Aug. 11.	John Coollidge & Mercy his wife made publick Confeſsion of their sin & owned y ͤ Covent.

1728/9,	Feb. 23.	Phebe Palfrey.
1729.	May 17.	Nathanael Jennison & Abigail his wife made publick Confession of their sin & owned y{e} Covenant.
	31.	Susanna Whitney.
1731.	March. 28	Peter, a Negro man of M{r} Stone's entered into Covent.
	April. 11.	Joshua Learned & Elizabeth his wife made publick Confession of their sin & he owned y{e} Coven{t}.
	Dec{r} 5	Susanna Holdin made publick Confession of her sin & owned y{e} Covent.
1731/2	Feb. 27.	Ruth underwood made publick Confession of her sin & was rec{d} into Favour
1732.	July 16.	Edward Harrington & Anna his wife made publick Confession of their sin & owned y{e} Covenant
	Aug{st} 13.	William Goddin Jun{r} & Martha his wife
1732/3.	Feb. 25.	Allen Brown made publick Confession of his sins and Ruth Brown Made Confession
	March. 18.	Hephzibah Berry made publick Confession of her sin
	April. 29.	Allen Brown
	May. 13.	John Brown
1734.	Sep{t} 8.	Henry Bond Jun{r} & Mary Bond made publick Confession of y{e} sin and on 22. Day they owned y{e} Covenant.
	Oct{r} 20.	Joseph Wellington & Dorcas Wellington owned y{e} Covenant

[10]

1734.

	Nov{r} 24.	Susanna Cutting
1734/5	Feb. 9.	Ebenezer Wellington made Confession of his sin w{c} was accepted, & y{n} he was dismissed to y{e} C{hh} in Stoughton.
	16.	Samuel Barnard
		Margaret Wafson made confession of her sin & then owned y{e} Covenant.
1734/5	Jan{ry} 26.	John Lawrence
	Feb. 8.	Stephen Sawin

[11]

The Following Persons have Owned y{e} Covenant since I was ordained.   Dan{l} Adams

1778

May 17{th}	Will{m} Warren and his wife Robe
June 28{th}	Moses Cooledge & Hannah his wife
June 28{th}	Susanna y{e} wife of Nath{l} Bright

[12]

The following persons have owned the Covenant since I was ordained.   R. R. ELIOTT, Viz

1780
Nov^r   Lucy & Elizabeth Bond

1781
March 10th   Benj^a Capan & his Wife Elizabeth

1782
July 29th   Moses Warren & his Wife
Feby 17.   John Bullard & his Wife
Novr 3.   Willm Beals & his Wife
    17   Hugh Mason & his Wife

1783
Augt 24   Andrew Stimpson & his Wife
Novr 16   Abijah Stone & his Wife
    30.   Daniell Jackson
Decr 7   Joseph Bright & his Wife

1784
Feby 1.   Lucy the Wife of Daniel Jackson
May 2.   Nathaniell Bemifs & Wife
Octr 17   Jonathan Stone
Decr 26   Joseph Coolidge & his Wife

1785
Augt 21   Francis Faulkner & his Wife
Octr 30   Thomas Vose & his Wife
Novr 6   Susana the Wife of John Cooke Junr

1786
Augt 7.   Lydia the Wife of Nathan Porter

1787
March 4.   Kate the Wife of Stephen Harris Junr

1788
July 27   Thomas Clarke & his Wife
Novr 23   Benjamin Hastings & wife

1789
Octr 11   John George

1792
March 4   Moses Mason

1793
June 2   Kathy Wife of Ezekiel Whitney Junr
     Charles Bond & Wife

1794
March 9   John Vinal

[13]

                1794
    March 30   Sarah Saunders
                1795
    June 21   Sukey Norcrofs
    Oct' 16   Elizabeth Coolidge Freeman
                1796
    July 17   Joshua Underwood & wife
    Sep' 11   Peter Clark & wife
    Oct' 2   Joshua Grant & wife
                1797
    June 4   Sarah Wife of Isreal Cooke
                1798
    Jan' 7   John Durant & wife
    May 13   Phinehas Hovey & wife
    June 24   Luke Bemis
                1801
    June 7   John Tucker & Wife
                Joseph Pierce & wife
    July 12   William Bond & wife
                James Simmons & wife
    Aug' 2   Jonathan Alden & wife
                1803
    Oct' 2   Elisha Livermore & wife
        23   Luther Coolidge & Wife
                1805
    Sep' 6   Jofeph Russell & Wife
                Paul Kendal & wife
    Nov' 10   Andrew Blackmer & wife
                1808
    May 14   Jonathan Robbins

[14]

    May 22   Tyler Bigelow & Wife
                Henry Dalrymple & Wife
    June 19   Nathaniel R. Whitney Jun. & Wife
    Oct' 1   Charles Whitney & Wife
        23   Afa Stone & wife and Luther Barrett
                1809
    Oct' 29   Jonathan Child & Wife
    Nov' 5   Isaac Patten & Wife
                1810
    June 3   Levi Thaxter
    Nov' 4   Thaddeus Cole & Wife

1811

Jany 20	Seth Bemis & wife
June 23	John Trull & Wife
July 26	Anna Bent
Sepr 22	Nathaniel Harrington & wife

1812

	Jany 5	Joseph Bird & wife
1813	Nov 14	Phebe S. Stone
1814	Sepr 18	Mary Rand, Sophia Leath
1815	July 16	Mary Robbins
	30	Sarah Robbins
1816	April 21	Jonathan Stone Junr & wife
		Julianna Wife of Charles Stone

[Pages 15 to 41 inclusive blank.]

[42] Marriages

Novr 23^d 1780. Phineas Stearnes & Esther Sanderson were married
Decr 7th 1780 John Sangar & Ame Trask were marr^d
Decr 28. 1780 Isaac Parkhurst & Lucy White were married

The following account of persons baptized by the Revd Mr Seth Storer was soon after his Decease, transcribed from his interleaved Almanaks by his Nephew Eben^r Storer Esqr. An account of the persons baptized by Mr Storer previous to the 18th of April 1773 is entered in this Book. See page [222.]

1773

May 23	Susanna Daughter of John Hunt Junr
July 25	Phineas Son of Thomas Learned
Augt 8	Katherine Daugh^t of Nathl Sparhawk at Cambridge Village
Sep^t 30	Elizabeth Daughter of Samuel Soden
Octr 17	Parnel Daugh^r of Jonathan Learned Junr
	Lucy Daugh^r of John Stratton
31	Elisha Son of Amos Livermore

[43]

Novr 21	Susannah Daughter of Joshua Kendall

1774

Feby 20	Frances Daughter of William Fuller
	Christopher. Son of Christopher Grant Junr
27	Thomas Son of Dan^el Cornwall
March 13	Elizabeth Daughter of Josiah Bright
	Lois Daughter of Josiah Bright
	James Son of William Learned
	Israel Son of Israel Whitney

	20.	Rhoda Daughter of David Coolidge
	27	Lydia Daughter of Henry Sanderson
May 8		David & Susana Twins of Jonas Barnard
	15	William Son of Nathaniel Rogers }
		Abigail Daughter of Phineas Robbins }
		at Newton
June 12		Lucy Daughter of Pennel Park
	26	Grant Son of Jedediah Learned
		Joseph Son of Jonathan Whitney
July 10		Grace Daughter of Elkanah Wales
	31	Kezia Daughter of Zachariah Shed
		Edmund Son of Edmund Fowle

[44]

Aug. 14		Nathaniel Son of John Tainter Junr
		Moses Son of Josiah Norcrofs
	21.	Daniel & John the Sons }
		Sarah & Hannah the Daughters of }
		of Daniel Bond
	28	Relief Daughter of John Wellington
Sep^t 11.		Hannah Daughter of Amos Bond
Octr 2.		John Son of Ezekiel Hall
		Mary Daughter of Joseph Gardner
	23	Benjamin Son of Phineas Jinnison
		Sybill Daughter of Wm Chenery
Novr 6		Aaron Son of Wm Sanger
		Abner Son of Abner Craft
		Rebecca Daughter of Eyris Tainter
		Lucy Daughter of Stephen Whitney

[45]

The following account of persons rec^d into full communion by the Revd Mr Storer was also transcribed from his interleaved Almanacks

1773

May 23	Charity Capen
July 25	Josiah Bisco
Decr 19	Samuel Barnard & Elizabeth Barnard

1774

April 17	Jonas Barnard & Abigail Barnard
	Mary Coolidge & Dorothy Coolidge
24	Amos Bond
May 22	Mercy Coolidge
June 5.	Sarah, Elizabeth, & Mary Fisk

See page [304.]

[46] Form of the Covenant to be administered to those who join in full Communion with the Church.

You do now in the presence of the great God, and this christian Assembly, profess your belief in the holy Scriptures, that they are the word of God, and the only rule of our faith and obedience. You believe that the Lord Jesus Christ, is the Son of God and the only Mediator between God and Man, and with all your heart, you desire to give up yourself to God, in an everlasting covenant, and to accept of Jesus Christ as your Saviour and Redeemer, in the way prescribed in the Gospel, and solemnly promise [47] that by the help of divine grace, you will sincerely endeavour to conform to the rules & precepts of our holy religion, to forsake the sins and vanities of this evil world, and to approve yourself a true diciple of Jesus Christ, in all good behaviour, towards God and towards man. And, particularly, you promise, that you will endeavour to walk with this Church, while you have opportunity, in the exercise of christian affection, in conforming to the regulations, and submitting to the discipline of the Church, in all things, agreeably to what you do know, or may hereafter know, to be your duty.

Do you make this profession, and take upon you the obligation of this Covenant? I then declare you to be a Member in [48] full Communion with the Church of Christ, and we who are members of the Church, do promise and engage, that by the help of the divine Spirit, we will make it our sincere aim and endeavour, to treat you in every respect, as a member of the same body with ourselves, watching over you and that for your good, with a spirit of meeknefs, love and tendernefs, earnestly praying, that the Lord God, the great Head of the Church, would dwell among us, that his blessed Spirit, may be upon us, and that his glorious kingdom may be advanced by us. Amen.

[49] Form of the Covenant to be administered to these who own the Covenant.

You do now in the presence of the great God, and this christian Assembly, profess your belief in the holy Scriptures, that they are the word of God, and the only rule of our faith and obedience: You believe that the Lord Jesus Christ is the Son of God, and the only Mediator between God and Man, and with all your heart, you desire to give up yourself to God, in an everlasting Covenant, and to accept Jesus Christ as your Saviour and Redeemer, in the way prescribed in the Gospel, and you solemnly promise, that by the help of divine grace you will sincerely endeavour to conform to the rules and [50] precepts of our holy religion, to forsake the sins and vanities of this evil world, and to approve yourself a true disciple of Jesus Christ in all good behaviour towards God, and towards man. And you likewise submit to the government and discipline of Christ in his Church, and engage to walk in all things, agreeably to what you do know, or may hereafter know, to be your duty.

Do you thus profess and promise? I then declare you to be entitled to all the privileges which are usually given by this Church, to those, who take upon them the obligations of this Covenant.

[51 to 61 inclusive] all blank.

[62]

An Epitaph upon my Dear Wife's Tomb Stone in Watertown in N. E.   made by Mr Moodey:

> Pious Lydia made and given by God
> As a most meet help to John Bailey
> Minister of ye Gospel—
> Good betimes, Best at last,
> Lived by Faith, Dyed in peace
> Went oft singing, Left us weeping,
> Walked wth God till transflated in y^e
> 39 yeare of her age April 16, 1691
> Read her Epitaph in Prov. 31, 10, 11, 12, 28, 29, 30, 31.

[See page 292]

[63]

Epitaph upon 2 or 3 psons I were acquainted with, Brother Thomas and my D^r wife Lydia.

An Epitaph upon Mr Sherman in Watertown in N. E. In my time, my Honorable predecessor, made by Mr Willard.

" Johannis Shermanni, Maximæ Pietatis, Gravitatis, & Candoris Viri
In Theologia plurimum versati, In concionando vere Chrysostomi,
In Artibus Liberalibus præcipue Mathematicis incomparabilis;
Aquitamensis Ecclesiæ in Nova Anglia fidelissimi Pastoris,
Collegii Harvardini Inspectoris & Socii,
Qui postquam annis plus minus XLV Christo fuit
YIIIIPETIIS [i.e. under rowers y^u steer ye ship towards heaven,] in Ecclesia Fidus—Morte Matura transmigravit
et a Christo palma Decoratus est,
A.D. MDCLXXXV, Augusti. 8.
   Ætatis. Suæ LXXII.
   Memoriæ."

This is better written in ye end of my Concordance.

An Epitaph upon my Brother Thomas Tomb Stone, In Watertown in N. E.   Made by Mr Moody.

> " Here lyes ye precious dust of
>   Thomas Bailey,

A painful preacher,	A Most desirable neighbour,
An Exemplary Liver,	A pleasant Companion,
A Tender Husband,	A Common Good,
A Careful Father,	A Cheerful doer,
A Brother for Adversity,	A patient Sufferer,
A Faithful Friend,	Lived much in a little time.

A Good Copy for all Survivors,
Aged 35 years
Slept in Jesus 21 of January 1688."

[Epitaph in the Granary Burial Ground of Boston,
"Here lyeth interred the Body of the
Reverend and Faithful Minister
Of the Gospel in Boston
M[r] John Bailey
aged 54 years who
Deceased the 12 of December 1687"]

[64] Blank

[65]

A Legacy being left, by M[rs] Ann Mills late of Watertown to the Church in the East part of this Town, which Legacy consisted of Two Hun[d]. Eighty Three p[ds] 10[s]. The Church chose a Committee to let the same out upon Interest; which Interest was to be paid to the Minister & Deacons to be disposed of by them according to the last will of y[e] s[d] M[rs]. Mills.

The account of what has been received, & to what objects of Charity disposed of, follows.

1730.
		£	s	d
May. 13.	Received of the Churches Comittee which was disposed of to the following Persons Viz.	7.	11.	3
	To M[rs] Chamberlain 40/	2.	00.	00
	To the widow Sarah Perry. 20/	1.	00.	00
	To the wife of Sam[ll] Warren 20/	1.	00.	00
	To Martha Whitney 20/	1.	00.	00
	To the widow Ruth Coollidge	1.	01.	3
	To M[r] Tho[s] Coollidge for the widow Webb	1.	10.	0
		£7.	11.	3

Dec. 13

		£	s	d
	Received of the Churches Comittee which was given to the following persons viz.	9	00	0
	To the wife of Ebenezer Biggelow	3	00	0
	To M[r] Eph. Cutter Sen[r]	1	05	0
	To his wife Bethiah Cutter	1	05	0
	To Martha Whitney	1	00	0
	To M[r] Benj[a] Chadwick	1	07	0
	To widow Ruth Coollidge	1	05	0
		£9	00	0

1731.

July 26. Received of the Churches Comittee
Eighteen pounds five Shillings & six pence } 18. 05. 6
of w^c was given To ye widow Susanna

Benjemin	3. 00.	00
To Ep. Cutter Senr	1. 00.	00
To Martha Whitney	1. 00.	00
	£5. 00.	00

1732/3

March. 5th Rec. of the Churches Committee, by

ye Minister & Deacons.	14.	12.	1
To Eph. Cutter	00.	18.	0
March. 5. To Margrett Warren	01.	10.	0
Sam^{ll} Warrens Wife	1.	10.	0
Martha Whitney	2.	00.	0
Benj^a Chadwicks Wife	3.	00	0
Wm Goddin Senr	1.	5.	5
Widow Susanna Benjamin	2.	00.	0
	£12.	3.	5

[66 to 77] Occupied with the continued account of this fund.

[78] Blank

[79]   1798

A List of the persons who have contributed towards the support of the Communion Table, in Watertown with the sums by them respectively paid. Viz–

John Remington	£0 3	0
Josiah Mixer	2	3
Ruth Stone	1	6
Easter Cook		9
Daniel Sawin	1	6
Jedediah Leathe	3	0
Daniel Whitney	3	0
Samuel White	3	0
Richard Clark	1	6
Moses Coolidge	3	0
Susanna Bond	1	6
Eunice Coolidge	1	6
Mary Stearnes	1	6
Sarah Clark	1	6
Sibil Livermore	1	6
Amos Bond	3	0
Joanna Cook		9

[80 to 85] occupied with continuation of this list.

[86 to 89] Blank.

[90 to 119] "Texts."

[120 to 127] Blank.

[128]

At a meeting of the Church belonging to the East part of Watertown January. y⁴ 22ⁿᵈ 1728/9

The Following votes were pafsed viz⁴

Voted. 1. Wether the Church be of the mind to chufe a Committee to receive what is due to this Church by vertue of the last Will and Testamont of Mʳˢ Anne Mills, late of Watertown deceafed. It pafsed in the affirmative.

Voted. 2. That Lieuᵗ Samˡˡ Stearns, Deacon John Coollidge Deacon Joseph Mafon, Lieuᵗ Joseph Coollidge & Mʳ Nathⁿ Harris be the Church's Comittee to act on their behalf in referrence to the aforsaid Legacy.

Voted. 3. Whether the Church doth invest the faid Comittee with full Power to recover and receive, in their behalf, the whole that is or fhall be due to this Church by virtue of the aforsaid last Will and Testament of Mʳˢ Anne Mills, of the Executors of faid Will, or of fuch of them as.fhall be furviving, and in the name of the Church to give faid Executors a Difcharge or Difcharges

It pafsed in the affirmative.

Voted. 4. Whether the Church doth empower the aforesaid Comittee to let out upon Lawful Interest, they having fuch Security as they think fufficient, that part of the eftate of the abovesaid Anne Mills, which doth or fhall belong to this Church, which Interest fhall be paid in yearly to the Minister or Ministers and Deacons. It pafsed in the affirmative.

Voted. 5. That if the Minister or Ministers and Deacons of this Church fee need to call for part or all of the Principal of the above mentioned Eftate, as well as for the interest of it we do acknowledge that they have full power to do it, and their receipt shall be the Comittee's Difcharge for fuch Sum or Sums as they receive of them. Atteft. SETH STORER Paftor.

[129]

At a Meeting of The Church belonging to the Eaſt part of Watertown. October 13ᵗʰ 1731.

1. Put to vote, whether the Church be of the mind that Daniel Whitney, (he having explicitly owned the Covenant among, and fubmitted himself to the Watch and Difcipline of thofe who acted as a third Church in Watertown, and having a Child baptized by Mʳ Robert Sturgeon after the Refult of the Council of Churches met at watertown on May 1. 1722.) could juftly claim the privilege of Baptifm for his Children, before he had made Satisfaction.

It pafsed in the negative.

2. Put to Vote whether the Church do leave it with the Minister and Deacons to receive fuch Satisfaction, from s'd whitney, as they shall think fufficient, and that in behalf of the Church.
It pafsed in the affirmative.

July. 15. 1736.
At a meeting of the Church of Chrift in the Eaft part of Watertown in order to make choice of fome fuitable Perfon to the office of a Deacon in faid Church, the Bretheren voted & chofe Mr Joseph Mafon to faid office, and he declared his acceptance thereof.
Atteft. SETH STORER Paftor.

May. 29. 1741.
At a meeting of the Church of Chrift in Watertown in Order to make Choice of fome fuitable perfon to the office a Deacon in faid Church, the Bretheren voted & chofe Mr Joseph Coollidge to faid office, who accepted thereof.
Atteft. SETH STORER Paftor.

June 27th 1749.
At a meeting of the Church of Chrft in Watertown in Order to make Choice of fome fuitable Perfon to the office of a Deacon in faid Church, the Bretheren voted & chofe Mr Samuel Fifk to faid office & he accepted thereof
Atteft. SETH STORER Paftor.

[130]

July. 14th 1749.
At a Meeting of the Church of Chrift in Watertown An account was exhibited to faid Church by fome of the faid Committee, chofen to let out on Intereft Mrs Ann Mills's Legacy to faid Church, of their difcharging the Truft repofed in them as the Churches Committee for the Time paft; after reading whereof, it was put to vote, vizt.
Voted. 1. Whether the Church be fatisfied with the account given unto the Church by faid Committee?
It paft in ye Affirmative.
Voted. 2. Whether the Bretheren of the Church give their Thanks to faid Committee for their faithful Care in the Difcharge of their office as the Churches Committee?
It paft in ye Affirmative.
Voted. 3. Whether the Church be of the mind to chufe two perfons to fupply the vacancies made in the Churches Comittee to let out Mrs Ann Mills's Legacy, in the Room of two of faid Committee removed by Death?   It paft in ye Affirmative.
Voted. 4. Voted & chofe Deacon Samuel Fifk to be one of the Churches Committee to let out the Legacy left to this Church by Mrs Ann Mills.   Atteft SETH STORER Paftor
Voted. 5. Voted & chofe Capt. John Tainter to be one of the Churches Committee to let out on Intereft the Legacy left to this Church by Mrs Ann Mills.   Attest. SETH STORER Paftor.

June 12. 1761. At a Meeting of the Church of Christ in Watertown in order to make choice of some suitable Person to be a Deacon in said Church, the Bretheren voted & chose Capt John Tainter to said office; and he declared his acceptance thereof.

Attest Seth Storer Pastor.

Voted. 2. Whether the Church be of the Mind to chuse a Person to supply the vecency made in the Churches Comittee to let out Mrs Ann Mills's Legacy. in the Room of Nathl Harris Esqr removed by Death.   It past in the affirmative.

Voted. 3. Voted & chose Nath^r Stone to be one of ye Churches Comittee for the service aforesaid.

Attest Seth Storer Pastor.

[131]

June 12th 1761. At a Church Meeting, Deacon Samuel Fisk rendred An Account of the Churches Comittee's Discharge of their Trust in letting out Mrs Ann Mills' Legacy to said Church & their receiving the Interest due thereon to the middle of last July, which was accepted by the Bretheren.

Voted. The Bretheren of the Church voted s^d Comittee Thanks for their faithful discharge of their office.

Attest Seth Storer Pastor

1777. Novr 22^d. Mr Nathaniel Stone was Chosen to the office of Deacon in the Church, of which he accepted.

The Same Day Mr Sam^{ll} White was Chosen one of the Com^{tee} to take care of the Legacy Left to this Chh: by Mrs Ann Mills.

Att^t Sam^{ll} Fisk Moderator

1780 Octr 27th

At a meeting of the Chh of Christ in Watertown The following Votes were passed, Viz.

Vote 1^{ly} That all Confessions & acknowledgements for Crimes committed should hereafter be mad before the Chh and not before the Congregation.

Vote 2^d. That all persons who have stood propounded the usual time & against whom no objections have been offered, should be received into the Chh by the Pastor without an express Vote of the Chh they publickly assenting to the holy Cov^t.

Attest Richard R. Elrot Pastor

[132]

1793

April 3. At a meeting of the Chh of Christ in Watertown the following Votes were passed Viz—

Voted. That a Committee of the Chh be chosen to take care of the monies belonging to the Chh, to collect any Debts which may be due to the Chh, to receive any monies belonging to the Chh which may now be in the hands of any person or persons, — & apply them for the use of ye Chh in such a manner as they may think proper, unless they are the procedes of certain donations heretofore made to the Chh. in which Case the Committee are to apply the money to fuch uses as have been exprefsly pointed out by the Donors.

Voted. That Deacon Leathe, Dea{n} Whetney & M{r} Soden be a Commit{e} to act in behalf of the Chh, in respect to the Matters which are mentioned in the preceeding vote—

at{t} RICHARD R. ELIOT Pastor

[133]

1795
June 28. At a meeting of the Chh of Ch{t} in Watertown

Voted. That Roger Adams & his Wife be dismissed from this Chh, & be recommended to the Church under the pastoral Care of the Rev. M{r} Greenough of Newton. They having signified to the Chh that it is their desire to receive fuch a Dismission.

At a meeting of the Church of Christ in Watertown on Monday the 21{t} of Oct. 1799, the following Votes were passed Viz.

1. Voted, that all persons who have or shall hereafter own the Covenant shall enjoy the Privilege of having their Children Baptized.

2. Voted, that all the Flagons & other pewter vessels belonging to the Church, shall be fold as foon as may be & that two Silver Tankards shall be purchased for the use of the Church, with the money belonging to the Church which has not been otherwise appropriated. & that Dea{n} Leathe & Dea{n} Whitney be requested to purchase them.

[134]

Vote 3{d}. Voted, that in all future Contributions of the Church for the fupply of the Communion Table, the Members of the Chh present shall contribute 25 Cents each, & that the money then contributed be paid into the hands of the Deacons.

4. Voted That whenever the fums of money which have been contributed for the supply of the Communion Table shall have been expended, an account of such expenditure shall be rendered to the Pastor by the Deacons, & that a time be appointed by the Pastor for another Contribution to be held by the Church.

5. Voted that in all future Contributions of the Church, for the fupply of the Communion Table, which may be appointed by the Pastor, the amount of the fums thus Contributed be afsertained by the Pastor, & an account thereof be kept by him.

[135]

At a meeting of the Church of Christ in Watertown Feb{y} 10{th} 1802, in order to make choice of some fuitable person to the office of a Deacon in said Church—the Brethren Voted & chose Col. Moses Coolidge to said office. At the same meeting of the Church the following Votes were passed. Viz

Vote 1. That Dea{n} Coolidge be empowered to act as an agent in behalf of the Church, to fettle with the administrator of the Estate of Dea Daniel Whitney, relative to any sum or sums of money which may have been deposited in his hands, belonging to the Church, & which he had not an opportunity of appropriating to the use for which it had been committed to his care.

Vote 2ᵈ. That Col. Amos Bond be empowered in the Name & behalf of the Church

[136]

to take the pewter Vessels belonging to the Church, of the persons who have the care of them, & to dispose thereof to the best advantage in behalf of the Chh.

That the Sacrament of the Lord's Supper be administered in the Church on the first Sabbath of the month of april next, & on the first Sabbath of the seven following Months & that the administration of the sacrament be omitted, during the Space, intervening between the first Sabbath in Novʳ & the first Sabbath in aprill, annually.

At a meeting of the Church of Christ in Watertown August 7ᵗʰ 1805—held for the purpose ot choosing fome fuitable Person to fill the office of a Deacon in faid Church, the Brethren voted by written votes, upon counting of which it appeared that Col. Amos Bond was unanimously chosen to faid office.

[137]

At a meeting of the Church of Christ in Watertown Decʳ 21ˢᵗ 1814, the following votes were passed, Viz.

Vote 1 That the Sacrament of the Lords-Supper be administered in future on the first Sabbath of every month in the year.

Vote 2 That a Sacramental Lecture on each Friday preceeding the first Lords-Day of the following month, Viz, January March, May, July, September & November

Vote 3 That the Treasurer of the Church be requested, to obtain a renewal of all the Notes belonging to the Church now in his pofsession as foon as may be after the first of January next.

Vote 4. That the Treasurer be requested to adjust his account, as foon as may be, & give a Note upon Interest for the ballance, & keep the fame on file, with the other Notes belonging to the Church.

[138]

At a meeting of the Church of Christ in Watertown on the 18ᵗʰ of Decʳ 1815 they pafsed the following Vote, Viz—

That whenever any three members of the Church desire that a meeting of the Church be holden, they shall agree upon the time & place of such meeting & fhall make application to the Pastor, to furnish them with a notification for the purpose, & shall proceed to notify all the members of the Church accordingly.

At a meeting of the Church of Christ in Watertown on the 17ᵗʰ of Novʳ 1817, in order to make choice of some fuitable person to the office of a Deacon in said Church the meeting was opened with Prayer the Brethren voted & chose Mʳ John Tucker to said office.

[139 to 161] Blank.

[162 & 163] [Meditations upon Bible texts.]

[164]

1800 March 17th

Deacon Jedediah Leathe to the Chh in Watertown   Dr.
To Cash contributed by sundry Persons & deposited
  in your hands   £11-13-7-
To Cash paid by the Chh.   1-5.-0-

                                           £12-18-7

1800 March 17

Deacon Daniel Whitney to the Chh in Watertown   Dr
To cash contributed by sundry Persons and de-
  posited in your hands   £12-7-11
To Cash paid by the Chh   —9-11

                                           £12-17-11

[165]

1800 March 17th   Cr
By sundry payments & expenditures in behalf
  of the Chh   £12-18-7

By sundry payments & expenditures in behalf
  of the Chh   £12-17-11

[166-187] Blank.

[188] [Religious Thought.]

[189]

    To full communion in the church at Watertown was admitted, 1637 (or previously) Capt Patrick, once of the prince of orange's guards and made a member of the church in order to receive the rights of a freeman and be qualified to take the command of the Massachnsetts men in the Pequod War—see Hutchinson Vol. 1 p 76.

[190]

    Such as I admitted in Watertown to ye Lds supper.

    Ye 5 of December 86. I admitted 9 to full comunion, mr Samuell Thacher & his wife Mary, Sarah Sawin, & Judith Sawin (ye wives of Muning & John) Margret Taylor (ny maid)—Joseph Underwood, mis Train, Joseph Whitney's wife viz Martha, & Joanna Stone. Before yr Admission, I sd 3 things to all present, (1) I showed wt made ym worthy & yt before Gd, & men, as to yr former only grace did, & as to ye later both knowledge, & a blameless life (2) yt all these were able to give me a particular account of gds dealing wth yr soules-(3) yt I had desired ym all to say something if ye could at yr Admission for ye edification of others but y̅ᵉ being neither able nor free, I told y̅ᵐ all I durſt not Impoſe it on y̅ᵐ having no warrant for it—y̅ⁿ I read briefly w̅ᵗ had paſsed betwixt y̅ᵐ & me as to y̅ʳ grace—y̅ⁿ called for y̅ⁿ vote of y̅ⁿ ch & had it, & y̅ⁿ y̅ᵘ pmiſed to cary becomingly, & y̅ᵉ were Admitted, & after y̅ᵗ briefly adviſed to ſomethings, eſp to y̅ʳ family, & tongue Govern̅ᵗ

Y̅ᵉ 30ᵗʰ of January 1686/7 I admittted 11, viz Tho. Whitney, Eliz. Fiſk, Eliz. Balham, Eliz. Goffe, Ann Stone, John Edy, Nich. With & his wife, young James Cornith, Eliz. Barnard, Rebekah Farnworth [Remarks made at admissions from here on generally omitted]

Y̅ᵉ 27ᵗʰ of March 1687 I admitted 14 (w̅ᶜʰ was remarkable) viz Sarah Philips, Mary Philips, Elizabeth Underwood, M̅ʳ Abiah Sherman, Joſeph Maſon, M̅ʳ Wil. Bond, (Justice of peace) old M̅ʳ Jo. Biſcoe, Thomas Ryder, George Lawrence, Anna Livermore, Elizabeth Deeks, Judith Jenningſon, Sarah Warren, & Sarah Mixer

Y̅ᵉ 8ᵗʰ of May 87. I admitted 6, viz Lidia Bowman, (y̅ᵉ wife of young Francis Bowman) Thomas Strait, Benjamin Pearſe & his wife Hannah, M̅ʳˢ Grace Sherman, & Sarah Whitney, y̅ᵉ wife of Nathanael Whitney this day Nat. Holland openly acknowledged his lye

Y̅ᵉ 19 of June 87, I admitted 6, viz Eliz. Tanter (y̅ᵉ wife of Tanter) Margret Warren, Eliz. Lawrence (y̅ᵉ wife of George Lawrence) Abia Sanders (y̅ᵉ wife of Jon. Sanders) Richard Cutting, & Jo. Bacon. I hinted at Cor. 8. 5

[191]   Such as I baptized in Watertown 1686.

Y̅ᵉ 6 of October 1686 I was ſolemnly ſett y̅ᵗ for y̅ᵉ Paſtorall work at Watertown, w̅ᵗʰout Imposition of Hands. I am ſick of it, & unfitt for it, but y̅ᵉ many particulars y̅ᵗ attend this work I wholly omitt

Oct. 17. 86. I baptized 3 viz Iſraell Pierce, y̅ᵉ child of Joſeph Pierce, about a year old. And Mercy Begulah y̅ᵉ child of John Begulo, a young child. And Thomas Milling a young man who Pſeſſed his Faith in X & obed to him

Y̅ᵉ 24 of Oct. 86. I baptized 10 all of y̅ᵐ under a year old Samuell Livermores child called Nathanaell. William Bonds called Diliverance. John Parkis called George. Juſtinian Holden's called Elizabeth. Tho. Hamon's, called Thomas. John Cutting's called George. Michaell Flegs called Abigall. Thomas Bonds called Sarah all theſe related to the church, but y̅ᵉ other 2 were not, only formerly M̅ʳ Sherman baptized their children, viz Samuell Thacher's called John, & Theophilus Philips, called Mary

Y̅ᵉ 7 of November 86, I baptized 6 viz Stephen Willis child (who belongs to y̅ᵉ church in Brantrey) viz Benjamin, & Jonathan Stimpſons child viz Rebecca, & Tho. Williams child (who at preſent lives in Wooborn his wife formerly lived in this town & owned y̅ᵉ Covenant) viz Damaris, all of y̅ᵐ under a year old.

Alſo I baptized James Knopp a young man, & John Price a young man, & alſo Mary Price his Siſter, but ſhe is maryed & her huſband from her above theſe 2 yeares, ye Ld bleſs this ord to y^m

Y^e 14th of November I baptized 3 children, viz Abraham Geals child (who is a member ye church) viz Ebenezer, it was young. & Abigall Townſends child (her huſbands name I know not) viz Martin. & John Bonds child, called Abigall, not a fortnight old

Y^e 21. of November 86 I baptized 12, viz Tredaways child called Joſiah, & John Chinerys child (who owned ye Cov^t) called Sarah, & 5 of old Simon Millings children, viz Simon, Richard, Mary, James, & John. & David Fiſks wife viz Elizabeth (in order to Admiſsion) & her child David. & George Adams wife Martha who owned ye Cov^t, & her child called George. & Mary Adams who is his Siſter, who owned ye Cov^t

Y^e 28 of Nov. 86 I baptized 9 viz 4 children of Tho. Underwood (who owned ye Cov^t privately, & his wife publickly) viz Thomas, Jonathan, Mary & Elizabeth. And Jonathan Smithes wife viz Jane. And Sarah Jane and her child Jonathan, & Widow Fiſks daughter viz Elizabeth. And Sarah Sanders, viz William Sanders daughter. And Samuell Severn ye widows ſon

Y^e 5 of December 86. I baptized 7, viz 6 of John Aplin who owned ye Cov^t, viz John, Thomas, Mary, Hannah, Baſhuah, Abiah. & Benjamin Davis who owned ye Cov^t

[192]

Such as were Admitted by me to Full Communion In Waterown—1687

Y^e 31 of July 1687 I admitted 6, viz Tho. Cutler, Thomas Millings, Benjamin Goddard, Sarah Cuttings, Abiah Leaſon, & Elizabeth Willington, I ſpent ſome time in a word in Benj. Goddards relation, viz a child of ye Covn^t, oh y^t g^d wid bleſse it for much good. Eliz. Willington is ye wife of Joſeph Willington

Y^e 13th of November I admitted 7, viz Philip Shattock, Benjamin Flegg, Jonathan Stimſon, Abigaill Townſend (ye wife of Martin Townſend) Elizabeth Chinery (ye wife of John Chinery) Suſanna Grout (ye wife of Joſeph Grout) Elizabeth Nevenſon (ye wif of John Nevinſon, whom I admitted wthout a Relation her huſband who is of ye church of England wid not ſuffer it, but ye church was ſatiſfyed in her wthout it), I hope g^d will bleſse y^m, & make y^m bleſsings

Y^e 8th of January I admitted 3, viz Mr William Goddard, Abigail Fox (ye wife of Iſaac Fox, of Miſtick, or Medford as it is called) & Bithia Satle

Y 4th March 1687/8 I admitted 3 viz Calib Church, Stephen Cook, & Abraham Brown I had ſaid ſomething largely to y^m but y^t I had other matters y^t day

Ye 15th of Aprill 1688 I admitted one viz Samuell Bigelow.

Y 19 of Auguſt 1688 I admitted 6, viz young John Warren & his wife Elizabeth, Benjamin young Richard Child, Martha Fiſk, Thomas Thornton.

Yᵉ 11ᵗʰ of November 1688 I admitted 4 viz John Ball & his wife, John Aplin, & Walter Taylor. now admitted by me 76

Yᵉ 3ᵈ off February 1688/9 I admitted 7 viz John Whitmore of Miftick, young Henery Spring, Sufannah Cook (viz Gregory Cooks wife) Samuell Stearnes, John Child (who was baptized by me a year ago) Elizabeth Gale (yᵉ wife of John Gale) & Mary Grant, who was baptized by me not long a gon—now 83.

Yᵉ 17ᵗʰ of March 1688/9 I admitted 6 viz Rebeka Shattuck (i.e Philips wife,) Hepzibah Bond, (i. e young Williams wife) Elizabeth Stimfon (i. e Jonathans wife) Benjamin Taylor, Danyell Stone & his wife, to whom I fd fomething.

[193]

Such as were baptized by me in Watertown. 1686.

Upon yᵉ 26 of December 86 I baptized 13, viz Jofeph Grants child (who owned yᵉ Covᵗ fome old bufinefs brought againft him, but nothing proved) viz Mary. Ebenezer Stones child who lives in Cambridge village, viz Ebenezer, & Allin Fleggs child (who owned yᵉ Covᵗ) viz Sarah, & Sarah Thropp, & Mary Throp, & Elizabeth Goodwin, & Margaret Fisk, & Elizabeth Dill, all wᶜʰ owned yᵉ Covenant & Jofeph Mafons wife, yᵗ both of yᵐ ftood acknowledging & taking shame to yᵐfelves for   her name was Mary, baptized 2 of yʳ children viz Mary & Hefter. I baptized John Knop, & his child Sarah, he & his wife alfo ftood as it were in yᵉ ftool of repentance for yᵉ fame Folly, much was sd to yᵐ wᶜʰ I now pafs by

Yᵘ 2ᵈ of January 86/7 I baptized 3. viz Nathanell Brights child called Nathanaell, & Muning Sawins child called Abigall, & Mary Gregg who owned yᵉ covenant.

Yᵉ 9 of January 86/7 I baptized 4 children viz Tho. Cutlers (who had formerly owned yᵉ covent) viz James, & 2 of Jo. Harringtons (who now owned yᵉ covenant, viz John, & Hannah, & one of Nat. Bonds whofe wife owned yᵉ covenant, viz Nathanaell.

Yᵉ 16 of January 86/7 I baptized 9, viz 5 of Jofeph Whitney's (fhe lately Joyning herfelf to yᵉ cʰ) viz Jofeph, John, Ifaac, Abigall, & Martha. alfo I baptized yᵉ wife of Daniell Pierfe viz Elizabeth, & 3 of her children, viz John, Hannah, & Benjamin, he viz Danyell Pierfe owned yᵉ covᵗ.

Yᵉ 20ᵗʰ February 86/7 I baptized one, viz a grand child of Simon Stone, fhe lives at Dedham, her hufbands name is Comfort Starr, yᵉ childs name was Mary

Yᵉ 27ᵗʰ of February 86/7 I baptized one, viz Hannah Johnfon yᵗ lived at Mʳ Bonds, I hope a good girle.

Yᵉ 20ᵗʰ of March 86/7 I baptized 5 young perfons (yᵉ Ld blefe it unto yᵐ) viz Henery Stretcher who lives wᵗʰ Mʳ Bridge, & Hefter Sanders, yᵉ daughter of Edward Sanders, & Hefter Bullard yᵉ daughter of Jonathan Bullard, & Bethia Meatox, & Mary Meatox yᵉ daughters of Danyell Meatox.

Yᵉ 10ᵗʰ of Aprill 86 I baptized 4 children of Abiah Leafon (yᵉ wife of young William Leafon) who owned yᵉ covᵗ, yʳ names were

William, Joseph, John, & Elizabeth. I sd something to y^m from Mark 10. 14

Y^e 17 of Aprill 87 I baptized 3, viz 2 of Jo. Fisks children who owned ye covenant viz Abigall, & Elizabeth, & also I baptized Ruth Garfield ye daughter of widdow Garfield. she also owned ye Cov^t.

[194]
Such as was admitted to ye Lds Supper, or to full Comunion in Watertown in my time. A. D. 1689.

Y^e 18 of August 1689 there was admitted 2 women viz Mary Mason i. e. Josephs wife, & Mary Tufts i. e. Johns wife of Mistick.

Y^e 29 of September 1689 there was only one admitted viz Elizabeth Flegg, ye wife of Allin Flegg.

Y^e 20th of October 1689 I did in ye name of ye church admitt Deacon Stephen Cooke to full comunion wth us being a member of ye church of X in Mendon, he being cast by Pr^dence here, & had his dismission from thence.

Y^e 2^d of February 1689/90 I admitted 2 viz Mr Edw. Procter of Boston, (he being my countreyman had ye advantage others had not. I grtly rejoyce I shid be usefull to him, oh y^t Lancashire might live in ye light.) & Sarah Wait, ye wife of Thomas Waite. I hope y^t wth ye rest will walk worthy.

Y^e 27 of Aprill 1690 I admitted 4. viz Mr Hen. Gibbs who hath some time preached for me here & now this quarter of a yeare liveth wth me, Phebe Cutler (who publickly owned her aggravated sin before ye congregation, Amos Merrett, & Mehetabell Child who at present lives wth me as a serv^t. Here have an hundred save one given vp y^mselves to ye Ld since my comeing hither.

Y^e 22th of June 1690 there were 5 Admitted, viz Thomas Flegg (& oh w^t a mercy & wonder of mercy is it y^t ever I shid see him thus presenting of himself, often was I affrayed to heare of his drowning or hanging of himself, but I see ye foundation of gd standeth sure, & he is a prayer hearing gd. it was worth my comeing for N. E but to convert such a man I hope much good was don at ye reading of his Relation, & by those words y^t were occasionally dropt by me. Blessed be gd, Let all say Amen & Amen) & Isaac Stearnes, & Abigail Stratten (ye wife of young John Stratten my Neighbour) & Bithia Merrett, (ye wife of Amos Merrett) & Sarah Fanning &c. Now 104

Y^e 3^1 of August 1690 there were 5 admitted, viz Mary Flegg (who publickly took shame to herself before ye Ld & his people for her sin & Freely offered herself thus publickly to give glory to gd, & not only so, but desired full comunion wth this church she had so offended & grieved, & obtained it). & Tho. Hammond, & Samuel Whitmore of Cambridge Farmes

[195] Such as were Baptized by me in Watertown 1687.

Y^e 24 of Aprill 87 I baptized 10, viz Philip Shattocks child, called Joseph, & Jonathan Coolidge child called Mary, & ye child of Sufannah Grout (Jofeph Grouts wife) who owned ye Cov^t, it was called Jonathan. I likewife Sarah Mofse & her child called James, fhe is ye wife of Jeremye Mofse. fhe owned ye cov^t. John Garfield, & Mercy Garfield ye children of Widdow Garfield, ye both owned ye Cov^t. William Rowe, who lives at Phil. Shattocks, & Elizabeth Child, & Mary Child, who owned y^r Cov^t y^e are ye children, i. e. ye young daughters of John Childs, their mother is now maryed to Nath. Fifk.

Y^e Firft of May 87. I baptized 3 children of Jonathan Philips viz Sarah, Elizabeth, & Ruth

Y^e 22 of May 87 I baptized 9, viz 2 children of Danyell Harrington who owned ye Cov^t, viz Danyell & Robert — & a child of Rich. Childs, viz John, & a child of John Fifks viz John, & a child of George Adams viz Mathew — & 4 young folks who gave vp y^mfelves to ye Ld, viz John Johnfon, Thomas Johnfon, Mary Johnfon, & John Child

Y^e 5th of June 87 I baptized 9, viz 3 of Tho. Chadwicks children, (who owned ye covn^t, & tho he had committed folly at ye firft long agon, yet Satiffaction was given to ye church at Newbury, where he had 4 children baptized fince, & I could not but think once Satiffaction is enough for one fault) viz Elizabeth, Lidia, & Richard. I baptized 4 of Nathanaell Fifks (who alfo owned ye covenant) viz Nathanaell, John, Hannah, & Sarah. I baptized alfo one of his wives children by a former hufband, viz Danyell Child, ye vndertook for ye bringing it of it up. I alfo baptized Jofeph Childs child, viz Mary

Y^e 19 of June 87 I baptized 14, viz 6 of John Deeks children, viz Elizabeth, John, Edward (or Edmond) Jofeph, Abigaill, & Debora, a child of Jofiah Jones who owned ye Covenant (he never did it have before) viz John, and 2 children of John Gale's, (fhe having formerly owned it) viz Anna & Abigaill, I baptized Danyell Stone's wife (who owned ye Covenant) viz Joanna, & her 3 children viz Danyell, David, & Dorcas. I also Baptized a child of John Harringtons viz Mary

Y^e 10th of July 87 I baptized 11, viz 4 of Caleb Church his children (who folemnly owned ye Cov^t), viz Caleb, Jofhua, Ifaac, & Rebekah, alfo a child of Jo. Balls called Abigaill, alfo I baptized Ifaac Lamb, Abigaill Sanders & Mary Laurence, all wch 3 owned ye Coven^t, I baptized 3 of George Dills children, (he himfelf taking fhame to himfelf for his sin   ) his children were called Thomas, Sarah and James

[196]

Such as were admitted to Full communion in Watertown N. E by me Anno domoni 1690

Sarah Edy, & Hannah Johnfon.

N ow 109

Y^e 1^{ft} of March 1690/1 I admitted one, viz Thomas Underwood, y^r was John Bond and wife alfo, but he was buryed juft 3 houres (or y^r abouts) before he was to be admitted, ftupendious Providence, he dyed of ye small pox. He was a thriving man both as to this world & another, & likely to have been of gr^t vſe to this ch & town, he dyed comfortably, I formerly ſtirred him vp to this duty, but his feares & Temp^t kept him, & now was eager vpon it. He ſent me word to warn all others by him y^t ye looſe no opportunity putt into y^r hands, for now he wid but muſt not ptake of ye ord This thing this evening I largely ſpoke to (wch now I paſse by) ye L^d bleſse it

Y^e 12 of Aprill 1691 I admitted 5, viz John Woodward, an ancient man of 70 yeares, John Bemis, John Moſse, Rich Bloſse, & Grace Bond, i. e, ye wife of Jonas Bond Now 116 wth John Bond & his wife who were as good as admitted.

I had thought to have ſd ſomething here further as to it, but my D^t Lyddy is dead & ſo am wholly indiſpoſed to everything.

Y^e 24 of May 1691 I admitted 2 viz Roſe Norcroſse i. e young Richards wife, & Elizabeth Berſham I took an occaſion to take leave of ch members, & gave ſome ſerious hints from 2 Tim. 2. 19. I ſuppoſe I ſhall admit no more   118

[197]

Such as were Baptized by me in Watertown 1687

Y^e 17 of July 87. I baptized 11, viz a child of Joſeph Shermans called Elizabeth, 2 children of Thomas Biſcoe's (who owned ye covn^t) called John, & Elizabeth, 2 children of Jonathan Tanters called Jonathan & Benjamin, a child of Nathanaell Whitney's called Samuell, a child of Jonathan Smiths called Zechariah, & 2 young women, viz Lidia Corley y^t owned ye covenant, ſhe lived y^n wth John Ball, & Lidia Smith, who formerly was called Zipparah, ſhe lives at Father Satle I wiſh ſhe may have ye New name indeed

I have now already baptized an Hundred Forty-nine

Y^e 31 of July 87 I baptized 2 children, viz Sam. Livermor child called Lidia, & John Stratten (vp in ye town) child, called Mercy

Y^e 14 of Aug., 87 I baptized William Shattocks child, called Benjamin

Y^e 21 of Auguſt 1687 I baptized 2 children of Joſeph Willingtons (his wife being lately admitted) called Thomas, & Elizabeth

Y^e 28 of Auguſt 87 I baptized a child of Danyell Harington's (who formerly owned ye cov^t) called David

Y^e 4 of September 87 I baptized a child of Samuell Stearnes (his wife Mehetabell ſolmely owning ye Covn^t) called Samuell

Y^e 11th of September 87   I baptized 3 children, viz Joſeph Pearſse child called Elizabeth, & Joſhuah Bigulows child called Elizabeth, & Thomas Harringtons child (his wife Rebekah who ſolemnly owned ye Covenant) called Ebenezer

Y^e 2^d of October 1687 I baptized 2, viz John Rowe who owned ye Covn^t, he lives wth his Father in ye Farmes of Cambridge, & ye child of Enoch Satle called Suſannah, his wife Suſannah owned ye Covn^t

Yᵒ 16 of October 87 I baptized yᵉ Mother & child, viz yᵉ wife of Samuell Shattock who owned yᵉ covenant, called Abigaill, & her child was called Abigaill

Yᵉ 23 of October 1687 I baptized 5, viz Elizabeth Beamis (who folemnly owned yᵒ covenant) yᵉ wife of Ephraim Beamis, & her 4 children, viz Elizabeth, Sarah, Rebekah & Abigaill

Yᵉ 6 of November 1687 I baptized a child of David Church (who had owned yᵉ covn in Mʳ Shermans time) called John

Yᵒ 4ᵗʰ of December I baptized 7, viz 5 of Jofeph Smith's (who had owned yᵉ Covnᵗ in Mʳ Shermans time) viz Jofeph, John, Danyell, Hanah & Rebekah & 2 of John Haftings, viz Elizabeth & Hephzibah he had formerly owned yᵉ Covᵗ

[198]   Admifsions to full Communion in yᵉ Eaſt Chh of Watertown p H. Gibbs.

1697.

Dec.	12.	David Stone
	19.	Samll Eddy
Febr.	6.	Elizabeth Eddy, Abigail Benjamin
	13.	Elizabeth Stone

1698.

May.	29.	Edward Goddard, Benjamin Eddy
Septʳ.	18.	Rebecka Train
Jan.	8.	Mary Hasting Mary Rice Sufanna Fifk

1699.

June	25.	Sarah Chadwich
Oct.	15.	Josiah Goddard, Nathan Fifk, John Coolidge, Sarah Fifk
Decʳ	10.	Nathaniell Coolidge junʳ Lydia Coolidge, his wife, Abigail Bacon, Rachel Goddard
Febr.	4.	Nathaniell Bright. Mary Bright. Rebecca Barftow. Martha Whitney

1700.

Apr.	7.	Lydia Spring
May	26.	Hephzibah Stone
July	28.	Elizabeth Train
Jan.	5.	Mʳ Jonas Bond
	12.	Timothy Barron

1701.

Apr.	27.	Sufanna Goddard
Aug.	27.	Deliverance Eddy

[199]   Such as were Baptized by me in Watertown—1687.

Yᵉ 11ᵗʰ of Dec. 87. 2 children, viz Serj. Garfields called Mehatabell, & a child yᵗ Jo. Flegg adopted, I fuppofe a baſtard of Matthew Humſteds, called Jabez

Y^e 25th of Dec. 87 ye child of John Bacon, called Mary

Y^e 22 of Jan. 1687/8 4 young pſons, viz Joſeph Memory who lives wth Martin Townſend who vndertook for him, wth ye other 3 Owned ye Covenant, viz Mary Memory who lives wth Lt Winſhipp, & Mary Grant who lives wth Mr Goddard, & Ann Leaſon, who lives wth her Mother

Y^e 29th of January 1687/8 John Moſse child, called Nathanaell

Y^e 5th of February 1687/8 a child of Thomas Bond's called William

Y^e 12th of February 1687/8 a child of Joſeph Vnderwood called Sarah

Y^e 4th of March 1687/8 a child of Benjamin Willingtons called Mehetabell

Y^e 18th of March 1687/8 a child of Joſeph Grant called Sarah

Y^e 8th of Aprill 1688 2 young Pſons who owned ye covenant, viz William & Hannah Sanderſon, ye children of William Sanderſon

Y^e 15th of Aprill 1688 7, viz 4 of Stephen Cooks called Stepheen, Iſaac, John, & Mary. John Parkis child called Samuell. & Samuell Bigulows child called Abigaill, & Nathanaell Fiſks child called Lydia

Y^e 22 of Aprill 1688 a child of John Winters called Sarah

Y^e 29th of Aprill 1688 3 viz a child of Benj. Pearſe called Sarah, & one of Martin Townſends called Jonathan, & one of young John Warrens called Jonathan

Y^e 6th of May 1688 4, (viz) a child of Sam. Thacher called Anna, one of James Begulow's called James, one of Henery Springs called Lidia, & one of Jeremy Moſse called Jonathan

Y^e 20th of May 1688 3 children, a child of Samuell Jenniſons called Lidia, & 2 of Sarah Sanderſons (ye wife of William Sanderſon) who owed ye Covenant, viz Joſeph & Lidia

Y^e 17th of June 1688 3 children & a Melotto, a child of Tho. Cutler called Jonathan, a child of Tho. Hammond called Elizabeth, & a child of Comfort Starrs of Dedham called Lidia—& Melotto called Walter Taylor, living wth Capt. Wade living at Miſtick

Y^e 24th of June 1688 I baptized a child of Jon. Stimſon called Joſeph

Y^e 8th of July 1688 2 children, viz one of Theophilus Philips called Theophilus, & one of John Aplins called Mehetabell

[200] Blank.

[201] Such as were baptized in Watertown 1688

Y^e 29th of July 1688 a child of Jonathan Tanters called Joſeph

Y^e 19th of Aug. 1688 2 children, viz one of my Brother Thomas Bayly's called Thomas, & one of John Chinery's called Sarah

Y^e 26th of Auguſt 1688 a child of Joſeph Garfield called Grace

Y^e 2^d of Sept, 1688 a child of John Bond's called Sarah

Y^e 14th of October 1688 a child of Joſeph Maſon called Joſeph

Y^e 21th 1688 a child of John Tuſte's of Miſtick called Mary, both he & his wife owned ye Covenant

Y^e 25th of November 1688 a child of John Fifk called Jonathan
Y^e 9th of December 1688 a child of Joseph Willingtons called Mary
Y^e 23 of December 1688 a child of William Jones called Caleb
Y^e 6th of January 1688/9 a child of Jofiah Tredway's called Severanna
Y^e 13th of January 1688/9 Mary Sanderfon ye daughter of William Sanderfon, fhe owned ye Covenant
Y^e 27th of January 1688/9 a child of Stephen Cooke called James
Y^e 3^d of February 1688/9 a child of John Knops called John
Y^e 3^d of March 1688/9 11 children, viz one of Philip Shattucks called Nathanaell, one of Tho. Harringtons called Sufannah, 4 of Ifaac Fox his children (of Miftick) called Ifaac, John, Abigaill, & Samuell, & 5 of John Beamis (who acknowledged his fin in ye publick, & owned ye Covenant both he & his wife) called Jofeph, John, Sufannah, Bethia, & Mary
Y^e 10th of March 1688/9 2 children, viz one of Nathanaell Whitneys called Hannah, & of George Adams called John
Y^e 17th of March 1688/9 Danyell Benjamins child called Danyell
Y^e 31th of March 1689 a child of Michaell Flegs called Michaell
Y^e 7th of Aprill 1689 5 children, viz one of Jonathan Coollidge called Jonathan, one of Nathanaell Bright's called John, one of Thomas Chadwicks called Danyell, one of Jonathan Smiths called Elizabeth, & one of Samuell Shattucks called Samuell

[202] Blank.

[203] Such as were baptized by me in Watertown in N. E.
1689

Y^e 14th of Aprill 1689 2, viz a child of Danyell Harringtons called Jonathan, & a young woman one Sarah Grant who lived at Mrs Shermans, fhe owned ye Covenant
Y^e 21st of Aprill 1689 a child of Abraham Gales called Marah
Y^e 28th of Aprill 1689 a child of Enoch Satle called Richard
Y^e 12^t of May 1689 a child of widdow Hannah Bifco's who owned ye Coven^t (her hufband Tho. Bifcoe being lately dead) called Thomas
Y^e 14 of July 1689 6 children, viz one of John Chadwicks called Benjamin, one of Francis Bowmans called John, one one of Jonathan Sanders called Hannah, one of widdow Gales (viz Johns) called Alfah, one of Ephraim Beamis called James, & one of Allen Fleggs called Mary
Y^e 28 of July 1689 a child of young John Strattens (who owned ye covenant) called John
Y^e 4th of Auguft 1689 a child of Jonathan Philips called Sarah
Y^e 18th of Auguft 1689 6 children, viz 4 of Ephraim Cutters (who owned ye covenant) viz Ephraim, Jonathan, Bethia, & Mary, a child of Muning Sawings called John, & one of Jofeph Childs called John

Y^e 1st of September 1689 3, viz a child of Jofeph Shermans called Martha, & a child of young John Warrens called Danyell, & a young woman y^t lives wth Philip Shattucks called Elizabeth Danyells, fhe owned ye Covenant.

Y^e 8th of September 1689 a grand child of ye wife of Ellis Barron called Benoni, his Father lives at Sherburn, viz Mofes Adams

Y^e 6th of October 1689 one child, of David Churche's called Sarah

Y^e 13 of October 1689 one child, of John Deex called Jane

Y^e 20th of Oct. 1689 a child of Danyell Stone called Hannah— tho I feare in haft I called Joannah

Y^e 27th of October 1689 a child of Jofeph Grout called Mehetabell

Y^e 3^d of November 1689 a child of Jofhuah Biggulo's called Jabez

Y^e 24th of November 1689 4 children, viz 3 of Thomas Smiths (who owned ye covn^t here as he had don formerly at Concord) called Samuell, Jofeph, & Benjamin, & one of William Price called William, his wife a member at Brantry

[204] Blank.

[205]

Such as were baptized by me in Watertown in 1689, & alfo 1690

Y^e 1st of December 1689 a child of Ifaac Foxe's called Ebenezer

Y^e 22 of December 1689 a child of John Fifks called Jonathan

Y^e 19th of January 1689/90 4 children of ye wife of Samuell Perrye (who owned ye Covenant) 3 of them by this hufband, called Samuell, John, & Ebenezer, & ye other by a former hufband (fhe being of yeares tho young owned ye Covn^t alfo) called Hefter Comye

Y^e 2^d of March 1689/90 a child of John Harringtons called Lidia

Y^e 30th of March 1690 a child of John Bacons called John

Y^e 13 of Aprill 1690 3 children, one of Jofeph Underwoods called Hannath, one of William Shattuck called Mary, & one of Mr Prouts called Eunice

Y^e 20th of Aprill 1690 3 children, one of Samuel Biggulo's called Ifaac, one of Nathanall Fifks called Mary, & one of young Nathanaell Coolidge (who owned folemnly & publickly ye Covenant) called Lidia

Y^e 18th of May 1690 a child of Jofeph Grant called Jofeph

Y^e 25th of May 1690 3 children, one of Jofiah Jones called Ifaac & 2 of young Richard Norcrofse (he & his wife Rofe publickly took fhame for their gr^t fin   I might have written this & many other things as y^t of Sarjeant Barnards, Nat, Holland, & other things by themfelves but w^t I write is only for myfelf & not others) called Richard, & y^o other Samuell

Y^e 22th of June 1690 7 children, viz one of young John Winters (who owned ye Coven^t) called Hannah, & 5 of Judith Stearnes (ye wife of John Stearnes, she was baptized by Mr Sherman at yeares of discretion, & I suppofed owned ye Coven^t) called George, Benjamin, Rebekah, Judith & Sarah, & one of Mary Earle's (who were baptized by me & y^n owned ye Covenant) called Mary
Y^e 6th of July 1690 3 children, viz one of John Bonds called Danyell, one of Jonas Bonds (who owned ye Covenant) called Sarah, & a child of one Stars of Dedham (I have formerly baptized some of hers) called Hannah
Y^e 13 of July 1690 3 children viz one of Theophilus Philips called Jonathan, one of John Haftings called William, & one of John Tufts called John
Y^e 27 of July 1690 2 children, viz one of young William Bonds called Marah, & one of Ephraim Cutters called Hannah

[206] Blank.

[207] Such as were Baptized by me in Watertown N. E. 1690.

Y^e 10th of Aug. 1690 one child (viz) of Abr-ham Pearfe, (he & his wife Ifabell came over wth me out of Ireland. I maryed them in Bofton, he was in church comunion) called Samuell. ye live at Salem
Y^e 28th of Sept. 1690 2 children viz one of Samuell Thachers called Marath, & one of Jonathan Stimfons called Benjamin
Y^e 23 of November 1690 5 children, viz one of Samuel Livermore's called Anna, one of Lt Ben. Garfields called Samuel, one of Tho. Hammonds called David, one of Danyel Benjamin's called John, & one of Nathanael Bonds called John
Y^e 30th of November 1690 2 children one of Mr Gafkell's called John, & one of Mary Flege called Marah, it was by Benjamin Davis
Y^e 7th of December 1690 3 children, viz one of Tho. Bonds called Mary, one of young Stephen Cooks called Samuel, & one of Abiah Leafons called Ifaac
Y^e 4th of January 1690/91 a child of Benjamin Willingtons called Jofeph
Y^e 1st of Feb. 1690/91 2 children one of Benjamin Fleggs called Benjamin, & one of John Chineryes called Elizabeth
Y^e 10th of May 91 2 children, one of Widdow Stratton's in ye woods called Samuel, ye other of Jonathan Smith's called Elifha
Y^e 17th of May 1691 10 children, one of Jonathan Coolidg called John, one of Jofiah Tredaways called Tabitha, one of Tho. Cutler's called Samuel, one of John Parkifse called Anna, one of Allen Fleggs called Allen, one of John Perryi's called Jofeph, one of young John Knops called James, one of John Whittamores, (she was of old a member of ye church at Yarmouth, of late at Charleftown, & now dwells where Amos Merritt did) called Daniel, one of Tho. Chadwick called Jonathan, & one of Nathanael Norcrofse (he folemnly owned ye Lords covenant) called Mehetabel

Y^e 24th of May 1691   4 children & a young woman, 3 children of Samuel Whitmore called Francis, Samuel, & Rebekah, one of Samuel Hagers called Sarah.   ye young woman was Abigail Fifk who owned ye Covenant

Y^e 31th of May 1691 5, 3 children of young John Mofse (formerly of Groton) called Elizabeth, John, & David.   one of Thomas Harringtons called Rebekah, & Mary Hawkins who folemnly owned ye Covenant

[208

Marriages Confummated p Henry Gibbs in Watertown

1697

Decr 7.   Francis Pearfe & Hannah Johnfon, both of Watertown were married in my Houfe

1698/9

Jan. 4.   The marriage of James Stimfon & Bethiah Manffield was confummated at ye Houfe of Deacon Barfham, both of Watert^n

18.   Benjamin Wellington & Lydia Brown, both of Watertown, were married att my Houfe

March. 10.   Timothy Barron and Rachel Jenifon were joined in Marriage in my Houfe.   both of Watertown

21.   Jonathan Stimfon & Mehetabel Spring were Married att my Houfe both of s^d Town

1699

Apr. 11.   Charles Chadwick & Sarah Whitney, both of Watertown, were married in my Houfe

Nov. 2.   Samuell Jennifon and Mary Stearns, both of Watertown, were joyned in marriage att my Houfe

7.   John Holdin & Grace Jennifon, both of Watertown, were married by me in my Houfe

15.   The Marriage of Thomas Coolidge & Sarah Eddy was confummated att my Houfe

Att ye Same time, was ye Confummation of ye Marriage of Jonathan Stone and Ruth Eddy   all Four of Watertown

Decr 20.   Sam^{ll} Stratton & Sarah Perry were Married att his Fathers Houfe

Sam^{ll} Severns & Rebecca Stratton were Married at ye same time and place all belonging to Watertown

Jan. 2.   Henry Houghton of Lancafter, and Abigail Barron of Watertown, were married at my Houfe

16.   The Marriage of John Coolidge & Margaret Bond, both of Watert^n was confummated at my Houfe

1700

Apr. 2.   Ebenezer Allen & Elizabeth Eddy, both of Watertown, were married att my Houfe

4.   Samuell Barnard and Mary Sherman were married att Mrs Shermans Houfe; both of y^m belonging to Watertown

May. 2.	Samuell Jones and Mary Woolfon, both of Watertown, were married in my Houfe
Dec. 12.	Mr Hananiah Parker of Redding & Mrs Mary Bright of Watertown, were married, att her Houfe.
March 12.	The marriage of Richard Barnes Senr of Marlborough & Elizabeth Stimfon of Watertown, was Solemnized at my Houfe

1701

July. 10.	Sam^{ll} Haftings & Sarah Coolidge were marryed at Mr Nath^{ll} Brights Houfe, both of y^m of Watertown
Aug. 5.	Amos Waight & Elizabeth Cutting, both of Watert^n were Marry'd in my Houfe

[209]   Baptized p H Gibbs in Watertown

1697

Nov. 7.	William & Jonathan, fons of William Bond
	Samuell & Elizabeth, Children of Dan^{ll} Benjamin
	Sarah, the Daughter of Henry Spring
	George, the Son of Munnings Sawin
	John, the Son of John Stacy
14.	John, the Son of Richard Coolidge, who Owned ye Cov^t
	Ebenezer the son of John Chenery
	Hannah Barftow, who being adult owned ye Covenant
21.	Simon, Son of Isaac Stearns
28.	Elizabeth, Daughter of Sam^{ll} Hastings, who own'd ye Cov^t
Decr 12.	Ruth Maddock, Wife of John Maddock. She owning ye Cov^t
	Sarah, Daughter of Andrew White, who Own'd ye Covenant
Jan. 16.	Mercy, Daughter of Sam^{ll} Thacher

1698

Apr. 13.	John, Son of James Ball, his Wife owning the Coven
May 8.	Jonathan, Son of Abel Benjamin, He owned ye Cov^t
15.	Edward, Son of Edward Goddard, He owning ye Cov^t
June 5.	George, Son of George Lawrence
26.	Isaac, Son of Thomas Bond
July 10.	Nathaniell & John, Sons of Widow Mary Hastings, She own'd ye Cov^t
17.	Mehetabel, Daughter of Henry Spring
24.	Benjamin, Son of Nathaniell Bright
Aug. 28.	Joshua, Abigail, Elizabeth, children of Joseph Grant
	Jonathan, Robert, Sons of William Shattuck
	Abigail, Daughter of Obadiah Coolidge He owning ye Cov^t

	Oliver, Son of Daniel Livermore, He alſo owning yᵉ Covᵗ
Septʳ 18.	John Train junʳ who owned yᵉ Covᵗ
	Thomas, Margaret, Rebecka, Children of Jnᵒ Train Senʳ who own'd yᵉ covᵗ
	Abigail, Mary, Daughters of John Stratton junʳ
	Simon Beers, who own'd yᵉ covenᵗ
Oct. 2.	John, Ruth, Mary, Sarah, Children of John Maddock
	Curtis, Son of Mary Halloway
30.	Henry, Son of John Maddock
	Samuel, Son of Samuell Haſtings
	Joſeph, Son of Rachel Jenniſon
Nov. 13.	Joſeph, Joſiah, Sons of Jonathan Coolidge
20.	Mary, Daughter of Joseph Grant
Dec. 4.	Sarah, Daughter of Nathan Fiſk
25.	Deborah, Daughter of Thomˢ Train
Jan. 15.	Henry Knop, Adult & owning yᵉ Covᵗ
March. 5.	Isaac, Son of Joſeph Child
26.	Elizabeth, Daughter of Nathan Fiſk

1699

Apr. 30.	Richard, Son of Richard Coolidge
	Rachel, Daughter of Josiah Goddard, He owning yᵉ Covᵗ
May. 21.	Hephzibah, yᵉ Daughter of Deacon Bond
28.	Nathaniell son of John Stone, He owned yᵉ Covenᵗ
June. 11.	Abigail, Daughter of Widdow Anna Thare, She owning yᵉ Covᵗ
18.	Eſther, Elizabeth, Daughters of John Kinningham, He owning yᵉ Covᵗ
July. 9.	Margaret My third Daughter
	Mercy, the Daughter of Nicholas Wyeth
Sept. 10.	Lydia, Daughter of Daniell Benjamin
	Abigail, Daughter of Abel Benjamin
Oct. 8.	Lydia, Suſanna, Daughters of Samᵘˡ Holdin, He owning yᵉ Covᵗ
22.	Elizabeth, Daughter of James Ball
Dec. 3.	Sarah, Daughter of Samˡˡ Thacher
Feb. 11.	Samuell, Son of Munnings Sawin
	Lydia, Daughter of Obadiah Coolidge
25.	Suſanna, Daughter of Edward Goddard

[210] Blank.

[211]   Baptisms
1700

March. 31.	Samuell, Son of John Stacy
Apr. 7.	Francis, Son of Francis Pearſe
May. 19.	Mercy, Daughter of Nathaniell Bright
26.	Sarah, the Daughter of Samˡˡ Eddy
June. 30.	Timothy, Son of Timothy Barron

July. 28.	Mary, Daughter of Dan Livermore
Sept. 8.	Sarah, Daughter of Thomas Coolidge
22.	Abigail, Daughter of Nath{ll} Coolidge jun{r}
	Shadrach, Son of Jonathan Whitney
Oct. 27.	John, Son of John Wellington, He owning y{e} Cov{t}
Nov. 3.	Elizabeth, Daughter of George Lawrence
	John, Son of John Kinningham
10.	Samuell, Son of Sam{ll} Livermore, he own'd y{e} Cov
24.	Benjamin, Son of Sam{ll} Hastings
	Hannah, Daughter of Joseph Grant
Dec. 29.	Andrew, Son of Andrew White
Jan. 19.	Ebenezer, Son of Ebenezer King, He owned y{e} Cove{nt}
March. 2.	Abigaill, Daughter of John Chenery
16,	Caleb, Son of John Maddock
	Mary, Daughter of Sam{ll} Jenison, S{d} S. Jennison & his wife owned y{e} Cov{t}

1701

30.	Jabez, Son of John Stratton
Apr. 6.	Elizabeth, Daughter of Henry Spring
	Elizabeth, Daughter of Ebenezer Allen
	Elizabeth, Daughter of Sam{ll} Severns
	Bethiah, Daughter of James Stimson
	y{e} S{d} Severns with his wife & S{d} Stimson w{ith} his wife own'd y{e} Cov{t}
May 4.	Josiah, Son of Josiah Jones. He owned y{e} Cov{t}
June 22.	Sarah, Daughter of James Ball
July. 13.	Josiah, Son of Josiah Goddard
20.	Nathaniell, Son of Deacon William Bond
Aug. 3.	Jonathan, Son of Jonathan Whitney
17.	Sam{ll} son of Sam{ll} Eddy jun{r}
Oct. 5.	Samuell, son of Sam{ll} Holdin
26.	Patience, Daughter of Dan{ll} Benjamin
Nov. 16.	John, Sarah, Mary, Abigail, children of John Perry jun{r} He owning y{e} Covent
Dec. 7.	Rebecca, Daughter of Tho{s} Train
Jan. 25.	Caleb, y{e} Son of Abel Benjamin
Feb. 22.	Simon, y{e} Son of Edward Goddard
March 3.	Nathan, y{e} Son of Nathan Fiske
15.	Nathaniel, y{e} Son of Richard Coolidge
22.	Henry, y{e} first Son of y{e} Rev{d} M{r} Henry Gibbs

1702

29{th}	Sarah, y{e} Daughter of Caleb Grant, he owning y{e} Covenant
April. 19.	Sam{ll} y{e} Son of Ebenezer King
May. 31.	Henry, y{e} Son of Henry Houghton of Lancaster his wife Abigail owning y{e} Covenant
July y{e} 19.	Hannah, y{e} Dauter of Sam{ll} Jenison
26.	Daniel & Benjamin y{e} Sons of Sam{ll} Hastings

Augt 2. Peter ye Son of Timothy Barron
16. Hannah Priest was Baptized ſhe owning ye Covenant
Sep^t 6. Deborah, Daûter Munnings Sawin
20. Mercy, ye Daûter of Joſeph Grant
Octob. 4. Jonathan, ye Son of Jonathan Stone
11. Joanna, ye Daûter of John Maddocks
Nov. 1. Anna, ye Daûter of Jonathan Whitney, Palsgruve, ye Son of John Wellington, Hannah ye Daûter of Francis Peirce, & Abigail ye Daûter of James Ball
8. Tabitha, ye Daûter of Tho. Coollidge, & Abraham, ye Son of Jer. Mors
Decem. 6. Anna, ye Daûter of Daniel Livermore
20. William, ye Son of Andrew White

1703

Jan. 3. Rebecca, ye Daûter of John Chadwick
17. Matthew, ye Son of Sam^{ll} Livermore
31. James, ye Son of James Stimpſon
Feb. 28. John, ye Son of George Lawrence
March. 21. Mary, ye Daûter of Thos Spring
May. 2. Samuel, ye Son of Sam^{ll} Stratton, he owning ye Covenant
30. Elizabeth, ye Daûter of John Perry
June. 6. Jacob, ye Son of Jerim: Mors

[212 to 221 inclusive Blank.]

[222]

I was called to the work of the Miniſtry, by the Church & Congregation in the Eaſterly Precinct in Watertown, on February ye 3rd 1723/4. and was ſolemnly ſet apart to that work by prayer & the Impoſition of the hands of the Preſbytery on July 22nd 1724.

A Record of Baptiſms p Seth Storer.

1724

Augst 30. Jonathan, Son of Jonathan Brown
October. 4. Silas, Son of Henry Bright
Enoch Son of John Haſtings
Novr 8. Eliſha and Seth, Sons of George Harrington
15. Hannah, Daûter of Sam^{ll} Peirce
Eunice Daûter of John Haſtings
29. Priſcilla Daûter of John Phillips
Lydia, Daûter of David Sanger

1724/5

Jan^{ry} 10. Phinehas, Son of Thos Bond
24. Simon, Son of Richd Beers
John, Son of David Sanger
31. Daniel, Son of Oliver Livermore
Feb. 7. Hannah, Daûter of John Tainter
14. Mary Daûter of Henry Spring jun^r
21. Abigail, Daughter of George Lawrence Junr

March. 7. Obadiah, Son of Daniel Bond
Mofes Son of Jofhua warren Junr
14. Grace Daûter of George Cutting
Elizabeth Daûter of Daniel Stearns
28. Ann, Daûter of Nath^ll Bond

1725

May. 16. At Wells, Abigail Daûter of Jofeph Hill Junr
18. at Wells, it being Lecture Day, I baptized Jofeph, Son of Bro^r John Storer
June. 13. Jonathan, Son of Jofeph Holdin
July. 18. Mary Daûter of Ebenezer Chenery
Hannah Daûter of Sam^ll Hager
Sarah, Daû of Eben^r Stone
Sep^t 26. Mercy, Daûter of Thos Learned
Samuel, Son of Timothy Harris
Octo^r 10. Thomas, Francis, Sarah & Prifcilla, Children of Nath^ll Harris
Novr 14. Efther, Dauter of Jofeph Mafon
Ruth, Daûter of Jon^a Coollidge
21. Jon^a Son of widow Hannah Stone
Decr 5. Nathan, Son of Sam^ll Warren, in private

1725/6

Jan. 2. Samuel, Son of Sam^ll Parry
9. Lydia, Dauter of Obadiah Coollidge
Feb. 6. Elizabeth, Daûter of John Ormes
20. Lydia, Dauter of Eben^r Wellington
March. 6. Sarah, Dauter of Dan^ll Haftings

[223]

1726

May. 1. Elizabeth, Daûter of Jon^a Harrington
8. Mindwell, Daûter of Jon^a Benjamin Senr
Abijah, Son of Jabez Stratton
June 5. Mary, Dauter of John Phillips
12. Samuel, Son of And^r White Junr
Aug. 14. Jonas, Son of Jonas Bond
21. Amariah, Son of Thos. Learned
Sep^t 11. Stephen, Son of Daniel Sterns
18. At wells, Dauter of Gerfhom Balfton
Octr 2. Nathanael, Son of Nath^ll Bond
16. Jofhua, Son of Jofhua Warren Junr
30. Uriah, Son of Nath^ll Norcrofs
Novem^r 13. Hannah, Dauter of Eben^r Stone
20. Abraham, Son of Dan^ll Bond
27. Abraham, Son of Jon^a Brown
Decem^r 4. Benjamin, Son of John Stearns Senr
12. Hannah, Dauter of Thos Hamond, in private
25. Sarah, Dauter of Nath^ll Bright

1726/7

- Jan. 15. Elisha, Son of John Haftings
- Samuel, Son of Sam¹ Benjamin
- 22. Samuel, Son of Henry Spring Ju^r
- Feb^{ry} 12. Mary, Daûter of Benjamin Haftings, in private
- March. 5. Samuel, Son of Peter Oliver
- Joshua, Son of Joshua Grant
- 12. Mary, Daûter of Jofeph Coollidge
- 26. John, Son of John Maddock
- 19. Millefcient, Daûter of Henry Bright

1727

- April. 9. Abraham, Jonas, Edward & Joshua, fons of Edward Jackfon
- 23. Jofiah, Son of George Cutting
- May 28. Ruth Daûter of Oliver Livermore
- David, Son of David Sanger
- June. 11. Samuel, Son of Jon^a Stone Junr
- 25. Nathanael, Son of Nath^{ll} Norcrofs
- July. 9. At wells, Mercy, Daûter of Benjamin Hatch
- Augst 27. Stephen, Son of Daniel Haftings
- Mary, Dauter of Timothy Harris
- Sep^t 17. Oliver, Son of Sam^{ll} Stratton
- Octo^r 15. Nathaniel, Son of Nath^{ll} Clark
- 22. At Newton, Daniel Son of John Hamond
- Novr 5. Daniel, Son of John Sawen
- 12. Lydia, Dauter of Joseph Mafon
- Sarah, Dauter of George Harrington
- Decr 3. Abijah, Son of Thomas Bond, John, Son of John Dix, Submit, Kezia & Sarah, Dauters & Abijah, Son of Charles Chadwick, Elizabeth, Dauter of Hannah Cutler
- 31. Dorcas, Dauter of Jofiah Perry
- Eunice, Dauter of John Stratton

1727/8.

- Jan^{ry} 14. Abigail, Dauter of Caleb Benjamin
- 28. Benjamin, Son of George Lawrence Junr
- Feb. 4. Isaiah, Son of Dam^{ll} Stearns
- March. 24. Ruth, Daûter of And^r White Junr

1728

- May. 19. Ebenezer Son of Eben^r Nutting, Mofes, Son of John Stearns Junr, Abigail, Dauter of Eben^r Chenery
- June 2. Eunice, Daûter of George Cutting
- July. 14. Jofiah, Son of John Bond, Sufanna, Daûter of John Tainter, James, Son of John Stowel, in private
- Augst 11. Lucey, Daûter of John Coollidge
- 25. Elijah, Son of Jonas Bond
- Sep^t 8. Jonas, Son of Thomas Learned
- Daniel, Son of Benjamin Haftings
- 22. Thomas, Son, Martha & Ruth ye Daughters of Richard Clark

Octo' 6.	Jonathan, Son of Nath'' Bond
13.	Jonathan, Son of Jon" Benjamin Jun'. Josiah, Son of Nath'' Norcrofs, Nathan, Son of Jabez Stratton
20.	Margeret, Daûter of Eben' Stone
Nov' 3.	Hannah, Daûter of John Coollidge
	Nathaniel, Son of Isaac Child
10.	Ather, Son of John Haftings
24.	Ruth, Daûter of Sam'' Pierce
	Lydia, Daûter of Henry Spring Ju'
Decem' 8.	Nathaniel, Son of Nath'' Coollidge
22.	Benjamin, Son of Jofhua Warren Ju'
29.	Lydia, Daûter of Jofhua Grant Jun'

1728/9.

Feb. 9.	Prifcilla, Daûter of Nath'' Harris
	Sarah, Daûter of Jon" Benjamin Sen'
23.	Phebe, Palfrey was baptized, fhe having first owned y" Covenant
March. 23.	Jonas, Son of James Barnard, in private

1729.

March 30.	Sarah, Daûter of Sam'' Benjamin
	Mary, Daûter of John Dix
June. 1.	Caleb, Son of Caleb Benjamin was baptized by Rev. Emerfon, Malden.
29.	Jonathan, Son of John Fisk
July 6.	Mary & Rebecca, Daûters of Jon" Coollidge
Aug'' 3.	Mary, Daûter of William Ozment
17.	William, Son of David Sanger
	Mary Daûter of Sam'' Warren in private
23.	Rachel, Daûter of Oliver Livermore
	Lydia, Daûter of Jon" Brown
Sep' 14.	Mary Daûter of Nath'' Clark
28.	Sufanna, Daûter of Joseph Mafon
Nov' 16.	Josiah, Son of Jon" Stone Jun'
Dec' 14.	Abigail, Daûter of John Stratton

1729/30.

Feb. 8.	Amariah, Son of W'" Williams
	Anna, Daûter of Timothy Harris
March. 15.	Sarah, Daûter of John Bond
	Mary, Daûter of James Nutting

1730.

Aprill. 12.	Abijah, Son of John Sawen
	Peter, Son of Elizabeth Gibbins
19.	Jedidiah, Son of Henry Spring Jun' was baptized by Rev'' Jenifon
26.	Elizabeth, y" Daûter of Jos. Holdin was baptized by y" Rev'' Warham Williams
May. 3.	Mofes, Son of Eben' Biggelow
10.	Benjamin, Son of John Stowel

17. Josiah, Son of Nath{ll} Jenifon
    Thomas Bifhop having first owned y{e} Covent
31. Sufanna, Daûter of John Whitney

[225]

June. 7. William, Son of John Maddocks
         Sarah, & Martha, y{e} Daûters of And{r} White Jun{r}
     21. Jofeph, Son of Simon Coollidge
Aug{st} 9. Mercy, Daûter of Nath{ll} Norcrofs
Sep{t} 13. Mary, Daûter of Eleazer Biggelow
Oct{r} 11. William Son of   Shattuck dec{d}
     25. Elias, Son of Jabez Stratton
Nov{r} 1. Jerufha, Daûter of John Stearns Jun{r}
     15. Mary, Daûter of John Leppington
         John, Son of Eben{r} Chenery
     22. Samuel, Son of George Cutting
Dec{r} 6. Joanna, Daûter of John Tainter by Rev. M{r} Jenifon
     13. Abigail, Daûter of John Coollidge Jun.
         Abigail, Daûter of Nath{ll} Bond
     20. Sufanna, Daûter of Nath{ll} Coollidge

1730/1.

Jan{ry} 24. Mary, Daûter of Sam{ll} Benjamin
         William, Son of David Sanger
Feb. 7. Sarah, Daûter of John Haftings
    14. Elizabeth, Daûter of Tho{s} Dana of Cambridge
    21. Samuel, Son of Sam{ll} Peirce
        Ruth, Daûter of Jofhua Grant Jun{r}
March. 17. John, Son of John Whitney in private
       21. Elizabeth, Daûter of Edmund Dix

1731.

28. Peter, negro man of M{r} Jon{n} Stone, entered into Cov{t}
    & rec{d} baptifm
April. 11. Mary, Daûter of Nath{ll} Bright
           Mofes, Son of Isaac Child
       18. Kezia, Daûter of Caleb Benjamin
       25. Benjamin, Son of Nath{ll} Harris
           Mary, Daûter of John Maddocks
May. 16. Elizabeth, Daûter of Jofhua Learned
     23. Thomas, Son of David Learned,
         Elizabeth, Daûter of Nath{ll} Jenifon
June. 6. Daniel, Son of Jon{a} Benjamin
         Hopestill, Son of Eben{r} Biggelow
July. 4. Benjamin, Son of Benjamin Haftings
     18. Mary, Daûter of Daniel Bond
Aug{st} 1. Elijah, Son of Jofhua Warren Jun{r}, Lydia, Daûter
           of John Dix, Martha, Dauter of Sam{ll} Dix
       1. Mary, Betty & Martha, Dauters of Nath{ll} Sherman
      15. Kezia, Dauter of Eben{r} Stone
          Ifaac, Son, & Sarah, Dauter of Isaac Barnard

Sep^t 12. Mary, Dauter of Oliver Livermore
    19. Abel, Son of Sufanna Benjamin
Octr 17. Jonathan, Son of Jon^a Learned
    24. Benjamin, Son of Nath^{ll} Clark, by Rev. Mr Cotton
Novr 21. Hannah, Dauter of Jonas Bond
Decr 12. Abigail, Dauter of Jonathan Brown

1731/2.

Jan^{ry} 2. Lydia, Dauter of Simon Coollidge
    16. Hannah, Dauter of And^r White Junr
March. 5. Ebenezer, Son of Jofeph Mafon

1732.

Aprill. 16. John, Son of Henry Spring Junr
    23. At Wefton, Jonathan, Son of Abijah Upham
    30. Jonathan, Son of John Whitney

[226]

May. 7. at Marlborough, Mary, Dauter of James Brown
    14. Efther, Dauter of William Williams
    21. James, Son of Ruth Underwood
June. 18. at Wells, Reuben, Son of Daniel Chaney
July. 16. Richard, Son of Richard Clark
    23. Uriah, Son of Nath^{ll} Norcrofs
       Mary, Dauter of Edward Harrington Junr
Augs^t 6. Robert, Son of Jofhua Learned
    13. Martha, Dauter of William Goddin
       John, Son of John Tainter
Sep. 3. Silence, Dauter of Eben^r Biggelow
    24. William, Son of Edmund Dix
Octr 8. Eliakim, Son of Samuel Gearfield
       John, Son of John Stratton
    29. Elizabeth, Dauter of John Haftings
       Sufanna, Dauter of John Bond
Novr 5. Samuel, Son of Eben^r Thatcher
    26. Abijah, Son of Timothy Harris
Decr 10. Mary, Dauter of Jonathan Bond
    31. Hezekiah, Son of John Stowel
       Ezekiel, Son of Sam^{ll} Stearns Junr

1732/3

Feb. 4. Elizabeth, Dauter of Nath^{ll} Bond
    18. Anna, Dauter of Sam^{ll} Benjamin
       Daniel, Son of John Coollidge Junr
       Amariah, Son of Jon^a Learned
    25. Elizabeth, Dauter of Ruth Brown
March. 25. John, Son of Adam Pattefon
       David, Son of David Learned
       Hannah, Dauter of Benj^a Haftings.

1733.

April. 15. Hannah, Dauter of Nath^{ll} Harris
Joshua, Son of Eleazer Biggelow
29. Joseph, Son and } of Eben^r Hastings
Ruth & Hannah Dauters }
May. 13. Abigail, Dauter of John Brown
27. Abigail, Dauter of John Dix
July. 22. Mary, Dauter of Benj^a Whitney Junr
29. Thaddeus, Son of Nath^{ll} Warren
Augst 5. Mary, Dauter & } of Dan^{ll} Stearnes
Daniel, Son }
19. Rachel, Dauter of Oliver Livermore
Lydia, Dauter of And^r White Junr
Mary, Dauter of Sam^{ll} Stratton
Sep^t 16. At Newton, Abigail, Dauter of   Murdock
Nov. 4. Nathaniel, Son of David Sanger
Moses, Son of Edwd Harrington Junr
18. Isaac, Son of Dan^{ll} Bond
Lois, Dauter of Simon Coollidge
Decr 9. Ruth, Dauter of Daniel Stearns

1733/4.

Jan^{ry} 13. Jonas, Son of Josiah Reed
Feb. 17. Elizabeth, Dauter of Joshua Warren Junr
24. William, Son of Jonas Bond
Benoni, Son of Richard Clark
Sarah, Dauter of Eben^r Thatcher

1734.

Aprill. 14. George, Son of David Mc Connoughey
Eunice, Dauter of Isaac Child

[227]

May. 26. Abraham & Elijah, Sons of Eb^r Biggelow
June. 5. Lucey, Dauter of Jon^a Brown
23. David, Son of John Fisk
Ebenezer, Son of Eb^r Chenery
30. Josiah, Son of Nath^{ll} Norcross
July 14. Joseph, Son of Allen Brown
21. At Newton, Rachel, Dauter of Thos Fuller
Augst 4. Thomas & Fanning, Sons of Jon^a Learned
Sep^t 1. Ann, Dauter of John Tainter
Octr 13. Josiah, Son of Jos. Mason
17. Samuel, Son of Henry Bond jun^r
20. Mary, Dauter of Nath^{ll} Coollidge
Novr 10. Phinehas, Son of William Williams
Amos, Son of John Whitney
Samuel, Son of Sam^{ll} Jenison
17. Ephraim, Son of John Craft
Elizabeth, Dauter of Edmund Livermore

	Joseph, Son of Jos. Wellington
Dec' 1.	Sarah, Daughter of Jabez Stratton
22.	Seth, Son of Nath'l Bond
	Elizabeth, Dauter of Joshua Learned

1734/5.

Jan'y 5.	Convers, Son of Henry Spring Jun'
12.	At Menotomy 3 Three Children
	Hubert, Son of David Dunster
	Abraham, Son of Zecharias Hill
	Jason, Son of Bathrick
26.	William, Son of Thos. Saltmarsh
Feb. 2d	At Camb. Villige, Sarah, Dauter of John Ellis
9.	Jerusha, Dauter of John Stowel
	Jedediah, Son of And' White Jun'
	Phineas, Son of Josiah Stearns
16.	Sarah, Dauter of Sam'l Benjamin
	Mary, Dauter of Jon'a Benjamin
	Adam, Son of Adam Patterson
	Jonathan, Son of Stephen Sawen
	Lethie, Dauter of Margaret Wason
March. 2.	At Menotomy three children
	Aaron, Son of Jason Winship
	Joseph, Son of Ebenezer Swan
	Jonathan, Son of George Cutter

1735.

30th.	William Murch owned the Covenant, & Lydia his Dauter & Mercy, Dauter of Mercy Stratton & Simon, Son of Benjamin Hastings were baptized
May 25.	Edward, Son of Edw'd Harrington Jun'
June. 29.	Stephen, Son of Nath'l Harris
	Susanna, Dauter of Sam'l Barnard

[228]

July. 6.	Stephen, Son of John Dix
20th	Oliver, Son of Oliver Livermore
27th	Lucey, Dauter of David Learned
Sep' 21st	Sarah, Dauter of John Hastings
	Samuel Stearns Jun' owed y'e Coven'
Octob' 12th	Jonathan Barnard & Hannah Barnard own'd y'e Coven'
19th	Jonathan Son of Jon'a Barnard
26th	Abigail & Lydia, Dauters of Jos. Crackbone
	Sarah, Dauter of Sam'l Stearns Jun'
Nov' 2.	Thomas Wellington & Margaret Wellington owned y'e Cov'
16th	James, Son of James Barnard
Dec' 7th	William Lawrence & Mary Lawrence owned y'e Coven'
	Abraham, Son of John Whitney

14th Thomas, Son of Thos. Wellington Junr
21st Samuel, Son of William Lawrence

1735/6

Jan. 4. Mary, Dauter of Eb^r Thatcher
Isaac, Son of Isaac Stearns } were baptized at Weſt
Anne Dauter of Sam^ll Fiſk } Chh by S. S.
Fey^ry 15. Nathaniel, Son of Daniel Stearns
29. Phebe, Dauter of Jon^a Barnard
March. 14. Elizabeth, Dauter of Thos Wellington.

1736

April. 25th Jonathan, Son of Jonathan Bond
June. 6th. Samuel, Son of David Sanger
13th. Abigail Sawen owned ye Coven^t
July 4th. John Sawen Junr owned ye Covenant
Elijah, Son of Joſhua Warren Junr
Silas, Son of John Coollidge were baptized
Aug^st 15th. Thomas, Son, & Martha Dauter of Jos. Harrington
Jonathan Church & Thankful Church owned ye Coven^t
29. Hannah, Sarah & Ruth, Dauters of Rich^d & Ab. Sawtle
Benjamin, ye Son of Benjamin Whitney
Sep^t 5. Mary, Dauter of Jon^a Church
19. Simon & Daniel, Sons }
Joanna, Abigail, Mary } of Daniel Whitney
Dorothy, Dauters }
William, Son of Wm Murch
Samuel, Son of Stephen Sawen
Ruth, Dauter of Eb^r Cheany in private
Oct^o 3^d. Samuel, Son of Edmund Livermore
Jedediah, Son of Jon^a Learned
17. Ruth & Elizabeth, Dauters of Jo^s Harrington
31. William, Son of William Godding Junr
10th Abigail, Dauter of Sam^ll Jeniſon
Nov' 21. Annah, Dauter of Simon Coollidge
28. Abijah, Son of Jon^a Brown
Decr 12. Lucy, Dauter of Andrew White jun^r
19. Jabez, Son of Eleazer Biggelow
Elizabeth Sawen owned ye Coven

[229]

1736/7

Jan^ry 23rd Jonas, Son of Benj^a Haſtings
Ephraim Perry owned the Covenant
Feb^ry 6th Martha, Dauter of Sam^ll Haſtings
20. Anna, Dauter of John Stearns
Jonas, Son of Joſiah Stearns
27. Bathſheba, Dauter of Eb^r Swan of Cambridge

March. 6th		Sarah, Dauter of Henry Spring Jun'r
		Jemima, Dauter of John Stowell
		Thomas, Son of Tho's Saltmarsh
	20.	Samuel, Son of John Tainter

1737

	27.	Nehemiah, Son of Caleb Fuller of Newton
April. 3rd		Catharine, Dauter of Jonas Bond
		Elizabeth, Dauter of John Bond
		Joshua, Son of Daniel Whitney
May. 22nd		Fullam, Son of Nath'll Harris
June. 12th		Beulah, Dauter of Edw'd Harrington
	19.	Samuel, Son of Sam'll Barnard
July. 3rd		Jesse, Son of William Williams
	24.	Sarah, Dauter of John Lawrence
	31.	Amos, Son of Oliver Livermore
		Mercy, Dauter of Joshua Learned
August. 7.		Elizabeth Benjamin owned ye Cove't
		Rachel, Dauter of Eliza Benjamin
	14.	Samuel, Son of Sam'll Benjamin
		Elisha, Son of David Learned
	28.	Ebenezer, Son of Eb'r Thatcher
Sep't 4.		Jonathan, Son of John Dix
		Rebecca, Dauter of Jos'e Wellington
	11th	Samuel Clark owned ye Covenant
		Samuel, Son of Sam'll Clark
Octo. 16.		Thomas Quiner & Sarah Quiner owned ye Cove't
Nov'r 6th		Eliza Bright owned ye Cove't
		Josiah Son } of Jos'e & Eliza Bright
		Elizabeth, Dauter }
	27.	Jonathan Child & Elizabeth his Wife owned ye Cove't
		Anna, Dauter of Jonathan Church
		John, Son of Tho's Wellington Jun'r
		Sarah, Dauter of Tho's Quiner

1737/8

Jan'ry 8		William, Son of Jonathan Benjamin
		Elizabeth, Dauter of Jon'a Child
	29th	Pero, negro of Cap't Bowman owned ye Cove't & was baptized

[230]

Feb. 12.		Francis, Son of Benj'a Dana of Cambridge
	19	Joseph Whitney & Mary his wife owned ye Cove't
		Samuel, Son of Stephen Sawen
		Flemming, Son of Jon'a Barnard
March. 5th.		Sarah Tom, an Indian Woman owned ye Covenant & was baptized
		Abigail, Dauter of Jos. Bright
	19th	Joseph, Son of Jos. Whitney
		Lydia, Dauter of Sam'll Prentis

1738

26. Peter Stears, Mary Tainter & Mary Bemis owned y[e] Coven[t]
April. 9. Margaret, Dauter of Sarah Tom, by Rev. M[r] Cotton
16. Mary, Dauter of Nath[ll] Norcrofs
John, Son of Tho[s] Bifco
Sarah, Dauter of John Steward
30. Elizabeth Berry entred into Coven[t] & was baptized
May. 28. Samuel, Son of Eb[r] Biggelow
July. 16. Pegg, Molatto Serv[t] of Oliver Livermore entred into Cov[t] & rec[d] Baptifm
August. 13. Sarah, Dauter of Simon Coollidge
20. Abigail, Dauter of And[r] White jun[r]
Sept. 3rd Sufanna, Dauter of Thos Wellington
Mofes, Son of John Whitney
24th Eunice, Daughter of George Lawrence
October. 22nd William, Son of Jon[a] Learned
Nov. 5th Sarah, Dauter of John Brown
Dec[r] 3rd John, Son of Tho[s] Saltmarfh
31. Henry, Son of Daniel Whitney
Jofiah, Son of Edmand Livermore

1738/9

Feb[ry] 4. Jonathan Coollidge, Son of W[m] Godding
11. Efther, Dauter of John Hoar
Rebecca, Dauter of Benj[n] Whitney
18. Samuel, Son of Nath[ll] Coollidge
25. Mary, Dauter of Eben[r] Swan
John, Son of Zechariah Hill
March. 11. Mary, Dauter of Benj[n] Haftings
25. Jofiah, Son of John Bowman of Lexington

1739

April 15. Mary Sawen, & Lydia Sawen owned y[e] Covent
29th Ann, Dauter of Ephraim Cooke ⎫
Philemon, Son of Jofeph Winship ⎬ at Menotomy by S. S.
Mary, Dauter of Jofeph Robbins ⎭
May. 13. Alpheus, Son of Henry Spring Jun[r]
Anna, y[e] Dauter of Oliver Livermore
Abigail & Mercy, Dauters of W[m] Lawrence
20. Zachariah, Son of Jof. Morfe, at Newton by S. S.
David, Son of James Barnard, by Rev[d] M[r] Cotton
27. Jemima, Dauter of John White
June. 10. Elijah, Son of John Coollidge
17. Mary, Dauter of David Learned

[231]

July. 1. Mary, Dauter of David Coollidge
8. Sufanna, Dauter of Eb[r] Thatcher
29. Sarah, Dauter of Daniel Stearns
Samuel, Son of Samuel Stratton

Sept. 2. John, Son of John Veleau
Elizabeth, Dauter of Sam^ll Benjamin
Oct° 21. John, Son of Eb^r Chenery
28. Abigail, Dautr of John Stearns
Nov. 4. Noah, Son of Joſh. Warren Junr by Rev. Warham Williams
18. Samuel, Son of Sam^ll Stearns

1739/40

Feb. 3. Thomas, Son of Jon^a Bond by Rev. Mr Cooke
17. Paul, Son of Joſhua Learned
Benjamin, Son of Stephen Sawen
March. 9. Aſa, Son of Nath^ll Norcrofs
Sarah, Dauter of Jon^a Bemis
Grace, Dauter of Edwd Harrington
John, Son of John Gleaſon
16. Sarah, Daughter of John Sawen Junr
23. Eunice, Dauter of Simon Coollidge
Mary, Dauter of Chriſtopher Grant

1740

30. Jonathan, Son of Sam^ll Hager
David, Son of John Stowel
Dorcas, Dauter of Joſeph Wellington
Dorothy Gleaſon owned ye Covenant
April. 6. Daniel, Son of John Maddock
Joſiah, Son of Edmund Livermore
Lydia, Dauter of Jon^a Church
May 11. Abigail, Dauter of Thos. Saltmarsh
27. Abigail Godding owned ye Covenant
June. 1. Ann, Dauter of Eleazer Bigelow, by Rev. Mr Cooke
Aaron, Son of Sam^ll Swan } at Menotomy
Samuel, Son of Nehemiah Cutter } by S. S.
20. Joſiah, Son of Thos Biſco
Noah, & Aaron, Sons of Benj^a Chadwick
Aug^st 17. Solomon, Son of David Sanger
24. Iſrael Meed owned ye Covenant
Sept. 14. Mary, Dauter of Thos Quiner
Novr 23. Jonas, Son of Hephzibah Steward
30. Ephraim, Son of Ephraim Winſhip, at Menotomy by S. S.

1740/1

Jan^ry 4. Anna, Dauter of John Brown
Samuel, Son of James Grimes
11. Benjamin, Son of Benj^a Dix
25. David, Son of Joſeph Whitney, by R^d Mr Cotton
Efther, Daughter of Jon^a Edmunds, at Newton by S. S.
March. 1. Aaron, Son of Ephraim Cooke, at Menotomy by S. S.

1741

April. 5. Elizabeth, Dauter of Sam^ll Prentice
12. Ezekiel, Son of John Whitney
Hannah, Daughter of Sam^ll Barnard
Josiah, Son of Jonathan Barnard

[232]

April. 12. Ebenezer Bullard } owned the Covenant
Samuel Coollidge
19. Abigail, Dauter of Oliver Livermore
26. Joanna, Dauter of Wm Godding Junr
Hannah, Dauter of Jon^a Learned
May. 3. Andrew, Son of Andrew White Junr
10. Hannah Tainter owned ye Covenant
24. Arminna, a negro Woman owned the Covenant
31. David Gleason owned the Covenant
June. 7. William, Son of Wm Lawrence
Ruth Livermore owned the Covenant
14. Dorcas Perry owned the Covenant
28. Ephraim Mailet & Robert Crowell entered into Cov
& were baptized
Daniel Livermore, Bethiah Bond & Abigail Bond
owned ye Cov^t
Mary, Dauter of Sam^ll Jenison
July 5. Sarah, Dauter of David Coollidge
Jonathan Stone Junr, Lois Stearns
Anna Stearns, Abigail Sawtle } owned y^e
Sarah Harrington & Abigail Whitney } Covent
12. Daniel Peirce, Jos Child jun^r, Moses Stone
& Hannah Hastings
19. John Cooke, Benjamin Hastings } owned ye Cov^t
Henry Sawtle, Ann Bond
Elizabeth, Dauter of Sam^n Cooke
Mary, Dauter of Sam^n Child
26. Avres, Son of John Tainter
Abigail, Dauter of Eb^r Goddard
Grace Bond, & Jerusha Bond owned ye Covenant
Aug^st 2. Seth Hastings owned ye Covenant
16. Israel, Son of Daniel Whitney
Anthony, a molatto entered into Cov^t & was baptized
Abijah Stearns, Hannah Godding owned ye Covenant
Octr 4. Samuel, Son of John Dix
11. Isaac, son of Jsaac Sanderson
25. Joshua, Son of Josiah Perry Junr
Nov. 1. Hepzibah, Dauter of John Stearns
Decr 27. John, Son of Sam^ll Nutting

1741

May. 29. Joseph Coollidge was chosen to the office of a Deacon

[233]

1741/2

Jan^ry 3^d. Simon, Son of Simon Coollidge
    10. William, Son of Benj^a Haftings
        Sarah, Dauter of David Learned
    17. Jonathan, Son of Edwd Harrington
    31. Elitha Biggelow and Mary Biggelow owned ye Covenant
Feb. 7. Nehemiah, Son of Nathl^l Norcrofs
    21. Hannah Sawen owned ye Covenant
    28. Marfhall, Son of Henry Spring Junr
        Eunice, Dauter of Jon^a Bond

1742

April. 11. Lydia, Dauter of Sam^ll Benjamin
    25. Samuel, Son of Benj^a Whitney
May. 9. Katherine, Dauter of John Hunt
June. 13. At Newton, Mofes, Son of Thos. Parker
July. 4. William, Son of Eb^r Chenery, by R^d War. Williams
    11. Sarah, Dauter of Sam^ll Stratton
Aug^st 1. David, Son of Benj^a Dix
    8. Peter, Son of Josiah Stearns
Sep^t 5. At Wefton, Ruth, Dauter of Thos Upham
        Ruhamah, Son of Jofiah Wellington
    12. Anna, Dauter of John Velau
        Deborah, Dauter of Thos Saltmarfh
Octr 10. Joseph Mafon Junr owned the Covenant
        Rachel, Dauter of Eb^r Goddard
        Daniel, Son of John Coollidge
        Grace, Dauter of Jof Mafon Junr
    31. At Lexington Betty, Dauter of Daniel Tidd
Nov. 28. John, Son of Stephen Sawen
Decr 5. Mary, Dauter of Jof Wellington

1742/3.

Jan^ry 9. Stephen, Son of Sam^ll Cooke
    16. Ebenezer, Son of Eb^r Thatcher
        Abigail, Dauter of Jon^a Church
Feb. 6. Mary, Dauter of Daniel Searns
    13. At Newton, Elifabeth Dauter of Michael Jackfon

1743

March. 27. Jonathan, Son of Oliver Livermore
        Eunice, Dauter of Andrew White
April. 10. Lydia, Dauter of Daniel Whitney
        Cornelius, Son of Aaron Brown
    17. Jerufha, Dauter of Jona Learned
        Jonathan, Son of Jos. Whitney, by Revd. W. Williams
May. 29. Jacob Caldwell owned the Covenant
June. 5. Lydia, Dauter of David Sanger
        John, Son of Jacob Caldwell

July. 3. Edmund, Son of Jon^a Barnard
10. Margaret, Dauter of John Clark ⎱ at Newton
Mary, Dauter of Jon^a Trowbridge ⎰ by S. S.
24. Elifabeth, Dauter of Daniel Bond

[234]

Augst 7. James Hackleton owned the Covenant
Stephen, Son of John Whitney
John, Son of James Hackleton
Jofiah, Son of Isaac Sanderson
21. Nathan, Son of Benj^a Hastings, by Rev. W. Williams
28. Mary Chenery owned ye Cov^t & Mary her Dauter was baptized
Sep^t 4th Jofiah, Son of Jofiah perry Junr, by Rev. War. Williams
Oct^o 2. Phineas, Son of Sam^{ll} Jenifon
9. Mary, Dauter of David Coolidge
16. Jofiah & Ebenezer, Sons of Eb. Goddard
30. Mary, Dauter of John Beath
Nov. 13. Hepzibah, Dauter of Simon Coollidge
Decr 11. Phineas, Son of Edward Harrington
18. Abigail, Dauter of Jofh. Learned

1743/4

Jan^{ry} 8. Jonas Coollidge, James Dix & Sarah Dix owned the Coven^t
Oliver, Son of David Learned
Sarah, Dauter of James Dix
22. Lucy, Dauter of Sam^{ll} Clark ⎱ at Camb. Village
Sarah, Dauter of Jon^a Fefsenden ⎰ by S. S.
Feb. 5. Chriftopher, Son of Chriftopher Grant
12. Jonas, Son of Jonas Coollidge
26. Sarah, Dauter of James Grimes, by Rev. War. Williams

1744

April. 8. Elifabeth, Dauter of Wm. Coollidge
22. Hannah, Dauter of Jofe Mafon Junr
May. 13. Katherine, Dauter of John Hunt
June. 3. Jonathan, Son of Abijah Wheeler at Wefton ⎱
10. Dorothy, Dauter of Jofiah Stearns ⎰
July. 8. Edward, Son of Edward Park at Newton
Augst 5. Peter, Son of Wm Godding Junr
Sept. 9. Mary, Dauter of Uriah Clark
16. Sarah, Dauter of Sam^{ll} Nutting
30. Sarah, Dauter of Gerfhom Cutter Junr at Menotomy
Octr. 14. John, Son of Benjamin Haftings Junr
21. Rebecca, Dauter of Jacob Caldwell
28. Samuel, Son of Nath^{ll} Coollidge
Grace, Dauter of Daniel Whitney
Novr. 4. Katherine, Dauter of Thos. Saltmarfh
11. Uriah Biggelow owned ye covenant

Dec.r 30. David Livermore & Abigail Livermore owned ye Covenant
Sufanna, Daûter of John Young

1744/5.

Jan.ry 20. Hepzebah, Dauter of John Hackleton
27. Samuel, Son of Wm Downe }
Samuel, Son of Alexander Thompfon } at Camb. Village by S. S. B.
March. 3. David, Son of Stephen Sawen }
Abigail, Daûter of David Livermore } by R^d War. Williams
17. Smith Prentice owned ye Cov^t
Benjamin, Son of f^d Prentice
24. Katey, Dauter of Sam^{ll} Benjamin

[235]   1745.

April. 7. Jofiah, Son of Thos Wellington
Margaret, Dauter of John Beath
21. John, Son of John Velau
May 26. Jofeph, Son of Daniel Bond
Elijah, Son of Andrew White
July. 14. Amos, Son of Amos Bond
Aug. 11. Anna, Daûter of James Dix
25. Hannah, Dauter of Sam^{ll} Stratton
Margaret, Daûter of Jos. Wellington
Sept. 1. Kezia, Daûter of Isaac Sanderfon
15. Cornelius, Son of Jon^a Barnard
Henry, Son of Henry Sawtle
Oct.r 20. Benjamin, Son of Jon^a Learned, by R. S. Cooke
27. Samuel, Son of John Hunt
Nov. 3. Elizabeth, Dauter of Eb^r Goddard
10. Ebenezer, Son of James Coollidge
Dec.r 8. Mofes, Son of Sam^{ll} Miller at Newton by S. S.
Sarah, Dauter of Eb^r Thacher, by R^d Mr Cotton
29. Elifha, Son of James Hackleton

1745/6.

Jan.ry 12. Nathaniel, Son of Oliver Livermore
Henry, Son of Benj^a Whitney Junr
19. Robert, Son of Sam^{ll} Cooke
Feb. 23. Benjamin, Son of Jofiah Shattuck
March. 2. Henry, Son of Henry & Sarah Bright
9. Daniel Sawen owned Covenant
23. Elifha, Son of Wm Wellington, at Menotomy by S. S.
Jefse, Son of David Learned, by R^d Mr Cooke

1746

30. Jonathan, Son of John Dix
April. 13. Aaron, Son of John Whitney, in private
20. Lucy, Dauter of Sam^{ll} Jenifon
Hepzibah, Dauter of David Coollidge

27.	Sufanna, Dauter of Josiah Stearns
May. 4.	Jennet, Dauter of Wm Fullerton
June. 8.	William, Son of John Tainter
15.	Jofiah, Son of Benj^a Whitney
July. 6.	Mary, Dauter of Henry Spring Tertius
27.	Martha, Dauter of James Cutler, at Menotomy by S. S.
	Sufanna, Dauter of Nath^{ll} Norcrofs, by R^d Mr Cooke
Augst. 10.	Uriah, Son of Uriah Clark
24.	Sarah, Dauter of Jos. Mafon Junr
Sep^t. 14.	Elifabeth, Dauter of Jos. Kelly
Nov. 2.	Hannah, Dauter of Bezaleel Learned
16.	Henry, Son of Wm Godding Jun
23.	Abigail, Dauter of Benj^a Haftings
30.	Elifabeth, Daûter of Jos. Whitney
	John, Son of John Young
Decr. 7.	Seth, Son of Thos. Saltmarfh
	Anna, Dauter of Jacob Caldwell
	Jofhua & Isaac, Sons, &
	Hannah, Dauter, of Daniel Stearns
	Nymphos, my Negro, entered into Cov^t & was baptized.

[236]   1746/7.

Jan^{ry} 11.	William, Son of Edward Harrington
18.	Prifcilla, Dauter of David Livermore
Feb. 1.	John, Son of John Hunt
8.	Daniel, Son of Daniel Hofmer, at Concord by S. S.
15.	Mehetabel, Daûter of Simon Coollidge
22.	Nathaniel, Son of Amos Bond
March. 8.	Elifha, Son of Benj^a Whitney
15.	Elizabeth, of Benj^a Cheny } at Camb. Village
	Sarah, Dauter of John Cheny } by S. S.
22.	Jofeph, Son of Henry Sawtle

1747

April. 19.	Sarah, Daûter of Eb^r Goddard
May. 10.	Phinehas, Son of Sol. Robbins, at Cam : Vil : by S. S.
17.	Mary, Dauter of Smith Prentice
24.	Elizabeth, Daûter of Jonas Coollidge
31.	Silas, Son of John Train at Wefton by S. S.
June. 28.	Lydia, Daûter of Sam. Fifk
July. 26.	Hannah, Dauter of Nathan Perry
Augst 2.	Eunice, Dauter of Jonas Pierce of Concord by S. S.
23.	Elijah, Son of James Dix
Oct^o 18.	Edmund Fowle owned ye Covent
	Sufanna, Daûter of Sam^{ll} Hager
	Abigail, Daûter of Edmund Fowle
	Lydia, Dauter of Benj^a Whitney Junr
Novr 22.	David, Son of Nath^{ll} Stone
	Mary, Dauter of Mofes Stone
29.	Daniel, Son of Jos. White, at Brooklin by S. S.

Dec' 27. Henry, Son of Isaac Sanderson
Edmund, Son of Edmund Fowle

1747/8.

Jan'y 3. Smith, Son of Benj' Haftings
    10. Nathaniel, Son of Edw'd Thwing at Camb. Village by S. S.
    17. Elifabeth, Dauter of John Tainter
Eunice, Dauter of W'm Coollidge
Feb. 28. Samuel, Son of Henry Bond
Sufanna, Dauter of Jofiah Shattuck
March. 6. Mary, Dauter of W'm Dana at Camb. Vil: by S. S.
    13. Mary, Dauter of Sam'll Nutting
Palfgrave, Son of Jos. Wellington

1748

April. 3. William, Son of Josiah Stearns
    10. Jofeph, Son of Jon'a Barnard
    17. Jerufha, Dauter of Bezaleel Learned
    24. Ruth, Dauter of Uriah Clark
May. 15. Samuel Warren Jun' owned y'e Covenant
    22. Mary, Daûter of Nath'll Harrington
June. 5. Mary, Daûter of Sam'll Warren Jun'
    12. Sarah, Dauter of Sam'll Jenifon
Lydia, Dauter of Henry Spring Ter'us
July. 6. Ruth, Daughter of John Whitney
Jonathan, Son of Jon'a Stone
    24. Ruth, Daûter of Jon'a Stone Tertius
    31. Isaac, Son of Tho's Saltmarfh
Aug'st 21. Samuel, Son of James Hackleton by R'd M' Cotton
Mofes, Son of Jofiah Greenwood at Newton by S. S.
    28. Ruth, Daûter of John Hunt
Sept. 11. Mehetabel, Daûter of Sam'll Benjamin
Daniel, Son of John Young

[237]

Oct° 16. Nathaniel, Son of Sam'll Stratton
Nov' 6. Jacob, Son of Jacob Caldwell
    20. Lucey, Dauter of Afa Warren at Waltham by S. S.
Dec' 11. Sufanna, Dauter of Sam'll Cooke
    25. Jonas, Son of Jos. Mafon Jun'

1748/9.

Jan'y 29th. Lucy, Dauter of Sam'll Hager
Feb. 26. Hannah, Daûter of Nath'll Bright
March. 19. Thomas, Son of David Coollidge

1749

    26. Mary, Dauter of Jonas Coollidge
April. 9th. Releif, Dauter of Jofiah Stearns
Amos, Son of Amos Bond
Daniel, Son of David Livermore
    30. Lydia, Dauter of Daniel Bond

May. 7. Sufanna, Dauter of Jofiah Hall at Newton by S. S.
28. David, Son of Sol. Robbins at Camb. Village by S. S.
June. 4. Hannah, Dauter of Nathan Perry
11. Mercy, Dauter of Simon Coollidge
18. Mofes, Son of Mofes Stone
27. Samuel Fifk was chofen to ye office of a Deacon
July. 2. Lucey, Dauter of Daniel Whitney
Smith, Son of Smith Prentice
9. Spencer, Son of Wm Godding
16. William, Son of James Dix
Augst 13. Elifabeth, Daûter of Abraham Cutting at Camb. Vil. by S. S.
Sept. 3. Jofiah, Son of Nath^{ll} Stone
10. Sarah, Dauter of Benj^a Whitney Junr
17. Francis, Son of Henry Spring Ter^{ts}
Oct^o 8. William, Son of Wm Coollidge
Abigail, Daûter of Abigail Bifco
15. At Waltham, William, Son of Jofiah Biggelow
29. Mary Prieft owned ye Cov^t & Sarah, her Daûter was baptized
Oct^o 19. Jonas, Son of Daniel Knap } at Newton by S. S.
ye Son of Wm Cheney } at Newton by S. S.
Mary, Dauter of Sam^{ll} Child } at Newton by S. S.
Decr 3. Mary, Dauter of Edmund Fowle
10. Bezaleel, Son of Bezaleel Learned
24. Anna, Dauter of Edward Harrington
Nathaniel Warren Junr owned ye Covenant

1749/50

Jan^{ry} 14th William, Son of John Hunt
28. At Brookline, Thankful ye Daûter of Sam^{ll} Gleafon
Feby 4th Matthias Stone was difmifsed from this Church & recomended to the Church of Chrift in Worcefter
11th Samuel, Son of Benj^a Haftings
18th James Dafcombe entered into Covenant & was baptized
March. 4th Benjamin, Son of Jon^a Barnard
18. Joseph, Son of Sam^{ll} Coollidge

1750.

April. 15. Jonas Barnard owned the Covenant
May. 20th Jonas White owned the Covenant
27. Abijah, Son of Jonas White
13. Sufanna, Dauter of John Warren was baptized, he & his wife Sufanna having at ye fametime owned ye Covenant

[238]

June 10th Thankful Gearfield difmifsed & recomended to the Church of Chrift in Concord, whereof the Revd Mr Lawrence is Paftor

July. 8th		Sufanna, Dauter of John Sawen Junr
		Richard & Thomas, Sons of Uriah Clark
Augst 5th		Nathaniel, Son of Nathll Harrington
		William & Abigail, Children of Wm Gammage
		Abigail, Daûter of Samll Warren Junr
	19th	Martha, Daûter of Jonn Stone Junr
Sept. 9th		Jeduthan, Son of Jos. Wellington
		Daniel, Son of Wm Gammage
	16th	At Camb: Village Lydia, Daûter of John Dana
	23d	William, Son of Samll Jenifon
		Seth, Son of Isaac Sanderfon
	30th	Mary, Daûter of Seth Haftings
		Joshua, Son of Stephen Stearns
October. 7.		William, Son of Mofes Stone
		John, Son of John Randall
	28.	Sarah, Daûter of Samll Fifk
Novr 18th		Sarah, Daûter of Samll Stratton
Decr 2d		Anne, Daûter of Nathll Bright
		Sarah, Dauter of Jacob Caldwell
		Jonathan, Son of Jona Stone Tertius
	23d	Daniel, Son of Nath. Stone

1750/51.

Janry 6.		Lucey, Dauter of Wm Coollidge
	20.	Lydia, Dauter of David Livermore
March. 3.		Mary, Dauter of James Hackleton
	24.	Abijah Stearns was difmifsed & recomended to ye Chh in Lunenburgh

1751.

	31.	Nathan, Son of Nathan Perry
May. 5.		Hannah, Daûter of Samll Cooke
		Efther, Dauter of Jona Bemis Junr
June. 2.		At Newton, Achfah, Dauter of John Woodward
July. 14.		Thomas, Son of Amos Bond
	21.	At Wefton Isaac ye Son of John Stratton
		Hannah, Daûter of Nathll Williams
Augst 11.		Deborah, Dauter of James Dix
		Elifabeth Hay owned ye Covenant
	18.	Samuel, Son of Samll Coollidge
Sept. 15.		At Waltham. Jonathan, Son of Joseph Hager
		Mary, Dauter of Josiah Harrington, Mary, Dauter of Richd Cutting, Elifha, Son of Samll Harrington, Abraham, Son of Abraham Bemis, Sarah, Dauter of Elifha Livermore & Abraham, Son of Wm Lackey

[239]

Sept 29th		William White Junr owned ye Covenant
		William, Son of Wm White
		Abigail, Dauter of James Hay

	Jonathan Bond & Lydia Twitchell were difmifsed & recomended to ye C^{lh} of Chrift in Weftboro, whereof ye Revd Mr Parkman is Paftor
October. 6.	Katharine, Dauter of John Hunt
20.	Thomas, Son of Smith Prentice
Decr 8th	Jenny, Negro Woman of Sam^ll Parry owned ye Cov^t & was baptized
	Nathan, Son of Jon^a Barnard
	Nymphas, Son of Nymphas & Jenny
29.	Israel, Son of Israel Meed
	John, Son of John Warren

1751/2.

Jan^ry 12th	George Lawrence was difmifed & recommended to the Church of Chrift in Waltham
19th	Margaret, Daûter of Eb^r Hinds
Feb 2^d	Benjamin, Son of Benj^a Whitney
	Dorothy, Daûter of Edmund Fowle
March. 22^d.	Katharine, Daûter of Bezaleel Learned

1752.

April. 12.	At Newton George, Son of Thos Brown Junr
26.	At Camb. Village Mary, Dauter of John Stratton
May. 3^d.	John, Son of William Dockum of Bofton
	Elizabeth, Daûter of John Randall
	Mofes, Son of Joseph Peters
10th	Peter, Son of Nath^ll Harrington
24th	Daniel, Son of John Cook
June. 21st	Jonas, Son of Jonas White
28th	Hannah Mafon of Bofton owned the Covenant
July. 12th	Benjamin, Son of Timothy Austin of Charlestown
26th	At Natick Mofes ye Son of James Man
	Abigail, Dauter of Enos How
Aug^st 2^d	Hephzibah, Daûter of Jos. Stevens of Bofton
9th	John, Son of John White of Bofton
	David, Son of David Mafon of Bofton
16th	At Camb. Village Ebenezer ye Son of Eb^r Storer of Bofton
23^d	Mary, Daûter of Edwd Harrington
	Nathaniel, Son of Nath^ll Bright
30th	Jonas, Son of Jon^a Learned
	Samuel, Son of Wm Gammage
	Uriah, Son of Uriah Clark
	John Kimball Junr owned the Covenant
	Jofiah Berry, John Bond & Sarah Perry were difmifsed & recomended to the Church of Chrift in Worcester
Sep^t 24th	At Waltham Aaron, Son of Isaac Brown
	Lydia, Dauter of Jonathan Hammond

[240]

Oct° 1st	Lydia, Daûter of Samll Warren Junr
8th	Anna, Daûter of Wm Coollidge by Revd Mr Woodward
15th	Mary, Daûter of Jonathan Peirce
22d	Abijah, Son of Nathll Stone
Novr 5th	Benjamin, Son of Benjamin Felton
12th	Mary, Daûter of Henry Bacon ⎫
	Thomas, Son of Thomas Sowen ⎪
	Sufee, Daûter of Hezekiah Allen ⎬ at Natick
	Ethel, Son of James Battle ⎪ by S. Storer
	Jacob, Son of Timothy Sparhawke ⎪
	Hannah, Daûter of Joseph Paughonot ⎭
19th	Peter Parker owned ye Covenant at Brookline
December.17th.	Sufanna, Daûter of Nathll Coollidge Junr
	Charles, Son of Samll Nutting
31st	Seth, Son of Jona Stone Junr

1753

Jany 7th	At Lexington, Joseph, Son of Jos Fifk
14th	At Brookline, Samuel, Son of Samll Clark Junr
21st	Enoch, Son of Jacob Caldwell
Febry 4th	Jonathan, Son of Mofes Stone
18th	Nymphas, Son of my Negro Man
March. 4th	At Waltham Ruth, Daûter of Stephen White
	Henry, Son of Danll Pierce by Rev. Mr Cufhing
April. 15th	Elifabeth, Daûter of James Hay
22nd	Jofhua & Mercy, Children of Samll Jenifon
May. 6th	Daniel, Son of James Hackleton
13th	At Newton Amos Son of Jonas Stone
June 17th	Elifabeth, Daûter of Isaac Sanderfon
July. 1st	Mary, Daûter of Israel Meed
15th	Mofes, Son of Samuel Coollidge
	Mercy, Daûter of Smith Prentice
22d	Elifabeth, Daûter of Samuel Fifk
Augst 26th	At Cambridge Village Caleb Son of Joseph Cook
Sept: 9th	John Stratton, Mary Stratton & Abigail Barnard owned ye Covent
	Jonas, Son of Jonas Barnard
October 7th	Abel Benjamin & Elizabeth Benjamin owned ye Covenant
14th	Edward, Mofes & Richard, Sons of Edwd Richardfon
21st	William, Son of William & Jane Baldwin
Novr 11th	Elifabeth, Daûter of Joseph Wellington
18th	Thomas Son of Seth Haftings by Revd Mr Cotton at Newton Elifabeth Daûter of Edward Durant
Decr 2.	Peter, Son of Edward Richardfon

[241]

1754.

Janry 13th	Mary Daûter of Josiah Stearns

Feb^ry 10th	John Son of Nath^ll Bright
	Samuel Son of Abel Benjamin
March 17th	Abraham Son of Abraham Brown
24th	Ebenezer Smith Son of Edmund Fowle
31st	Hannah Dauter of David Livermore
	Samuel Son of Henry Spring Junr
	Stephen Son of John Cook
May. 5th	William Son of James Hay
June 2^d	Thomas Son of Francis Wells at Camb. Village
23^d	Thankful Dauter of Jon^a Bemis jun^r
July 21st	Joel, Son of Jonas White
Aug^st 18th	Mercy Dauter of Joseph Coollidge
25.	Thomas Giles & Mary Giles owned the Covenant
Sep^t 15th	Abigail Dauter of Eb. Hinds
22nd	Thomas Son of John Hunt
	Samuel Son of John Randall
	David Son of David Bemis
Octob^r 6th	Thomas Son of Thos Giles
	David ye Son of Sufanna Fofter
27th	Ann Rainger entered into Covenant & was baptized
Novr 24th	Rebecca Dauter of Uriah & Ruth Clark
Decr 1st	Ann Dauter of Sam^ll Warren Junr
8th	Mary Dauter of Nath^ll Coollidge Junr
22^d	Martha Dauter of Daniel Peirce

1755.

Jan^ry 19th	Phillis, Dauter of Nymphas a Negroe
Feb^ry 2nd	Samuel, Son of Jonas Barnard
16th	John Remington & Mary Remington owned ye Covenant
23^d	John, Son of Israel Meed &
	Efther, Dauter of John Warren
March. 2^d	Stephen Harris & Sarah Harris owned ye Covenant
9th	John Son of John Remington
23^d	Nathaniel, Son of Stephen Harris
30th	At Camb. Village, Nathaniel Son of Nath. Sparhawke
May. 4th	Jeddediah Leath & Hannah Leath owned the Covenant
11th	Sufanna, Dauter of Edwd Harrington
18th	Mary, Dauter of Samuel Fifk
25.	James, Son of James Hay
June. 1st	At Lexington Thomas, Son of Thos Blogget
July. 27th	Thaddeus, Son of Henry Bond
Aug^st 3rd	Jonathan, Son of Jon^a Winchefter } at Brooklin
	Solomon, Son of John Newell
	Elifha Gardner owned the Covenant
31st	Katharine, Dauter of Nath^ll Harrington
Sep^t 14th	David, Son of Smith Prentice

28th	Joseph Hay & Hannah Hay owned ye Covenant
	Hannah, Dauter of Joseph Hay
October 5th	Elizabeth, Dauter of John Hunt
Novr 16.	Elijah, Son of Samll Hager
Decr 7.	Sufanna, Dauter of Josiah Shattuck
28th	John Tainter Junr owned the Covenant
Novr 23d	Mary Shattuck owned ye Covenant

1756

Janry 4th	Mary, Dauter of John Tainter Junr
11.	David Sanger & Lucy Sanger owned the Covenant
18th	Efther, Dauter of Joseph Patterfon
Febry 22nd	John, Son of Edmund Fowle
	David, Son of David Sanger
March. 21st	Jonathan, Son of Abel Benjamin
28th	Molly, Dauter of Daniel Sawen
April. 4th	Amariah Learned & Hannah Learned owned ye Covenant
	Daniel, Son of Amariah Learned
11th	William Sanger & Abigail Sanger owned ye Covenant
	John, Son of Willm Sanger
	Ebenezer, Son of Ebr Hinds
May. 2nd	Mary, Dauter of John Cooke
	Abigail, Dauter of Edwd Richardfon
9th	Elifabeth, Dauter of Nathll Stone
23rd	John, Son of Jedediah Leathe
30th	Lucy, Dauter of Benjamin Felton
	Daniel, Son of Nathll Coollidge Junr
June 6th	Abraham, Son of John Randall
	Samuel, Son of John Whitney Junr
	Mary Whitney owned the Covenant
27th	Mary, Dauter of James Hay
July. 18th	Edward Harrington & Anna Harrington owned ye Covenant
August. 8th	Phinehas, Son of Edwd Harrington Junr
15th	William, Son of Josiah Prieft } at Waltham
	Elitha, Son of Daniel Stearns } by S. S.
	Sufanna, Dauter of John Coffeen by Rt Cufhing

[243]

Sept 12th	Samuel, Son of Jonas Coollidge
19th	Thomas, Son of Jedediah Spring
26th	Sufanna, Dauter of Samuel Soden
Octo 10th	Lois, Dauter of Jonas White
	Katharine, Dauter of Jons Bemis Junr
	Abigail, Dauter of Jonas Barnard
17th	Sarah, Dauter of John Hunt
31th	Jacob Boynton & Mary Boynton owned ye Covenant
	Elifabeth, Dauter of Jacob Boynton

Nov.r 2:st Cornelius, Son of Eben.r Stone Jun.r
Dec.r 5th Daniel, Son of Dan.ll Dana, at Camb. Village
26th Nathaniel, Son of David Bemis

1757.

Jan.ry 16th Elifabeth, Dauter of Joseph Coollidge
23d Abigail, Dauter of Joseph Hay
Feb.ry 27th Abijah, Son of W.m Brown ⎫ Cambridge Village
Ebenezer, Son of Eb.r Brown ⎬ by S. Storer
Lydia, Dauter of John Stratton ⎭
March. 13th Tabitha, Dauter of Jonas Learned
Kate, Dauter of Nymphas (my Negro)
May 8th Daniel, Son of Dan.ll Sawen ⎫ by Rev.d S. Bald-
Anna, Dauter of Stephen Harris ⎬ win.
15th Samuel, Son of Sam.ll Warren Jun.r
22d Jonathan, & Sufanna Raymond owned y.e Covenant
Sufanna, y.r Dauter baptized
29th Kezia, Dauter of John Spring of Bofton
June 5th Hannah, Dauter of Jon. Mirick at Newton by S. S.
12th Lucey, Dauter of John Remington
July. 10. Lydia, Dauter of Smith Prentice
17th Hannah, Dauter & William, Son of James Dix
24th Lucey, Dauter of W.m Park by Rev. N. Potter
Oct.o 9th John Son of John Cook
16th Elifabeth, Dauter of ——— Dunah at Roxbury by S. S.
23d Abraham, Son of Abraham Crawley
Nathan Son of Jacob Boynton
Nov.r 6th Ruth Dauter of John Warren
20th Anna Tainter owned the Covenant
28th Grace, Dauter of Benj.a Whitney in private
Dec.r 4th Deliverance, Dauter of Benj.a Whitney
11. Samuel, Son of John Savage

[244]

1758

Jan.ry 1st Sufanna, Dauter of John Tainter Jun.r
15th Thomas, Son of David Sanger
22d Mofes Harrington & Mary Harrington owned y.e Covenant
Feb.ry 5th John Son of Abel Benjamin
12th Abigail, Dauter of W.m Sanger
26th Jofiah Norcrofs & Elifabeth Norcrofs owned y.e Covenant
Nathaniel, y.e Son baptized
March. 5th Samuel, Son of Sam. White
12th Abijah, Son of Mofes Harrington
April. 2nd Sarah, Dauter of Jonas Barnard
9th Thomas, Son of James Hay
30th Mary, Dauter of Isaac Sanderfon.
May. 14th Mary, Dauter of Mofes Biggelow
21st Mary Biggelow owned y.e Covenant

	Edward, Son of Edwd Harrington Junr
June. 18th	James, Son of Nath^{ll} Stone
25th	Nathaniel, Son of Nath^{ll} Harris Junr
July. 2nd	Lucey, Dauter of Sam^{ll} Fifk
	Mary, Dauter of Amariah Learned
	Jofiah Bright owned ye Covenant
9th	Abraham, Son of Abr. Cutting, at Camb. Village by S. S.
16th	John, Son of Edwd Richardson
	Isaac, Son of John Randall
23^d	Jonathan, Son of Jon^a Bemis Junr
	Hannah, Dauter of Jedediah Leathe
August. 13th	Lucey, Dauter of Edmund Fowle
	Thomas, Son of Samuel Soden
Sep^t 3rd	Samuel, Son of Sam^{ll} Mafon
17th	Jonathan, Son of John Remington
24th	Jofiah & Jonathan (Twins), Sons of Jofiah Bright
Oct^o 15th	Hannah, Dauter of Jofiah Thompfon at Medford
Novr 12th	Ephraim, Son of John Hunt
	Jofiah, Son of Jonas White
26th	Isaac Sparhawk, Son of Isaac Gardner Junr at Brookline

1759.

Feb^{ry} 11th	John, Son of Daniel Sawen
18th	Kezia, Dauter of Jofhua Jackfon at Newton by S. S.
March. 25th	Nathaniel Ruggles, Son of Simon Whitney
	Abijah, Son of Abijah Brown

[245]

April. 29th	Lucey, Dauter of John Stratton of Camb. Village
May. 27th	Charles, Son of Nath^{ll} Harrington
June. 24th	Elifabeth, Daûter of James Dix
July. 29th	Josiah, Son of Jedediah Spring
Augst 12th	John, Son of Joseph Hay
26th	Oliver Livermore owned the Covenant
	Katharine, Daûter of Oliver Livermore
	Mofes, Son of Mofes Biggelow
	Matthew, Son of Matthew Johnfon
Sep^t 16th	Samuel, Son of Edwd Jackfon at Camb. Vil: by S. S.
23^d	Joshua, Son of Joseph Coollidge
30.	Lucy, Dauter of Sam^{ll} White by Revd Lawrence
Oct^o 14th	Luke, Son of David Bemis
Nov. 25th	Sufanna, Daûter of Edwd Harrington Junr
Decr 2^d	Lucey, Daûter of John Cook
30th	Elifabeth, Daûter of Smith Prentice

1760.

Jan^{ry} 6th	Sufanna, Daûter of William Brown at Camb. Village
27th	Elifabeth, Dauter of Josiah Norcrofs
Feb. 3^d	Benjamin, Son of Benj^a Bridge at Brooklin

March. 9th	Sarah, Dauter of John Tainter Junr
April. 6th	Benjamin, Son of Simon Haftings
27th	Daniel, Son of Jonas Barnard
May. 4th	Nathaniel, Son of Nath[ll] Coollidge Jun[r]
18th	Nathaniel, Son of David Sanger
25th	Lucey, Dauter of Sam[ll] Warren
June 15th	James Barnard & Sarah Barnard owned y[e] Covenant
July. 6th	Hannah, Dauter of Stephen Harris
13th	Ebenezer, Son of Edw[d] Richardfon
	Lucey, Dauter of Daniel Sawen
27th	Nathaniel, Son of Nath[ll] Stone
	Anna, Dauter of Daniel Pierce
	Jacob, Son of John Randall
	Dorothy, Dauter of Simon Whitney
Aug[st] 10th	Abigail, Dauter of Jonas White by Rev. Meriam
17th	David, Son of James Barnard
24th	At Waltham Tabitha, Dauter of Afa Warren
31st	Joseph, Son of Josiah Bright

[246]

Sep[t] 28th	Sarah, Dauter of Jedediah Leathe
	Lydia, Dauter of Will[m] Sanger
Oct[o] 12th	Eli, Son of Amariah Learned
	John, Son of James Hay
19.	At Cambridge Charles, Son of Thadeus Wyman
	Sarah, Dauter of Jonathan Cooper Jun[r]
26th	Jonathan, Son of Jon[a] Bemis Jun[r]
Nov. 2nd	Ann, Dauter of Henry Bond
9th	Sarah, Dauter of James Bryant at Camb. Village
Decembr 21st	Jeremiah, Son of Edmund Fowle

1761.

Jan[ry] 18th	Samuel, Son of Sam[ll] Soden'
	Samuel Sanger & Grace Sanger owned y[e] Covenant
Feb[y] 11th	Mary, Dauter of Abraham Crawley
8th	Ebenezer Mafon & Elifabeth Mafon owned y[t] Covenant
March. 1st	Elijah, Son of Samuel Mafon
	Samuel, Son of Sam[ll] Sanger
15th	Ebenezer, Son of Eben[r] Mafon
May. 3rd	Joseph Gardner owned Covenant
	Thomas, Son of Joseph Gardner
June 7th	Jonas, Son of James Dix
21st	At Wefton Samuel, Son of Isaac Whittemore
28th	At Newton Mofes, Son of Jonas Jackfon
July. 19th	Jonathan, Son of John Remington
	Abigail, Dauter of Samuel White
Aug[st] 9th	Lucey, Dauter of Edwd Harrington
30th	Samuel, Son of Mofes Biggelow
	William Saltmarfh & Eliz[a] Saltmarfh owned y[e] Covenant

Sep.t 13th Mary, Daûter of Simon Haftings
20th Oliver, Son of Oliver Livermore
Oct.o 25th Israel, Son of John Cook
John, Son of W.m Saltmarsh
Nov. 8th Joseph, Son of Joseph Coollidge
Decemb.r 6th Sarah, Daûter of James Gray

1762.

Jan.ry 10th Mary, Daûter of Simon Whitney
Feb.ry 28th Benjamin, Son of David Sanger
Jonathan, Son of Jon.a Coollidge Godding
March. 7th Edward, Son of Edw.d Prentice at Camb. Village
28th Lydia, Daûter of Jonas Barnard

[247]

April. 4th Joanna, Daûter of John Tainter Jun.r
25th Josiah, Son of Josiah Norcrofs
May 2nd Josiah, Son of Josiah Bright
9th John, Son of Jon.a Bemis Jun.r
Samuel, Son of Daniel Sawen
16th Sarah, Dauter of James Hay
30th Stephen, Son of Stephen Harris
June 13th Jonathan, Son of David Bemis
July 25th John Stearns & Martha Stearns owned y.e Covenant
Katharine, Daûter of John Stearns
Aug.st 8th Thomas Learned owned the Covenant
Josiah & Paul, Sons of Tho.s Learned
22.d John, Son of John Stearns
October: 10th Samuel, Son of Sam.ll Fifk
31.st John, Son of Abraham Crawley
Joshua, Son of Smith Prentice
Elias Mafon was difmifsed from this Chh & recomended to the C.hh of Ch in Woodftock, y.e firft Society
Nov.r 14th Abijah, Son of Sam.ll Warren
24th Martha, Daûter of John Rogers at Newton
Dec.r 12th William, Son of Eb.r Mafon
26th Samuel, Son of Edmund Fowle
Sarah, Dauter of Joseph Gardner

1763.

Jan.ry 2.d Mercy Amelia, Dauter of Convers Spring
23.rd Grace, Dauter of Sam.ll Sanger
30th At Camb. Village John, Son of W.m Bowles
Feb.ry 6th Achfah, Dauter of Jedediah Leathe
April. 24th William, Son of W.m Sanger
May. 22.d Frederick, Son of John Remington
29th James, Son of James Bryant, at Camb: Village
June 12th Sarah, Dauter of Edw.d Richardfon
Sally Dauter of Daniel Edes
July. 17th Grace, Dauter of Simon Whitney

	Isaac, Son of Abijah Hammond
31st	Eleanor, Dauter of Sam^{ll} White by Revd Mr Cushing
Augt 21st	Grace, Dauter of Nath^{ll} Coollidge
	Hannah, Dauter of John Draper
Sep^t 4.	Daniel, Son of Simon Hastings
October. 9th	Katharine, Dauter of Nath^{ll} Sanger
23^d	Eunice, Dauter of Joseph Coollidge
2^d	Day, William, Son of Wm Saltmarsh
Nov. 6.	Peter, Son of Jon^a Coollidge Godding

[248]   1764

Jan^{ry} 1st	Joshua, Son of John Stratton
8th	Esther, Dauter of Thos Johnson
22nd	Abijah, Son of Daniel Sawen
	Thomas, Son of John Stearns
	Daniel, Son of Oliver Livermore
Feb^{ry} 12th	Lois, Dauter of Jonas White
26th	Amos, Son of John Thwing at Camb. Village
March. 4th	Hannah, Dauter of Sam^{ll} Soden
25th	Spencer, Son of Nath^{ll} Sanger
April 8th	Josiah Convers, Son of James Thomas of Boston
22^d	Lucey, Dauter of David Sanger
29th	Nathaniel, Son of Josiah Norcrofs
	Susanna, Dauter of Edwd Harrington Junr
May. 27th	At Camb. Village 4 Children vizt,
	Bridger, Dauter of Isaac Ridgway of Boston,
	Edward^t Son of Edwd Peirce of Boston
	Edmund, Son of Richard Dana } of Cambridge
	Mary, Dauter of Thomas Thwing Junr } bridge
June 3rd	James, Son of Jonas Barnard
	Elisabeth, Dauter of Sam^{ll} Jenison Junr
July. 8th	Convers, Son of Convers Spring
22^d	Ephraim Wheeler owned ye Covenant
	Elizabeth, Dauter of Ephraim Wheeler
29th	Elisabeth, ye Dauter of Abraham Crawley
Augst 5th	Enoch Son of Eb^r Mason } by Revd Mr Cushing
	Moses, Son of Moses Bigelow }
26th	Moses, Son of Josiah Bright
	Joshua, Son of Thos Learned
	Samuel, Son of Sam^{ll} Jenison Junr
Sep^t 2^d	Grace, Dauter of Daniel Fuller
	Priscilla, Dauter of Sam^{ll} Calderwood
	Sarah, Dauter of Elisha Learned
9th	Anna, Dauter of David Bemis
16th	Lucretia, Dauter of Sam^{ll} Fisk
October. 14th	Amos Livermore owned ye Covenant
	Amos, ye Son of Amos Livermore was baptized
21st	Rebecca, Dauter of Wm Godding Junr
28	Abraham Brown & Mary Brown were dismissed from this C^{hh} & recomended to ye C^{hh} of C^t in Grafton

Novr 4. Mary, Dauter of John Remington
25th Cherry, Dauter of Jon^a Stone
December 2^d James Barnard & Sarah Barnard were difmifsed from this Ch^h & recomended to the Ch^h in Acton
9th Jonathan Learned Junr & Sufanna Learned owned ye Covenant
30th Anna, ye Dauter of Jon^a Learned Junr

[249]   1765

March. 3rd Jofeph, Son of Jofeph Hay
10th Jedediah & Betty White owned ye Covenant
Diadama, Dauter &
Jedediah, Son of Jedediah White
23rd At Newton Fanny, Dauter of   Parker
April. 7th Nathaniel, Son of Sam^ll Warren
May 5th Reuben, Son of Jedediah White by Rev^rd Mr Cufhing
19th Rhoda, Dauter of Nathl Stone
Sarah, Dauter of Stephen Harris
June 2nd Frances, Dauter of Jedediah Leathe
Samuel, Son of John Tainter Junr
July. 14th Mary, Dauter of Thos Hovey, at Camb. Village
Aug^st 11th Jonathan Harrington owned ye Covenant
18th Hannah, Dauter of Benjamin Fefsenden
Sep^t 22nd Joseph, Son of John Stearns
Elizabeth, Dauter of Wm Saltmarfh
29th Thomas, Son of Sam^ll Soden
Sarah Gray was difmifsed from this Ch^h & recomended to the Church of Chrift in Stockbridge
October. 6th Grace, Dauter of Jon^a Harrington
13th William, Son of Edwd Richardfon by Rev. Mr Meriam
Novr 17th Hannah, Dauter of Jofeph Gardner
December 8th At Roxbury, Sarah, ye Dauter of Thaddeus Partridge
29th Josiah Bifco, Wm Chenery, & Sybbil Chenery owned ye Covenant
Daniel Whitney, Son of Josiah Bifco
William, Son of William Chenery

1766

Jan^ry 5th Seth Son of David Sanger
26th Nathaniel, Son of Oliver Livermore
Feb^ry 2nd At Camb: Village Mary Dauter of Richd Dana
Rachel, Dauter of Jonathan Dana
9th Daniel, Son of Jon^a Stone
March. 2nd At Waltham John Son of John Pierce
At Watertown Samuel, Son of Ephraim Wheeler in private
9th Richard Coollidge, Son of John Stratton
23rd Elifha, Son of Elifha Learned
April. 6th Francis, Son of Jofiah Bright

	Elisabeth, Dauter of Simon Hastings
20th	Ebenezer Stutson & Keziah Stone } owned ye Covenant.
May. 11th	Joseph, Son of Daniel Sawen
	Abigail, Dauter of Samll Jenison Junr
	Anne, Dauter of James Hay
25th	Benjamin Felton, Son of Ebn Stutson
	Jemima, Dauter of Josiah Norcross

[250]

June. 22nd	Mary, Dauter of William Sanger
July. 6th	Samuel, Son of Abraham Crawley
	Lois & Katharine, Dauters of Phinehas Child
13th	Abraham Hews & Lucey Hewes owned ye Covenant
	David Coollidge & Dorothy Coollidge owned ye Covenant
	Abraham, Son of Abraham Hews
20th	Jonathan Whitney & Susanna Whitney owned ye Covenant
	Susanna, Daûter of Jona Whitney
27th	Samuel Brown & Lois Brown owned ye Covenant
Augst 3rd	Susanna, Dauter of David Coollidge Junr
10th	Lucey, Dauter of Joseph Coollidge
17th	Jacob, Son of Samll Brown
24th	Daniel, Son of Samuel Mason
	Silas Son of Convers Spring
	Richard Walker & Elizabeth Walker owned ye Covenant
Sept 7th	John, Son of Thomas Patten
	Jonas, Son of Jona Coollidge Godding
14th	At Camb. Village Caleb, Son of Caleb Dana Junr
21st	Josiah, Son of Samll White
	Richard, Son of Richard Walker
Octor 12th	Lizzey, Dauter of John Tainter Junr
Decr 7th	Nathan, Son of Nathaniel Coollidge by Revd Cushing
28th	Isaac, Son of David Bemis

1767

Janry 4th	Mary, Dauter of Stephen Harris
25th	Mary, Dauter of John Draper
Febry 1st	Mary, Dauter of Jedediah Leathe
	Anna Dauter of William Chenery
22nd	Elizabeth, Dauter of Benja Fessenden
March. 1st	Samuel, Son of Thos Learned
29th	Lydia, Dauter of Jona Harrington
April. 5th	William & Anna Learned owned the Covenant
12.	Hannah, Dauter of Jona Learned jur
May. 17th	William, Son of Wm Learned
31st	Josiah, Son of John Stearns
June. 28th	James, Son of Ephraim Wheeler
Augst 2d	Simon Coollidge owned ye Covenant

Sep[t] 6th Sufanna, Dauter of Elifha Learned
       Mary, Dauter of Simon Coollidge
Oct[o] 4th Grace, Dauter of Jedediah White
       Grace, Dauter of Josiah Bifco
    11. Jonas Coollidge j[r] & Anna Coollidge owned the Coven[t]
       Sarah Saunders owned y[e] Covenant
       Sarah, Dauter of Mofes & Sarah Saunders
       Elifabeth, Dauter of Jonas Coollidge ju[r]

[251] [Notes upon Baptism and y[e] Covenant in Abraham.]
[252]
1767
October. 18th At Cambridge Village Sufanna Dauter of Benj[a] Hill
         & Mofes, Son of Joshua Thomas
    25th Lucey, Dauter of Simon Whitney
Nov[r] 1st Jonas, Son of Jon[a] Stone
    15th Elizabeth, Dauter of Edw[d] Richardson
       William, Son of Sam[ll] Warren
Dec[r] 13. Hannah, Dauter of John Tainter jun[r]
       Jonas, Son of Jonas Barnard

1768
Jan[ry] 3[d] Mary, Dauter of Tho[s] Patten
       Lucey, Dauter of Amos Livermore
    17th William Son of David Coollidge ju[r]
       Mary, Dauter of Jon[a] Whitney
Feb[y] 7th Jefse, Son of David Sanger
    14. At Camb Village Martin, Son of Jon[a] Fefsenden ju[r]
    21. Nancy, Dauter of Josiah Bright
April. 10th Jofeph, Son of Chriftopher Grant ju[r]
    17th Elifabeth, Dauter of Josiah Norcrofs
    24th At Waltham Betty, Dauter of Uriah Cutting
May. 1st At Newton Henry, Son of Sam[ll] Craft
    22[d] Eunice, Dauter of Mofes Biggelow
    29th Benjamin, Son of Daniel Sawen
June 12th Phinehas Stearns & Hannah Stearns owned y[e] Coven.
       Hannah, Dauter of Phinehas Stearns
       Amafa, Son of Sam[ll] Brown
July. 17th Henry, Son of Convers Spring
       Jemima, Dauter of Israel Whitney
Aug[st] 14. Lucey, Dauter of James Hay
Oct[r] 2. Benjamin, Son of Joseph Gardner
Nov. 6th At Camb. Village Nathan, Son of Nath[l] Sparhawk
    13th Martha, Dauter of W[m] Godding
       Henry, Son of W[m] Learned
    27. Richard, Son of W[m] Sanger

[253]
Dec[r] 4th Elifabeth, Dauter of Ayres Tainter
    18. Jsaac, Son of Samuel Mafon

1769

Jan^ry 8th	Lucy, Dauter of Jedediah Leathe
	Charles, Son of John Stearns
29th	Thomas, Son of Jonas Barnard
Feb^ry 12.	Anna, Dauter of Sam^ll Sanger
19th	Mary, Dauter of David Bemis
March. 5th	Rebecca, Dauter of Benj^a Fefsenden
	Lucey, Dauter of Thomas Learned
	Jon^a Stone & Martha Stone were difmiffed from this Church to ye 1st Church in Shrewsbury
12.	Mary, Dauter of Sam^ll Soden
April. 2^d	Lucey, Dauter of Stephen Harris
16th	John, Son of Joseph Coollidge by ye Revd Mr Cufhing
30th	Andrew, Son of Jedediah White
May 7th	Lucretia, Dauter of Josiah Bright
	Spencer, Son of Jon^a Coollidge Godding
21.	Joseph, Son of Jon^a Learned ju^r
June. 4th	Thomas Draper & Elifabeth Draper owned ye Covenant
11.	John, Son of Elifha Learned
	Hephzibath, Dauter of Simon Coollidge
	Elifabeth, Dauter of Thomas Draper
25th	Eunice, Dauter of Sam^ll White } by Revd Cufhing
	John, Son of John Draper }
July. 15.	Anna, Dauter of Jonas Coollidge
23^d	Anna, Dauter of Simon Whitney
	John Hackleton & Bethiah Hackleton owned ye Covenant
30th	Thomas, Son of Thomas Patten
Sep^t 10th	Thomas, Son of Jofiah Bifco
	John, Son of John Hackleton
24th	John Durant & Sarah Durant owned ye Covenant
Novr 19th	Phinehas Jenifon & Sufanna Jenifon owned ye Coven^t
26th	Sufanna, ye Dauter of Phinehas Stearns
Decr 17th	Jonathan, Son of Jon^a Whitney
23th	Lucey, Dauter of Edwd Richardfon

1770

Jan^ry 14th	Phinehas Son & Sufanna Dauter of Phinehas Jenifon
Feb^ry 25th	Ifaac Son of John Stratton
	Amos, Son of William Dawes
	Mary Dauter of Ifrael Whitney
March. 4th	Abigail Dauter of Abijah Hammond
	Mary Dauter of Seth Saltmarfh
	Peter Son of David Coollidge Junr
	Seth Saltmarfh & Sufanna his Wife owned ye Covenant

[254]

April 29th	John, Son of John Tainter ju^r
May 6th	Jofeph, Son of Jofeph Gardner

27th	John, Son of Josiah Norcross
July 1st	Joseph, Son of David Sanger
8th	Elijah, Son of Jonathan Bemis
	Silas, Son of William Learned
22nd	Elisabeth, Dauter of Samuel Brown
29th	John, Son of James Hay
August. 12th	George, Son of Benjamin Fessenden
Sept 2nd	Lucey, Dauter of Ayres Tainter
16th	Martha, Dauter of John Stearns
23rd	Susanna, Dauter of Daniel Sawen
30th	Elijah White & Hannah White owned ye Covenant
October. 14th	Lucey, Dauter of Daniel Fuller
28th	Luke, Son of Convers Spring
Novembr. 4th	Nathaniel, Son of Saml Jenison junr
18th	Hannah, Dauter of Elijah White
	John Bond was dismissed from yr Chh of Ct in Watertown & recomend to ye Chh of Ct in Conway
Decemb'r. 9th	Elisebeth, Dauter of John Remington
	Sarah, Dauter of Josiah Bright
	Elisha, Son of William Chenery
30th	Sarah, Daughter of Christopher Grant junr
	Stephen Whitney & Relief Whitney owned ye Covenant

1771

Janry 6th	William, Son of Phinehas Stearns
27.	Stephen, Son of Stephen Whitney
Feb. 3.	Josiah Warren & Abigail Warren owned the Covenant
24.	Isaac, Son of Thos Patten
March. 10.	Hannah, Dauter of Thos Learned
31.	Josiah, Son of Josiah Warren
April. 7th	Hephzibah, Dauter of Amos Livermore
21.	Elisabeth, Dauter of Saml Sanger
	Seth Hastings & Hannah Hastings were dismissed from this Chh & recomend to ye 1st Chh of Ct in Cambridge.
May 31.	Ann Dauter of Elisha Learned
July 14.	Elisabeth, Dauter of Jonas Barnard
August. 4.	Benjamin Shattuck Son of Joshua Kendall
11.	Simon, Son of Simon Hastings, by Revd Merriam
25.	Hannah, Dauter of David Bemis

[255]   1771

Sept 22.	Susanna, Dauter of Jona Learned junr
Octo 6.	At Cambridge Village Francis, Son of George Dana
	Nathan, Son of Jona Winthip
27.	Stephen, Son of Saml Warren
	Sarah, Dauter of Jos. Coollidge
Nov. 3.	Moses & Aaron, twin Sons of Simon Coollidge junr
10.	Mary, Dauter of John Stratton
	Samuel, Son of Phinehas Robbins

17. Dorothy, Dauter of Israel Whitney
24. Mary, Daûter of John Hunt jun^r
Decr 15. Chriſtopher, Son of Jedediah Learned

1772.

Jan^ry 26. At Cambridge Village Andrew, Son of Eben^r Seaver & John Son of Andrew Ellis
Feb. 2. Elijah, Son of Wm Learned
Dorothy, Daûter of David Coollidge
Apr. 5. Abraham, Son of William Sanger
26. Thomas, Son of Benjn Feſsenden
Elias, Son of Phinehas Jeniſon
May. 10. At Camb. Village Thomas Son of Jon^n Feſsenden
17. Henry Saunderſon & Charity Saunderſon owned the Covenant
Abigail Daûter of Josiah Bright
31. Anna, Dauter of Ezekiel Hall
June 7. Hannah, Daûter of Jon^n Coollidge Godding
28. Abigail, Dauter of Josiah Norcroſs
July. 12. At Camb. Village William Son of Moſes Robbins
Josiah, Son of Josiah Feſsenden
19. William, Son of Ayres Tainter
Jonas, Son of Jonas Coollidge
26. Francis, Son of Zacharias Shed
Sibyl, Daûter of Sam^ll White
Charity, Dauter of Henry Sanderson
Aug^st 2. At Newton Amaſa, Son of John Murdock
16. Mary, Daûter of Edwd Richardſon
23. Edmund, Son of Thos Wellington
Jacob, Son of Edward Harrington ju^r
Sep^t 13. Henry, Son of William Godding
27. Eliſabeth, Dauter of Jos. Gardner

[256]

Oct^o 4. Abigail, Dauter of Josiah Warren, at Camb. Village
11. Anna, Dauter of Sam^ll Brown
18. Mary, Dauter of Josiah Capen Junr
Novr 15. Relief, Daûter of Stephen Whitney, by Rev^d Cuſhing
Decr 6. Elifabeth, Daûter of Daniel Sawin
13. William, Son of Thos Patten

1773

Jan^ry 17. Mary, Daûter of John Remington
31. Isaac, Son of Simon Haſtings
Feb^ry 26. William, Son of Phinehas Stearns, in private
28th Mary, Dauter of John & Martha Stearns
March 14. Daniel, Son of Sam^ll Sanger
Eliſabeth, Dauter of Eliſha Learned
April. 4th Leonard, Son of Josiah Biſco

18ᵗʰ Moses, Abigail, Jerutha & Aaron, Children of yᵉ widow Abigail Learned, she being rec'd into Chh Fellowship

Elisabeth, Daughter of Convers Spring

[Continued on Page 42.]

[257] Blank.

[258]

I was called to yᵉ work of yᵉ Ministry by yᵉ church and congregation in Watertown on Novʰʳ 24ᵗʰ 1777, and was ordained April 29ᵗʰ 1778.

[He died of dysentery Sept. 16, 1778, ae. 32.]

A Record of Baptisms by Danˡ Adams.

1778

May 10.   Samˡ Son of Willᵐ Chenery
June 7ᵗʰ Roba, Daughter of Willᵐ Warren
June 14ᵗʰ Polly, Daughter of Jonᵃ Crosby
June 28ᵗʰ Susanna, wife of Nathˡ Bright
June 28ᵗʰ Eunice, Daughter of Josiah Capen
July 12ᵗʰ Cate, Daughter of Danˡ Bond
Aug. 2ᵈ   Nathˡ Son of Nathˡ Bright
Aug. 2ᵈ   Susanna, Daughter of Nathˡ Bright

1779

Augˡ 8ᵗʰ Samˡ Son of Nathˡ Bright, by Mʳ Cooke

[259]

I was called to the work of the Ministry by the Church & Congregation in Watertown on March 13ᵗʰ 1780 & was Ordained June 21ˡ 1780.

A Record of Baptisms by R. R. Eliot.

1780

Augˡ 20ᵗʰ   Sally, Daughter of George Brown
Sepʳ 10ᵗʰ   Hannah, Daughter, & Elijah Son of William Harrington
Sepʳ 10   Lucy, Daughter of Smith Adams
Nov 5ᵗʰ   Mary Kimbal & Katharine, Daughters & Daniel son of Daniel Whitney
Nov 26   Charles son of Daniel Whitney
            Lucy & Elizabeth Daughters of Willᵐ Bond
Decʳ 17ᵗʰ   Isaac son & Polly Daughter of Roger Adams

1781

Janʸ 7ᵗʰ   Rhoda, Daughter of Moses Stone Juʳ
Janʸ 14   Polly, Daughter of Elijah Mead
March 4   Edward, son of Edward Harrington Junʳ
March 11ᵗʰ Alexander, son of Benjᵃ Capen
March 25   David, son of Benjᵃ Capen
            Charles, son of Charles Nutting

June 24. Ruth, Daughter of William Chenery
July 1. Hannah, Daughter of Nath¹ Bright
July 29. Lucy, Daughter of Josiah Sanders
Samuel White, ſon of Moses Warren
Augᵗ 12. Betsy, Daughter of Elijah Meads
Sepᵗ 16. Henry Son & Hannah Daughter of Jedediah Learned

[260]

Sepʳ 30. Benjamin, Son of Phinehas Jenniſon
Josiah, Son of Phinehas Jenniſon
Octʳ 21. Betsy, Daughter of Abner Craft
Nancy, Daughter of Stephen Whitney
Hephza, Daughter of Roger Adams
Oct 28. George Waſhington, ſon of Phinehas Stearns
Benjamin, ſon of Henry Whitney
Novʳ 25. William, Son of William Warren
Decʳ 9. Isaac, Son of Sam¹ Barnard
Joseph, Son of Moses Coolidge
Decʳ 30. William, Son of William Harrington

1782

Janʸ 6 Richard, Son of Simon Whitney
March 10ᵗʰ Rebecca Cooke, Daughter of Henry Bradshaw
April 21 Amos, Son of Amos Bond
June 23 Betsy, Daughter of Elkanah Wales
July 21 George, Son of George Brown
Augᵗ 25 Israel, Son of Daniel Whitney
Octʳ 28 Moſes, Son of Moses Warren
Novʳ 3ᵈ Adino Bullfinch, ſon of Willᵐ Beals
Decʳ 15 Martha Clark, Daughter of Hugh Maſon
19 Samuel, Son of Sam¹ Spring

1783

Janʸ 12 Cornelius, ſon of Moſes Stone Junʳ
Febʸ 23. Francis, Son of Sam¹ Spring
April 6 Marcy, Daughter of Roger Adams
27. Lydia, Daughter of Amos Bond
May 4 John, Son of Josiah Mixer
11 Isaac, Son of Elijah Mead
June 6 Charles, Son of Willᵐ Warren
Augᵗ 24 William, Son of Nath¹ Bright
Lucy, Daughter of Andrew Stimpson
31 Ebenezer, Son of Moses Coolidge
Septʳ 7 Polly, Daughter of William Harrington
Octʳ 5 Samuel, Son of Thomas Patten
12. Abigail, Daughter of William Stone
Novʳ 16 Lucy, Daughter of Abijah Stone
30 Josiah, Son of Josiah Sanderson
Henry, Son of Daniel Jackson
Sukey, Daughter of William Beals

[261]
Decr 7 Polly, Daughter of Phinehas Stearns
Hannah, Daughter of Joseph Bright

1784

Feby 1. Nancy, Daughter of Abner Craft
15 Polly, Daughter of Nathaniel R. Whitney
March 21 Richard Clarke, Son of Hugh Mason
May 2 Samuel, Son of John Botang
David, Son of Jonathan Bemifs
June 20 Nathaniel, Son of Nathaniel Bemifs
July 11 Sally, Daughter of Eayres Tainter
Septr 5 Nathaniel Pierce, Son of Samuel Hoar
12 Dorothy, Daughter of Daniel Whitney
Samuel, Son of Elkanah Wales
19 Betsy, Daughter of Henry Bradfhaw
Octr 17 Sally, Daughter of Jonathan Stone
24 Richard Hunnewell, Son of Charles Nutting
Nov 14 William, Son of Jonas White Junr
Decr 12 William, Son of Phinehas Jennison
26 Joseph, Son of Joseph Coolidge

1785

Feb^{ry} 16 Charles, Son of George Brown
27 Carolina Matilda, Daughter of Willm Warren
Joseph, Son of Joseph Bright
May 22 Samuel, Son of Elijah Mead
29 Betsy, Daughter of Joshua Kendal
June 12 Roger, Son of Roger Adams
July 30 Mary, Daughter of Joseph Coolidge
Augt 27 Polly, Daughter of Hezekiah Metcalf
Sepr 4 Daniel, Son of Daniel Jackson
Octr 9th Moses Gill, Son of Edmund Fowle
Charles, Son of Francis Faulkner
23 Clarissa, Daughter of Shubal Downes
30 Polly, Daughter of Thomas Vose
Nov 6 Nancy, Daughter of John Bullard
John & Samuel, Sons of John Cooke Junr
13 Phinehas, Son of Charles Nutting
20 Dolly, Daughter of John Tainter
Betsy, Daughter of William Harrington
27 Josiah, Son of Abijah Stone
Decr 18 Susanna, Daughter of John Stimpson

[262]

1786

Jany 29. Anna, Daughter of Henry Bradshaw
Feby 5. Elizabeth, Daughter of Jonathan Bemifs
March 12 Katy, Daughter of Willm Beals
26 James Bradish, Son of Nathaniel R. Whitney
April 23 Caleb, Son of Caleb Cooke

May 14	Joseph, Son of Hugh Mason
June 11	Charles, Son of Abner Craft
July 23	Lucy, Daughter of Phinehas Stearns
30	Lydia the Wife & Lydia, Nabby & Nathan, the Children of Nathan Porter
Sep 24	Asaph, Son of Moses Stone Jun
Oct 22	Ephraim, Son of Jonathan Harrington
Nov 5.	Hannah Stowel, Daughter of Mofes Coolidge
	Samuel Mafsay, Son of Samuel Holt
19	Marcy, Daughter of Joseph Coolidge
26	Jonathan, Son of Joseph Bright
Dec 31	Lois, Daughter of Josiah Mixer

1787

Jan 21	Eleanor, Daughter of Moses Warren
28	Hannah, Daughter of Roger Adams
March 11	Samuel, Son of Katharine Harris
18	Jofiah, Son of Jonas White Jun
	Jonathan, Son of Jonathan Stone
April 8	Rebecca Boylston, Daughter of Edmund Fowle
	Francis, Son of Daniel Jackson
29	Lucy, Joel, Edward, Children of Phinehas Harrington
June 17	Charles William Henry, Son of William Warren
July 1.	Naby & Lydia, Daughters of Elijah Meads
29.	Grace, Daughter of Elkanah Wales
Aug 5.	Hannah, Daughter of Stephen Harris Jun
30	Elizabeth Swift, Daughter of Sam. Babcock
Oct 7.	Sally, Daughter of Thomas Vose
28	Richard, Son of William Stone
Nov 4	Isaac, Son of William Harrington

[263]

Nov 4	Elizabeth, Daughter of Hugh Mafon
11.	Abigail, Daughter of Abijah Stone
Dec 30	Lydia, Daughter of Samuel Wellington
	Eleanor, Daughter of Moses Warren

1788

Jan 13	Elizabeth Thomson, Daughter of Henry Crane
Feb 3.	Josiah, Son of Joshua Kendal
24	Betfy, Daughter of John Stimpson
March 2	Francis, Son of Francis Faulkner
	Jonathan, Son of Jonathan Bemifs
16	Nabby, Daughter of Charles Nutting
April 27	Elizabeth, Daughter of Moses Coolidge
May 25	Samuel, Son of Joseph Bright
July 6.	George, Son of Abner Craft
	Francis, Son of Nath¹, Ruggles Whitney.
27	Sarah, Daughter & Thomas Son of Thomas Clark
Aug 2	Nancy, Daughter of Joseph Coolidge

31 Lydia Stratton, Daughter of Josiah Sanderson
Aaron, Son of Moses Stone Junr
Novr 9 John, Son of Thomas Clarke
23 Betsy, Daughter of Roger Adams
Daniel, Son of Benjamin Hastings

1789

Jany 25 Grace, Daughter of Daniel Whitney
March 22 Hephzibah, Daughter of William Stone
29 Charles, Son of Nathaniel Bemis
April 12 Katy, Daughter of Jonathan Harrington
Charles, Son of Jonathan Stone
26 Henry, Son of Jonas White Junr
June 7 Amos, Son of Hugh Mason
July 12 Thomas, Son of Thomas Soden
Sep. 13 Mary Henshaw, Daughter of Daniel Jackson
Lucretia, Daughter of William Harrington
Sally, Daughter of Samuel Babcock

[264]

Octr 4. George, Son of William Warren
18. William Main, Son of John George
Nov. 1. Gregory, Son of Daniel Cooke

1790

Jany 10 Katy, Daughter of Samuel Wellington
17 Joseph, Son of Moses Coolidge
Charles, Son of Benjamin Hastings
Eunice, Daughter of Joseph Coolidge
31 Nathaniel, Son of Charles Nutting
Feby 14 Charlotte, Daughter of Jacob Sayer
May 9 Hannah, Daughter of Joshua Kendal
23 Polly, Daughter of Joseph Bright
Augt 15 Lucretia, Daughter of James Robbins
Sepr 26 John & Stephen, Sons of Israel Cooke
Octr 24 Patty, Daughter of Roger Adams
Novr 7 Joseph, Son of William Stone
Decr 16 Seth, Son of Josiah Sanderson

1791

Jany 6 Seth, Son of Hugh Mason
16 Hannah Bond, Daughter of Thomas Clarke
March 27 James, Son of Jonathan Bemise
April 3. Hannah Balch, Daughter of Tilly Buttrick
Elizabeth, Daughter of Benjamin Hastings
May 1 Leonard, Son of Jonathan Harrington
June 31 Samuel, Son of Jona^t Whitney
July 3 Samuel, Son of Jonathan Stone
John, Son of John George
10 Hannah, Daughter of Nathl Ruggles Whitney
31 Leonard, Son of Daniel Jackson

[265]

  Sepr 4. Nathaniel, Son of Josiah Mixer
  Octr 9. Daniel Parker, Son of Abner Craft
          Juliana Maria, Daughter of Willm Warren

1792

  Feb 19 Elisha & Kata, Son & Daughter of Joseph Bright
  March 6. Moses, Isaac, Hannah, Aaron, Children of Moses Mason.
  April 1. Sophia, Daughter of Moses Warren
  May 6 Nancy, Daughter of Moses Stone Ju^r
  June 3 James, Son of Samuel Babcock
  July 8 Nancy, Daughter of Nathaniel Bridge
    29 Elisha, Son of Daniel Whitney
        Eliza, Daughter of Stephen Crane
  Sepr 16 Betsy, Daughter of William Stone
  Decr 2 John Jacob, Son of John Jacob Salga
    9 Nathaniel, Son of Charles Nutting
       Sally Main, Daughter of John George
    16 James, Son of James Robbins
       Mary, Elizabeth, Samuel & George, Children of Samuel Coolidge

1793

  March 31. David, Son of Joshua Kendal
  June 2 Charles Bond an Adult was Bap^d having own'd the Cov^t
       Samuel, Son of Charles Bond
       Sally, Daughter of Moses White

[266]

  June 2 Frank & Leonard, ſons of Ezekiel Whitney Junr
  July 21 Lydia, Daughter of Thomas Clark
  Augt 25 George Call, Son of Nathl Ruggles Whitney
  Sepr 22 Richard Clarke, Son of Benj^a Haſtings
  Octr 6 Susanna, Daughter of Willm Stone
       Francis, Son of Jonathan Bemis
  Decr 15 Henry, Son of Jonas White Junr

1794

  March 9 Mary Oliver, Daug^r of John Vinal
    16 Mary Little, Daughter of Tilly Butterick
    30 Sally Williams, Daughter of Abner Craft
  April 6 Joel, Son of Moses Stone Junr
    13 Josiah, Son of Joseph Bright
  May 11 Polly Goddard, Daughter of Sarah Saunders
  July 6 Joseph, Son of Joseph Nison
  Septr 14 Mary Ann, Daughter of John George
       Sally Dorrs, Daughter of Enoch Hide
       Abigail, Daughter of Ezekiel Whitney
       Nancy, Daughter of Willm Barry

21 Lucy, Daughter of Daniel Jackson
Novr 16 Rebecca, Daughter of Samuel Babcock

1795

Feby 1 Rebeccah, Daughter of Jonathan Stone
15 George, Son of James Robbins
April 12 Samuel, Son of John Hunt
May 31 Mary, Daughter of Benjamin Haftings
June 14 Eliza, Daughter of Willm Stone

[267]

June 21 Sukey, Helen, Charlotte & Polly, Children of Seth Norcrofs
July 5 Lydia, Daughter of Shubal Smith
Octr 18 Elizabeth Coolidge Freeman was Baptiz^d having this day owned the Covenant
25 William, Son of Nathl R. Whitney
Decr 6 Sally, Daughter of Charles Nutting
20 Marshall, Son of Moses Warren

1796

Jany 3 Charles, Son of Charles Bond
March 3 Mary, Daughter of Thomas Clark
May 22 Lucy, Daughter of Samuel Coolidge
June 19 Charles, Son of Joshua Kendal
Lucy, Daughter of Amos Livermore Junr
Sep^t 11 Lucy Jones, Daughter of John George
Decr 4 Joshua, Son of Joshua Grant

1797

Jany 1 Sarah, Daughter of Benj. Hastings
15 Seth, Son of Willm Stone
Feby 27 Augustus Frederick, Son of Jona. Bemis
March 5 George, Son of Shubal Smith
May 7 Joseph Watson, Son of Jonathan Stone
June 1 Francis, Son of Israel Cooke
Sepr Hannah Rawson, Daughter of Israel Cooke
Octr 1 Phinehas, Son of Charles Bond
Leonard, Son of William Winchester
Novr 5 Simon, Son of Nathl R. Whitney
Decr 18 Henry Ward, Son of John Durant

[268]

1798

March 11 Columbus Jackson, Son of Moses Stone
May 13 Unice & Sally, Daughters of Phinehas Hovey
June 3 Thomas, Son of Amos Livermore J^r
10 Josiah, Son of Thomas Clark
24 David, Son of Nathl Bemis
Robert Eddy, Son of Luke Bemis
July 15 Thomas, Samuel & Daniel, Sons of Paul Learned
22 Henry Williams, Son of Saml Coolidge

   28 Sally, Daughter of Artemas Moredock
Aug.t 12 Otis, Son of Ezekiel Whitney J.r
   26 Sarah Grant, Daughter of Peter Clark
Oct.r 14 Patty Remington, Daughter of Daniel Jackson
   28 Hepsibah, Daughter of Joshua Grant

1799

Jan.y 20 Jane White, Daughter of James Robbins
   27 Mary, Daughter of W.m Winchester
Feb.y 3 Mary Ann, Daughter of Shubial Smith
March 3 David, Son of David Livermore
   24 Eliza Brown, Daughter of Phinehas Hovey
Ap.l 7 John, Son of John Durant
    Anna, Daughter of Joseph Bright
June 23 Everline & Caroline, Daughters of W.m Stone
July 28 Hannah, Daughter of Charles Nutting
Aug.t 4 Benjamin, Son of Benjamin Hastings

[269]

Dec.r 8 Polly, Daughter of Israel Cooke
  22 Horace, Son of Artemas Moredock

1800

March 9 Lucy Parkhurst, Daughter of Moses Warren
   16 Luke, Son of Luke Bemis
    Sibil, Daughter of David Livermore
April 6 Anna, Daughter of Jonathan Stone
June 8 Jonathan Mayhew, Son of Ebenezer Vose
July 27 Sarah, Daughter of William Winchester
    Sarah Dennis, Daughter of John Durant
Aug.t 3 Moses Davis & Aaron Davis, Children of Moses White
    Hannah, Daughter of Amos Livermore Jun.r
    Hannah, Daughter of Charles Bond
Sep.t 21 William, Son of Samuel Coolidge
   29 Charles, Son of Joshua Grant
Oct.r 20 John, Son of Nath.l R. Whitney
Nov.r 9 George & Eliza Wheaton, Children of James Robbins

1801

April 19. James Robbins, Son of Francis Faulkner
July 12 Mary Eddy, Daughter of Luke Bemis
    Josiah Sanderson, Son of Thomas Clark
  19. William Bond, a Adult
    Moses, Lucy, & Hitta, Children of William Bond
     [Continued upon page 320.]

[270 to 290] Some hints upon Bible texts.

[291] Blank.

[292]

My Dr wife dyed April 16. 1691. I wil since her death take notice of some things I layd out, payed, bought, sold since yt. I have & shall forgett many.
Funerall charges.

For Gloves bought of Mr Kilenys - - -	9- 6 0
For ye Coffin - - - - - -	1 11 0
To Mrs Kay, for Candles, Tobacco, & pipes -	0 5 3
To Mr Gibbins for Mourning - - - -	0 7 6
To Deacon Eliot for Man & horse - -	0 5 0
To Margaret Bulman, for bread - -	0- 0 8
To Mr Allison for 8 Gold Rings - - -	1 0 0
To Capt. Townsend for wine - - -	6 15 0
To John Knox for digging ye grave - -	0- 0-3
To Dearing for mourning stockins &c - -	0 9-0
For a Mourning hatt - - - - -	1 2 0
For Black Crape 1 - - - - -	0- 2-0
For a Mourning coat of 25s pr yard -	5- 9-0
For Crape for my Hatt - - - -	0- 5-0
For the Bricking of her Grave or Tombe -	0-12-0
For mourning Breeches - - - -	1- 3 8

For a Tombe stone, as followes, yt came one June 21. 92 from Connecticut, ye fright cost 8s. Carting it cost a ls. Carying it to ye Grave from Boston, Something for stones & Lime 10s. ye building it vp was given me by Mr Willis.

The engraving of it cost me to Jos. Whittemore 12s. wch is but ye half of wt is vsuall viz, a penny a letter, he took an halpeny a letter. Wt ye Epitaph was is to be found elsewhere in this book. see p. [62]

For ye Stone is sett I gave £2-5s. I payed it to Mr John Hemlin of Midleton y 14 day of June 1693.

[293]

What things of hers I gave to friends, 1692, Aprill

Ap. 16 gave Mrs Beeres wt was about her wn dead, she washed & Layd her out.

April. 17 a new pair of shoes to Mary Smith

April. 23 gave Mrs Kay a very good Crape Mantua, & petticoat, & shift.

Ap. 25 gave Mrs Kay a good Allamode Scarfe, to Lidia Kay a Mantua & Petticoat.

Ap. 27 a paire of her Lethern gloves to Mr Kay.

Ap. 27 I gave to Nurse Barber a good Petticote of cloth sarg.

Ap. 27 gave Mary Smith a Rideing gown of hers.

Ap. 27 gave Mehetabel Child a good black Hood & Scarf of hers.

Ap. 27 gave Mary Smith one of her Gower hoods.

Ap. 29 gave Sister Baily an Allamode Hood, & set of head.

May 11. gave Sister B. a new pair of her thred Gloves, for me.

June, I gave her Girt old Psalm book to Deacon Stearns wife.

Her straw Hatt to Mrs Beeres, besides many other pety things to others as spoons, Lumpe &c to M. Child & others. A rich neck lace to Sister Baily.

To Lidia Kay her Silver Thimble. To Sifter Baily her beft morning Gown wch was bought in & brought from London for her.

To Benjamin Taylor I gave cloth for 2 fhirts, wch was 13^s.

To Ifabel Pearfe (who is very low, & a member of X) I gave her good Sarg Mantle, a good pair of yarn stockins, fome night capps & forehead clothes.

To Sifter B. a Gofe cap, her Rideing coat (or gown) of half Silk, a good one.

To Mis Kay her Rideing hood, a good warm one.

[294] Blank.

[295] What I fold after her Death. 1691. April. N. E.

Aprill. 2 Calves to John Langdon, wch came to	1- 0-0
Ap. 25 Jo. Langdon fold a red cowe for me at Charlftown for	2-10-0
May 12 I received of Mr Gibbs for 2 months boarding I did not defign to take it, but my ftraites forceth me. Books.	2- 0-0
June. fold Baxters Call for 16^s. 2 Brafs candlefticks 15^s	0-16-4
June. fold Burroughs Rare Jewell wth walking wth g^d 5^s-6^d & sk .... 9^d	0-14-6
June. fold a Eawer 9^d, botle 5^d, Lockyers pills 2^s, cheefe prefse 4-6	0- 7-8
July fold Cowes for £4-10^s, for Barrells 5^s-6^d, old clofe, ftool 3^s	4-18-6
Sold a gr^t Table for 20^s	1- 0-0
July 27 I fold my bed (y^t bed I have for above 19 years layd vpon wth My D^t Bedfellow, who is now in glory. I had not fold it but y^t I could never any more reft vpon it. It grtly greeved me to fee it caryed away, but no more of y^t), to Capt. Sewal for £8.	8- 0-0
a quart pott 16^d, Stone botle 5^d, two pewter difhes 8^s	0- 9-9
a Tin Cullinder 6^d, a chaftindifh & pan 5^s, Stone botle 10^d	0- 6-4
a paire of Brafse fcales 3^s, an Iron chaftindifh 1^s	0- 4-0
a brafse Morter 4^s, Twelve Leathern chaires i. e. Rufhia £3-12^s	3-16-0
4 Glafse bottles 16^d, Bees & hives 15^s, a jugg 4^d, two Stands 4^s-6^d	1- 1-2
2 Earthen pots 1^s, a Limbeck £1-10^s, ye pott to it 6^s, pair beliows 2^s	1-19-0
a glafse botle 2^s, two Juggs 1^s, Tuneel & pott 1^s, tin pan 5^d,	0- 4-5
Earthen pan 6^d, a Table 20^s, one blanket 6^s, a candleftick 4^s,	1-10-0
Ladle 1-6^d, driping pan 2^s-6^d, box & heater 5^s, pitch fork 1^s,	0-10-0
a Tray 2^s-3^d, two cufhings 10^s-6^d, tubbs 2^s-6^d, green curtains 2^s-6^d,	1-15-9
a Squabb £1-8^s,	1- 8-0
To Mr Thrafher 2 fhirts for his boyes 13^s, for tongues 2^s	0-15-0
A Table 14^s, Hand Irons 14^s, a prel 2^s	1-10-0

Books

Barlow vpon Timothy 8ˢ, Lee's Sol. Temple 7ˢ, Lee's Trivmph 3ˢ	0-18-0
Steeles Hufbandry 3ˢ. for other bookes £3-11ˢ-6ᵈ.	3-14-6
Roberts Claris 17ˢ, Ufhers divinity 5ˢ, Ames de confcientia 2ˢ-6ᵈ, Owen on yᵉ 130 pfalme 5ˢ-6ᵈ, Leighs body of divinity 15ˢ.Cartwright on Pv. 4ˢ-6ᵈ, Ambrofse work 22ˢ	
For books, viz Vrfirs Catechifm, & Wendelins Divinity	0- 8-0
For a warming pann 8ˢ, for a piece of cloth 7ˢ-6ᵈ	0-15-6
For Bookes 9ˢ viz Sanderfons fermons 6ˢ,Wilkins preaching 2ˢ, praying 1ˢ,	0- 9-0
Sold to Jo. Langdon an Hefer, it was but poor, it came to 30ˢ, I took it out in better beefe for my winter Pvifion	1-10-0
Sold to Sam. Grey yᵉ 31 of March 1692 a Ketle	4- 0-0
For Bookes, Cars bible 10ˢ, a Scotch bible 6ˢ	

[296] Blank.

[297] What I layd out in lefser things fince her death, April, 1691, N. E.

Aprill, att Boston in fmall things 8ˢ, to Mⁱˢ Bafsam, a fhilling	0- 9-0
Apr. 23 at Boston p fifter B, 7ˢ-4ᵈ, to widdow Faning for Butter 6ˢ	0-13-4
Ap. to Mʳ Knight for yᵉ horfes 3ˢ, for Butter 1ˢ-6ᵈ To Betty Deex	0-10-0
That of Betty Deex was for half a quarter, my wife gave her 10ˢ before.	
I payd Mʳ Thornton for a Shute of clothes for Wil. Pain, befides Hatt & fhoes, but yᵉ weeke after he had an opportunity to go for England, & I let him go tho I had need of him at prefent to pay for his cloths by working, but I gave him all for yᵉ fake spy of his wife who loved, pittyed, wept, & prayed often for him.	2- 2-8

Things go but crofsly wᵗʰ me, let god fanctify all, & its well.

At Knights 3ˢ 0ᵈ to Allifon 1ˢ-8ᵈ, Rum 8ᵈ, Barber 8ᵈ	0- 6-0
To Boatman 8ᵈ, to Tho. Chadwick for working	0- 4-8
Att Boston 2ˢ, To John Kimball for Barrell 6ˢ	0- 8-0
May 12 I payd Mary Smith for half a years fervice fhe had receaved of my wife 15ˢ before, my wife Pmifsing her (as fhe fd) £5 p annum, wᶜʰ is a grt deall, for this halfe year I did it. but will give no fuch wages, for my Dear wife' fake I now do it.	1-15-0
May 12 for meat 2ˢ, to ———. C a 1ˢ-18ᵈ, for gathering herbs 5ˢ	0- 9-8
For Rum 16ᵈ, for fhoeing & other things 2ˢ, for meat 14ᵈ, for Mault 9ˢ-8ᵈ	0-14-4
May 28 for fome things 2ˢ-8ᵈ, to Mis Beeres 4ˢ-4ᵈ	0- 7-0
May 27 I payd Sifter Baily (having borrowed near £30 of her)	17-0-0

May 30 I payd Sifter Bayly £3 more of w^t I owed, wch make it now £20, thire is ftill neare £7 behind -   - 3- 0-0
June 4 to W. Shattock for weaving (an old bufinefs) 12^s- 6^d - - - - - - - - - - - 0-18-0

As for this p^t, Ile Pceed no further, its enough to make a man madd to take notice of dayly expenfes. Finis.

[298]

The following perfons were received into full Communion with the firft Church of Chrift in Watertown.   ⅌ *Seth Storer.*

1724/5

Feb. 27.   Elizabeth Cunningham & Mary Childs
28th.   Rebecca Tainter

1725

April. 25.   Elizabeth Holden & Abigail Benjamin
June. 20.   Elizabeth Shattuck & Lydia Phillips
Octob. 3.   Nathaniel Harris & Joseph Holden
10th.   Ephraim Cutter Senr, Mary Grant & Annabel Benjamin
Dec^t 5.   Abigail Holden

1725/6

Jan. 25.   Mary Hammond

1726.

March 31.   Jonathan Stone Jun. & Huldah Coollidge
May. 15.   Samuel Stearns
July 10.   Elizabeth Sawtel
Sep^t 11.   William Jenifon & William Ozmont
October 30.   Hannah Smith
Decem^r 25.   Josiah Convers, Sam^{ll} Coollidge & Mary Hastings

1726/7

Feb. 19.   George Lawrence Junr, Mercy Stratton & Anna Stearns

1727

June. 18.   Mary Jenifon, Hannah Stone & Hephzibah Bond
Decemb^r 3.   Elnathan Whitney, Jonathan Brown, Sarah Hastings, Efther Barnard & Mary Church

1727/8

Jan. 28.   Andrew White Junr, Sam^{ll} Dix, Sarah White, Kezia Spring, Eliz^a Harrington, Jane White, Joanna Tainter, Grace Coollige, Hannah Thatcher, Abigail Thatcher, Mehetabel Harris, Abigail Stearns & Abigail White
March. 17.   Jabez Stratton, James Symms, Sam^{ll} Jenifon Junr, Jonathan Learned, Rebecca Pierce, Lydia Bond, Ann Bright, Chary Stone, Eliz^a Brown, Tabitha Stratton, Mary Dix, Sarah Bowman, Anna Cooke, Lydia Dix, Hannah White & Abigail Dix

[299]

March. 24. Joshua Warren Sen[r], Joshua Grant Jun[r], Josiah Livermore, Rebecca Warren, Eliz[a] Ormes & Ruth Chenery

1728

April. 7th Mercy Nutting
May. 19. Benjamin Hastings & Anna Child
July. 28. Nath[ll] Clark, dismissed from & recomended by y[e] old C[hh] in Boston
Sep[t] 1. Daniel Bond & Ruth Underwood
December. 22. Sarah Eddy & Ruth Eddy

1729

Aug[st] 3. Richard Clark & Mary Clark

1729/30

Jan. 18. Ebenezer Thatcher, Henry Fisk, Edmund Livermore, Edmund Dix, Daniel Fisk, David Learned, Mercy Perry & Mary Mason
March. 15. Samuel Benjamin, Ebenezer Goddard & John Jenison
22. Joshua Learned, Mary Bond & Deborah Coollidge

1730

May 10. Jonathan Bond
Novem[r] 1. Thomas Wellington & Rebecca his wife
Dec[r] 27. Nath[ll] Jennison

1731.

April. 4th Benj[a] Whitney Sen
June 6th Jon[a] Perry
13th Timothy Harris

1731/2

Jan[y] 23 Mary Benjamin
March 12th Joseph Stearns

1732

July 2nd John Tainter

1732/3

March. 11. Nath[ll] Harrington being dismissed & Recomended to us by y[e] C[hh] in Wells
25 Adam Patterson & Isabel Patterson

1733

Nov[r] 18. Elizabeth Whitney

1733/4

Jan[ry] 20. Andrew White Sen[r]
March. 10. Joshua Biggelow, Edw[d] Harrington & Eleazer Biggelow being dismissed & Recomended by y[e] west Church

[300]

1734
July. 7. Hannah Benjamin being difmifsed & Recomended to us by ye new North C^{hh} in Bofton
Novr 24. Lydia Cutting & Hannah Stearns

1734/5
Feb. 9th Nathaniel Stone, Benj^a Dix & Sufanna Cutting

1735
April. 13. Jofiah Stearns & Sufanna Stearns
Sep^t 21st Isaac Holden

1736
June. 13th Peter ye Negro man of Mr Jon^a Stone
27. Abiah Coollidge
July. 4th Mary Stone
Oct^o 17. Amos Bond & Elizabeth Learned
Decr 19. Abigail Jenifon ye wife of Sam^{ll}
Lydia, Abigail & Mercy Jenifon

1736/7
Feb^{ry} 13. Mehetabel Saunderfon

1737
April 3rd Nathaniel Coollidge, Ruth Haftings, Abigail Mafon & Ruth Stone
June 5th Abigail Sawen
July. 17. Sarah Stowell
Sep^t 18th Elizabeth Goddard
25th William Lawrence

1737/8
Jan^{ry} 8. Hannah Bright
Feb. 19th Chriftopher Grant
March. 12th Margaret Wellington

1739
July. 29th Sam^{ll} Stratton
Sep^t 2nd Elizabeth Child
Decemb^r 31. John Kimbal

1740
June. 29. Elifabeth Fifk
December 14 John Sawen Junr

1740/1
Feb^{ry} 1. Ruth Haftings

1741
April. 5. Samuel Child, Uriah Clark, Elifabeth Child & Eliz^a Brown
May. 29. Joseph Coollidge was chofen to the office a Deacon in this Church

May. 24. John Bond, Nehemiah Underwood, Matthias Stone, Ruth Bond, Mary Lawrence, Sufanna Cooke, Sarah Harris, Mary Perry, Mary Bemis, Mary Kimbal, Mary Parry, & Sufanna Parry
     31. Dorothy Whitney & Ruth Bond
July. 19. Oliver Livermore, Samuel Whitney, Benj^a Bond, Ebenezer Bullard, Joanna Clark, Mary Bond, Hannah Tainter, Love Stone, Thankful Stowel, & Eunice Underwood

[301]
July. 26. Ifrael Meed, Daniel Livermore & Martha Clark
Sep^t 13. Sarah Chadwick, Rebecca Clark, Submit Chadwick, Sarah Harrington & Lois Stearns
     20. Jon^a Child, John Fifk Junr, Samuel Coolidge, Elias Mafon, John Cooke & David Gleafon
Novr 8. Nehemiah Mafon, Mofes Stone, Hannah Godding & Arminna, a negro woman
     15. Kezia Spring & Sarah Stowel

1741/2
Jan^{ry} 3rd Jon^a Stone Junr, Eunice Jenifon & Lydia Sawen
     10. Abijah Stearns
Feb. 28. Joseph Harrington & Martha Harrington

1742
March. 7. Elizabeth Barnard
April. 25. Sufanna Thatcher
August 15. Mary Goodenow
     22. Mary Sawen
Dec. 5th Stephen Cooke & Rebecca Gage

1743
March. 27. Hannah Fifk & Hannah Haftings

1744
April. 22. Jeremiah Beeth
August. 19. Anna Stearns

1745
July. 14. Hannah Sawen
Novr 3. Rebecca Capens

1746
April. 13. Elifha Coollidge
June 15. Ruth Hunt & Rebecca Tainter
     22. Mary Stearns
Nov. 30. Samuel Stearns & Margaret Bright

1746/7
Jan^{ry} 25. Daniel Peirce
March 22. Nathan Stone

1747

May. 17. Samuel Fiſk and Lydia Fiſk
Novr 1. John Bond Junr & Abigail Bond

1747/8

Feb^{ry} 28. Nathan Perry & Eliſabeth Harrington

1748

April 17. Jon^a Stone Junr, Daniel Sawen, Martha Stone, Suſanna Maſon, & Ruth Clark
June. 12. David Bemis & Abigail Stowel

1749

June. 27. Samuel Fiſk was choſen to the office of a Deacon
Oct^o 22. Eunice Stratton & Abigail Stratton

1750

Ap. 22^d Mary Kelly
Augst 5. Moſes Biggelow
Decr 2^d Jonathan Bemis & Anna Bemis were admitted as members of the Church of Chriſt in Watertown being diſmiſsed & recommen^d to us by the C^{hh} of Chriſt in Waltham

1751

July. 14. Anna Bemis Junr
Octr 27. Nathaniel Bright

[302]

1752

April. 9th Seth Haſtings & Hannah Haſtings
October. 15. Suſanna Tainter
Novr 5. Joseph Peters & Abigail Peters were admitted as Members with this C^{hh} being diſmiſsed & recomended to us by the ſecond Church in Mendon.

1753

Decemb^r 30th Abraham Brown, Mary Brown & Eliſabeth Learned j^r

1756

Jan^{ry} 11. Lucey Bradford
Feby 1st. Thomas Learned & Martha Pierce
15th Lydia Baldwin
March. 28th Joanna Cooke

1757

April. 24th Lydia Coollidge
Novr 13th Simon Haſtings
Decr. 4. Nathaniel Coollidge Junr

1758

Jan^{ry} 22^d Simon Whitney, Mary Whitney & Mary Bemis
July. 2^d Rachel Bright

Novr 19th   Samuel Hager
Decr 31st   Hannah Coollidge

1759
Feb^ry 4th   Abijah Brown, Nathan Coollidge, & Sarah Brown
Aug^st 5th   Sarah Johnson

1760
Decr 7th   Mary Hunt

1761
Feb^ry 1st   Hannah Learned
April. 12th   Mary Biggelow
     19th   Alpheus Spring
Aug^st 9th   Sarah Gray
Decr 27th   Hannah Godding

1762
Jan^ry 17th   James Barnard & Sarah Barnard
May 9th   Thomas Saltmarsh

[303]
1763
June 5th   Kezia Saunderson, Susanna Barnard Junr & Hannah Barnard
July. 24th   Abigail Walker

1764
July. 1st   Grace Whitney
     22.   Elisha Learned & Sarah Learned
Aug^st 12th   Jedediah & Hannah Leathe, & Mary Hager
     26th   Abigail Goddard
Octr 21st   Susanna Barnard

1765
Feb^ry 10th   Ayres Tainter
April. 14th   Samuel White

1767
June 10.   Israel & Jemima Whitney
July 19th   Joseph Gardner & Susanna Whitney

1768
April. 17.   Samuel Hunt & John Hunt ju^o
Aug^st 14th   Nathaniel Bond

1769
Feb^ry 5th   Samuel & Grace Sanger

1770
August 5th   Elisabeth Remington

1771
Jan^ry 20th   Moses Stone jun^o
July 31.   Dorothy, Ruth, Katharine & Elisabeth Hunt
Sep^t 22.   Hannah Phillips

1772

March. 8th Hannah & Ann Bright
Augst 23. Edward Harrington
Sep^t 27. Daniel Whitney
Oct^o 11. Josiah Capen jun. & Mary Capen

1773

April 18th Abigail Learned

[Continued upon Page 45.]

[304]   1775

Octo^r 15. Solomon & Hannah Prentice, Being Dismissed & Recom^d from the first Ch^h in Cambridge

1778

December Richard and Mary Clark, being Dismissed & Recommended from the Second Church in Cambridge

[305]

The Following Persons were Admitted into full Communion w^t ye Ch^h of X in Watertown   P^{er} Danl Adams

1778

July 12th Nathl Bright & Susanna his wife

[306]

The following Persons were received into full Communion, with the Church of Christ in Watertown   p^r R. R. Eliot

1780

Augt 20. Wm Harrington & Esther his Wife
Octr 22. Danl Whitney & Mary his Wife
Novr 12th Moses Coolidge & Hannah his Wife
Decr 3. Roger Adams & Hepsibah his wife
           Elijah Meads & Abigail his wife
           Lucy Bond & Elizabeth Bond

1781

Feby 25th Anna Sanger
Octr 28 Hannah Whitney

1782

Novr 24th Lydia the Wife of Samuel Spring

1786

Decr 31 Thankful Harrington

1787

March 4 John Remington Junr

1788

Feby 10 Keziah, the Wife of Nathan Coolidge

[307]   1789
April 19th   Samuel Soden
May 31.   Abigail, the Wife of Moses Stone Junr
July 12.   Sibil White
      19.   Mary Stowel
Octr 4 Esther the Wife of Daniel Cooke
     18.   Susanna the Wife of Phinehas Jennison
     25.   Lucy Bowman

                               1790
Sepr 5. Hannah the Wife of Israel Cooke

                               1791
June 5   Lucy, the Wife of Bradbury Robinson

                               1792
Feby 12 Phinehas Jennison
Octr 7   Mary the Wife of Samuel Coolidge
Novr 4   Lucy Bond

                               1793
March 17   John Remington

                               1794
Feby 16 Hannah Soden
Novr 9   Jerusha Norcrofs

                               1796
Jany 10 Frederick Remington

                               1797
Sepr 24. Nathan Tilton

                               1798
Jany 7   Murriah a Negro Woman
July 15.   Paul Learned & Anna his Wife
Aug. 26.   Sally Coolidge

[308]   1803
June 5   Jonathan Stone & Sally his wife
     26   Thomas Clarke & his Wife
Augt 7th Christopher Grant & Sarah his wife
Sepr 1st Jonathan Alden

                               1805
June 2   Sophia Mellen
July 7   Phineas Page
     21   Mary Trowbridge
Decr 15 Daniel Jackson

                               1806
Sepr 28 Lucy Jackson

                               1807
May 3¹ Sarah Salter Scudder

1809

July 30   Peter Clark & Wife
Sepr 3   Hephzibah Grant, Elizabeth Bowes Coolidge, Hannah Stowel Coolidge & Elizabeth Mason Coolidge

[309]   1810

May 27   Mary Hunt & Sarah Postell Hunt
July 30   James Robbins was received at his own house being very sick
Augt 5.   Lois Robbins
Sepr 7   Hannah Bond at her Fathers house being very sick
Octr 7   Lois Curtifs & Marthe Robbins
Nov 25   Ann Bond

1811

Jany 13.   Sally Tainter & Martha Chenery
April 7.   Levi Thaxter
       28   Elizabeth the wife of Clinton Thayer at her house, being very sick

[310]

May 19.   Eleanor the Wife of Thaddeus Cole
June 2   Nathaniel Bemis & Wife, Luke Bemis & Wife, John Richardson & Wife, & Ann Richardson
      23.   Katharine Hunt
Octr 6   Jonathan Child & Wife & Susan the Wife of Paul Kendal

1814

Feby 19   Sally the Wife of Israil Whitney at her house being very sick
April 3   Nathaniel Weld & Nathaniel Ruggles Whitney & Wife
      10   Thomas Learned & wife
June 5   John Tucker

[311]

Novr 6.   Elizabeth Babcock & Grace Winchester

1815

Jany 29   Josiah Learned & Wife, Richard Sanger & Wife, Joseph Cole & Wife, Luther White & Wife & Grace Dana
Feby 26   Amos Livermore Junr
May 4   Sarah Russell
June 11. Eleanor Warren
       25 Elizabeth Sanger & Hannah Norcrofs
Aug 6   Ann Hilliard

1816

May 5   Daniel Sawin & Daniel Bond & Wife

[312]
June 16. Jonathan Brown
Nov' 3. Mary C. & Catherine M. Stearns

1817
July 15 Mary, the Wife of John Fowle, at his house, being very sick.
Sep' 16 Elizabeth Saunderson at Leonard Bond's, being dangerously sick
Nov' 9th Elizabeth, the Wife of Elijah Ray
30th Nathaniel Ruggles Whitney Jun' & Wife

1819
Feb 3¹ Susanna Bright at her Father's House being very sick by the Rev. Mr. Ripley of Waltham

[313 to 319] Blank.

[320] [Baptisms continued from Page 269.]

1801
Betsy, William & Simon Edgell, Children of W'ᵐ Bond
July 19 John, Sally, Ebenezer & William, Children of John Tucker
Joseph Pierce an Adult
William, John Minott & Elvira, Children of Joseph Pierce
Aug' 2 Sarah & Mary, Children of James Simmons
Jonathan Alden an Adult & Sally, Nancy & Jonathan, his Children
Nov' 6 William Smith, Son of Joseph Bright

1802
Feb' 8 Harriot, Daughter of Moses Stone

[321]
Feb' 21 Anna, Daughter of William Stone
March 7 Samuel White, Son of David Livermore
Jonathan, Son of Jonathan Alden
28 Henry, Son of Ebenezer Voce
Oct' 31. Daniel, Son of William Winchester
Dec' 12 Nelson, Son of Shubael Smith

1803
Jan'y 9 Sarah Clark, Daughter of Joshua Grant
23 Dwight Foster, Son of Francis Faulkner
Feb'y 13 George, Son of Charles Bond
20 Edward, Son of Jonathan Stone
March 6th Anna, Daughter of James Simmons
20 Margaret, Daughter of John George
April 24 Isaac, Son of James Robbins
May 15. Julia, Daughter of Artemas Murdock
29. Eliza, Daughter of Amos Livermore Jun'

June 12. Jane, Daughter of Moses White
July 24 Martha & Hannah, Children of Luke Bemis
Sep{r} 25 Elizabeth Atherton & Mary Call, Children of John Tucker
Oct{r} 23 Luther Coolidge an Adult
James Patterson & his Son
Nov{r} 27 Joseph Nathaniel, Son of Joseph Pierce

1804

Jan 22 Susanna Thayer, Daughter of Will{m} Bond

[322]

May 20 Peter, Son of Peter Clarke
June 17{th} William, Son of Thomas Clark
June 24 Elisha, Son of Elisha Livermore
July 8. Anna, Daughter of Paul Learned
Oct{r} 7 Addison, Son of Ebenezer Vose
Nov{r} 4 Hannah Foster, Daughter of John Tucker
18 James, Son of James Simmons

1805

Feb. 10 Josiah, Son of David Livermore
April 14 William Emerson, Son of Francis Faulkner
June 23. Rebecca Clark, Daughter of William Winchester
30 Susan, Daughter of Charles Bond
Aug{t} 4 Maria Bethune & Jane Lee, Daughters of Jane, the Widow of William Hunt
Hellen Maria, Sophia Ann, Daughters of Sophia the Widdow of Leonard Mellen
Oct{r} 20 Edmund, Lucy Pierce & Charles, Children of Edmund Troubride

[323]

Oct{r} 20 Henry Lewis, Son of Paul Kendal
Jane Ann Kendal, Daughter of Joseph Russell
Nov{r} 17 Sally Wife & Andrew Craige, Sally Joan Turner, Eliza White, George Turner, & Roxana Richardson, Children of Andrew Blackman
Martha Blake, Daughter of Joseph Pierce

1806

Feb{y} 2. Isaac Grant, Son of Peter Clark
16. Amos Henry, Son of Amos Livermore
Lucy, Daughter of Joseph White
April 13 Luke, Son of Luke Bemis
Aug{t} 3. Samuel Bright, Son of Elisha Livermore
Dec{r} 7 Stephen, Son of James Simmons
14 Nancy Daughter of William Winchester
28 Charlotte Daughter of Ebenezer Vose

1807

Jan{y} 25 Lydia Sanderson Daughter of Thomas Clarke
Feb{y} 8 Moses Son of Jonathan Stone

March 1 Sufan Curtis Daughter to Paul Kendall
May 3   Daniel Lewis, Son of Daniel Scudder

[324]

July 5   Lucy Stimpson Daughter of Joseph Russell
Aug[t] 16 George Washington Son of John Tucker
Nov[r] 1 Mary Daughter of Charles Bond
     15 Hannah Saunderson Daughter of David Livermore
Dec[r] 6 Harriot Rebecca Daughter of Peter Clark
     17 Abigail Jenkins Daughter of Israel Cook

1808

Feb[y] 21 Adeline Daughter of Joseph White
May 8   Mary Daughter of Jonathan Robbins
June 5 Clarissa, Wife & Clarissa Andrews, Daughter of Tyler Bigelow
         James Son of Edmund Trowbridge
         William Henry, Son of Henry Dalrymple

[325]

June 26 Nathaniel Ruggles Son of Nathaniel Ruggles Whitney Jun[r]
Oct[r] 1. Martha Daughter of John Tucker,
       8 Sibil Chenery Daughter of Charles Whitney
      23 Luther Gustavus Son of Luther Barrett
Nov[r] 6 William Coolidge Son of Afa Stone
Dec[r] 25. Jane Ann Daughter of Elifha Livermore

1809

April 9 Grace Saunderson Daughter of Amos Livermore
     16 Lucretia Daughter of Ebenezer Vose
July 2 Hiram Son of Paul Kendal
         Gustavus Son of Joseph Russell
Oct. 15 Rachel Daughter of Joseph White
      22 Rufus Howard Son of Tyler Bigelow
         Lydia Daughter of Jonathan Robbins

[326]

Oct[r] 29. Martha Minot Daughter of Jonathan Child

1810

Feb[y] 25 Lucretia, Wife of Isaac Patten, & Isaac his Son
March 25 Sarah Grant Daughter of Peter Clarke
April 22. Caroline Ann Daughter of Thomas Clark
May 6   Alexander Son of Nathaniel R Whitney
June 3   Lydia Ann Daughter of Levi Thaxter
July 15 Charles Son of Charles Whitney
Aug[t] 12. Mary Daughter of Afa Stone
      26 Ann Maria Daughter of Edmund Trowbridge
Sep[r] 30 Thomas Son of Isaac Patten
Oct[r] 28 Benjamin Dana Son of Daniel Leverett
Nov[r] 25 Isabella Daughter of John Frazer

[327]

Decr 9. Thaddeus Cole an Adult was Baptized
& Eleanor, Mary Ann, William, Andrew, Harriot & John his Children

1811

Jany 13. Martha Chenery an Adult
20 Jonathan Wheeler Son of Seth Bemis
April 14 George Tyler Son of Tyler Bigelow
28 George Clinton & Charles Sons of Clinton Thayer
June 2 Jonathan Stone Son of Nathaniel R. Whitney Junr
William Eaton Son of Jonathan Robbins
23. Thomas Dawes More Son of John Trull

[328]

July 21 Mary Ann Daughter of Amos Livermore Junr
28 Archibald Son of Michael Bent
Martha Daughter of Luther White
Augt 5 Eloisa Daughter of Thaddeus Cole
Eliza Carter Daughter of Paul Kendal
25 Eliza Crocker Daughter of Joseph Russell
Benjamin Robbins Son of Benjamin Curtifs
George Son of Polly Newhall
Sepr 8. Abigail Minott & Mary Boothe, Daughters of Joseph Pierce
Sarah Wiswell Daughter of Luther Barrett

[329]

Octr 6 Hannah Saunderson, Daughter of Jonathan Child

1812

Jany 26 Marshall Bond & Joseph Sons of Joseph Bird
April 26 Hannah Bemis Daughter of John Richardson
May 24 Charles Son of David Livermore
June 14 Delia Ann Daughter of Micah Bent
28 George Howard Son of Abijah White
Sepr 20 Sarah Wheeler Daughter of Seth Bemis
Octr 4 Anna Aspinwall Daughter of Charles Whitney
25 William John Son of John Trull

1813

March 7 George Ticknor Son of Benjamin Curtifs
May 16 Walter Son of John Fraser
July 4 George Henry Son of Asa Stone
George Son of Paul Kendall
18 James Frothingham Son of Nath R. Whitney Ju^r

[330]

July 18 Elizabeth Meriam Daughter of Joseph Bird
24 Martha Minot Daughter of Jonathan Child
Augt 1. Charles Henry Son of Tyler Bigelow

	John Hosmer, Son of Jonathan Robbins
22	Mary Adeline Daughter of Thaddeus Cole
	Adeline Daughter of Luther Barrett
Sep' 5	Adeline Mariah Daughter of Amos Livermore Jun'
	Calvin Son of Luther White
Oct' 31.	Richard Roswell Eliot, Son of Isaac Patten
Nov' 28	Mary Bellows & Harriot Louisa, Daughters of Leonard Stone

1814

Feb'y 19	Sarah Barnard & Mary Ann, Daughters of Israel Whitney
April 24	Hiram Son of Micah Bent

[331]

May 22.	Thomas & Edward Winship Son of Thomas Learned
June 26	Horace Son of Joseph Bird
Aug' 14	Charles Henry Son of Tyler Bigelow
	Lydia Daughter of Alfred Smith
Sep' 25	Harriot Augusta & Elbridge Dexter, Children of Samuel Rand
	Ann Geyer Daughter of John Leathe
Oct' 2	Martha White Daughter of David Livermore
Nov' 6	Jonas White Son of Levi Thaxter
13	Seth Son of Seth Bemis

1815

Jan'y 1.	Joseph Russell Son of Charles Bradford
29	Joseph Cole & Elizabeth his wife
	Grace wife of Caleb Dana
June 11.	William Son of John Tucker
25	Elizabeth Sanger, & Hannah Norcrofs Adults

[332]

June 25.	William, Richard Eliot, Anne, George Washington & Samuel Edward, Children of Richard Sanger
July 9.	Edward Son of Nath R. Whitney Jun'
16	Josiah Learned, Samuel, & James, Children of Joseph Cole
23	Lois Jane Daughter of Mary Robbins
Aug' 27	William Son of Paul Kendall
	Lucy Coolidge Daughter of Asa Stone
Oct' 15	Sarah the Wife of James Robbins & Lois his Daughter
22	Mary Deneale Daughter of Isaac Patten

[333] 1816

April 28	Juliana Wife of Charles Stone, & Ann Rebecca Watson, Daughter of Jonathan Stone Jun'
May 19	Francis Son of Thaddeus Cole
	Mary Cutter daughter of Joseph Bird

June 2   Catharine, Eliza Ann, Jane, Edward, George & Daniel, Children of Daniel Bond
16   Jonathan Brown an Adult
July 7   George Newell Son of Thomas Learned
Augt 11.   Lucy Ann Daughter of Luther Barrett
Sepr 8   Lucy White Daughter of Levi Thaxter
22   Harriot Daughter of Tyler Bigelow
Novr 17   Warren Fay Son of Joseph Stone

1817

Jany 12   Abner Foster Son of Edward Loud Junr

[334]

May 25   Harriot Louisa Daughter of Amos Livermore Junr
June 22   Martha, Daughter & Bradshaw, Son of Charles Whitney
Sepr 7   Sarah Watson Daughter of Nathaniel R. Whitney Junr
Octr 12   Juliana Danforth Daughter of Isaac Patten
Novr 16   Benjamin Franklin, Son of Paul Kendall
Decr 7   Caroline Daughter of Thaddeus Cole

1818

Feby 8th Lucy White Daughter of Levi Thaxter
March 15   Charles Banks Son of John Fraser
April 26   Samuel Sargent Son of Thomas Learned
May 10   Asa Son of Asa Stone
Aug. 9   Nathaniel Carter Son of Daniel Sanger

[335]

Octr 4th Mehetable Bond, Dauter of Joseph Bird

1819

Jan. 6th Mary Harrington an adult at her House being very sick by the Rev. Mr. Ripley of Waltham
Feb. 3   Susanna Bright an adult at her Father's House, being very sick by the Rev. Mr. Ripley of Waltham

[336-373] Blank.

[374-384] Meditations upon Bible Texts.

[384-418] Blank.

[419]

Sacramentall phrafes, or exprefsions vfed at ye L^{ds} Table in breaking & pouring out. [While at Limerick in Ireland.]

    The firft facrament we ever had together was on June 15. 79. I fd much, but now have forgotton it. as oh for a broken h— its a fearfull thing to fall into ye hands of ye living g^d Thus wid our fines have ferved us—its precious, pleading, juftifying blood. Exhortation was given afterward to y^m.

[All from here on to page 495 omitted, alternate pages being blank.]

[495]

The 46th Sac was on Jan yo 13. 87 in ye morning at Mr W. Jo. Currye & his wif, & Ann Collett was admitted at yt Table, I sd nothing before it, bec, I was at one of clock to preach at Mr C. in ye Irish town, But I have now nothing to say to this days worke, for I was Imprisoned in yt afternoon & so I suppose it may be ye last Sac, yt I may give, many things were sd at yt Table weh I now being vnder confinment forbear to speake, we sung pt of yt 118 psm—ye collection was 30—I exhorted ym to prove yr things yt are Acceptable to ye Ld.

[October 6 1686]

I coming for N. England, after some time, was sett apt for ye church of Watertown viz on Oct. 6. 86—wt out ye Imposition of hands, I preached, others prayed &c I pmised to be of wt vse I could dureing my continuance amongst ym &c. ye particulars are too long &c.

The first Sacmt by me in W. was on ye 31 of Oct. 86. many yr &c. I preached on Cant. 8. 6, on ye first Doct &c. At ye begining I exhorted ym to ye right Sanctifying of ye name of gd in this Ord. wt was sd at it I have forgotten, esp becauſe I purposed never more to putt down wt I sd, & wt I may do for ye future shall be very short. After ward I exh ym to walk as yt redeemed of ye Ld, & as such as had renewed yr Cov & in particular these 3 things, viz yt yr wid lay in, for sufferings, & lay vp for death, & lay out for gd in ye places gd had sett ym & yn spake to ye Spectators (who were very many) asking ym some Questions, as whether yr had no need, no love, no feare, no shame yr Father ptaking in yt place, & yt ye place, linnen & cups shid rise vp in Judgmt agnst ym, it was blesed for much good &c we sung ye Song of ye Lamb.

[From here to page 509 omitted.]

[509]

The 9 Sacrmt we had vpon ye 20th of November '87. ye weather proving better yn I thought for &c, very many yr, from Dedham, Wooborn, Bastable, Cambridge, old church in Boston, & yt New church in Boston, Cambridge Village, Concord, Dorchester, Roxbury, Newbury, Charlstown, Waymouth, &c ye text was in Col. 3. 11. ye dayes being short I only sd before we begunn, yt our work was now to Remember X, & it ought to be 2 wayes, viz wth Joy, & wth Conformity &c Gal. 6. 24. After we had donn (for I passe by wt was dropped all a long over ye Elemts) I spoke both to Partakers & Spectators in one, viz This was Crying blood, as all blood is, & it cryes these 3 wayes, (1) It cryes after yt, I ere I stood vp & spake to ye Spectators (wch were very many on every side) & held ye cup in my hand, & sd this blood cryed to ym, and yt for 3 things (which were pressed) viz yt yt wid Come to it, yt ye wid drink of it, yt yt wid wash in it, it cryes as in Ps. 9. 2 to 8 v. I sd, can y be sived wthout this blood? This bleeding X cryes come, drink, wath & be pardoned, sanctifyed & Saved for ever. Its ye blood of G^d y^t cryes after y all both on ye right, & left hand & before me in both Galleryes. & will y, can y, dare y refufe this X, & his blood, y^t this bowll fhall rife vp in judgm^t agnft y, & fo fhall alfo this good company, and y^r poor Minifter &c. Is y^r any vnbeleeving Thomas amongft Y, This Dear X faith, come & thruft in y hands vp to ye Elbowes in my blood &c—come, oh come all Watertown to this blood, come tho ye worft of finners, y are Welcome—G^d, X, ye H. G. Angells, Minifters, & all good xtians bid y welcome—And if y will not come, y^n ye blood fhall go for it—oh let all thefe feates, pofts, & galleryes bear witnefse agnft y, & all ye old Fathers of this ancient church take notice of this 20 of Nov. 87 y^t I thus invited y to X, nay let all ye young folks y^t have been admitted of late bear wit- nefse y^t y will not come to ye blood of X—I befeech y, nay charg y by all ye loves of X, ye beautyes of X, & his bitter Agonyes y^t y come in to X.

(2) This blood cryes for y, now to ye doubting communicant, tho y fins fpeaks high, & fometimes y can fay nothing for yfelf, it cryes for 3 things, viz pardon, peace, & purging &c.

(3) This blood will cry agnft y, if fleighted or refufed by y, it efp cryes agnft 3 things (y^t were opened) viz Indifferency, Infi- delity, & Enmity, oh faith X, y^r are fome here y^t have flain me (i. e by y^r rafh & vnworthy ptaking) & others have fleighted me, as if I were not worth ye minding—& to all y y^t fleigh his fon, & ordinances, G^d faith or may fay My curfe be on y^m, & my fons blood &c.

[511]

oh faith all heaven, let y^m never profp in y^r bafkett nor ftore, in foull nor body, time nor eternity y^t defpife fuch a matchles offer of love. Heaven, Earth, & Hell cryes out Anathema &c, let y^m be damned fayn & damned for ever y^t fleight fuch blood, ye all pray as I may fo fay agnft y, ye H. G. faith, L^d fhall I never ftrive wth y^m more &c, ye Angells faying, fhall I go & take off y^r heads of thefe dead doggs, & Devills incarnatt &c—ye very Seates & galleryes crying fhall I let y^m fall & break y^r necks, & let y^m go quick into y^r pitt, &c ye devills faying, let us have y^m, we never finned agnft this blood thus, oh y^t I had good ground to Imagin, y^t y are all thinking to fay, oh Dear Sir, y have fd enough, fay no more of it, we will go home & clofe wth X & wafh in his blood &c—y^n will I fay no more. But I leave all this wth I. X. to take an Anfwer from y this night, whether y will receave or rejèct him &c.

we fung ye Song of ye Lamb &c.

[All from here to page 543 omitted.]

[543] [At a third from the bottom.]

VPon ye 31 of May 1691 we had our 34 Sacrm^t & very likely our laft, a rayny day—at ye begining I raifed Notes from Math, 26.29, I pafse y^m by tho I had no Notes, vyd Dykfon. I defired Partakers to dept from iniquity. Spectators I reproved y^r trifling & only read Math 22- 14 & Lu. 14. 24 to y^m &c. Baptizing fome afterward, took my leave from 2 Cor. 13. 11. I did pticularly bid farewell to my houfe, old walker, all ye 3 ptes of ye town. My Afiftant Gibbs, ye Schoolm^r, Deacon, Selectme, military P^fons, 2 Cunftables, ye burying place, my Servt y^t lived wth me formerly, this old Ch, ye 3 or 4 meetings in ye town, this neighbourhood of mine, Snts but finners efp, old but young efp, all my children wch grieved me moft, Friends and foes, ye fweet finger of Ifrael, all widdowes & fatherles familyes, all moralized pons, all y^m y^t heard me not now, ye pulpit pues, feats & galleryes, & cufhion I left as a token of my love, all my adminiftrations, him y^t digs ye graves, Neighbouring townes & ch,

[544] Adminiftrations of ye L^d fupper att ye Eaft Chh in Watertown, Dec. 12, 1697 to Oct. 19, 1701.
 [Dates of administration.]

[545-560] [Here some scattering entries, but mostly blank.]

[561-576] [An imperfectly made index of the contents of the book.]

[Finis.]

East Precinct and Pastors' Records.

Index to Persons.

Abbot, John 23
Adams, Benjamin 173
" Daniel 104, 186
" George . . 120, 123, 127
" Hannah 172
" Hepza 170
" Hepsibah 186
" Isaac 169
" John 100, 127
" Joseph 97
" Lucy 169
" Marcy 170
" Martha 120
" Mary 124
" Matthew 123
" Moses 128
" Patty 173
" Polly 169
" Roger 116, 169, 170, 171, 172, 173, 186
" Smith 169
Addington, Thomas 1
Alden, Jonathan . . 106, 187, 189
" Nancy 189
" Sally 180
Allen, Dea. 101
" Ebenezer 133
" Elizabeth . . . 130, 133
" Hepsibah 133
" John 97
" Joseph 91, 97
" Judith 21
" Peter 109
" Susee 133
Allison, Mr. 177
Angier, Ephraim 38
Anthony (a mulatto) . . . 116
Applin, Ablah 120
" Bashuah 120
" Hannah 120
" John . . 120, 121, 126
" Mary 120
" Mehitable 126
" Thomas 120
Arminna a negro) . . 116, 183
Austin, Benjamin 154
" Timothy 154
Avered, Abigail 98
Babcock, Elizabeth 188
" Elizabeth S. . . . 172
" James 174
" Rebecca 175
" Sally 173
" Samuel 172, 173, 174, 175

Bacon, Abigail 125
" Henry 155
" John 126, 128
" Joseph 119
" Mary 125, 155
Bailey, Bayley, Elizabeth . . 84
" James 89, 91, 93
" John 87
" Rebecca 101
" Sister . 177, 178, 179, 180
" Thomas 126
Baker, John 88, 89
Baldwin, Jane 155
" Lydia 184
" Rev. S. 158
" William 155
Ball, Abigail 123, 154
" Eliza 152
" James . 131, 132, 153, 154
" John 92, 121, 123, 124, 151
" Sarah 133
Bulston, Gersham 125
Barbour, Peter 88
Barker, Elizabeth 101
" Nurse 177
Barnard, Abigail . 158, 155, 157
" Benjamin 152
" Cornelius 149
" Daniel 160
" David . . 108, 111, 160
" Edmund 148
" Elizabeth 108, 119, 167, 183
" Esther 180
" Fleming 143
" Hannah . 111, 116, 185
" Isaac . . 113, 138, 170
" James 71, 137, 141, 144, 160, 162, 163, 185
" Jonas 108, 152, 155, 157, 158, 160, 161, 162, 165, 166, 167
" Jonathan 137, 141, 142, 143, 146, 148, 149, 151, 152, 154, 156
" Joseph 151
" Josiah 146
" Lydia 131
" Nathan 154
" Phebe 112
" Samuel 65, 86, 104, 108, 109, 111, 114, 146, 176, 170
" Sarah 108, 138, 140, 152, 185
" Susanna . . 138, 111, 185
" Sergt. 125

Barnard, Thomas 166
Barnes, Richard 131
Barrett, Adeline 193
" John 100
" Lucy A. 194
" Luther . 106, 191, 192, 193
" Luther C. 191
" Sarah 98
" Sarah W. 192
Barron, Abigail 130
" Benoni 128
" Elliz 128
" Peter 134
" Timothy 23, 125, 130, 132, 134
Barry, Nancy 174
" William 174
Barsham, Anna 171
" Captain . . . 5, 6, 7
" Dea. 6, 7, 130
" Elizabeth . . 119, 124
" Nathaniel 2, 5, 7, 8, 9, 10, 11, 15, 17, 18, 19, 22, 23, 24, 26, 27
Bristow, Hannah 131
" Micael 2
" Rebecca 125
Bassam, Mis 179
Basset, Elizabeth 97
Bathrick, Jason 141
Battle, Ethel 155
" James 155
Beals, Adino B. 170
" Katy 171
" Sukey 170
" William . . 105, 170, 171
Beath, Beeth, Jeremiah . . 183
" John 148, 149
" Margaret 149
" Mary 148
" Walter 91
Becks, John 92
Beers, Jabez 11, 101
" John 90
" Mis 177, 179
" Sergeant 6, 7
" Simon 132, 134
Bemis, Abigail 125
" Abraham 153
" Anna 162, 184
" Augustus F. 175
" Bethia 127
" Charles 173
" David 156, 158, 159, 161, 162, 164, 166, 167, 171, 175, 184
" Elijah 167
" Elizabeth . . 125, 171
" Ephraim . . . 125, 127
" Esther 153
" Francis 174
" Hannah . . . 167, 190
" Isaac 164

Bemis, James 127, 173
" John . . . 124, 127, 161
" Jonathan 90, 92, 94, 145, 153, 156, 157, 159, 160, 161, 167, 171, 172, 173, 174, 175, 184, 194
" Jonathan W. . . . 192
" Joseph . . , . . 127
" Katharine 157
" Luke 106, 159, 175, 176, 188, 190
" Martha 190
" Mary 127, 144, 166, 183, 184
" Nathaniel 105, 153, 171, 173, 175, 188
" Rebecca 125
" Robert E. 175
" Samuel . . . 149, 151
" Sarah 125, 145
" Sarah W. 192
" Seth . . 107, 192, 193
" Susannah 127
" Thankful 156
Benjamin, Abel 131, 132, 133, 139, 155, 156, 157, 158
" Abigail . 103, 125, 136, 180
" Anna 139
" Annabel 180
" Caleb 103, 133, 136, 137, 138
" Daniel 10, 18, 19, 23, 96, 127, 129, 131, 132, 133, 138
" Elizabeth 91, 131, 143, 145, 155
" Hannah 182
" John . . 96, 97, 129, 158
" Jonathan 90, 92, 131, 135, 137, 138, 141, 143, 157
" Katy 149
" Kezia 138
" Lydia 132, 147
" Mary . 103, 138, 141, 181
" Mehitabel 151
" Mindwell 135
" Patience 133
" Rachel 143
" Samuel 103, 131, 136, 137, 138, 139, 141, 143, 145, 147, 156, 181
" Sarah 97, 137
" Susannah . 103, 112, 139
" William 143
Bennet, Susanna 100
Bent, Anna 107
" Archibald 192
" Delia A. 192
" Hiram 193
" Micah 172, 193
" Michael 192
Berry, Elizabeth 144
" Hephzibah 104
" Josiah 104

Bigelow, Abigail	. . . .	126
" Abraham	. . . .	140
" Ann	. . . .	145
" Charles H.	. . . 192,	193
" Clarrissa	. . . .	194
" Clarrissa A.	. . . .	194
" Ebenezer	111, 137, 138, 139, 140, 144	
" Eleazer	138, 140, 142, 145, 1st	
" Elijah	. . . .	140
" Elisha	. . . .	147
" Elizabeth	. . . .	124
" Eunice	. . . .	165
" George T.	. . . .	192
" Harriet	. . . .	194
" Hopestill	. . . .	138
" Isaac	. . . .	128
" Jabez	. . . 128,	142
" James	. . . 97,	126
" John	. . . 97,	119
" Joseph	. . . .	124
" Joshua	. 128, 140,	181
" Josiah	. . . .	152
" Mary	. 138, 147, 158,	185
" Mercy	. . . .	119
" Moses	137, 158, 159, 160, 162, 165, 184	
" Rufus	. . . .	194
" Samuel	120, 126, 128, 144, 160	
" Silence	. . . .	139
" Tyler	106, 191, 192, 193, 194	
" Uriah	. . . .	118
" William	. . . .	152
Bird, Elizabeth M.	. . . .	192
" Horace	. . . .	193
" Joseph	. 107, 192, 193, 194	
" Marshal B.	. . . .	192
" Mary C.	. . . .	193
" Mehitabel B.	. . . .	194
Bisco, Abigail	. . . .	152
" Daniel W.	. . . .	163
" Grace	. . . .	165
" Hannah	. . . .	127
" Jno.	. . . .	2
" John	. . . 23,	111
" Jo.	. . . .	119
" Josiah	108, 145, 163, 165, 166, 168	
" Leonard	. . . .	168
" Thomas	2, 79, 127, 114, 115, 163	
Bishop, Thomas	. . . 90,	138
Blackman, Andrew	. . . .	190
" Eliza W.	. . . .	190
" Roxana R.	. . . .	190
" Sally J. T.	. . . .	190
Blackmer, Andrew	. . . .	103
Blake, Sarah	. . . .	164
Blanchard, Geo.	. . . .	98
Blogget, Thomas	. . . .	156
Bloyse Blosse, Richard	. . 90,	124

Bond, Abigail	. 120, 138, 146, 184	
" Abijah	. . . .	146
" Abraham	. . . .	183
" Amos	92, 93, 108, 112, 117, 149, 150 151 153, 170, 182	
" Ann	103, 135, 146, 160, 184	
" Benjamin	. . . .	183
" Bethiah	. . . .	146
" Betsey	. . . .	180
" Cate	. . . .	169
" Catherine	. . . 113,	194
" Charles	105, 174, 175, 176, 189, 190, 194	
" Corporal	. . . .	2
" Daniel	17, 50, 51, 90, 108, 129, 135, 138, 140, 148, 149, 154, 160, 184, 188, 194	
" Deacon	. . . .	6, 7
" Deliverance	. . . .	119
" Edward	. . . .	194
" Elijah	. . . 88,	126
" Eliza A.	. . . .	194
" Elizabeth	23, 105, 136, 143, 148, 169, 186	
" Eunice	. . . .	147
" George	. . . 189,	194
" Grace	. . . 124,	146
" Hannah	108, 139, 176, 188	
" Hephzibah	105, 121, 132, 189	
" Henry	57, 64, 74, 77, 80, 82, 90, 92, 93, 101, 119, 151, 156, 160	
" Hitty	. . . .	170
" Isaac	. . . 134,	140
" Jan	. . . .	194
" Jerusha	. . . .	146
" John	2, 90, 91, 108, 120, 123, 125, 129, 136, 157, 159, 143, 151, 167, 183, 184	
" Jonas	7, 8, 9, 15, 17, 18, 19, 22, 23, 24, 25, 26, 27, 28, 29, 30, 31, 32, 34, 35, 36, 37, 38, 39, 41, 42, 43, 44, 45, 46, 47, 54, 57, 59, 61, 63, 64, 65, 66, 67, 68, 70, 74, 80, 81, 82, 84, 89, 124, 125, 126, 126, 129, 140, 143	
" Jonathan Jona	134, 137, 142, 145, 147, 154, 181	
" Joseph	. . . .	149
" Josiah	. . . .	196
" Leonard	. . . .	184
" Lieut.	. . . .	3, 6
" Lucy	105, 169, 176, 183, 187	
" Lydia	. 131, 139, 189	
" Margaret	. . . .	100
" March	. . . .	190
" Mary	104, 108, 139, 181, 182, 194	

Bond, Moses 176
" Nathaniel 90, 92, 103, 121,
129, 133, 135, 137, 138,
139, 141, 150, 185
" Obadiah 135
" Phineas 134, 175
" Ruth 183
" Samuel . . 140, 151, 174
" Sarah 108, 119, 126, 129, 137
" Sergt 5
" Seth 141
" Simon E. 189
" Susan 190
" Susanna . . 112, 139, 190
" Thaddens 156
" Thomas 23, 41, 47, 50, 52, 54,
55, 56, 90, 119, 126,
129, 131, 134, 136,
145, 153
" Widow 91
" William 2, 3, 8, 9, 11, 12, 13,
18, 19, 23, 26, 27, 28,
29, 31, 32, 33, 36, 43,
97, 98, 106, 119, 126,
129, 131, 133, 140, 169,
176
Botang, John 171
" Mary E. 176
" Samuel 171
Bowen, Thomas 155
Bowles, John 161
" William 161
Bowman, Capt. 143
" Francis 119, 127
" John 127, 144
" Josiah 144
" Lydia 119
" Lucy 187
" Sarah 180
Box, John 88
Boynton, Elizabeth 137
" Jacob 157, 158
" Mary 157
" Nathan 158
Bradford, Charles 193
" Joseph R. 193
" Lucy 184
Bradshaw, Betsey 171
" Henry 170, 171
" Rebecca C. 170
Bridge, Benj. 159
" Mr. 121
" Nancy 174
" Nathaniel 174
Briggs, William 102
Bright, Abigail 143, 168
" Ann 180, 186
" Anna 153, 176
" Benjamin 131
" Elisha 174
" Elizabeth . . . 107, 143
" Francis 163

Bright, Hannah 151, 170, 171, 182,
186
" Henry 31, 38, 43, 45, 46, 48,
54. 59, 60, 63, 67, 134,
136, 149
" John 3, 81, 84, 90, 92, 93,
127, 156
" Jonathan 159
" Joseph 90, 91. 93, 105, 143,
171, 172, 173, 174,
176, 189
" Josiah 88, 107, 143, 159, 160,
161, 162, 166, 167, 168,
174
" Kata 174
" Lois 107
" Lucretia 166
" Margaret 183
" Mary . . 125, 131, 138
" Mercy 132
" Millescient 136
" Moses 162, 163
" Nathaniel 2, 5, 6, 7, 9, 10,
12, 18, 19, 21, 22,
23, 24, 25, 26, 27,
28, 29, 30, 31, 32,
33, 36, 38, 39, 40,
41, 43, 44, 46, 47,
51, 55, 66, 69, 80,
90, 92, 93, 94, 104,
121, 125, 127, 131,
132, 135, 138, 151,
153, 154, 156, 169,
170, 183, 186
" Polly 173
" Rachel 184
" Samuel . . . 169, 172
" Sarah . . . 135, 149, 167
" Silas 89, 134
" Susanna 104, 169, 186, 189,
194
" William 170
" William S. 189
Brown, Aaron, ... 154
" Abigail . . . 139, 140
" Abijah 142, 158, 159, 185
" Abraham 36, 37, 38, 39. 41,
120, 135, 136, 162,
184
" Allen 104, 140
" Amasa 165
" Anna 145, 168
" Charles 171
" Ebenezer 158
" Elizabeth 96, 139, 167, 168,
182
" George 154, 169, 170, 171
" Isaac 154
" Jacob 164
" James 139
" John 71, 90, 92, 104, 140,
144, 145

Brown, Jonathan	2, 77, 78, 79, 80, 93, 96, 97, 134, 135, 137, 139, 140, 142, 180, 189
" Joseph	110
" Lois	134
" Lucy	110
" Lydia	139, 157
" Mary	139, 162, 184
" Patience	97
" Ruth	104, 139
" Sally	169
" Samuel	66, 67, 69, 70, 71, 71, 77, 79, 80, 90, 164, 165, 167, 168
" Sarah	114, 185
" Susanna	159
" Thomas	1, 154
" William	104, 158, 159
Bryant, James	160, 161
" Sarah	169
Bullard, Eben	116, 183
" Hester	121
" John	103, 171
" Nancy	171
Bulman, Alex.	100
" Margaret	177
Butler, Peter	102
Butterfield, Mary	99
Buttrick, Hannah B.	173
" Tilly	173
Calderwood, Priscilla	162
" Samuel	162
Caldwell, Anna	150
" Enoch	155
" Jacob	93, 147, 148, 150, 151, 153, 155
" John	117
" Rebecca	118
" Sarah	153
Caner, H.	88
Capen, Alexander	169
" Benj.	105, 169
" Charity	108
" Elizabeth	105
" Eunice	169
" Josiah	168, 169, 186
" Mary	168, 186
" Rebecca	183
" Samuel	104
Chamberlain, Alex.	88, 89
" Mrs.	111
Checkley, Hannah	109
" John	109
" Dr. Richard	56
Chadwick, Aaron	115
" Abijah	106
" Benjamin	90, 111, 112, 127, 145
" Charles	103, 130, 156
" Daniel	127
" Elizabeth	124
" John	9, 10, 13, 14, 18, 19, 127, 134

Chadwick, Jonathan	190
" Kezia	106
" Lydia	127
" Noah	115
" Rebecca	14
" Richard	123
" Sarah	103, 127, 135, 183
" Sergt.	6
" Submit	145, 183
" Thomas	127, 128
Cheney, Chenery, Abigail	103, 163
" Anna	164
" Benjamin	150
" Daniel	150
" Ebenezer	66, 69, 70, 77, 78, 103, 131, 145, 6., 148, 149, 142, 145, 117
" Elisha	167
" Elizabeth	120, 120, 150
" John	2, 23, 120, 126, 129, 131, 133, 138, 145
" Martha	188, 1 2
" Mary	145
" Ruth	103, 139, 142, 170, 184
" Samuel	160
" Sarah	120, 123, 150
" Sybil	138, 143
" Widow	94
" William	108, 117, 132, 165, 164, 167, 169, 174
Child, Anna	184
" Dan'l	123
" Elizabeth	123, 114, 182
" Experience	184
" Eunice	140
" Hannah	157
" Hannah S.	192
" Isaac	71, 132, 137, 138, 140
" John	104, 121, 126, 127
" Jonathan	92, 93, 105, 115, 185, 188, 191, 192
" Joseph	71, 72, 90, 91, 93, 94, 127, 152, 140
" Katharine	184
" Lois	164
" Martha M.	191, 192
" Mary	124, 116, 152, 189
" Mehitabel	122, 177
" Moses	14
" Pamias	184
" Richard	126, 127
" Samuel	92, 96, 116, 152, 182
Church, Abigail	147
" Caleb	185, 124, 123
" David	3, 12, 128
" Isaac	90, 91, 122
" John	123
" Jonathan	98, 142, 145, 147
" Jos'h	184
" Lydia	90, 145
" Mary	142, 184
" Rebecca	139

Church, Sarah 128
" Thankful 142
Clark, Benjamin 139
" Benoni 140
" Caroline A. 191
" Daniel 155
" Hannah B. 173
" Harriet R. 191
" Isaac G. 190
" John . . . 93, 148, 173
" Josiah 175
" Josiah S. 176
" Lucy 148
" Lydia 174
" Lydia S. 190
" Margaret . . . 148
" Martha . . . 103, 136
" Mary . 137, 148, 175, 181
" Nathaniel 75, 90, 136, 137, 139, 181
" Peter 106, 176, 188, 190, 191
" Rebecca . . . 156, 183
" Richard 90, 91, 93, 112, 136, 139, 140, 153, 181
" Ruth . 136, 151, 156, 184
" Samuel . . 90, 143, 148
" Sarah . . . 112, 172
" Sarah G. . . . 176, 191
" Thomas 100, 103, 136, 153, 172, 173, 174, 175, 176, 187, 190, 191
" Uriah 93, 148, 150, 151, 153, 154, 156, 182
" William 190
Clargett, William 97
Coffin, Coffeen, John . . . 157
" Susanna 157
Cole, Andrew 192
" Caroline 194
" Eleanor . . . 188, 192
" Eloisa 192
" Harriet 192
" James 193
" John 192
" Joseph . . . 188, 193
" Josiah L. 193
" May A. . . . 192, 193
" Samuel 193
" Thaddeus 106, 188, 192, 193, 194
" William 192
Coleman, Elizabeth . . . 103
" Rebecca 101
Collins, Daniel 101
" Rose 97
Comye, Hester 128
Cornish, James . . . 97, 119
" Joshua 100
Convers, Convarse, Josiah 91, 93, 162, 180
" Widow 91
Cornwall, Daniel 107
" Thomas 107

Coolidge, Aaron 167
" Abigail . . 131, 133, 138
" Abiah 182
" Annah . 142, 155, 165, 166
" Daniel . . . 139, 147, 157
" David 92, 93, 108, 144, 146, 148, 149, 151, 164, 165, 166, 168
" Deborah 181
" Dorothy . . 108, 164, 168
" Ebenezer 149, 170
" Elijah 144
" Elisha 93, 183
" Elizabeth 148, 150, 158, 165, 172, 174
" Elizabeth B. 188
" Elizabeth M. 188
" Eunice 112, 145, 151, 162, 173
" George 174
" Grace 162, 180
" Hannah 104, 137, 185, 186
" Hannah S. . . . 172, 188
" Henry W. 175
" Hepzibah . . 148, 149
" Huldah 180
" James 149
" John 2, 15, 21, 26, 28 29, 31, 36, 37, 38, 40, 41, 42, 45, 46, 49, 71, 73, 75, 79, 80, 82, 83, 84, 88, 90, 91, 93, 103, 113, 129, 130, 131, 136, 137, 138, 139, 142, 144, 147, 166
" Jonas 148, 150, 151, 157, 165, 166, 168
" Jonathan 3, 127, 129, 132, 135, 137
" Joseph 19, 23, 29, 31, 36, 38, 43, 45, 47, 48, 49, 50, 52, 53, 54, 55, 57, 60, 63, 65, 66, 69, 71, 72, 83, 84, 90, 91, 105, 113, 132, 136, 138, 146, 152, 156, 158, 159, 162, 164, 166, 167, 170, 171, 172, 173, 182
" Joshua 159
" Josiah 132
" Kezia 186
" Lois 140
" Lucy . 136, 153, 164, 175
" Luther . . . 106, 190
" Lydia 125, 128, 132, 135, 139, 184
" Martha . . . 91, 92
" Mary 108, 122, 136, 137, 140, 144, 148, 151, 156, 165, 171, 174, 187
" Mehitabel 150
" Mercy 103, 108, 152, 156, 172
" Moses 104, 112, 116, 155, 167, 170, 171, 172, 173, 186

Coolidge, Nancy 172
" Nathan . . 164, 185, 186
". Nathaniel 2, 19, 82, 83, 84,
90, 98, 125, 128,
133, 137, 138, 140,
144, 148, 155, 156,
157, 160, 162, 164,
182, 184
" Obadiah 11, 131, 132, 135, 182
" Peter 166
" Rebecca 137
" Richard 7, 11, 16, 18, 22, 23,
24, 25, 26, 28, 30, 31,
47, 50, 54, 55, 67,
131, 132, 133
" Rhoda 108
" Ruth 111, 135
" Sally 187
" Samuel 93, 144, 148, 152, 153,
155, 157, 174, 175, 176,
180, 183, 187
" Sarah 131, 133, 144, 146, 167
" Sergt. 7, 41
" Silas 142
" Simon 90, 92, 93, 103, 138,
142, 144, 145, 147, 148,
150, 152, 164, 165, 167
" Stephen 2
" Susanna . . 138, 155, 164
" Tabitha 134
" Thomas 11, 12, 13, 19, 20, 21,
24, 26, 28, 29, 31, 33,
43, 57, 90, 111, 130,
133, 134, 151
" William 93, 148, 151, 152,
153, 155, 165, 176
Cook, Aaron 145
" Abigail J. 191
" Ann 114
" Anna 180
" Caleb 155, 171
" Daniel . . 154, 173, 187
" Easter 112
" Elizabeth 146
" Ephraim . . 144, 145
" Esther 187
" Francis 175
" Gregory . . 2, 99, 173
" Hannah . . 153, 175, 187
" Isaac 126
" Israel 106, 161, 166, 173, 175,
176, 187, 191
" James 127
" Joanna . . . 112, 184
" John 105, 126, 127, 146, 154,
156, 157, 158, 159, 161,
171, 173, 183
" Joseph 155
" Lucy 159
" Mary . . . 126, 157
" Polly 176
" R. S. 149
" Rev. Mr. . . . 145, 150

Cook, Robert 169
" Samuel 92, 93, 129, 146, 147,
149, 153, 171
" Sarah 166
" Stephen 25, 90, 91, 120, 122,
129, 147, 156, 173, 183
" Susanna 105, 121, 151, 183
Corley, Lidia 124
Cooper, Jonathan 169
" Sarah 169
Cotton, Rev. Mr. 139, 144, 145, 149,
151, 155
Crackbone, Abigail 141
" Joseph 141
" Lydia 141
Craft, Abner 108, 170, 171, 172, 174
" Betsey 170
" Charles 172
" Daniel P. . . . 174
" Ephraim 141
" George 172
" Henry 165
" John 141
" Nancy 171
" Sally 174
" Samuel 165
Craige, Andrew 190
" Sally 190
Crane, Eliza 174
" Elizabeth T. . . . 172
" Henry 172
" Stephen 174
Cravath, Eliz 103
Crawley, Abram 158, 160, 161, 162,
164
" Elizabeth 162
" John 161
" Mary 160
" Samuel 164
Crosby, John 169
" Polly 169
Crowell, Robert 116
Cunningham, Elizabeth . . 180
" John 90
Currye, Jo. 195
Curtis, Benjamin 192
" Benjamin R. . . . 192
" Geo. T. 192
Cushing, Rev. Mr. 155, 157, 162, 163,
164, 166, 168
Cutler, Ann 99
" Elizabeth . . . 136
" Hannah . . 103, 136
" James . . . 121, 170
" Jonathan . . . 126
" Martha 170
" Phebe 122
" Samuel 129
" Thomas . . 120, 126, 129
" Timothy 88, 89
Cutter, Bethia . . . 111, 127
" Ephraim 19, 41, 49, 50, 54,
55, 70, 71, 84, 90,

Cutter, Ephraim, *Continued.*
   111, 112, 127, 129, 180
Cutter, George 141
" Gershom 148
" Hannah 129
" Jonathan . . . 127, 141
" Mary 127
" Nehemiah 145
" Samuel 145
" Sarah 148
Cutting, Abraham . . . 152, 159
" Betty 165
" Elizabeth . . 92, 131, 152
" Eunice 136
" George 90, 119, 135, 136, 138
" Grace 135
" John 119
" Josiah 136
" Lydia 182
" Mary 153
" Richard . . . 119, 153
" Samuel 138
" Sarah 120
" Susanna . . . 104, 182
" Uriah 165
" Zec. 90
Dalrymple, Henry 191
" Wm. H. 191
Dana, Benj. 143
" Caleb 164, 193
" Daniel 158
" Edmund 162
" Elizabeth . . . 128, 138
" Francis 143
" George 167
" Grace 188, 193
" John 153
" Jonathan 163
" Lydia 153
" Mary 151
" Rachel 163
" Richard 162
" Thomas 138
" William 151
Danforth, Gov. 99
Dascomb, James 152
Davis, Benj. 120, 129
Dawes, Amos 166
" William 166
Dearing 177
Dill, Elizabeth 121
" George 123
" James 123
" Sarah 123
" Thomas 123
Dix, Deeks, Abigail 103, 123, 140, 180
" Anna 149
" Benjamin . 145, 147, 182
" Betty 179
" David 117
" Deborah 153

Dix, Edmund 90, 123, 138, 139, 181
" Elijah 150
" Elizabeth 77, 119, 123, 138, 159
" Hannah 158
" James 92, 93, 148, 149, 150, 152, 153, 158, 159, 160
" Jane 128
" John 103, 123, 128, 136, 137, 138, 140, 141, 143, 146, 149
" Jonas 160
" Jonathan . . 143, 149
" Joseph 123
" Lydia 138, 180
" Martha 138
" Mary . . 103, 137, 180
" Samuel 90, 103, 138, 146, 180
" Sarah 148
" Stephen 141
" William . 139, 152, 158
Dockum, John 154
" William 154
Downes, Clarissa 171
" Samuel 149
" Shubal 171
" William 149
Draper, Elizabeth 166
" Hannah 162
" John 162, 166
" Thomas 166
Drue, Ann 101
Dunah, Elizabeth 158
Dunster, David 141
" Herbert 141
Durant, Edward 155
" Elizabeth 155
" Henry W. 175
" John . . 106, 166, 175, 176
" Sarah 166
" Sarah D. 176
Earle, John 99
" Mary 129
Eddy, Benjamin . . . 23, 125
" Deliverance . . . 125
" Ebenezer 91
" Elizabeth . . 125, 130
" John 119
" Ruth 130, 181
" Samuel 2, 17, 19, 23, 132, 133
" Sarah 123, 130, 132, 181
Edes, Daniel 161
" Sally 161
Edmunds, Jonathan . . . 145
" Esther 145
Elding, Read 103
Elliston, Jonathan . . . 102
Eliot, Richard R. 105, 115, 116, 186
" Dea. 177
Ellis, Andrew 168
" John 141, 168
" Sarah 141

Index to Persons.

Fairbanks, Jona. 99
Fairfield, Tryphena 98
Fanning, Elizabeth 2
" Sarah 122
" Widow 179
Farnsworth, Rebecca . . . 119
Faulkner, Charles 171
" Dwight F. 189
" Francis 105, 171, 172, 176, 189, 190
" James R. 176
" William E. 190
Felton, Benjamin . 155, 157, 164
" Ebenezer 164
" Lucy 157
Fenton, Thomas 97
Ferris, William 98
Fessenden, Benj. 163, 164, 166, 167, 168
" Elizabeth 164
" George 167
" Hannah 163
" Jonathan . 148, 165, 168
" Josiah 168
" Martin 165
" Rebecca 166
" Sarah 148
" Thomas 168
Fiske, Abigail . . . 122, 130
" Anna 142
" Daniel . . . 91, 156, 181
" David . . . 120, 140
" Elizabeth 108, 119, 120, 122, 132, 155, 182
" Hannah 123, 183
" Henry 91, 181
" John 90, 91, 123, 127, 128, 137, 140, 183
" Jonathan . 127, 128, 137
" Joseph 155
" Lucretia 162
" Lucy 159
" Lydia . . 126, 150, 183
" Margaret 121
" Martha 120
" Mary . . 108, 128, 156
" Nathan 2, 6, 7, 8, 11, 12, 13, 17, 18, 21, 22, 23, 24, 25, 26, 28, 29, 30, 31, 36, 38, 45, 46, 47, 49, 51, 53, 68, 73, 74, 75, 79, 91, 123, 125, 132, 133
" Nathaniel . 123, 126, 128
" Samuel 92, 93, 114, 115, 142, 150, 152, 153, 155, 159, 161, 162, 183, 184
" Sarah . . 108, 125, 132, 153
" Susanna 125
Fitzhugh, Robert 102
Flag, Fleg. Abigail . . . 114
" Allin . . 122, 127, 129

Flag, Benjamin . 99, 120, 124
" Elizabeth 124
" Jo. 125
" Mary 127, 124
" Michael . . . 119, 127
" Sarah 124
" Thomas 124
Forbes, James 88
Foster, David 156
" Susanna 156
Fowle, Abigail 150
" Dorothy 154
" Ebenezer 156
" Edmund 98, 108, 150, 151, 152, 154, 156, 157, 159, 160, 161, 171, 172
" Jeremiah 110
" John 157, 159
" Lucy 159
" Mary 152, 189
" Moses G. 171
" Rebecca B. 172
" Samuel 161
Fox, Abigail 120, 127
" Ebenezer 128
" Isaac . . 120, 127, 128
" John 127
" Samuel 127
Frazer, Charles B. 191
" Isabella 191
" John . . . 191, 192, 194
" Walter 192
Freeman, Elizabeth . . 108, 175
" Hannah 109
Fullam, Francis 35, 36
Fuller, Caleb 113
" Daniel 162, 167
" Francis 107
" Grace 162
" Lucy 167
" Nehemiah 113
" Rachel 140
" Thomas 140
" William 107
Fullerton, Jennet 170
" William 170
Gage, Rebecca 183
Gale, Abiah 127
" Abigail 123
" Abraham . . . 120, 127
" Anna 123
" Elizabeth . . . 120, 124
" John 90, 124
" Marah 127
Gamage, Abigail 143
" Daniel 154
" Samuel 154
" William . . 93, 143, 144
Gardner, Benjamin . . . 175
" Elisha 186
" Elizabeth 188
" Hannah 183

Gardner, Joseph 108, 160, 161, 163, 165, 166, 168
" Mary 108
" Sarah 161
Garfield, Benjamin . . . 4, 129
" Eliakim 139
" Grace 120
" John 98, 123
" Joseph 126
" Mehitabel . . . 125
" Mercy 123
" Ruth 122
" Samuel . . . 129, 139
" Serg. 125
" Thankful 152
Garrett, Hannah 102
Gaskell, John 129
George (a negro) 101
" John, 105, 173, 174, 175, 189
" Lucy 175
" Margaret 189
" Mary 102
" Mary A. 174
" Sally M. 174
" William M. 173
Gibbins, Elizabeth 137
" Mr. 102, 177
" Peter 137
" W. 97
Gibbs, Henry 3, 4, 5, 6, 7, 8, 21, 22, 24, 25, 31, 33, 37, 38, 52, 122, 125, 130, 134
" Mr. 178
Giles, Mary 156
" Thomas 156
Gleason, David . . 92, 146, 183
" Dorothy 145
" John 92, 145
" Samuel 152
" Thankful 152
Goddard, Abigail . . . 146, 185
" Benjamin 120
" Ebenezer 57, 63, 64, 66, 69, 70, 71, 77, 146, 147, 148, 149, 150
" Edward . 125, 131, 132, 133
" Elizabeth . . . 149, 181
" Josiah 10, 17, 18, 20, 21, 23, 28, 30, 31, 125, 132, 133, 148
" Rachel . . 125, 132, 147
" Robert . . 5, 23, 27, 28
" Simon 133
" Susanna . . . 125, 132
" William . . . 2, 120
Godding, Abigail 145
" Hannah 146, 168, 183, 185
" Henry 90, 92, 93, 150, 168
" Joanna 146
" Jonas 164
" Jonathan C. 144, 161, 162, 164, 166, 168

Godding, Martha . 104, 139, 165
" Peter 148, 162
" Rebecca 162
" Spencer . . . 151, 166
" William 89, 90, 91, 92, 93, 104, 112, 139, 142, 144, 146, 148, 150, 151, 162, 165, 168
Goffe, Elizabeth 119
Goodenow, Mary 183
Gooding, Elizabeth 99
Goodwin, Elizabeth 121
Grant, Abigail 91, 131
" Caleb 2, 133
" Charles 176
" Christopher 2, 92, 107, 145, 148, 165, 167, 182, 187
" Elizabeth . . . 131
" Hannah 133
" Hepsibah . . . 176, 188
" Joseph 2, 6, 10, 19, 28, 126, 128, 131, 132, 133, 134, 165
" Joshua 50, 64, 65, 90, 106, 131, 136, 137, 138, 175, 176, 181, 189
" Lydia 137
" Mary 91, 92, 121, 126, 132, 145, 180
" Mercy 134
" Ruth 138
" Sarah 126, 127, 133, 167, 187
Gray, James 161
" Samuel . . . 101, 179
" Sarah . . 161, 163, 185
" Thomas 101
" William 103
Grefte, Hannah 96
Gregg, Mary 121
Greenfield, Ann 97
Greenough, Rev. Mr. . . . 116
Greenwood, Josiah 151
" Moses 151
Grimes, James . . . 92, 145, 148
" Samuel 145
" Sarah 148
Grout, Jonathan 123
" Joseph . . 120, 123, 128
" Mary 99
" Mehitabel 128
" Susanna . . . 120, 123
Grover, Thomas 90
Hackleton, Bethiah . . . 166
" Daniel 155
" Elisha 149
" Hepzibah 149
" James 92, 148, 149, 151, 153, 155
" John . . . 148, 149, 166
" Mary 153
" Samuel 151

Index to Persons.

Hagar (a negro) 101
" Abigail 97
" Elijah 157
" Hannah 135
" Jonathan . . . 145, 153
" Joseph 153
" Lucy 151
" Mary 185
" Mehitabel 97
" Samuel 90, 92, 93, 130, 135,
          145, 150, 151, 157, 185
" Sarah 130
" Susanna 150
" William 97
Hall, Anna 168
" Ezekiel . . . 108, 168
" John 108
" Josiah 152
" Susanna 152
Halloway, Curtis 132
" Mary 132
Hamlin, John 177
Hammond, Hamont, Abigail . 166
" Abijah . . . 162, 166
" Daniel 136
" David 129
" Elizabeth 126
" Hannah 135
" Isaac 162
" John . . . 2, 5, 15, 136
" Jonathan 154
" Mary 180
" Thomas 119, 122, 126, 129, 135
Hancoks, Samuel 77
Hanna, Hannah, Robert . . 102
" William 103
Hapgood, Mary 98
" Shadrack 98
Harrington, Abijah 158
" Anna . . . 104, 152, 157
" Beulah 143
" Betsey 171
" Charles 159
" Daniel . . . 123, 124, 127
" David 124
" Ebenezer 124
" Edward 37, 38, 45, 59, 60, 61,
        62, 63, 64, 71, 77, 78,
        95, 104, 139, 141, 143,
        145, 147, 148, 150, 152,
        154, 156, 157, 159, 160,
        162, 168, 169, 170, 171,
        172, 181, 186
" Elijah 169
" Elisha 134, 153
" Elizabeth 135, 142, 180, 184
" Ephraim 172
" Esther 186
" George . . . 134, 136
" Grace . . . 145, 163
" Hannah . . . 121, 163
" Henry 130
" Isaac 172

Harrington, Jabez 94
" Jacob 168
" Joel 172
" John 103, 121, 123, 128, 163
" Jonathan 127, 135, 147, 163,
              164, 172, 173
" Joseph 52, 55, 56, 64, 90, 91,
              93, 99, 142, 183
" Josiah 153
" Katy 157, 173
" Leonard 173
" Lucretia 173
" Lucy 172
" Lydia . . . 128, 164
" Martha . . . 142, 183
" Mary 123, 139, 151, 153, 154,
              158, 194
" Moses . . . 140, 158
" Nathaniel 93, 107, 151, 153,
              154, 157, 159, 181
" Peter 154
" Phineas . . 148, 157, 172
" Polly 170
" Rebecca . . . 124, 150
" Robert 123
" Ruth 142
" Samuel . . 153, 159, 160
" Sarah . 98, 136, 146, 183
" Seth 134
" Susanna . . 127, 136, 162
" Thankful 186
" Thomas 124, 127, 130, 142
" William 150, 169, 170, 171,
              172
Harris, Abijah 139
" Anna 137, 158
" Benjamin 138
" Francis 155
" Fullam 143
" Hannah . . 140, 160, 172
" Kate 105, 172
" Lucy 166
" Mary 136, 164
" Mehitable 180
" Nathaniel 37, 38, 41, 43, 45,
              46, 47, 48, 49, 50,
              51, 52, 53, 54, 55,
              57, 59, 60, 61, 62,
              63, 64, 65, 66, 67,
              68, 69, 70, 71, 72,
              74, 76, 90, 91, 113,
              115, 135, 147, 158,
              159, 181
" Priscilla . . . 135, 157
" Samuel . . . 155, 172
" Sarah . 1, 5, 156, 163, 183
" Stephen 105, 141, 156, 158,
              159, 161, 163, 164,
              166, 172
" Thomas 165
" Timothy 93, 136, 157, 179, 181
Harrison, Prudence 98

Hastings, Abigail	. . . .	150
" Asher	. . . . .	137
" Benjamin	71, 90, 92, 93, 105,	
	133, 136, 138, 140,	
	141, 142, 144, 146,	
	147, 148, 150, 151,	
	152, 160, 173, 174,	
	175, 176, 180	
" Charles	. . . .	173
" Daniel	46, 52, 53, 103, 133,	
	135, 136, 162	
" Ebenezer	66, 71, 75, 77, 79,	
	80, 82, 84, 90, 92,	
	140	
" Elisha	. . . . .	136
" Elizabeth	125, 131, 139, 164,	
	173	
" Enoch	. . . . .	134
" Eunice	. . . . .	134
" Hepzibah	. . . . .	125
" Hannah	140, 146, 167, 183,	
	184	
" Isaac	. . . . .	168
" John	38, 45, 46, 51, 63, 74,	
	75, 76, 77, 79, 90, 91,	
	125, 129, 131, 134, 136,	
	137, 138, 139, 141	
" Jonas	. . . . .	142
" Joseph	. 2, 91, 140, 148	
" Martha	. . . . .	142
" Mary	91, 125, 131, 136, 144,	
	153, 161, 175, 180	
" Nathan	. . . . .	148
" Nathaniel	. . . 91, 131	
" Richard C.	. . . .	174
" Ruth	. . . 140, 182	
" Samuel	23, 96, 131, 132, 133,	
	142, 152, 173	
" Sarah	103, 135, 138, 141, 175,	
	180	
" Seth	93, 146, 153, 184	
" Simon	141, 160, 161, 162, 164,	
	167, 168, 184	
" Smith	. . . . .	151
" Stephen	. . . . .	136
" Thomas	. . . 96, 155	
" William	. . . 129, 147	
Hatch, Benjamin	. . . .	136
" Mercy	. . . . .	136
Haward, Mary	. . . . .	99
Hawkins, Mary	. . . . .	130
Hay, Abigail	. . . 153, 158	
" Anna	. . . . .	164
" Elizabeth	. . 153, 155	
" Hannah	. . . . .	157
" James	153, 155, 156, 157, 158,	
	160, 161, 164, 165, 167	
" John	. . . 159, 160, 167	
" Joseph	. 157, 158, 159, 163	
" Lucy	. . . . .	165
" Mary	. . . . .	157
" Sarah	. . . . .	161

Hay, Thomas	. . . . .	158
" William	. . . . .	156
Hayman, Samuel	. . . . .	1
Hewes, Abraham	. . . .	164
" Lucy	. . . . .	164
Hicks, Elizabeth	. . . .	101
Hide, Enoch	. . . . .	174
" Sally D.	. . . . .	174
Hill, Abigail	. . . . .	135
" Abraham	. . . .	141
" Benjamin	. . . .	165
" John	. . . . .	144
" Joseph	. . . . .	135
" Susanna	. . . . .	165
" Thomas	. . . . .	78
" Zechariah	. . 141, 144	
Hilliard, Ann	. . . . .	188
Hinds, Abigail	. . . . .	156
" Ebenezer	. 154, 156, 157	
" Margaret	. . . .	154
Hoar, Esther	. . . . .	144
" John	. . . . .	144
" Nathaniel P.	. . . .	171
" Samuel	. . . . .	171
Holden, Holdin, Holding, Abigail		180
" Elizabeth	. 119, 137, 180	
" Isaac	. 23, 90, 92, 182	
" John	. . . . .	130
" Jonathan	. . . .	135
" Joseph	23, 47, 57, 59, 63, 64,	
	66, 69, 70, 75, 76, 90,	
	135, 137, 180	
" Justinian	. . . .	119
" Lydia	. . . . .	132
" Phineas	. . 192, 193	
" Samuel	. 23, 132, 133	
" Susanna	. . 104, 132	
Holland, John	. . . . .	90
" Nathaniel	. . 119, 128	
" Ruth	. . . . .	99
Holman, Deborah	. . . .	98
Homans, Thomas	. . . .	91
Hosmer, Daniel	. . . .	150
Holt, Samuel	. . . . .	172
" Samuel N.	. . . .	172
Houghton, Abigail	. . . .	133
" Henry	. . . .	133
Hovey, Eliza B.	. . . .	176
" Eunice	. . . . .	175
" Mary	. . . . .	163
" Phineas	. 106, 175, 176	
" Sally	. . . . .	175
" Thomas	. . . . .	166
How, Abigail	. . . . .	154
" Enos	. . . . .	154
Humphrys, Rebecca	. . . .	97
Humsteds, Jabez	. . . .	125
" Matthew	. . . .	125
Hunt, Dorothy	. . . . .	185
" Elizabeth	. . . .	185
" Jane	. . . . .	190
" Jane L.	. . . . .	190

Index to Persons.

Hunt, John 91, 147, 148, 149, 150,
   151, 152, 154, 156, 157,
   159, 168, 175, 185
" Katherine 147, 148, 154, 185, 188
" Maria B. 190
" Mary . . . 168, 185, 188
" Ruth . . . 151, 183, 185
" Samuel . . . 149, 175, 185
" Sarah 157
" Sarah P. 188
" Susanna 107
" Thomas 156
" William . . . 152, 190
Jackson, Abigail 103
" Abraham 136
" Daniel 105, 170, 171, 172, 173, 175, 176, 187
" Edward . . 103, 136, 159
" Elizabeth 147
" Francis 172
" Henry 170
" Jonas 136, 160
" Joshua 136, 159
" Kezia 159
" Leonard 173
" Lucy . . 105, 175, 187
" Mary H. 173
" Michael 147
" Moses 160
" Patty R. 176
" Samuel 159
Jane (a negro) 102
Jeffreys, George 102
Jenny (a negro) 154
Jennison, Abigail 104, 142, 164, 182
" Benjamin . . 108, 170
" Elias 168
" Elizabeth . . 138, 162
" Eunice 183
" Grace 130
" Hannah 133
" John 181
" Joseph 132
" Joshua 155
" Josiah 138
" Judith 119
" Lucy 149
" Lydia 126, 182
" Mary . . 133, 146, 180
" Mercy 155, 182
" Nathaniel . . 138, 167, 181
" Phineas 108, 148, 166, 168, 170, 171, 187
" Rachel 130, 132
" Rev. 137, 138
" Samuel 12, 15, 17, 18, 20, 23, 51, 52, 54, 56, 103, 126, 130, 133, 140, 142, 146, 148, 149, 151, 153, 155, 162, 164, 167, 180, 182, 224
" Sarah 151

Jennison, Susanna . . 166, 187
" Sergt. 41
" William . 153, 171, 180
Johnson, Esther 162
" Hannah . . 121, 123, 130
" John 123
" Mary 123
" Matthew 159
" Sarah 185
" Solomon 96
" Thomas . . . 123, 162
Jones, Caleb 127
" Deborah 123
" Isaac 128
" Josiah . 98, 123, 128, 133
" Lydia 98
" Samuel 131
" William 127
Kate (a negro) 154
Kay, Lydia 177, 178
" Mary 97
" Miss 177
" Thomas 97
Kelly, Elizabeth 150
" Joseph 150
" Mary 184
Kendall, Benjamin F. . . . 194
" Benjamin S. 167
" Betsey 171
" Charles 175
" David 174
" Eliza C. 192
" George 192
" Hannah 173
" Henry L. 190
" Hiram 191
" Joshua 107, 167, 171, 172, 173, 174, 175
" Josiah 172
" Paul 106, 188, 190, 191, 192, 193, 194
" Susan C. 191
" Susanna 107
" William 193
Kimball, John 2, 90, 91, 93, 154, 179, 182
" Mary 183
King, Ebenezer 133
" John 77
" Richard 92
" Samuel 133
Kinningham, Cuningham, Elizabeth 132
" Esther 132
" John 132, 133
Knap, Knop, Daniel . . . 152
" Henry 132
" James 120, 123
" John . . 2, 121, 127, 129
" Jonas 152
" Sarah 121
" Thomas 99
Knight, Mr. 175

Knox, John 177
Lamb, Isaac 123
Langdon, John 178
"   Jo. 179
Lawrence, Abigail . . 134, 144
"   Benjamin 136
"   Edmund 142
"   Elizabeth . . . 119, 133
"   Eunice 144
"   George 23, 99, 103, 119, 131,
          133, 134, 136, 144, 154,
          180
"   John . . . 104, 134, 143
"   Mary . 99, 123, 141, 183
"   Mercy 144
"   Rev. Mr. . . . 152, 159
"   Samuel 142
"   Sarah 143
"   William 92, 141, 142, 144,
          146, 182
Learned, Larned, Aaron . . 169
"   Abigail . . 148, 169, 186
"   Amariah 135, 139, 157, 159,
          160
"   Anna 163, 164, 167, 187, 190
"   Benjamin 149
"   Bezalel 93, 150, 151, 152, 154
"   Christopher 168
"   Daniel 175
"   David 90, 92, 93, 140, 138,
          141, 143, 144, 147, 148,
          149, 181
"   Edward W. 193
"   Eli 160
"   Elijah 168
"   Elisha 143, 162, 163, 165, 167,
          168, 185
"   Elizabeth 93, 104, 138, 141,
          168, 182, 184
"   Fanning 140
"   George N. 194
"   Grant 108
"   Hannah 146, 150, 157, 164,
          167, 170, 185
"   Henry 93, 165, 170
"   James 107
"   Jedidiah 108, 142, 168, 170
"   Jerusha . . 147, 151, 169
"   Jesse 149
"   Jonas . . 136, 154, 158
"   Jonathan 90, 107, 139, 140,
          142, 144, 146, 147,
          149, 154, 163, 164,
          166, 167, 180
"   Joseph 166
"   Joshua 90, 92, 104, 138, 139,
          141, 143, 145, 148, 162,
          181
"   Josiah . . . 161, 188
"   Katherine 154
"   Lucy . . . 141, 166
"   Mary . . 71, 77, 144, 159
"   Mercy 135

Learned, Moses 169
"   Oliver 148
"   Parnel 107
"   Paul 145, 161, 175, 187, 190
"   Phineas 107
"   Robert 139
"   Samuel . . . 164, 175
"   Samuel S. 194
"   Sarah . . 147, 162, 185
"   Silas 167
"   Susanna . 163, 165, 167
"   Tabitha 158
"   Thomas 23, 38, 49, 59, 63, 64,
          107, 135, 136, 138,
          140, 161, 162, 164,
          165, 167, 175, 184,
          188, 193, 194
"   William 107, 144, 164, 165,
          167, 168
Leason, Abiah . . . 120, 121, 129
"   Ann 126
"   Elizabeth 122
"   Isaac 129
"   John 122
"   Joseph 122
"   William . . 121, 122
Leathe, Achsah 161
"   Ann G. 193
"   Frances 163
"   Hannah . . 156, 159, 185
"   Jedidiah 112, 118, 156, 157,
          160, 161, 163, 164,
          166, 185
"   John 157, 193
"   Jonathan 159
"   Lucy 166
"   Mary 164
"   Sarah 160
"   Sophia 107
Leckey, Abraham 153
"   Richard 97
"   William 153
Lee, William 93
Legg, Capt. 100, 103
"   Sabella 100
Leppington, John 138
"   Mary 138
Leverett, Benjamin D. . . . 191
"   Daniel 191
Little, Anne 101
Livermore, Abigail . . 146, 149
"   Adeline 193
"   Amos 107, 143, 162, 165, 167,
          175, 176, 188, 189, 190,
          191, 192, 193, 194
"   Amos H. 190
"   Anna . . 129, 134, 144
"   Charles 192
"   Daniel 23, 25, 132, 133, 134,
          146, 151, 162, 183, 189
"   David 92, 149, 150, 151, 153,
          156, 176, 190, 191, 192,
          193

Livermore, Edmund 91, 92, 141, 144,
    145, 181
"   Elisha . . . 100, 107, 153
"   Eliza 189
"   Elizabeth 111
"   Grace S. 191
"   Hannah . . . 99, 156, 176
"   Hannah S. 191
"   Harriet L. 194
"   Hepzibah 167
"   Jane A. 191
"   Jonathan 147
"   Josiah 91, 144, 145, 181, 190
"   Katherine 159
"   Lucy 165
"   Lydia 121, 153
"   Martha W. 193
"   Mary 133
"   Mary A. 192
"   Matthew . . . 134, 139
"   Nathaniel . . . 119, 149
"   Oliver 59, 60, 61, 63, 64, 66,
       67, 68, 69, 70, 71, 74,
       75, 80, 81, 90, 91, 92,
       103, 132, 134, 136, 137,
       139, 140, 141, 143, 144,
       146, 147, 149, 159, 161,
       162, 183
"   Priscilla 150
"   Rachel 137, 140
"   Ruth 136
"   Samuel 3, 8, 9, 11, 12, 13, 22,
       23, 24, 25, 26, 27, 28,
       119, 129, 133, 134
"   Samuel B. 190
"   Samuel W. 189
"   Sarah 153
"   Sibyl 112, 176
"   Thomas 175
Loud, Abner F. 194
"   Edward 194
Maccoys, Alex 77, 78, 79
Maddocks, Caleb 133
"   Daniel 145
"   Joanna 134
"   Henry 132
"   John 90, 131, 132, 133, 134,
       136, 138, 145
"   Mary 132, 138
"   Ruth 131, 132
"   Sarah 132
"   William 138
Mallet, Ephraim 146
Man, Hannah 102
"   James 151
"   Moses 154
Mansfield, Bethiah 130
Mason, Aaron 174
"   Abigail 182
"   Amos 173
"   Daniel 164, 165
"   David 154
"   Ebenezer 139, 160, 161, 162

Mason, Elias . . . 93, 161, 183
"   Elijah 160
"   Elizabeth . . . 160, 172
"   Enoch 162
"   Esther 135
"   Grace 117
"   Hannah   102, 118, 154, 174
"   Hugh 105, 170, 171, 172, 173
"   Isaac 165, 174
"   Jonas 151
"   Joseph 3, 30, 31, 33, 43, 44,
       45, 46, 51, 52, 54, 55,
       59, 60, 63, 66, 68, 73,
       75, 80, 81, 82, 83, 84,
       85, 91, 92, 113, 114,
       119, 126, 135, 136, 137,
       139, 140, 147, 148, 150,
       151, 172
"   Josiah 140
"   Lydia 136
"   Martha C. 170
"   Mary . 102, 121, 122, 181
"   Moses 105, 174
"   Nehemiah . . . 93, 183
"   Richard C. 171
"   Samuel . . . 159, 160, 164
"   Sarah 150
"   Seth 173
"   Susanna . . . 137, 184
"   William 161
Maverick, Elias 103
McCollister, Charles 84
"   John 94
McConnoughey, David . . . 140
"   George 140
McKilenys, Mr. 177
Mead, Abigail 186
"   Betsey 170
"   Elijah 169, 170, 171, 172, 186
"   Isaac 170
"   Israel 92, 93, 115, 154, 155,
       156, 183
"   John 156
"   Lydia 172
"   Mary 155
"   Nabby 172
"   Polly 103
"   Samuel 171
Meatox, Bethia 121
"   Daniel 121
"   Mary 121
Mellin, Helen M. 190
"   Leonard 190
"   Sophia 187, 190
Memory, Joseph 126
"   Mary 126
Merriam, Rev. Mr. . 160, 163, 167
Merritt, Amos 122, 129
"   Bethiah 122
"   Daniel 129
Messenger, Ebenezer . . . 97
Metcalf, Hezikiah 171
"   Polly 171

Miller, Moses		149
" Samuel		149
Millings, James		120
" John		120
" Mary		120
" Richard		120
" Samuel		120
" Simon		120
" Thomas		119, 120
Mills, Ann		110
" Henry		23
Mixer, Isaac		4
" Joanna		99
" John		170
" Josiah	112, 170,	172, 174
" John		170
" Lois		172
" Nathaniel		174
" Sarah		119
Moodey, Mr.		110
Morse, Abraham		134
" Daniel		130
" Elizabeth		130
" Jacob		134
" James		123
" Jeremye	123,	126, 134
" John	2, 99, 124,	126, 130
" Jonathan		126
" Joseph		144
" Nathaniel		126
" Sarah		123
" Zechariah		144
Murch, Lydia		141
" William	91,	141, 142
Murdock, Abigail		140
" Amasa		168
" Artemas		176, 189
" Horace		176
" John		168
" Julia		189
" Sally		176
Murriah (a negro)		187
Myrick, Abigail		97
" Hannah		158
" John		97
" Jonathan		158
Neggres, Mary		97
Nevenson, Elizabeth		120
" John		120
Newell, John		156
" Solomon		156
Newhall, George		192
" Polly		192
Nison, Joseph		174
Norcross, Abigail		168
" Asa		145
" Charlotte		175
" Elizabeth	158,	159, 165
" Hannah		188, 193
" Helen		175
" Jemima		164
" Jerusha		187

Norcross, Josiah 108, 137, 139, 158,		
159, 161, 162, 164, 165,		
167, 168		
" Mary		144
" Mehitabel		129
" Mercy		138
" Moses		108
" Nathaniel 90, 91, 97, 129, 135		
136, 137, 138, 139		
140, 144, 145, 147		
150, 158, 162		
" Nehemiah		147
" Polly		175
" Richard 2, 5, 96, 97, 124, 128		
" Rose		124, 128
" Samuel		128
" Seth		175
" Sukey		106, 175
" Susanna		150
" Uriah		135, 139
Nutting, Ebenezer		136
" Charles	155, 169,	171, 172,
173, 174, 175, 176		
" Hannah		176
" James		137
" John		146
" Mary		137, 151
" Mercy		181
" Nabby		172
" Nathaniel		173, 174
" Phineas		171
" Richard		4, 171
" Sally		175
" Samuel 92, 93, 148, 151, 155		
" Sarah		148
Nymphas (my negro) 150, 154, 155,		
156		
Oliver, Peter		136
" Samuel		136
Orms, Elizabeth		135, 181
" John	65, 66, 78,	90, 135
Ozment, Mary		137
" William		137, 180
Pain, Will		179
Page, Phineas		187
Palfrey, Phebe		104, 137
Park, Edward		148
" Lucy		108, 158
" Pennel		108
" William		158
Parker, Hananiah		131
" Fanny		163
" Jacob		91
" Moses		147
" Peter		155
" Thomas		147
Parkhurst, Isaac		107
Parkis, Anna		129
" George		119
" John		119, 126, 129
" Samuel		126
Parkman, Rev. Mr.		154

Patrick, Capt. 118
Partridge, Sarah 163
"   Thaddeus 163
Patten, Isaac . 167, 191, 193, 194
"   John 164
"   Juliana D. 194
"   Lucretia 194
"   Mary 165
"   Mary D. 193
"   Richard R. 193
"   Samuel 170
"   Thomas 164, 165, 166, 167,
              168, 170, 191
"   William 168
Patterson, Adam . . 139, 141, 181
"   Esther 157
"   Isaac 106
"   Isabel 181
"   James 190
"   John 139
"   Joseph 157
Paughonot, Hannah 155
"   Joseph 155
Pegg (a mulatto) 141
Pemberton, Hannah 103
"   Mr. 102, 103
Penneman, Widow 91
Pero (a negro) 113
Perry, Parry, Abigail . . . 133
"   Dorcas . . . 136, 146
"   Ebenezer 128
"   Elizabeth 134
"   Ephraim 142
"   Hannah . . . 150, 152
"   John . 2, 128, 129, 133, 134
"   Jonathan 91, 181
"   Joseph 129
"   Joshua 146
"   Josiah 23, 59, 61, 62, 64, 65,
              71, 72, 84, 90, 91, 92,
              93, 136, 146
"   Mary 133, 183
"   Mercy 181
"   Nathan . 150, 152, 153, 184
"   Samuel . 90, 91, 93, 128, 135
"   Sarah . 111, 130, 133, 154
"   Susanna 183
Peter (a negro) . . . 104, 138
Peters, Abigail 184
"   Joseph . . . 154, 184
"   Moses 154
Phillips, Elizabeth 123
"   Hannah 185
"   John . . . 79, 134, 155
"   Jonathan . . 123, 127, 129
"   Lydia 180
"   Mary 119, 155
"   Priscilla 134
"   Ruth 123
"   Sarah . . . 119, 123, 127
"   Theophilus . 119, 126, 124
Phillis (a negro) 156
Pierce, Pearse, Abigail M. . . 192

Pierce, Pearse, Abraham . . 129
"   Anna 161
"   Benjamin . . 119, 121, 126
"   Daniel 116, 155, 156, 160, 184
"   Edward 162
"   Elvira 189
"   Elizabeth . . . 121, 124
"   Eunice 150
"   Francis . . 130, 132, 134
"   Hannah . . 119, 121, 144
"   Henry 155
"   Isabel 129, 178
"   Israel 119
"   John 121, 163
"   John M. 189
"   Jonas 150
"   Jonathan 155
"   Joseph 99, 106, 119, 124,
              189, 190, 192
"   Joseph N. 190
"   Martha . . . 156, 184
"   Martha B. 190
"   Mary 155
"   Mary B 192
"   Rebecca 180
"   Ruth 157
"   Samuel 35, 36, 37, 38, 46, 57,
              59, 60, 63, 64, 65, 90,
              126, 129, 134, 137, 138
"   William 189
Pitman, Nathaniel 102
Place, Sarah 103
Poole, Matthew 101
Porter, Anna 102
"   Lydia 105, 172
"   Nabby 172
"   Nathan . . . 105, 172
Prense, Abraham 93
Prentice, Benjamin 149
"   David 157
"   Edward 161
"   Elizabeth . . 146, 159
"   Hannah 186
"   Joshua 161
"   Lydia 143, 158
"   Mary 170, 159
"   Mercy 157
"   Samuel . . 92, 93, 143, 146
"   Smith 93, 119, 170, 171, 155,
              157, 158, 159, 161
"   Solomon 186
"   Thomas 154
Price, John 129
"   Mary 129
"   William 128
Priest, Hannah 144
"   Josiah 157
"   Mary 152
"   Sarah 152
"   William 157
Proctor, Edward 122
Prout, Eunice 128
Quiner, Mary 145

Quiner, Sarah 143
"   Thomas . . . 143, 145
Rainger, Ann 156
Rand, Elbridge D. 193
"   Harriet A. 193
"   Mary 107
"   Samuel 193
Randall, Elizabeth 154
"   Isaac 159
"   Jacob 160
"   John 153, 154, 156, 157, 159, 160
"   Samuel 156
Ray, Elijah 189
"   Elizabeth 189
Raymond, Jonathan 158
"   Susanna 158
Reed, John 90
"   Jonas 140
"   Josiah 90, 140
Remington, Elizabeth . 167, 185
"   Frederick . . . 161, 187
"   John 112, 156, 158, 159, 160, 161, 163, 167, 168, 186, 187
"   Jonathan . . . 159, 160
"   Lucy 158
"   Mary . . 156, 163, 168
Rice, Rise, Ephraim 99
"   Mary 125, 162
Richards, Humphrey 102
Richardson, Abigail 157
"   Ann 188
"   Ebenezer 160
"   Edward 155, 157, 159, 160, 161, 163, 165, 166, 168
"   Elizabeth 165
"   Hannah B. 192
"   John . . 159, 188, 192
"   Lucy 166
"   Mary 168
"   Moses 155
"   Peter 155
"   Richard 155
"   Sarah 161
"   William 163
Ridgway, Bridget 162
"   Isaac 162
Ripley, Rev. Mr. . . . 189, 194
Robbins, David 152
"   Eliza W. 176
"   George 175, 176
"   Isaac 189
"   James 173, 174, 175, 176, 188, 189, 193
"   Jane W. 176
"   John H. 193
"   Jonathan 106, 191, 192, 193
"   Joseph 144
"   Lois 188, 193
"   Lois A. 193
"   Lois C. 188
"   Lois J. 193

Robbins, Lucretia 173
"   Lydia 191
"   Martha 191
"   Mary . 107, 144, 191, 193
"   Moses 163
"   Phineas . . . 150, 167
"   Samuel 167
"   Sarah 107, 193
"   Solomon . . . 150, 152
"   William 168
"   William E. 192
Robinson, Bradbury 187
"   Lucy 187
Rogers, Abigail 108
"   John 161
"   Martha 161
"   Nathaniel 108
"   Phineas 108
"   William 108
Rosse, Dorothy 97
Rowe, John 124
"   William 123
Royal, Joseph 103
Russell, Eliza C. 192
"   Gustavus 191
"   Jane A. K. 190
"   Joseph . 106, 190, 191, 192
"   Lucy S. 191
"   Sarah 188
Ryder, Rider, Thomas . . 10. 119
Salga, John 174
Saltmarsh, Abigail 145
"   Deborah 147
"   Elizabeth . . . 160, 163
"   John . . 144, 161, 163
"   Katharine 148
"   Mary 166
"   Seth 150, 166
"   Susanna 166
"   Thomas 92, 93, 94, 141, 143, 144, 145, 147, 148, 150, 185
"   William 141, 160, 161, 162
Sanders, Saunders, Abia . . 119
"   Abigail 123
"   Hester 121
"   Jon. 119
"   Josiah 170
"   Lucy 170
"   Moses 163
"   Polly G. 174
"   Sarah . 106, 120, 163, 174
"   William 120
Sanderson, Charity 168
"   Elizabeth . . . 155, 189
"   Esther 107
"   Hannah 126
"   Henry . . 108, 151, 168
"   Isaac 92, 93, 146, 148, 149, 151, 153, 155, 158
"   Joseph 126
"   Josiah . . 148, 170, 173
"   Kezia . . . 149, 185
"   Lydia . . 108, 126, 173

Sanderson, Mary . . . 127, 158
" Mehitabel 182
" Sarah 126
" Seth 153, 173
" William . . . 126, 127
Sanger, Aaron 108
" Abigail 157, 158
" Abraham 168
" Anna . . 166, 186, 193
" Benjamin 161
" Daniel . . . 157, 168, 194
" David 90, 92, 93, 134, 136,
137, 138, 140, 142, 145,
147, 157, 158, 160, 161,
162, 163, 165, 167
" Elizabeth . . 167, 188, 193
" George W. 193
" Grace . . 160, 161, 185
" Jesse 165
" John . . . 107, 134, 157
" Joseph 167
" Katharine 162
" Lucy 157, 162
" Lydia . . 134, 147, 160
" Mary 164
" Molly 157
" Nathaniel . 140, 160, 162
" Nathaniel C. 194
" Richard 188, 193
" Richard E. 193
" Samuel 142, 160, 161, 166,
167, 168, 185
" Samuel E. 193
" Seth 163
" Solomon 145
" Spencer 162
" Thomas 158
" William 108, 137, 138, 157,
158, 160, 161, 164,
168, 193
Savage, Ephraim . . . 102, 103
" John 158
" Samuel 158
Sawin, Abigail . . 121, 142, 182
" Abijah 137, 162
" Benjamin . . . 145, 165
" Daniel 112, 136, 149, 158, 159,
160, 161, 162, 165, 167,
168, 184, 188
" David 149
" Deborah 134
" Elizabeth . . . 142, 168
" George 131
" Goodman 2
" Hannah . . . 147, 183
" John 2, 79, 127, 136, 137, 142,
145, 147, 153, 159, 182
" Jonathan 141
" Joseph 164
" Judith 103, 118
" Lydia 144, 183
" Lucy 160

Sawin, Mary . . . 118, 144, 183
" Mononga- 2, 3, 9, 11, 12, 13,
21, 23, 24, 26, 27, 28, 29,
31, 32, 33, 100, 127, 131,
132, 134
" Samuel 122, 142, 143, 161
" Sarah 145
" Stephen 92, 104, 141, 142,
143, 145, 147, 149
" Susanna . . . 153, 167
Sawtell, Satle, Ab. . . . 112, 116
" Bethia 120
" Elizabeth 180
" Enoch 124, 127
" Hannah 112
" Henry . . 146, 149, 150
" John 150
" Richard 127
" Ruth 142
" Sarah 112
" Susanna 124
Sayer, Charlotte 173
" Jacob 173
Scudder, Daniel 191
" Daniel L. 191
" Sarah P. 187
Seaver, Andrew 168
" Ebenezer 168
Severn, Elizabeth 133
" Samuel . . 120, 130, 133
Sewall, Capt. 178
Shattuck, Shattock, Abigail . 125
" Benjamin . . . 124, 119
" Elizabeth 180
" John 3
" Jonathan 131
" Joseph 78, 122
" Josiah . . 149, 151, 157
" Mary 128, 139
" Nathaniel 127
" Philip . 4, 120, 127, 128
" Rebecca 121
" Robert 131
" Samuel . . . 23, 125, 127
" Susanna 151
" William 2, 6, 19, 22, 23, 24,
25, 28, 30, 38, 39, 41, 43,
49, 53, 63, 71, 90, 124,
128, 131, 138, 180
Shed, Francis 168
" Keziah 168
" Zecariah . . . 108, 168
Sherman, Abiah 119
" Betty 128
" Capt. 2, 3
" Corporal 5, 6
" Elizabeth 124
" Grace 119
" Joseph 5, 22, 23, 25, 26, 124, 128
" Martha 128, 188
" Mary 130

Sherman, Mr. 119
" Nathaniel 43, 45, 47, 51, 57, 138
" Pastor 2
Simmons, Anna 189
" James . . 106, 189, 190
" Mary 189
" Sarah 189
" Stephen 190
Smethurst, Mary 100
Smith, Alfred 193
" Benjamin 128
" Daniel 23, 125
" Elisha 129
" Elizabeth 127
" George 175
" Hannah 180
" James 98
" Jane 120
" John 125
" Jonathan 120, 124, 127, 129
" Joseph . . . 125, 128
" Lydia . . 124, 175, 193
" Mary . . . 2, 177, 179
" Mary A. 176
" Nelson 189
" Rebecca 125
" Samuel 128
" Sarah 103
" Sarah J. 120
" Shubael . . 175, 176, 189
" Thomas 128
" Widow 129
" Zechariah 124
Soden, Elizabeth 107
" Hannah . . . 162, 187
" Mary 166
" Samuel 107, 157, 159, 160, 162, 163, 166, 187
" Susanna 157
" Thomas . . 159, 163, 173
Sparhawk, Isaac 159
" Jacob 155
" Katherine 107
" Nathan 165
" Nathaniel . . 107, 156, 165
" Timothy 155
Spring, Abigail 99
" Alpheus . . . 144, 185
" Convers 141, 161, 162, 164, 165, 167, 169
" Elizabeth . . . 133, 169
" Francis . . . 152, 170
" Henry 18, 20, 23, 28, 36, 90, 91, 93, 121, 126, 131, 133, 136, 137, 139, 141, 143, 144, 147, 150, 151, 152, 156, 165
" Jedediah . . 137, 157, 159
" John 139, 158
" Josiah 159
" Keziah . . 158, 180, 183

Spring, Luke 167
" Lydia 125, 126, 137, 151, 186
" Marshall 147
" Mary . . . 134, 150
" Mehitable . . 130, 131
" Mercy A. 161
" Mr. 41
" Samuel . 136, 156, 170, 186
" Sarah . . . 131, 143
" Silas 164
" Thomas . . 134, 157
Stacy, John . . . 131, 132
" Samuel 132
Starrs, Star, Comfort . 121, 126
" Hannah 129
" Lydia 126
" Mary 121
" Peter 144
Stearns, Abigail . . . 145, 180
" Abijah . . 146, 153, 183
" Anna . 142, 146, 180, 183
" Benjamin . . . 129, 135
" Catherine M. 189
" Charles 166
" Daniel . 135, 136, 140, 142, 144, 147, 150, 157
" Dorothy 148
" Elisha 157
" Elizabeth 135
" Ezekiel 139
" George W. . . 129, 170
" Hannah . . . 165, 182
" Hepzibah 146
" Isaac . 122, 131, 142, 150
" Isaiah 136
" Jacob 182
" John 36, 38, 57, 59, 61, 63, 64, 65, 90, 92, 129, 135, 136, 138, 142, 145, 146, 161, 162, 163, 164, 166, 168
" Jonas 142, 165
" Jonathan . . 138, 165, 166
" Joseph 92, 93, 163, 173, 181
" Joshua . . . 150, 153
" Josiah 141, 142, 147, 148, 150, 151, 156, 164
" Judith 129
" Katharine 161
" Lois 146, 183
" Lucy 172
" Martha . 161, 166, 167, 168
" Mary 112, 130, 140, 147, 155, 168, 183
" Mary C. 189
" Mehitabel 124
" Moses 136
" Nathaniel . . 90, 92, 142
" Peter 147
" Phineas 107, 141, 165, 166, 167, 168, 170, 171, 172
" Polly 171

Stearns, Rebecca	129	Stone, John 3, 142
" Relief	151	" Jonas 155
" Ruth	140	" Jonathan 20, 21, 23, 30, 31,
" Samuel . 113, 121, 124, 139		36, 38, 49, 51, 54,
141, 145, 180, 183		59, 60, 61, 62, 63,
" Sarah . . 129, 141, 144		64, 65, 78, 79 93,
" Simon	131	104, 105, 107, 130,
" Stephen . 94, 135, 153		134, 135, 156, 157,
" Susanna . 150, 166, 182		138, 146, 151, 153,
" Thomas	162	155, 163, 171,172,
" William . 151, 167, 168		173, 175, 176, 180,
Stevens, Hephzibah . . . 151		182, 183, 184, 190,
" Joseph	154	193
" Thomas	103	" Joel 174
Steward, Hephzibah . . . 145		" Joseph . . 41, 175, 194
" John	144	" Josiah . . 137, 152, 171
" Jonas	145	" Johanna . . . 107, 193
" Sarah	144	" Keziah . . . 138, 164
Stimpson, Stimson, Andrew 105, 170		" Leonard 193
" Benjamin	129	" Love 183
" Bethiah	133	" Lucy 170, 193
" Betsey	172	" Margaret 157
" Elizabeth . . 121, 131		" Martha 153, 184
" James . . 130, 133, 134		" Mary . 150, 182, 191, 193
" John 171, 172		" Mathias . . 152, 160, 183
" Jonathan 119, 120, 129, 130		" Moses 146, 150, 152, 153,
" Joseph	126	155, 169, 170, 172,
" Lucy	170	173, 174, 175, 183,
" Rebecca	119	185, 187, 189, 190
" Susanna	171	" Nancy 174
Stoddard, Solomon	90	" Nathan 150, 152, 153, 155,
Stone, Aaron	173	183
" Abigail . . . 170, 172		" Nathaniel 93, 115, 177, 103,
" Abijah . 105, 155,170, 171		182
" Amos	155	" Phebe S. 107
" Ann . . . 101, 119, 193		" Rebecca 175
" Anna 176, 189		" Rhoda 163, 164
" Asa 106, 191, 192, 193, 194		" Richard 172
" Asaph	172	" Ruth . . 112, 151, 182
" Betsey	174	" Sally 171
" Caroline	176	" Samuel 156
" Charles . 107, 173, 193		" Sarah 157
" Chary 91, 180		" Seth . . . 173, 175
" Cherry	163	" Simon 3, 4, 5, 6, 7, 8, 10, 11,
" Columbus J. . . . 175		12, 15
" Cornelius . . 158, 170		" Susanna 171
" Daniel . 121, 123, 128, 153		" Warren F. 144
" David, 23, 90, 91, 133, 150		" William 154, 170, 172, 173,
" Dorcas 123, 125		174, 175, 176, 189,
" Ebenezer 23, 26, 31, 48, 66,		191
67, 70, 77, 78, 79,	Storer, Ebenezer 154
82, 83, 90, 91, 93,	" John 145
107,121, 135, 137,	" Joseph 145
138	" Seth 37, 38, 39, 40, 41 44,
" Eliza	175	46, 51 56 78, 90, 114,
" Elizabeth . 125, 157, 158		144, 184
" Eveline	176	Stoughton, William 1
" George H.	192	Stowell, Abigail 184
" Hannah 103, 128, 135, 180		" Benjamin 17
" Harriet L. . . . 189, 193		" David 115
" Hepzibath . . . 125, 173		" Hezekiah 17
" Joanna . . . 100, 118, 123		" Jemima 14
" James	150	" Jerusha 144

Stowell, John 84, 90, 92, 136, 137,
    139, 141, 143, 145
" Josiah 88, 92, 93
" Mary 181
" Samuel 92
" Sarah 182, 183
" Thankful 183
" Thomas 192
Stratton, Abigail 122, 132, 137, 184
" Abijah 135
" Elizabeth 138
" Eunice . . . 136, 184
" Hannah 149
" Isaac . . . 151, 153, 166
" Jabez 133, 135, 137, 138, 141,
    180
" John 3, 15, 23, 103, 107, 122,
   124, 127, 133, 136, 137,
   139, 153, 154, 155, 158,
   159, 162, 163, 166, 167
" Joshua 162
" Lucy 107, 159
" Lydia 158
" Mary 132, 140, 154, 155, 167
" Mercy . . 124, 141, 180
" Nathan 137
" Nathaniel . . 78, 151
" Oliver 136
" Rebecca 130
" Richard 163
" Samuel 77, 89, 90, 92, 95,
   129, 130, 134, 136,
   140, 144, 147, 149,
   151, 153, 182
" Sarah . . 141, 147, 153
" Tabitha . . . 103, 180
" Thomas 151
" Widow 91
Sturgeon, Robert 113
Stutson, Ebenezer 164
Swan, Bathsheba 142
" Ebenezer . . 141, 142, 144
" Joseph 141
" Mary 144
Sweet, Mrs. 101
Symms, James 180
Tainter, Tayntor, Ann . . . 140
" Anna 158
" Ayers, Eyris 108, 146, 165
   . 167, 168, 171,
   185
" Benjamin 124
" Dolly 171
" Elizabeth . . 119, 151, 165,
" Hannah 134, 146, 165, 183
" Joanna . . . 138, 161, 180
" John 90, 92, 93, 108, 114,
   115, 134, 136, 139, 140,
   143, 146, 150, 151, 157,
   158, 160, 163, 164, 165,
   166, 171, 181
" Jonathan 124, 126, 150, 151
" Joseph 126

Tainter, Lizzey 164
" Lucy 167
" Mary . . . 144, 157
" Nathaniel 108
" Rebecca . . 108, 180, 183
" Sally 188
" Samuel 143, 163
" Sarah . . . 160, 171
" Simon 90, 100
" Susanna . . 136, 158, 184
" William . . 150, 168
Tay, Isaac 103
Taylor, Benjamin . . . 121, 178
" Edward 97
" Margaret . . . 100, 118
" Walter . . . 121, 126
Thayer, Thare, Abigail . . . 132
" Anna 132
" Charles 192
" Clinton 188, 192
" Elizabeth 188
" George C. 192
Thacher, Thatcher, Abigail . 180
" Anna 126
" Ebenezer 139, 142, 143, 144,
   149, 181
" Ensign 7
" Francis 101
" Hannah 180
" John 119
" Marath 129
" Mary 142
" Mercy 131
" Mr. 178
" Samuel 2, 7, 14, 15, 17, 28,
   38, 39, 72, 74, 118,
   119, 126, 129, 131,
   132, 139
" Sarah . . 132, 140, 149
" Sergt. 5, 6
" Susanna . . 144, 183
Thaxter, Atherton 190
" Elizabeth 190
" George W. 191
" Hannah F. 190
" Jonas 193
" Levi 106, 188, 191, 193, 194
" Lucy W. 194
" Lydia A. 191
" Mary C. 190
Thomas, James 162
" Joshua 165
" Moses 165
" Richard 102
Thompson, Alexander . . . 149
" Hannah 159
" John 159
" Samuel 149
Thornton, Ebenezer . . . 91, 93
" Mr. 179
" Thomas 120
Throp, Mary 121
" Sarah 121

Thwing, Amos 162
" Edward 151
" John 162
" Mary 162
" Nathaniel 151
" Thomas 162
Tidd, Betty 117
" Daniel 117
Tilton, Nathan 187
Tobey, (a negro) 162
Tom, Sarah (a negro) . . 113
" Margaret (a negro) . 114
Townsend, Abigail 120
" Capt. 177
" Jonathan 126
" Martin . . . 2, 120, 126
Train, Trayne, Deborah . . 132
" Elizabeth 125
" John . . . 2, 132, 150
" Margaret 132
" Rebecca . 92, 125, 131, 133
" Silas 150
" Thomas . 2, 90, 132, 133
Trask, Ame 107
Tredaway, Josiah . 120, 127, 129
" Severanna 127
" Tabitha 129
Trowbridge, Anna 191
" Charles 190
" Edmund . . . 190, 191
" James 191
" Jonathan 118
" Lucy 190
" Mary 118, 187
Trull, John 107, 192
" Thomas 192
" William J. . . . 192
Tucker, Ebenezer 189
" John 106, 117, 188, 189, 190,
    191, 193
" Martha 191
" Sally 189
" William . . . 189, 193
Tufts, John 126, 129
" Mary 122, 126
Twitchell, Lydia 151
Underwood, Elizabeth . 119, 120
" Eunice 183
" Hannah 128
" James 139
" Jonathan 120
" Joseph 126, 128
" Joshua 106
" Mary 120
" Nehemiah 183
" Ruth . . . 104, 139, 181
" Sarah 126
" Thomas . . . 120, 123
Upham, Abijah 179
" Jonathan 129
" Ruth 117
" Thomas 117
Vila, Velah, Veleau, Anna . . 147

Vila, Velah, Veleau John . . . .
            105, 115, 117 . . .
Vinal, Elizabeth 88
" John . . . . 105, 1..
" Mary . . . . . . 1..
Vose, Addison . . . . . . 1..
" Charlotte . . . . 1..
" Ebenezer . 176, 189 190, 1..
" Henry . . . . . . 1..
" Jonathan 176
" Lucretia . . . . 1..
" Polly 171
" Sally 172
" Thomas . . 105, 171, 172
Wade, Capt. 126
Waight, Walt, Amos . . . . 1..
" Sarah 122
" Thomas 122
Wakefield, Susanna 162
Wales, Betsey 170
" Elkanah 108
" Grace 108
" Samuel 171
Walker, Abigail 187
" Elizabeth 161
" Richard 161
Ward, William 99
Warren, Abigail . . 153, 167, 168
" Abijah 161
" Ann 156
" Asa 151, 190
" Benjamin 157
" Carolina M. . . . 171
" Capt. 3, 4
" Charles . . . 170, 172
" Daniel . . . 4, 79, 128
" Eleanor . . . 172, 188
" Elijah 168
" Ephraim 93
" Elizabeth 120, 140, 142, 165
" Esther 156
" George 173
" John 120, 126, 128, 152, 154,
    156, 158
" Jonathan 126
" Joshua 90, 92, 93, 103, 125,
    137, 138, 140, 142,
    145, 181
" Josiah 167, 168
" Juliana M. 171
" Lucy . . . 151, 160, 173
" Lydia 155
" Margaret . . . 112, 110
" Marshall 170
" Mary 137 151
" Moses 105, 145, 170, 1..2,
    174, 175, 176
" Nathan 137
" Nathaniel . . 100, 132, 103
" Noah 145
" Rebecca 181
" Robt . . . . . . 10..
" Ruth . . . . . 1..

Warren, Samuel 90, 92, 93, 111, 112,
      135, 137, 151, 153,
      155, 156, 158, 160,
      161, 163, 165, 167,
      170
"   Sarah 119
"   Sophia 174
"   Stephen 167
"   Susanna 152
"   Tabitha 160
"   Thaddeus 140
"   William 104, 169, 170, 171,
      172, 173, 174
Watson, Wason, Abraham . 99
"   Benjamin 101
"   Lethic 141
"   Margaret . . 104, 141
Weaver, Samuel 103
Webb, Mr. 111
"   Widow . . 100, 101, 102
Weld, Nathaniel 188
Wellington, Abraham . . 141
"   Benjamin 22, 126, 129, 130
"   Dorcas 104, 145
"   Dr. 5, 6, 7
"   Ebenezer . . 104, 135
"   Edmund 168
"   Elisha 149
"   Elizabeth 120, 124, 142, 155
"   Jeduthan 153
"   John . 108, 133, 134, 143
"   Joseph 92, 104, 120, 124,
      127, 129, 141, 143,
      145, 147, 149, 151,
      153, 155
"   Josiah 147, 149
"   Katy 173
"   Lydia 135, 172
"   Margaret . . 141, 149, 182
"   Mary 127
"   Mehitabel . . 126, 147, 168
"   Oliver 23
"   Palgrave 11, 15, 22, 23, 24,
      25, 26, 134, 151
"   Rebecca . . . 143, 181
"   Relief 108
"   Roger 3
"   Ruhamah 147
"   Samuel 172, 173
"   Susannah 144
"   Thomas 124, 141, 142, 143,
      144, 149, 181
"   William 149
Wells, Francis 156
"   Thomas 156
Wheeler, Abijah 148
"   Ephraim . . 162, 163, 164
"   Elizabeth 162
"   James 164
"   Jonathan 148
"   Samuel 163
White, Aaron 176
"   Abigail . . 144, 160, 180

White, Abijah 152, 192
"   Adeline 191
"   Andrew 90, 91, 92, 93, 94,
      131, 133, 134, 135,
      138, 139, 140, 141,
      142, 144, 146, 147,
      149, 166, 180, 181
"   Betty 163
"   Calvin 193
"   Daniel 150
"   Diadama 163
"   Eleanor 162
"   Elijah . . . 149, 167
"   Eunice . . . 147, 166
"   George 192
"   Grace 165
"   Hannah . . 139, 167, 180
"   Henry . . . 173, 174
"   Jane . . . 180, 190
"   Jedidiah 141, 163, 165, 166
"   Jemima 144
"   Joel 156
"   John . . . 144, 154
"   Jonas 152, 154, 156, 157,
      159, 160, 162, 171,
      172, 173, 174
"   Joseph . . 150, 190, 191
"   Josiah . . 159, 164, 172
"   Lois 157, 162
"   Lucy 107, 142, 159, 190
"   Luther . . 188, 192, 193
"   Lydia 140
"   Martha . . . 138, 192
"   Moses . . 174, 176, 190
"   Rachel 191
"   Reuben 163
"   Ruth 136, 155
"   Sally 174
"   Samuel 112, 115, 135, 158,
      159, 160, 162, 164,
      166, 168, 185
"   Sarah . . 131, 138, 180
"   Sibyl . . . 168, 187
"   Stephen 155
"   William . 134, 153, 171
Whitmore, Francis . . . 130
"   John 121
"   Rebecca 130
"   Samuel . . . 122, 130
Whittamore, Isaac 160
"   James 129
"   John 129
"   Joseph 177
"   Samuel 160
Whitney, Aaron 149
"   Abigail 121, 142, 146, 174
"   Alexander 191
"   Amos 140
"   Anna . . 134, 166, 192
"   Benjamin 90, 92, 93, 97, 140,
      142, 144, 147, 149,
      150, 152, 154, 158,
      170, 181

Index to Persons.

Whitney, Bradshaw 194
" Charles 106, 169, 191, 192, 194
" Daniel 90, 92, 94, 112, 113,
       116, 118, 142, 143,
       144, 146, 147, 148,
       150, 152, 169, 170,
       171, 173, 174, 186
" David . 145, 160, 168, 174
" Dorothy 112, 183
" Edward 193
" Eliezer 97
" Elisha 150, 174
" Elizabeth . . . 150, 184
" Elnathan 180
" Ezekiel 105, 116, 174, 176
" Francis 172
" Frank 174
" George 174
" Grace 148, 158, 161, 173, 185
" Hannah . . 127, 173, 186
" Henry . . . 144, 149, 170
" Isaac 121
" Israel 107, 116, 165, 166,
       168, 170, 185, 188,
       193
" James 171, 192
" Jemima 165, 185
" Joanna 142
" John 79, 90, 91, 93, 97, 98,
       121, 138, 139, 144, 146,
       148, 149, 151, 157, 176
" Jonathan 98, 108, 133, 134,
         139, 147, 164, 165,
         166, 173, 192
" Joseph 92, 93, 108, 121, 143,
         145, 147, 150
" Joshua 143
" Josiah 150
" Katy 105
" Leonard 174
" Lucy . . . 108, 152, 165
" Lydia 147, 150
" Martha 111, 112, 121, 125, 194
" Mary 140, 142, 143, 157, 161,
       165, 166, 169, 184, 186,
       193
" Moses 144
" Nancy 170
" Nathaniel 95, 106, 119, 124,
         127, 159, 171, 172,
         173, 174, 175, 176,
         188, 189, 191, 192,
         193, 194
" Otis 176
" Polly 174
" Rebecca 144
" Richard 170
" Relief . . . . 167 Jes
" Ruth 154
" Sally 188
" Samuel 124, 147, 157, 173,
         183, 186
" Sarah 119, 130, 152, 193, 194

Whitney, Sibil C. 194
" Simon 139, 160, 164, 165,
       166, 170, 175, 184
" Stephen 108, 148, 167, 168,
       170
" Susanna 104, 138, 161, 187
" Thomas 97, 110
" William 175
Wilkins, Mr. . . . 100, 101, 102
Williams, Amariah 167
" Damaris 149
" Esther 154
" Hannah 153
" Jesse 113
" Nathaniel 153
" Phineas 149
" Thomas 110
" Wareham 137, 143, 147, 148,
       149
" William 74, 80, 82, 90, 137,
       139, 140, 143
Willis, Benjamin 149
" Mr. 177
" Stephen 149
Willy, Sarah 98
Winchester, Daniel 184
" Grace 184
" Jonathan 156
" Leonard 175
" Mary 176
" Nancy 149
" Rebecca 184
" Sarah 176
" William 175, 176, 189, 190
Winship, Aaron 144
" Edward 98
" Ephraim 115
" Jason 144
" Jonathan 167
" Joseph . . . 98, 144
" Lient. 126
" Nathan 167
" Philemon 144
Winter, Hannah 124
" John 126, 144
" Sarah 126
Wisondonk, Elizabeth . . . 122
Witherspoon, Isabel 93
Woodward, Achsah 173
" John . . 2 98, 124, 153
" Rev. Mr. 175
" Rose 93
" Thomas 98
Woolson, Mary 121
Wyeth, Whett, John . . . 122
" Mercy 122
" Nicholas . . 112, 122
Wyman, Charles 180
" Thaddeus 100
Young, John . . . 149, 150, 154
" Susanna 144
" Daniel 154

Index to Places.

Acton 163	Mendon 122, 184
Antigo 97	Menotomey 96, 98, 141, 144, 145,
Barnstable 195	148, 149, 150
Boston 1, 18, 53, 88, 89, 96, 97, 98,	Middleton 177
99, 100, 102, 122, 129, 154,	Muddy River 98
158, 162, 179, 181, 195	Mystic 122, 126, 127
Bowling Green 103	Natick 154, 155
Braintree 119, 128	Newbury 195
Brookline . 150, 152, 155, 156, 159	Newton 108, 116, 136, 140, 143, 144,
Cambridge 52, 73, 86, 96, 98, 99, 107,	145, 147, 148, 149, 151, 152,
121, 124, 138, 141, 142,	153, 154, 155, 158, 159, 160,
148, 149, 150, 151, 152,	161, 163, 165, 168
156, 158, 159, 160, 161,	Piscataqua 102
162, 163, 167, 168, 186,	Plymouth 101
195	Roxbury . . . 103, 158, 163, 195
Charlestown 97, 98, 99, 129, 154,	Salem 101, 129
195	Sherborn 98, 128
Concord . . 99, 128, 150, 152, 195	Shrewsbury 166
Conway 167	Stockbridge 163
Dedham . . 98, 121, 126, 129, 195	Stoughton 104
Dorchester 101, 195	Sudbury 96, 97
Dublin, Ireland 96	Waltham 151, 152, 153, 154, 157, 160,
Grafton 162	163, 165, 184, 189, 194
Ireland 100, 194	Wells . . . 135, 136, 139, 181
Lancaster 99, 133	Westboro' 154
Lexington . . . 144, 147, 156	Weston 35, 139, 147, 148, 150, 160
Limerick 194	Weymouth 195
Lunenburg 153	Woburn 119, 195
Malden 137	Woodstock 161
Marlboro' 131, 139	Worcester 152, 154
Marshfield 101	Yarmouth 129
Medford 120, 159	

Index to Subjects.

Arms and Ammunition . . 85, 86
Assessment for finishing New Meeting House . . . 43
" rate of 5, 8
Auditors appointed . . . 16
Baptism by Rev. Robert Sturgeon, irregular . . . 113
Bailey, Rev. John's book . . 96
" bids farewell . . 124, 197
" end of his marrying in N. E. 99
" pastoral work, sick of 119
" records, private memoranda only 128
" remarks on admitting to Communion certain persons . . 118, 119, 122
" daily expenses . . . 179
" death of wife 110, 124, 177
" distributes what his wife left 177, 178
" funeral expenses of wife, 177
" marriage registration fee of 3 black dogs . . . 100
Bank 28
Bell 76, 78
" wheel 19
" ringing allowance for, 13, 46
" hanging of 71
Burying place 2
Certificates of attendance upon Church of England, 88, 89
Charles River 73, 84, 86
Church charity, upon whom bestowed 111
" meeting, held on desire of three . . . 117
" England, certificate of membership . . . 88, 89
" third in Watertown . . 113
" member, how received, 115
Clark 13, 15
Committee, appointed, against petition of sundry inhabitants . . . 22
" to buy land for use of minister 22
" to wait on General Court, 27
" to obtain helper for Mr. Gibbs 28
" for conference with the other congregation 30
" upon boundary between precincts . . . 31, 32
" for ordination of Seth Storer . . . 39, 40

Committee on building Meeting House 55
" to take care of Church funds . . . 115, 116
Communion service administered, when 117
Communion service vessels changed, 116
Communion table, support of, 112, 116
Confessions to be made before the Church 115
Congregational affairs end . . 33
Contributions, for expenses of ordination of Rev. S. Storer, 41
" for repairing buildings of Pastor Gibbs . . . 21
" to be papered, 5, 7, 9, 11, 12
Council of Churches, May, 1722, 113
Covenant, form of 109
" children of persons owning, 116
Doggs, 3 black, as marriage registration fee . . . 100
Epitaph on John Bailey . . 111
" on John Bailey's wife, 110
" on Thomas Bailey . 110
" on John Sherman . 110
Flagons, pewter, sold; silver tankards bought . . 116, 117
Full Communion, form of Covenant, 109
Funeral expenses of J. Bailey's wife, 177
Gibbs, Henry, called to ministry, 3
" " declines . . 4
" " gift to Church . 18
" " receipt for salary, 21
Glass, repairs, 6, 10, 18, 21, 64, 66, 69, 70, 71, 80, 82, 84
Great Bridge 73, 84
Grist Mill, old 10
Hearse cloth 2, 76
Land granted 86
Legacy from Mrs. Ann Mills, 111, 112, 113, 114
Marrying, end of for Mr. Bailey in N. Eng. 99
Masters brook 86
Meeting House, repairs, 6, 10, 27, 28
" " old, 1, 5, 6, 7, 29, 38, 42, 43, 44
" " middle . 1, 7, 21
" " new, 1, 4, 8, 12, 42, 49, 44, 45, 56
" " on School House Hill . 38, 50, 51

Meeting House, path to . 76, 78
  "   " pews in, 48, 58, 59, 60, 61, 62, 63, 94, 95
  "   " seating of, 65, 75, 76, 90, 91, 92, 93, 94
  "   " shutters to windows . . . 69, 70, 71
Military precinct 1
Mills, Ann, legacy, 111, 112, 113, 114
Minister, assessment for support of, 5, 6
  " Henry Gibbs chosen, 4
  " support of in the east and west parts . . . 1
  " advice of General Court, 24, 25
Ministeral place, 2, 37, 49, 52, 53, 55, 67, 71
  " alteration and repair of, 31, 53, 55, 56, 57, 67, 68
  " land and fence, 21, 22, 29, 83, 84
Notes belonging to the Church renewed 117
Ordination of Pastor Adams . 169
  "   " J. Bailey 119
  "   " Eliot . 169
  "   " Storer . 134
Owning the Covenant, form of, 109
  " " " " " for those, children of whom to be baptized . . . 116
Pequod War 118
Pew Committee 59, 62

Pew lots, disposal of, 48, 58, 60, 61, 62, 63, 64
Precinct affairs . . . 35, 86
  " assessors, allowance of, 45
  " lines 73, 74
Prince of Orange guards . . 118
Protest, town's voting in precinct affairs 30
Record book to be kept, 4, 9, 13, 14, 18, 22, 24, 39, 85, 86
  " transcribed from Almanacks 107
Sacraments, when to be administered 117
Sacramental phrases and expressions of J. Bailey, 194, 195, 196
  " lecture 117
Salary for Pastor, contributions for, on Sabbath days, 12, 14
  " of minister, 8, 11, 13, 37, 79
  " for sexton 14
Society to consider some method for placing meeting house, 19
Storer, Seth, chosen to be Gospel minister 37
  " " acceptance . . 39
  " " petition for increase of salary . . . 94
Town, division of, 72, 73, 84, 85, 86
Tombstone of Mrs. Bailey . 177
Treasurer's account book . . 82
Warning for precinct meeting, 10, 31
Ways layed out 86
Wood for Pastor . . 5, 6, 10, 31

www.ingramcontent.com/pod-product-compliance
Lightning Source LLC
Chambersburg PA
CBHW021805230426
43669CB00008B/637